FRO _ _ER'S
E _ _ _

W9-BYH-015

TO

VANCOUVER & VICTORIA

By
Joanne Sasvari

Easy Guides are ✦ Quick To Read ✦ Light To Carry
✦ For Expert Advice ✦ In All Price Ranges

FrommerMedia LLC

Published by
FROMMER MEDIA LLC

ISBN 978-1-62887-108-1 (paper), 978-1-62887-109-8 (e-book)

Editorial Director: Pauline Frommer
Editor: Billy Fox
Production Editor: Heather Wilcox
Cartographer: Roberta Stockwell
Cover Design: Howard Grossman

For information on our other products or services, see www.frommers.com.

Frommer Media LLC also publishes its books in a variety of electronic formats. Some content that
appears in print may not be available in electronic formats.

Manufactured in the United States of America

5 4 3 2 1

AN IMPORTANT NOTE

The world is a dynamic place. Hotels change ownership, restaurants hike their prices, museums
alter their opening hours, and buses and trains change their routings. And all this can occur in
the several months after our authors have visited, inspected, and written about these hotels,
restaurants, museums and transportation services. Though we have made valiant efforts to keep
all our information fresh and up-to-date, some few changes can inevitably occur in the periods
before a revised edition of this guidebook is published. So please bear with us if a tiny number
of the details in this book have changed. Please also note that we have no responsibility or liabil-
ity for any inaccuracy or errors or omissions, or for inconvenience, loss, damage, or expenses
suffered by anyone as a result of assertions in this guide.

CONTENTS

1 THE BEST OF VANCOUVER & VICTORIA 1

2 VANCOUVER & VICTORIA IN CONTEXT 12

3 SUGGESTED ITINERARIES 24

Iconic Vancouver in 1, 2 & 3 Days 24

Vancouver for Families 29

Vancouver for Foodies 30

Iconic Victoria in 1 & 2 Days 31

Victoria for Families 35

Victoria for Foodies 36

4 VANCOUVER 38

Essentials 38

The Neighborhoods in Brief 40

Getting Around 42

Fast Facts: Vancouver 45

Where to Stay in Vancouver 46

Where to Eat in Vancouver 61

Exploring Vancouver 81

Shopping 109

Entertainment & Nightlife 117

5 WHISTLER 122

Essentials 122

Where to Stay in Whistler 125

Where to Eat in Whistler 129

Outdoor Activities 131

Whistler After Dark 136

Sea-to-Sky Highway 136

6 VICTORIA 138

Essentials 138

The Neighborhoods in Brief 140

Getting Around 141

Fast Facts: Victoria 143

Where to Stay in Victoria 144

Where to Eat in Victoria 152

Exploring Victoria 162

Shopping 175

Entertainment & Nightlife 178

7 SIDE TRIPS FROM VICTORIA 180

Cowichan Valley 180

Gulf Islands 185

Tofino, Ucluelet & Pacific Rim National Park Preserve 190

8 PLANNING YOUR TRIP TO BRITISH COLUMBIA 202

ABOUT THE AUTHOR

Joanne Sasvari is a Vancouver-based independent writer who covers food, drink, travel, and other lifestyles topics for a variety of publications. She is the editor of "Flavours," a quarterly magazine about food and drink across Western Canada, and contributes regularly to "The Vancouver Sun," "Canadian Living," "Destination British Columbia," and others. Certified by the Wine and Spirits Education Trust (WSET), she has a special interest in spirits and cocktails and since 2006 has been the "In Good Spirits" columnist for "The Vancouver Sun." She is also the past president of the Travel Media Association of Canada as well as the former travel editor at "The National Post." She is the author of the culinary travel book "Paprika: A Spicy Memoir from Hungary."

ABOUT THE FROMMER'S TRAVEL GUIDES

For most of the past 50 years, Frommer's has been the leading series of travel guides in North America, accounting for as many as 24% of all guidebooks sold. I think I know why.

Although we hope our books are entertaining, we nevertheless deal with travel in a serious fashion. Our guidebooks have never looked on such journeys as a mere recreation, but as a far more important human function, a time of learning and introspection, an essential part of a civilized life. We stress the culture, lifestyle, history, and beliefs of the destinations we cover and urge our readers to seek out people and new ideas as the chief rewards of travel.

We have never shied from controversy. We have, from the beginning, encouraged our authors to be intensely judgmental, critical—both pro and con—in their comments, and wholly independent. Our only clients are our readers, and we have triggered the ire of countless prominent sorts, from a tourist newspaper we called "practically worthless" (it unsuccessfully sued us) to the many rip-offs we've condemned.

And because we believe that travel should be available to everyone regardless of their incomes, we have always been cost-conscious at every level of expenditure. Although we have broadened our recommendations beyond the budget category, we insist that every lodging we include be sensibly priced. We use every form of media to assist our readers and are particularly proud of our feisty daily website, the award-winning Frommers.com.

I have high hopes for the future of Frommer's. May these guidebooks, in all the years ahead, continue to reflect the joy of travel and the freedom that travel represents. May they always pursue a cost-conscious path, so that people of all incomes can enjoy the rewards of travel. And may they create, for both the traveler and the persons among whom we travel, a community of friends, where all human beings live in harmony and peace.

Arthur Frommer

THE BEST OF VANCOUVER & VICTORIA

The jagged, snowcapped peaks of the Coastal Mountains plunge down through hushed forests to sandy beaches. Idyllic islands float dreamily in the calm waters of the Georgia Strait. Lush gardens bloom even when the rest of Canada is still buried under snow. There's no question the southwest corner of British Columbia is one of the most breathtakingly beautiful places on the planet. And amid all this stunning natural beauty lie Vancouver and Victoria, two cities that may be physically close together but are miles apart when it comes to style and personality.

On the Mainland is Vancouver, the biggest metropolitan area in Western Canada. It is young and vibrant and bristling with the shiny modern towers that led hometown writer Douglas Coupland to label it the "City of Glass." Also known as Lotusland (as in Homer's "Odyssey," a land where the locals are befuddled by the narcotic lotus plant), Terminal City (for its place at the end of the transco ntinental railroad), and Hongcouver (for its huge ex-pat Chinese population), Vancouver is famously a city where you can snowboard in the morning, sail in the afternoon, and dine at a sophisticated restaurant in the evening. It consistently tops the lists of the world's most livable cities and is also the province's business hub, Canada's busiest port, and a center for creative industries such as film and animation.

On Vancouver Island, less than 100km (60 miles) to the west, is Victoria, the provincial capital. Smaller and cozier than Vancouver, Victoria is a government town, but one with a decidedly romantic ambience, thanks to its lush gardens, pretty views, and charming historic buildings. Its mild climate and slower pace have made it a popular retirement community, and it was once known somewhat dismissively as a place for the "newly wed and nearly dead." But today it's all about young families, with an exceptional local food scene and endless outdoor activities.

The great outdoors, of course, is what draws many people to this corner of the world. When the sun comes out, whatever time of year it is, everyone heads to the beaches, parks, bike paths, hiking trails, or out on the water for an afternoon of sailing or kayaking. In winter, visitors and locals alike head to the hills—the three ski hills on Vancouver's North Shore, or up the Sea to Sky Highway to Whistler, one of the top ski resorts in the world.

Any visit to Vancouver must surely begin in Stanley Park, a 400-hectare (1,000-acre) green space, much of it wild and untamed, right on the edge of the city's busy downtown. Surrounded by ocean and ringed by the popular Seawall paved pathway, it's home to the Vancouver Aquarium, as well as restaurants, gardens, swimming pools, playgrounds, a miniature railroad, a cricket pitch, and an outdoor amphitheater. The most popular attraction, though, is the cluster of totem poles at Brockton Point, a legacy of the First Nations peoples who lived here for thousands of years before the first Europeans arrived in the 18th century.

Similarly, any visit to Victoria must begin in the city's Inner Harbour, where pleasure craft, ferries, and float planes vie for space. Surrounding it are the city's most historic buildings—the BC Parliament Buildings and the ivy-clad Fairmont Hotel Empress—as well as the Royal BC Museum and a walkable downtown of irresistible shops and restaurants.

Victoria has a genteel ambience that's the legacy of its British heritage. Vancouver, on the other hand, is a bit brash, even a bit rough around the edges, just as it has been ever since it was a handful of shacks clustered around a tavern. Both cities have many adventures to discover. This book will help you find your own.

VANCOUVER'S best
AUTHENTIC EXPERIENCES

o **Checking out the spectacular views along the Seawall:** On a sunny day, everyone heads to the Seawall, a 22km (13.5-mile) paved pathway that starts at the Vancouver Convention Centre in Coal Harbour, then snakes around Stanley Park, and continues along English Bay and False Creek all the way to Kitsilano Beach. It's the place to stroll, run, cycle, skate, walk the dog, and check out the action. See p. 84.

o **Ordering the omakase at Tojo's:** Vancouver has sushi joints like the rest of Canada has donut shops, with one on practically every corner. The very best of them is where you will find the legendary master chef Hidekazu Tojo and his fresher-than-fresh seafood. Put yourself in his hands and order the chef's sampler known as *omakase* for an unforgettable dining experience. See p. 74.

o **Sleeping with the fishes:** Nope, it's not a "Godfather" movie—it's one of the most popular programs at the Vancouver Aquarium. Everyone has their favorite display at this world-leading research and education facility, and kids will love the sleepovers that feature special activities, guest speakers, and fishy ghost stories. See p. 86.

o **Buying fabulous footwear in Gastown:** Shoe designer John Fluevog is one of Vancouver's most famous hometown heroes and his shop is a must-visit when you explore the historic neighborhood of Gastown. Join famous Fluevogers, including Madonna, Woody Harrelson, and Scarlett Johansson, and slip your feet into one of his eccentrically designed but remarkably comfortable city boots or Mary Janes. See p. 113.

o **Taking tea in Chinatown:** Vancouver's historic Chinatown is going through an exciting period of revitalization, with new restaurants, bars, shops, and condo projects popping up like shiitake mushrooms. One of the most memorable experiences is still a visit to the Dr. Sun Yat-Sen Classical Chinese Garden, where, if you time it just right, you may be able to take part in a traditional Chinese tea ceremony. See p. 87.

o **Paddling around English Bay:** Rent a canoe, kayak, or standup paddleboard and explore this calm bay at the heart of the city by paddle power. See p. 103.

o **Savoring the sunset from the perfect patio:** When the weather is nice, and sometimes even when it's not, Vancouverites hit the city's patios to eat, drink, and catch up on the latest gossip. One to try is at **Dockside Restaurant** on Granville Island, overlooking the False Creek Marina. Enjoy the chicken satay and a glass of local wine after a tough day of browsing through the Granville Island Public Market. See p. 59.

o **Sharing your fish and chips with the seagulls at Spanish Banks Beach:** Vancouver is surrounded by beaches and there's one for every taste, from the hard bodies at Kits Beach to the naked ones at Wreck Beach. But one of the most popular beaches is this family-friendly one, with its casual vibe and endless sandy expanse. Don't even try resisting the deep-fried goodies at the concession stand; just watch out for the hungry gulls. See p. 102.

o **Climbing the Grouse Grind:** Cross the swooping span known as the Lions Gate Bridge and you will find yourself in the North Shore Mountains, with their dark forests, jagged peaks, and the brutal hike called the Grouse Grind. Also known as "Mother Nature's Stairmaster," this trail is only 2.9km (1.8 miles) long, but it goes straight up Grouse Mountain, with an elevation gain of 853m (2,800 ft.). Luckily, there's a beer waiting for you at the top. (*Note:* There's also a gondola for those who'd rather spare themselves the agony.) See p. 92.

o **Taking a selfie at the Olympic Cauldron:** In many ways, the 2010 Olympic and Paralympic Winter Games were Vancouver's coming-out party. One of the most memorable legacies of the Games is the striking cauldron at Jack Poole Plaza next to the Vancouver Convention Centre. It's become a popular meeting place and social hangout, and offers one of the city's most impressive views of the North Shore Mountains. It's a perfect backdrop for that photo you want to post on Instagram. See p. 82.

VANCOUVER'S best RESTAURANTS

o **Hawksworth Restaurant:** This swish spot has been Vancouver's buzziest resto since it opened in 2011. It is an elegant-but-funky art-filled space in the newly restored historic Rosewood Hotel Georgia, where Chef David Hawksworth cooks up exceptional West Coast fare with creative flair. A must for the extensive wine list and terrific cocktails. See p. 64.

o **Blue Water Cafe + Raw Bar:** Terrific seafood menu. Exceptional, award-wining wine list. Casual-elegant West Coast decor. Some of the best sushi in the city. In many ways, this high-end Yaletown eatery is the quintessential Vancouver dining experience. See p. 64.

o **Vij's:** Waiting in line at Vancouver's favorite Indian restaurant is something of a rite of passage. It's worth it, though, because once you finally get inside this jewel box of an eatery, you will discover fragrant and complex dishes unlike any you have ever experienced. Forget curry-in-a-hurry; this is some of Vancouver's best food, hands down. See p. 75.

o **Sun Sui Wah:** With its large Chinese population, it's no surprise that Vancouver has plenty of great places serving up noodles, dumplings, and stir-fries. This sophisticated Cantonese restaurant on Main Street is one of the best. Go for dim sum, the feast of small dishes served at lunch, so you can try as many tastes as possible. See p. 77.

○ **Cactus Club Coal Harbour:** Yes, it's a chain. But this chain has celebrity chef Rob Feenie at the helm and an exceptional sommelier choosing the wines. Besides, this location has one of the best views in the city, overlooking Coal Harbour and the North Shore Mountains from an enviable spot next to the Olympic Cauldron. See p. 67.

○ **Chambar Restaurant:** Hipsters and society types alike flock to this funky eatery, thanks to a great location in a historic building near the sports arenas and Queen Elizabeth Theatre. The cuisine is Belgian by way of North Africa, so expect terrific tagines and irresistible mussels, paired with Belgian beer, craft cocktails, and a great wine list. See p. 66.

○ **L'Abattoir:** Located at the oldest, most historic corner in the city, Gastown's Maple Tree Square, L'Abattoir serves up modern fare based on local ingredients, with just a touch of molecular madness to add some spice. Beautiful room, well-edited wine list, and some of the best cocktails in a city that takes its libations seriously. See p. 69.

○ **Burdock & Co.:** Even in a city obsessed with fresh, local, and sustainable fare, chef-owner-green-thumb Andrea Carlson stands above the rest. She opened this tiny room in 2013 after running some of the most demanding kitchens in Vancouver, and the lineups for her fried chicken and squash gnocchi haven't stopped since. See p. 78.

○ **Tojo's:** Before there was sashimi at the supermarket and all-you-can-eat *maki* at the mall, there was Hidekazu Tojo. His is still the best sushi in the city; his Golden Roll (crab, salmon, scallop, and shrimp in a paper-thin omelet) is one of the best things you'll ever eat. Order the *omakase*—chef's sampler—and one of the superb sakes. See p. 74.

○ **PiDGin:** Located as it is right on the edge of the sketchy Downtown Eastside, at first PiDGin attracted attention for the mobs of anti-poverty protestors outside. Now all anyone talks about is the exceptional and wildly innovative fusion cuisine. Don't ask what's in it—just order the tasting menu so you can try a little bit of everything. See p. 69.

VANCOUVER'S best HOTELS

○ **Rosewood Hotel Georgia:** Vancouverites breathed a sigh of relief when the Rosewood Group bought one of the city's oldest hotels and announced that they would be restoring it to its former glamor. Today, this is one of the most beautiful and luxurious places to stay in downtown Vancouver. See p. 50.

○ **Loden Hotel:** Located just slightly off the beaten path, but conveniently close to the business district and Coal Harbour, the Loden is a bit of a hidden gem. It's a modern boutique hotel with elegantly comfortable rooms and scenic views, perfect for business travelers. See p. 47.

○ **Opus Hotel:** Creative types and fashionistas love this personality-filled hotel. Bold, contemporary, even eccentric decor is housed in a historic Yaletown building, but top-notch amenities keep it fabulously functional. See p. 50.

○ **Four Seasons Hotel Vancouver:** This is one of the original Four Seasons locations, so you can expect quiet luxury in the guest rooms and exceptional service throughout. The updated Yew Seafood + Bar is one of the city's favorite meeting places. See p. 47.

○ **Fairmont Pacific Rim:** One of—count 'em—three Fairmont Hotels in downtown Vancouver, this is the newest, smallest, most flat-out gorgeous, and it has some of the best views in the city. See p. 46.

- **Sylvia Hotel:** A century-old hotel with a killer location right on English Bay; its guest rooms are pretty basic, but the low rates are almost as amazing as those spectacular views. See p. 58
- **Listel Hotel:** This comfortable, affordable, art-filled refuge is tucked amid the towers and shops of busy Robson Street, Vancouver's trendy shopping district. See p. 57.
- **Buchan Hotel:** Incredible location, incredible value. The Buchan is a three-story, family-owned, historic walkup in the leafy West End. Guest rooms aren't fancy, but they're clean, comfortable, and cheap. See p. 59.
- **The Burrard:** Recently restored to its retro 1960s cool, the Burrard is an old motor hotel that's been updated with all the modern conveniences and a whole lot of urban style. Great location and affordable rates. See p. 54.
- **Shangri-La Hotel:** The first North American location for the Asian luxury chain, this is a coolly elegant anchor for high-end Alberni Street. Expect the ultimate in hospitality. See p. 51.

VANCOUVER'S best FOR FAMILIES

- **Stanley Park Miniature Train:** More than 200,000 people each year climb aboard this tiny replica of Canada's first transcontinental passenger train for a short but scenic journey around a lagoon. See p. 84.
- **Vancouver Aquarium:** Kids big and small will love getting up close and personal with the dolphins, belugas, penguins, and other aquatic critters at this world-class research and education facility. See p. 86.
- **Science World at TELUS World of Science:** The fun never stops at this center at the far end of False Creek. Don't tell the kids they're actually learning something, too. See p. 91.
- **Playland at the PNE:** Whee! Every summer, the roller coasters roar and the Ferris wheels turn and the mini-donuts sizzle at the Pacific National Exhibition grounds. See p. 100.
- **Capilano Suspension Bridge:** No bored kids here, what with the Cliffwalk, Treetop Adventure, and, of course, the bridge, 140m-long (460-ft.) and swaying 70m (230 ft.) above the river. See p. 91.
- **Kids Market at Granville Island:** Not just toys, though there are plenty of those, too. This market offers loads of events like crafts and games to keep the little ones busy. See p. 99.
- **FlyOver Canada:** Buckle up and fly on an 8-minute journey inside a spherical screen—the spectacular film will make you feel as if you're literally soaring from coast to coast. See p. 82.
- **Carousel Theatre for Young People:** This Granville Island theater company puts on exceptional productions just for kids (and the grownups they allow to tag along). See p. 99.
- **Gulf of Georgia Cannery National Historic Site:** You'll find this fun and educational interactive experience out in the historic fishing village of Steveston, near the airport. See p. 98.
- **Maplewood Farm:** Head to the North Shore and play at being a farmer surrounded by horses, sheep, ducks, and chickens at this heritage dairy farm. See p. 100.

- **Stanley Park swimming pool and water park:** Keep your kids cool with two of the park's most popular features: the water park at Lumberman's Arch, and the heated outdoor pool at Second Beach. See p. 84.

VANCOUVER'S best OUTDOOR ADVENTURES

- **Snowboarding on Cypress Mountain:** Site of the Winter Olympics' snowboarding events, this small but mighty ski hill is only about 20 minutes from downtown Vancouver. See p. 107.
- **Ziplining on Grouse Mountain:** Soar across the peaks and canyons at this popular ski hill in the North Shore Mountains, and enjoy the views of the city sprawled below. See p. 92.
- **Hiking the Lynn Loop:** Lynn Headwaters Regional Park offers a number of hikes through meandering old-growth forest and alongside rushing Lynn Creek. See p. 97.
- **Doing the Sun Run:** This annual 10km (6-mile) run, held in April and organized by "The Vancouver Sun" newspaper, is Canada's largest 10K, with nearly 50,000 participants running through downtown. See p. 17.
- **Snowshoeing on Mount Seymour:** The North Shore's third ski hill has a snowshoe center, and offers snowshoe tours, lessons, and rentals, making it an ideal place to try this fast-growing sport. See p. 93.
- **Kayaking in Deep Cove:** Head up the scenic inlet called Indian Arm and you will find pretty, placid Deep Cove, one of the area's favorite places to paddle a kayak or canoe. See p. 103.
- **Biking the UBC Endowment Lands:** The University of British Columbia is surrounded by forests that are crisscrossed with quiet trails, perfect for an afternoon of mountain biking. See p. 96.
- **Swimming at Kitsilano Pool:** This huge, saltwater pool can be found on Vancouver's trendiest beach, and is a perfect place to while away a sunny afternoon. See p. 102.
- **Skating at Robson Square:** In winter, head to the heart of the city and you will find happy skaters whirling about this public skating rink—and best of all, while they charge for rentals, skating is free. See p. 82.
- **Exploring the Seawall:** Walk, run, bike, or skate part or all 22km (14 miles) of this paved seaside pathway that encircles much of downtown and False Creek. See p. 84.

VANCOUVER'S best CULTURAL EXPERIENCES

- **Museum of Anthropology:** This spectacular cliffside building at UBC houses one of the world's greatest collections of aboriginal art and artifacts. See p. 90.
- **Vancouver Art Gallery:** Home to one of the largest collections of works by the remarkable, Victoria-born painter Emily Carr, as well as an ever-changing series of traveling exhibitions. See p. 86.
- **Museum of Vancouver:** Discover fascinating glimpses of Vancouver's neon past, then take in a show at the planetarium next door. See p. 90.

- **Theatre Under the Stars:** What better way to spend a July or August evening than by watching musical theater at Malkin Bowl in Stanley Park? It's an essential local summertime tradition. See p. 84.
- **Vancouver International Wine Festival:** One of the biggest wine festivals in North America, and an absolute must on many Vancouverites' February calendars. See p. 17.
- **Commodore Ballroom:** Few experiences can compare to dancing to live music at one of the most influential clubs in North America, with its vintage sprung dance floor. See p. 119.
- **Dr. Sun Yat-Sen Classical Chinese Garden:** The first "scholars garden" built outside of China, this is a serene and beautiful oasis in bustling Chinatown. See p. 87.
- **TD Vancouver International Jazz Festival:** The biggest stars in the world of jazz music—and their fans—flock to Vancouver each summer for this multi-day festival of sizzling sounds. See p. 119.
- **Bard on the Beach Shakespeare Festival:** Every summer, men in tights descend on the tents in Vanier Park for a season of sword fights and wordplay. See p. 118.
- **Lunar New Year Celebrations:** Vancouver's huge Asian population makes the Lunar New Year one of the most exciting times of year, with banquets, parades, firecrackers, and lucky envelopes. See p. 17.

VICTORIA'S best
AUTHENTIC EXPERIENCES

- **Wandering among the floating houses at Fisherman's Wharf:** One of the best ways to explore Victoria's lively Inner Harbour is via the Victoria Harbour Ferries that zip from stop to stop including the colorful floating houses, shops, and eateries of Fisherman's Wharf. See p. 142.
- **Touring the Totem Hall at the Royal BC Museum:** The Totem Hall offers a haunting glimpse into British Columbia's First Nations heritage, but it is just one of the many intriguing exhibits, displays, and dioramas in in this engaging museum. See p. 166.
- **Searching for the elusive Himalayan poppy at Butchart Gardens:** This gorgeous display garden is one of the city's main attractions. Discover its heritage buildings, restaurants, and rare plants like the blue poppy from the mountainous reaches of the Himalayas. See p. 173.
- **Spotting an orca while whale-watching in the Salish Sea:** The magnificent black-and-white orca is just one of the many creatures you'll see while roaring across the sea in a Zodiac or cruiser. See p. 190.
- **Hanging with the ghost of Emily Carr at her family home:** One of the most iconic of Canadian painters, Emily Carr grew up in Victoria. Visit her childhood home to glimpse where her genius sprang from. See p. 165.
- **Taking tea at the Empress:** Afternoon tea at the Fairmont Hotel Empress is an essential tradition in this very English city. Expect a decadent feast and opulent setting right by the Inner Harbour. See p. 161.
- **Biking along Dallas Road:** Victoria is known as the "Cycling Capital of Canada," and this seaside path is one of the most popular, with a route that runs past gardens, totem poles, and unsurpassed scenery. See p. 170.

- o **Eating your way along Fort Street:** Fort Street has become a foodie mecca, with everything from cheese and charcuterie to Dutch cookies, artisan salts, and Asian noodles. Bring your appetite. See p. 37.

- o **Stocking up on great reads at Munro's Books:** Quite simply, one of the world's great bookstores. Housed in a glorious neoclassical building, staffed by passionate bibliophiles, and packed with extraordinary reads. See p. 175.

- o **Raising a pint at Spinnakers:** Victorians love their pubs, and there are many to choose from in just about every neighborhood. But this craft brew house with its exceptional cuisine is one of the best. See p. 154.

VICTORIA'S best RESTAURANTS

- o **Aura Waterfront Restaurant:** At the Inn at Laurel Point, chef Tak Ito brings creative flair and a touch of Asian fusion to high-end dining in a cool, modern room perched on the edge of the Inner Harbour. See p. 152.

- o **Ulla Restaurant:** Cool and modern—that describes both the food and the ambience. Pretty food prepared with creative flair, and an appealing mix of comfort cooking and fancy techniques. See p. 155.

- o **Veneto Tapa Lounge:** Variety is the name of the game in this lively hotspot known for exceptional cocktails, terrific wines, and tapas-style nibbles. See p. 157.

- o **Zambri's:** Chef-owner Peter Zambri has a knack for transforming the humble into the extraordinary at this chic Italian *boîte* with its ever-changing menu. See p. 157.

- o **Spinnakers Gastro Brew Pub:** Who knew that pub food could be this good? Start with the rich, creamy seafood chowder and finish with the house-made chocolates paired with the pub's craft beers. See p. 154.

- o **Café Brio:** At this romantic little Tuscan villa plopped in the middle of foodie Fort Street, the food has a Mediterranean flair, but the emphasis is on exceptional local ingredients. See p. 155.

- o **10 Acres Bistro + Bar + Farm:** When the restaurant owns the farm that produces its eggs and veggies, you know it's serious about cooking local. Great comfort food, and a fantastic patio. See p. 157.

- o **Willie's Bakery:** In Victoria, breakfast is practically an Olympic event. And one of the most popular brekkie joints is this historic bakery in LoJo. Definitely try the maple-syrup-glazed bacon. See p. 159.

- o **Bengal Lounge:** Tea a bit twee for you? Then head to this colonial-style lounge at the Fairmont Hotel Empress where you can relive the days of Imperial India with the curry buffet and a stiff gin cocktail. See p. 154.

- o **Bin 4 Burger Lounge:** Whether you prefer a basic beef burger or something more exotic, like, say, the pork-and-chorizo burger with apple and brie, this is the place to be if you like your food on a bun. See p. 158.

VICTORIA'S best HOTELS

- o **Inn at Laurel Point:** This coolly chic, modern hotel is unique amid Victoria's quaint old buildings. It's filled with art and light, with a peaceful Japanese garden and a gorgeous view of the harbor. See p. 146.

o **Fairmont Hotel Empress:** The grande dame of Victoria hotels, this historic property commands attention in the heart of the Inner Harbour. Expect a lovely blend of grandeur and coziness. See p. 165.

o **Magnolia Hotel and Spa:** Not only does this European-style boutique hotel have an ideal location near the Inner Harbour, it has sumptuously beautiful rooms and top-notch service. See p. 148.

o **Oak Bay Beach Hotel:** In 2012, this great old Craftsman-style hotel in posh Oak Bay was completely rebuilt. Now it boasts the charm of the old, with the comfort and luxury of the new. See p. 150.

o **Abigail's Hotel:** A slightly dated decor does nothing to diminish the comfort and charm of this romantic little inn in a quiet residential neighborhood. Plus the breakfast is fantastic. See p. 147.

o **Hotel Rialto:** This trendy and stylish boutique hotel has shrugged off its disreputable past as the city's most notorious dive to become its coolest new hangout. See p. 148.

o **Hotel Grand Pacific:** Victoria's best business-and-conference hotel is located right next to the BC Parliament Buildings, and features an exceptional fitness center where world-class athletes train. See p. 146.

o **Swan's Suite Hotel:** Located on lively Wharf Street, this is a fun place to stay, with its rambling, art-filled rooms and the popular brewpub right downstairs. See p. 149.

o **Hotel Zed:** Victoria's newest property is a bright, fun transformation of an old motel on the road into town. Think Palm Springs, bright colors, and retro cool, with a games room, casual eatery, and vintage VW van for your shuttle bus. See p. 151.

o **Sooke Harbour House:** Located in the quiet town of Sooke, about a half-hour drive from Victoria, this is a legendary inn, famous for leading the way in creating a West Coast cuisine based on local ingredients. It is beautiful, luxurious, rustic elegance at its finest. See p. 159.

VICTORIA'S best
OUTDOOR ADVENTURES

o **Cycling the Galloping Goose Trail:** This rail-to-trail conversion starts in Victoria at the south end of the Selkirk Trestle, and weaves the back roads through urban, rural, and semi-wilderness landscapes. Different access points, many with parking areas, mean you can explore for an hour, a morning, or the entire day. See p. 172.

o **Golfing at Bear Mountain:** Victoria, with its mild climate and Scottish heritage, is a golf-obsessed kind of place, with several public and private courses, including three in Oak Bay alone. It's also the gateway to the Vancouver Island Golf Trail, 250km (155 miles) of golfing paradise from Victoria to Campbell River, with 11 courses to choose from. One of the best places to swing a club is at the Bear Mountain Golf & Country Club just north of the city, where you will find 36 holes of Nicklaus Design golf, along with a Westin Resort and world-class Santé Spa. See p. 172.

o **Whale-watching:** The waters off Victoria's coast are teeming with marine wildlife, and the best way to meet the orcas, porpoises, seals, and eagles is aboard one of the many whale-watching tours that depart from the Inner Harbour. Some include a visit to Butchart Gardens. See p. 171.

o **Kayaking, canoeing, sailing:** This is boating paradise. Victoria has a proud maritime tradition that lives on in its vibrant sailing culture. And its many coves and bays, not to mention the calm waters around the nearby Gulf Islands, are perfect for paddling a canoe or kayak. There are numerous tour operators and rental agencies that can help you float your boat. See p. 173.

o **Hiking the Juan de Fuca Trail:** Victoria is a great walking city, surrounded by even greater hiking opportunities. Among them is the rugged Juan de Fuca Marine Trail, which travels from Botanical Beach out past Sooke all the way to the ferry terminal in Swartz Bay. If you do the whole thing, it's a 47km (29-mile) multiday hike, but you can easily do small portions of it in fairly easy day hikes. See p. 172.

VICTORIA'S best SHOPPING

o **Government Street:** Victoria's main shopping street downtown is a vibrant mix of tourist tat and funky boutiques. This is where you will find such quintessential local emporia as Munro's Books, Roger's Chocolates, and Murchie's Tea & Coffee. See p. 175.

o **LoJo:** LoJo is what the locals call the neighborhood that comprises Lower Johnson Street, Market Square, and bits of Yates and Wharf streets. You'll find lots of fashion boutiques here, housed in brightly painted historic buildings. See p. 177.

o **Victoria Public Market:** Brand new as of late 2013, the Victoria Public Market has a fantastic location on the main floor of a Belle Epoque building known as The Hudson. A great place to shop for foodie souvenirs and enjoy a grazing lunch. See p. 158.

o **Oak Bay Village:** Some of the most fun you can have is strolling along charming Oak Bay Avenue and browsing through the many boutiques selling gardening gear, candy, charcuterie, fashion, and more. See p. 178.

o **Fort Street:** Once known as Antique Row, Fort Street is better known these days for its foodie options. You can still pick up an Edwardian silver tea service, but you might find yourself spending more time sampling the terrines at Choux Choux Charcuterie. See p. 176.

VICTORIA'S best MUSEUMS & GALLERIES

o **Royal BC Museum:** This is one of the best regional museums in the world. It often hosts impressive visiting exhibits, like 2014's Vikings show, but is best known for its First Nations artifacts. See p. 166.

o **Emily Carr House:** A visit to the famous painter's childhood home offers a poignant look at the wellspring of her genius. See p. 165.

o **Art Gallery of Greater Victoria:** Half charming historic mansion; half contemporary exhibit space; all passionately committed to fine art. This great gallery features thousands of works from Asia, Europe, and North America, including several by Victoria's own Emily Carr. See p. 167.

o **Robert Bateman Centre:** Up on the second floor of the historic Steamship Terminal Building right on the Inner Harbour, you'll find this impressive collection of the famous wildlife painter's works. See p. 166.

- **Craigdarroch Castle Historic House and Museum:** Until you see it, it's hard to believe this place even exists—it's a four-story, 39-room, multi-turreted bonanza castle that dates back to the late 19th century, filled with antiques and surrounded by gardens. See p. 167.

THE best AUTHENTIC EXPERIENCES BEYOND VANCOUVER & VICTORIA

- **Riding the Peak 2 Peak Gondola at Whistler Blackcomb Resort:** Considered by many the best ski resort in the world, Whistler Blackcomb offers unforgettable experiences year round. It does, after all, have more than 200 ski runs and a world-class mountain biking network. But perhaps the most memorable experience is taking the record-shattering Peak 2 Peak Gondola between the two mountains. See chapter 5.
- **Whale-watching off Steveston Harbour:** The pretty little fishing village of Steveston is a great day trip from Vancouver, and getting out on the water to frolic with the porpoises and orcas is an unforgettable way to spend an afternoon. See chapter 4.
- **Discovering Pacific Rim National Park:** Vancouver Island's west coast is a world of old-growth temperate rainforests and surf-pounded beaches. It's also a place where you can experience both the primal glories of nature and the luxury of a first-class resort. See chapter 7.
- **Meandering through Vancouver Island's wineries:** Just 45 minutes north of Victoria, the Cowichan Valley is home to vineyards, cideries, cottage farms, and art studios. Touring it is as easy as following the burgundy-and-white Wine Route signs. See chapter 7.

VANCOUVER & VICTORIA IN CONTEXT

Two cities, only 100km (60 miles) apart, built on Canada's wild colonial frontier in the late Victorian era. Vancouver and Victoria have much in common—but they have even greater differences between them. Chalk it up to their origins: Well-mannered Victoria was created by merchants; rambunctious Vancouver by a handful of adventurers and a chatty saloonkeeper. Even today, while Vancouver is sleek, sophisticated, even glamorous, it can also be gritty and rough. Victoria, on the other hand, is quainter, quieter, and much less likely to break out in random acts of bad behavior. Still, both cities share a similar West Coast climate, laidback lifestyle, and spectacular natural beauty.

Vancouver, which is located on British Columbia's Lower Mainland, still has a few of its original late Victorian neighborhoods, but it is for the most part a sleek, contemporary, multicultural city that just happens to be surrounded by nature on a grand scale, thanks to the North Shore Mountains that tower over the city. Meanwhile, Victoria may be only a short ferry ride away over on Vancouver Island, yet it is a world apart, and that world is a charming, English one of Victorian and Edwardian low-rises surrounded by pretty gardens and serene coastal seascapes.

Different though they may be, both cities are active, outdoorsy places, with a deep-rooted eco-consciousness. That applies to the exciting food culture, too—these days, you have to try hard to find a place that isn't all about local, organic, sustainable, handcrafted fare, and in Vancouver especially, you'll find a delicious Asian influence thanks to a huge Chinese, Japanese, and South Asian population.

Visitors will want to bring good walking shoes and a spirit of adventure. They will want to take tea in Victoria and climb a mountain in Vancouver, to discover the haunting beauty of First Nations art, to relax in a beautiful garden, and to sip a pint of local craft beer on a sunny patio. They'll want to taste spot prawns and *xiao long bao*. They'll want to dance to the wee hours on Granville Street and take tea at The Empress. The one thing they may not want to do, though, is to leave.

VANCOUVER & VICTORIA TODAY

When people all over the world tuned into the 2010 Winter Olympic Games and caught their first glimpse of sunny Vancouver, they saw a city that was finally coming into its own. Surrounded by mountains and sea and dotted with parks and gardens, Vancouver has always been a pretty place, but only now is it realizing its potential as an urban powerhouse. It consistently makes the Top-10 lists of most-livable places on earth, and that's despite its ridiculously high housing prices. It's one of the world's greenest cities, where the air is fresh, the climate is mild, and the water is deliciously drinkable. (The cool people always order tap, and you should, too.) It is one of the world's most diverse cities, with more than half the residents speaking a first language other than English, mostly Mandarin and Cantonese. It is also home to a number of booming industries and escaped the recent economic downturn reasonably unscathed, which is why so many luxury brands are building their Canadian flagship stores here.

Vancouver proper is a fairly small city of about 600,000 people, and is one of the most densely populated in North America. But Greater Vancouver sprawls out into the Fraser Valley and up into the North Shore Mountains to create Canada's third-largest metropolitan area, with a population of 2.4 million. Forestry, fishing, and tourism are the big economic drivers here, with software development and biotechnology close behind, not to mention Canada's largest and busiest port. It's also known for a vibrant film industry, but unfortunately, the creative industries were among the few to be hard hit by the recession of 2008, and many of the once-lucrative film, animation, and video game jobs have since left town.

The city has always had a laidback, slightly eccentric, slightly rough-around-the-edges vibe, especially during the counter-culture heyday of the 1960s and '70s, when it earned the nickname "Lotusland." These days, though, that crunchy granola ambience is being replaced by a more sophisticated, slick sort of scene, with designer labels replacing Birkenstocks and glass towers overshadowing shaggy Craftsman-style houses.

An hour and a half away by ferry, the scene is quite a different one in Victoria. Once a quiet, proper, and slightly boring little city that was more British than Britain, today Victoria has fully embraced its inner hipster cool. Yes, it's still a government town—it is, after all, the provincial capital—and it's still a big retirement community. And it's still a small city, with a population of less than 350,000 in the entire urban area and only 80,000 in Victoria proper. But it's also a young, vibrant city, where every second person you meet seems to be working on some performance art piece or harvesting sea salt or building a still from scratch.

Victoria is actually Vancouver's older sister, and unlike her brash young sibling, has preserved its historic downtown. Those lovely old Victorian warehouses and homes make for beautiful shops and restaurants. And while Vancouver restaurants have been a leader in the farm-to-table movement, in Victoria, the farm is just up the road, and chances are the chef is the farmer as well, when he's not busy making his artisanal gin, of course.

LOOKING BACK AT VANCOUVER & VICTORIA

Compared to the world's great cities, Vancouver and Victoria are mere babies. Victoria only became a city in 1862; Vancouver in 1886. But long before Captain George Vancouver sailed into English Bay back in 1792, the First Nations people lived and fought and traded here. Their remarkable legacy still lingers on, despite their population being decimated by disease and their culture by regrettable government policies. Any history of the area has to start with their story.

In the late 18th century, Coast Salish villages dotted the lands all around Vancouver and Victoria, and archeological evidence suggests that they'd been settled here for some 10,000 years. Their society was a complex and sophisticated one, with a fascinating mythology. Different peoples had different traditions—the Haida, for instance, were known as great warriors, while others were known for their deftness in trading all up and down the coast. They lived richly off the bounty of the forest and sea, especially the salmon, which they enjoyed in celebratory feasts known as potlatches. And they were famous for their beautiful carvings and art, much of it made from cedar and copper.

When the Europeans arrived—led first by José María Narváez of Spain in 1791, then the British Captain George Vancouver a year later—they brought diseases that were unfamiliar and, as it proved, deadly to the indigenous people. It's estimated that smallpox killed all but 600 of the 10,000 First Nations people who lived around the southern coast. Then the Europeans drove the survivors off the lands they wanted for themselves. As time went on, they forced them into residential schools, demanding that they give up their language, their culture, even their stories. It was a dark blot in Canada's history, and it was only in 2008 that the federal government issued a formal apology for the system and its abuses.

Today, though, there is an upwelling of native pride, a revival of the old ways, and most of all, a brilliant resurgence in the art of the coastal peoples. Visitors can learn more about them at the Museum of Anthropology in Vancouver and the Royal BC Museum in Victoria, but their legacy is everywhere, from the welcome statues at Vancouver International Airport to the totem poles in Stanley Park and the First Nations shops and galleries in both cities.

Gold Rush & Boomtown

One can only imagine what it took for the explorer and fur trader Simon Fraser and his crew to make their way, back in 1808, through the rugged and dangerous canyons of what is now the Fraser River to become the first Europeans to set foot on the site of present-day Vancouver. They were soon followed by other trappers, traders, and merchants eager to take advantage of the richness of this new land. By the 1920s, the Hudson Bay Company had built forts in Victoria and Fort Langley, while the British, being no fools, had placed the whole region under their rule by the mid–19th century.

Then, in 1855, gold was discovered in the Fraser Canyon, and by 1861 the rush was on. Some 25,000 men, mostly from California, flooded into the region to prospect for the precious nuggets. They were followed by other business, most notably, Vancouver's first sawmills, which were kept busy processing timber for housing and shipbuilding. Vancouver wasn't even a community yet, and it was already booming. That's just what attracted a voluble saloonkeeper named John Deighton, better known as Gassy Jack.

He opened a bar called the Globe to serve the sawmill workers in the neighborhood we know today as Gastown. This would be the beginning of the city of Vancouver: a rough, tough, boozy settlement, originally named Granville.

Meanwhile, over on Vancouver Island, Victoria was already a prosperous city, quietly making its fortune as a supply base for explorers, traders, and gold miners. In 1866, it was politically united with the Mainland and 5 years later, when British Columbia became part of the Canadian Confederation, Victoria was named the provincial capital. It was a proper, well-heeled community, settled largely by the English and Scots, but it was also home to North America's second Chinatown and one of the continent's largest importers and processors of opium.

Although Victoria boomed again as a supply city during the 1898 Klondike Gold Rush, the city's reign as the province's commercial center ended in 1886. That's when the Canadian Pacific Railway terminus was built in what was now called Vancouver, not far from where Gassy Jack once served up tots of whiskey. In April of that year, Vancouver was incorporated as a city; 2 months later, it burned to the ground, but was quickly rebuilt, thus beginning its history as a city always in the process of reinventing itself.

Hippies & the Condo Boom

There is no underestimating the impact the railway had on Vancouver. Thousands of newcomers flooded in, including the Chinese who worked on building the railroad, and the city quickly became a key land and sea port. It also became a major driver of Canadian industries such as forestry, fishing, and shipbuilding, which attracted workers from Japan as well as Europe. By 1923, Vancouver was the third-largest city in Canada, and a glitzy, louche kind of town it was, with countless bars, dance halls, and saloons all aglow with neon lighting.

But it was still a remote outpost of civilization until the 1960s, when hippies and draft dodgers flooded in, especially to the neighborhood of Kitsilano. The era was marked by anti-war protests, peace rallies, marches, and the creation of Greenpeace in a Dunbar living room. A whole new Vancouver vibe emerged: a slightly flaky, hippie-dippy, lefty-leaning place, with the lingering aroma of really good marijuana.

Victoria, meanwhile, avoided most of the turmoil of the 20th century, and quietly developed a reputation as a major tourism destination, famous for its historic buildings, horse-drawn carriage rides, lush gardens, and afternoon teas.

On the Mainland, Vancouver was becoming a real economic powerhouse, and one with strong urban design and policies, thanks to visionaries like the city's modernist architect and urban planner Arthur Erickson. Unlike many major cities, Vancouver decided against putting a freeway through the city, a decision that has preserved its beauty and livability. It also transformed the industrial lands of Granville Island into a collection of food market, boutiques, restaurants, artist studios, and theaters that is considered one of the best urban development projects in North America. On the other hand, many gracious old homes were destroyed and replaced with soulless condo towers, leading hometown writer and artist Douglas Coupland to label it the "City of Glass."

Still, Expo '86, which coincided with Vancouver's 100th birthday, demonstrated just how far the city had come from its humble frontier-town beginnings. The World's Fair drew more than 21 million visitors and left a legacy that included the Skytrain rapid transit system and a new pride in the city. And in 2010, thousands of athletes, volunteers, and visitors descended on Vancouver once again, this time for the Winter Olympic and Paralympic Games, while billions of people watched on televisions the world over. And what they saw was a young, brash, and beautiful city that had just grown up.

WHEN TO GO

The best time to visit Vancouver and Victoria is during the warmer and drier months of April through October. But with their moderate, sunny summers and mild, rainy winters, both cities welcome visitors year round, especially Victoria, which receives about half as much rain as Vancouver.

In February, the first crocuses and daffodils appear. In March, thousands of cherry trees burst into bridal blossom, and by the end of the month, azaleas, rhododendrons, and magnolias are in bloom. By late April, the first cruise ships start to arrive, taking advantage of the beautiful spring weather.

Summer rarely gets too hot, or too humid, thanks to the cooling ocean breezes, and is rarely rainy, but the crowds can seem overwhelming, especially in the touristy parts of both cities. September and October are often the best times to visit, with their long, warm days, smaller crowds, and rarely a spot of rain. November sees the start of the rainy season, which continues through to March. Even in the depth of winter, neither city sees much snow or freezing temperatures; this is, after all, the mildest part of Canada.

Daily Average High Temperatures & Total Precipitation for Vancouver, BC

	JAN	FEB	MAR	APR	MAY	JUNE	JULY	AUG	SEPT	OCT	NOV	DEC
TEMP (°F)	41	45	50	57	64	70	73	73	64	57	48	43
TEMP (°C)	5	7	10	14	18	21	23	23	18	14	9	6
PRECIPITATION (in.)	5.9	4.9	4.3	3	2.4	1.8	1.4	1.5	2.5	4.5	6.7	7

Daily Average High Temperatures & Total Precipitation for Victoria, BC

	JAN	FEB	MAR	APR	MAY	JUNE	JULY	AUG	SEPT	OCT	NOV	DEC
TEMP (°F)	45	48	52	55	61	64	68	68	66	57	48	45
TEMP (°C)	7	9	11	13	16	18	20	20	19	14	9	7
PRECIPITATION (in.)	3.7	2.8	1.9	1.1	1	0.8	0.5	0.8	1	2	3.4	4.3

Holidays

The official British Columbia public holidays are New Year's Day (Jan 1), Family Day (third Mon in Feb), Good Friday, Easter, Easter Monday, Victoria Day (third Mon in May), Canada Day (July 1), British Columbia Day (first Mon in Aug), Labour Day (first Mon in Sept), Thanksgiving (first Mon in Oct), Remembrance Day (Nov 11), Christmas (Dec 25), and Boxing Day (Dec 26).

ATMs will work on all holidays, and most stores and many businesses remain open on all except Christmas Day and New Year's Day.

Vancouver & Victoria Calendar of Events

The dates below are approximate, and intended to help you plan your journey. For more information on events or help with planning, visit Tourism Vancouver (✆ **604/683-2000;** www.tourismvancouver.com), Tourism Victoria (✆ **250/953-2033;** www.tourismvictoria.com), or Destination BC (www.HelloBC.com).

JANUARY

Polar Bear Swim, Vancouver. Thousands of hardy citizens show up in elaborate costumes to dip into the icy waters of English Bay. Visit **http://vancouver.ca** for more information. January 1.

Dine Out, Vancouver. For 3 weeks starting in late January, Vancouver's hottest restaurants offer three-course dinners at bargain prices, as well as a variety of other cool foodie events. For info, visit **www.tourismvancouver.com**.

PuSh International Performing Arts Festival, Vancouver. An international performing-arts festival featuring over 100 groundbreaking performances. Check out **www.pushfestival.ca** for more info. Late January to early February.

FEBRUARY

Chinese (Lunar) New Year, Vancouver, Richmond, and Victoria. In Chinese cultures, the 2-week-long festival is the time to pay debts, forgive grievances, and feast on exceptional food. On the official night of the Lunar New Year, celebrations start with a bang—firecrackers, drums, dragon dances, and multi-course banquets. The biggest celebration is in Richmond, **www.tourism richmond.com**. Dates and events vary yearly.

Vancouver International Wine Festival. One of North America's biggest and most respected wine festivals offers the opportunity to taste hundreds of wines from all over the world. Call ℰ **604/873-3311** or 877/321-3121 or visit **www.vanwinefest.ca**. Mid-February.

International Bhangra Celebration, Vancouver. The city's vast South Asian population celebrates with lively folk music and dance that originates in the Punjab. Details at www.vibc.org. Mid-February.

Dine Out, Victoria. For 10 days, Victoria's most popular restaurants offer three-course dinners at great bargain prices. For details, visit **www.tourismvictoria.com**.

MARCH

CelticFest, Vancouver. For 5 days each year, the sounds of fiddles, bagpipes, bodhrans, dancing feet, and voices resound throughout the city in celebration of Celtic culture. Visit **www.celticfestvancouver.com**. Mid-March.

Pacific Rim Whale Festival, Pacific Rim National Park. Every spring, more than 20,000 gray whales migrate past Vancouver Island's west coast, and this fest celebrates with art shows, gala dinners, and whale-spotting excursions. Call ℰ **250/726-5164** or visit **www.pacificrimwhalefestival.com**. Mid-March to early April.

APRIL

Baisakhi Day Parade, Vancouver. The Sikh New Year is celebrated with a colorful parade around "Little India," where streets are packed with musicians, dancers, and stalls offering free traditional food. Visit **www.tourismvancouver.com**. Mid-April.

Vancouver Sun Run. Canada's biggest 10km (6.25-mile) race sees more than 60,000 runners, joggers, and walkers going through the city's West End to BC Place Stadium. Call ℰ **604/689-9441** or register at **https://register.vancouversunrun.com**.

MAY

Vancouver International Children's Festival. North America's premier annual festival of performing arts for young audiences features activities, plays, music, crafts, and celebrities throughout Granville Island. Call ℰ **604/708-5655** or visit **www.childrensfestival.ca**. Mid-May.

Swiftsure International Yacht Race, Victoria. Colorful and fast sailboats make for spectacular scenery on the waters around Victoria. Visit **www.tourismvictoria.com**. Third or fourth weekend in May.

JUNE

Rio Tinto Alcan Dragon Boat Festival, Vancouver. More than 150 local and international teams compete in this annual festival that also features music, dance, and Chinese acrobatics around False Creek. Visit **www.dragonboatbc.ca**. Third weekend in June.

TD Vancouver International Jazz Festival. More than 800 international jazz and blues players perform at 25 venues ranging from the Orpheum Theatre to free outdoor stages. Call ℰ **604/872-5200** or visit **www.coastaljazz.ca** for more information. Late June/early July.

Bard on the Beach Shakespeare Festival, Vancouver. One of the city's most popular festivals. Each year, four of Shakespeare's plays are performed in a tent overlooking English Bay. Call ℭ **604/739-0559** or visit **www.bardonthebeach.org**. Late May through late September.

Victoria International Cycling Festival. Canada's biggest cycling event features drag races, urban mountain biking events, and two-wheel tricks atop a floating barge, as well as activities for all the two-wheelers in the family. Visit **www.vicf.ca** for details.

JULY

Canada Day. In **Vancouver,** celebrate the country's birthday at an all-day celebration at Canada Place Pier, complete with music, dance, a 21-gun salute at noon, and fireworks. In **Victoria,** head to the Inner Harbour for music, food, and fireworks. But wherever you are, all communities will be celebrating. July 1.

Vancouver Folk Music Festival. Get your mellow on at this outdoor fest at Jericho Beach Park. Contact the Vancouver Folk Music Society at ℭ **604/602-9798** or visit **www.thefestival.bc.ca**. Second or third weekend in July.

Taste, Victoria. A festival of food and wine. Pairings, dinners, workshops, and the grand tasting with more than 100 selections all offer an irresistible sampling of Vancouver Island cuisine. Visit **www.victoriataste.com**.

Honda Celebration of Light, Vancouver. The night skies above English Bay explode with spectacular light shows in the world's biggest offshore fireworks competition. Visit **www.hondacelebrationoflight.com** for information. Three nights at the end of July to first week of August.

AUGUST

Victoria Symphony Splash. The city's beautiful Inner Harbour is transformed into a concert stage for the largest outdoor symphony event in Canada. There's music, food, fun, and all the bells, whistles, cannons, and fireworks of Tchaikovsky's "1812 Overture" performed by the Victoria Symphony. Visit **www.victoriasymphony.ca/splash**. First Sunday in August.

Vancouver Pride Parade & Festival. This huge and hugely popular gay- and lesbian-pride festival features numerous events throughout the week, but the highlight is, without a doubt, the exuberant parade through the city's West End. For more info, contact the Pride Society (ℭ **604/687-0955; www.vancouverpride.ca**). First Monday in August (BC Day).

Abbottsford International Air Show. Barnstorming stuntmen and precision military pilots fly everything from Sopwith Camels to Stealth Bombers in one of the biggest air shows in the world, held just outside Vancouver. Call ℭ **604/852-8511** or visit **www.abbotsfordairshow.com**. Second weekend in August.

Pacific National Exhibition, Vancouver. The city's favorite fair includes one of North America's best all-wooden roller coasters. Special events include livestock demonstrations, logger competitions, fashion shows, and a midway. Call ℭ **604/253-2311** or visit **www.pne.ca** for more details. Mid-August to Labour Day.

Classic Boat Festival, Victoria. Boaters from around the world converge in Victoria's Inner Harbour for this annual Labor Day weekend celebration, which includes races, a parade of steam vessels, a cruise up the Gorge Waterway, and vessels open for tours. For more information, call ℭ **250/383-8306** or visit **www.classicboatfestival.ca**. Last weekend in August.

SEPTEMBER

Vancouver Fringe Festival. This celebration of the performing arts features more than 600 original and innovative shows, performed throughout the city by groups from Canada and around the world. Call ℭ **604/257-0350** or check out **www.vancouverfringe.com** for more info. First and second week of September.

Victoria International Chalk Festival. Artists from around the world transform the streets of Victoria into a unique gallery of spectacular chalk art that must be seen to be believed. For info, visit www.victoriachalkfestival.com. Second weekend in September.

The Great Canadian Beer Festival, Victoria. Featuring samples from the province's best microbreweries, this event is held at Royal Athletic Park. For more information, call ☏ **250/383-2332** or visit **www.gcbf.com**. Early September.

OCTOBER

Vancouver International Writers and Readers Festival. Public readings by Canadian and international authors, as well as writers' workshops, take place on Granville Island and at other locations in the Lower Mainland. Call ☏ **604/681-6330** or check **www.writersfest.bc.ca** for details. Mid-October.

NOVEMBER

Cornucopia, Whistler. Ten days—including two weekends—of eating, drinking, sampling, and seminars that often coincide with the opening of the ski season at Whistler Mountain Resort. For tickets and info, visit **www.whistler cornucopia.com**. Mid-November.

DECEMBER

Carol Ship Parade of Lights Festival, Vancouver. Cruise ships decorated with colorful Christmas lights sail around English Bay, while onboard guests sip cider and sing their way through the canon of Christmas carols. For more info, call ☏ **604/878-8999** or check out **www.carolships.org**. First 3 weeks in December.

VISIONS OF VANCOUVER & VICTORIA

For a pair of cities that are so young and not terribly large, both Vancouver and Victoria have produced an impressive collection of creative people. Perhaps it's all that physical beauty that surrounds them. Or perhaps it's the legacy of all those adventurous folks that made their way here to the edge of the world. In any case, these are just a few of the artists whose works a visitor should seek out, and where to find them.

Arthur Erickson (1924–2009) is the Vancouver-born architect and urban planner who truly set the tone for Vancouver's design sense. He was best known for his elegant concrete modernist buildings, often modeled on the post-and-beam construction of Coastal First Nations buildings. His most famous buildings include the Vancouver Law Courts, Museum of Anthropology, and the Simon Fraser University campus.

Emily Carr (1871–1945) was one of the most remarkable people and greatest artists Canada has ever produced. Born in Victoria to a comfortable merchant family, she set society on its ears when she decided to become a painter. One of the legendary modernist painters, she was heavily influenced by both the nature and indigenous peoples of the West Coast and even traveled on her own to Ninstints on remote Haida Gwaii, where she created a series of iconic paintings. She was a contemporary of the Group of Seven—Lawren Harris told her, "You are one of us"—and spent time in Paris where she was influenced by the Post Impressionists and Fauvists. A true eccentric, and a Canadian legend, she spent her later years accompanied by her dog Billie and monkey Woo. You can find her works at the Vancouver Art Gallery and Art Gallery of Victoria.

Douglas Coupland (1961–present) became famous as the author who defined a lost generation when he published his first book, "Generation X: Tales for an Accelerated Culture," in 1991. Since then, he's written numerous other bestselling books, but has become just as well known for his artful design work. That's his "Digital Orca" sculpture you can see leaping up in Jack Poole Plaza near the Olympic Cauldron and Vancouver Convention Centre. His take on paintings by the famous Group of Seven artists is on display in the Rosewood Hotel Georgia, and other works are often exhibited at the Vancouver Art Gallery. He currently lives in West Vancouver.

Francis Mawson Rattenbury (1867–1935) was the architect who designed Victoria's most iconic buildings—the British Columbia Parliament Buildings (1898), the Fairmont Empress Hotel (1908), and the Steamship Terminal Building (1924), as well as the former courthouse that is now the Vancouver Art Gallery (1913). Self-trained as an architect, his designs were in the elegant Neoclassical and Romanesque styles fashionable at the turn of the last century. His personal life, though, was less graceful. In 1923, he very publicly left his wife and two children for another woman; in disgrace and poverty, he fled Victoria for England with his new wife and was later bludgeoned to death by her lover, their 18-year-old chauffeur.

Bill Reid (1920–98) was born in Victoria to an American father and a Haida mother of the Raven clan. He became one of the most significant artists among the Coastal First Nations, with works that include jewelry, paintings, and sculpture. Most importantly, he rediscovered the symbolism and traditions of the Haida, much of which had been lost after contact with the Europeans, and opened the door for other native artists as well. In 1951, he established a studio on Granville Island, and visitors can still see his carving shed there. His most famous works include the remarkable bronze sculpture, "Spirit of Haida Gwaii: The Jade Canoe," which is on display in the International Terminal at the Vancouver International Airport, as well as Chief of the Undersea World outside the Vancouver Aquarium, and numerous pieces at the Museum of Anthropology.

John Fluevog (1948–present) is a Vancouver-born-and-raised shoe designer known for some pretty fancy footwork. No one else designs shoes like Fluevog—which is why the Museum of Vancouver devoted a whole exhibit to him in 2010, and why Madonna famously sported a pair of his Munsters in the movie "Truth or Dare." Think handcrafted, eco-friendly, wildly colored platform Mary Janes for the ladies and pointy-toed punk oxfords for the gents, and you've got the general idea. You can become a "Fluevogger" by picking up a pair at his Gastown boutique.

Fred Herzog (1930–present) was born in Stuttgart, Germany, but emigrated to Vancouver in 1952, where he became famous as a photographer capturing scenes of everyday life, especially during the 1950s and '60s. He captured the city through its most dynamic changing years, and his later works have a distinctive sense of loss. His works have been compiled in books such as "Fred Herzog: Vancouver Photographs," and are frequently exhibited at various galleries, including the Vancouver Art Gallery.

Bing Thom (1940–present) was born in Hong Kong, but in 1950 immigrated with his family to Vancouver, where he became one of the city's most notable architects and urban designers. Known for his clean, cool lines and airy spaces, probably his two most iconic local works are the Aberdeen Centre in Richmond and the Chan Centre for Performing Arts at the University of British Columbia.

Jeff Wall (1946–present) is one of the artists who helped define what became known as the 1980s "Vancouver School" of art. He is best known for large scale, backlit cibachrome photographs that mix Vancouver's natural beauty with images of urban decay. His 1978 photograph "The Destroyed Room" was featured on a Sonic Youth album cover, and Wall shot the iconic image of Iggy Pop on the 1999 album "Avenue B." Other works are regularly displayed at the Vancouver Art gallery, and galleries around the world.

Robert Bateman (1930–present) is probably the world's most famous living wildlife painter. Although he spent the first part of his life in Ontario, where he was a geography teacher, he has in recent years made Salt Spring Island near Victoria his home. In 2013, he also opened the Bateman Centre in Victoria's Steamship Terminal

Building, which features a gallery displaying his famously detailed animal paintings, as well as the offices of the **Robert Bateman Foundation** (www.batemanfoundation.org), which works to promote conservation and awareness of global issues surrounding nature and wildlife.

Famous Faces, Famous Voices

"Wait, isn't that—?" If you were going to say Diana Krall or Michael Bublé, Sandra Oh, or Seth Rogen, well, it just might be. Plenty of famous folks call Vancouver and Victoria home, and you never know, you might just run into them while you're strolling around the Seawall.

Jazz chanteuse Diana Krall was born in Nanaimo, just up island from Victoria, and these days makes her home with husband Elvis Costello and their family in West Vancouver. Crooner Michael Bublé was born in the Vancouver suburb of Burnaby, mega rock star Bryan Adams grew up in North Vancouver, popster Carly Rae Jepsen in Mission, and Grammy Award–winning songbird Nelly Furtado hails from Victoria. Meanwhile, countless other musical performers have moved here to become honorary Vancouverites, including the Payolas' Paul Hyde, folk legend Sarah McLachlan, and country queen k. d. lang.

With a nickname like Hollywood North, it's not surprising that this is also home for many movie and TV stars. Around Victoria, you might run into actress Meg Tilly and her ex, Colin Firth, as well as director Atom Egoyan. In Vancouver, you never know when you'll see hometown kids Sandra Oh, Jason Priestley, Seth Rogen, Michael J. Fox, Joshua Jackson, Margot Kidder, or model Coco Rocha.

And maybe it's those gray days that make this such a popular place for writers to live. Among them, you might find the legendary sci-fi guys William Gibson and Spider Robinson, mystery writer William Deverell, poet Evelyn Lau, novelists Timothy Taylor, Douglas Coupland, and Wayson Choy, poet Evelyn Lau, and environmentalist David Suzuki.

VANCOUVER & VICTORIA ON A PLATE

Bring your appetite: There's some good eating to be had here. Vancouver especially has become one of the world's top dining destinations, while Victoria has carved out a niche for its DIY farm-to-table esthetic. This region doesn't have the centuries of history that, say, French or Chinese cuisine does, but what it does have is a bounty of terrific local ingredients, a vibrant multicultural community, and a batch of passionate, creative, and highly skilled chefs who are cooking up a cuisine that is uniquely of its place. Here are just a few things you'll want to taste while you're here.

Farm, Sea & Field-to-Table

"The 100 Mile Diet" was written here and Greenpeace was created here, so it shouldn't come as surprise that chefs take the whole local, seasonal, organic, and sustainable thing pretty seriously. Luckily, they have some great ingredients to choose from. There is, of course, the exceptional local seafood, from the finny salmon, tuna, and halibut to the crustaceans and shellfish including oysters, scallops, mussels, Dungeness crab, and, above all, sweet, buttery spot prawns, which come into a brief but luxurious season each May. With its rich, fertile soil and mild climate, this is also a terrific region for produce, especially sweet berries, tender greens, and, from the mountainous area around Pemberton, creamy potatoes. There's a lively foraging culture, too, and in spring and fall, chefs will often find boxes of wild mushrooms showing up at their back doors.

Local Heroes

Today's West Coast cuisine is wildly flavorful and innovative, but 2 decades ago, you wouldn't have found much more than simple fried fish or grilled steak on a menu. What changed it all? Two generations of passionate chefs. It started with a handful of gents who are still going strong: **Hidekazu Tojo,** who invented the California roll and introduced Vancouver to sushi; **Umberto Menghi,** who taught the city that real Italian food didn't come smothered in melted cheese; **Vikram Vij,** who proved that Indian food didn't mean curry in a hurry, and that it could pair perfectly well with good wine; and **John Bishop,** who was among the first, along with **Sinclair Philip** of Sooke Harbour House, to define what we now think of as West Coast cuisine. Since they came on the scene, they've passed on the whisk to a legion of creative chefs such as **David Hawksworth, Rob Feenie, Andrea Carlson,** and countless others.

Asian Influence

Better practice your chopstick skills. Chances are you'll be sitting down to a bowl of noodles, a plate of sushi, baskets of dim sum, or who knows, perhaps even a whole 10-course Cantonese banquet. With its huge Asian population, it's no surprise that Vancouver has absorbed many of that vast continent's culinary traditions. Chinese, Japanese, Indian, and Southeast Asian flavors abound, not just in ethnic eateries, but across menus of all sorts. Be prepared to enjoy their sweet, salty, sour, and hot mix of tastes.

Pub Culture

Victoria especially is famous for its lively pub culture, a legacy from its British and Scottish heritage. Today the best pubs serve terrific casual food, such as fish and chips, charcuterie, and burgers, along with craft ales and usually a respectable wine list. The atmosphere will always be casual and friendly, and the bill affordable.

Drink It In

Be sure to try a British Columbia wine with your meal. B.C. wines are exceptional, and this is likely the only place you'll get to try them—supply tends to be small, and local demand is big. The main wine region is the Okanagan Valley, and the best wines are cooler climate varietals, such as Chardonnay, Riesling, and Pinot Noir. That said, you can find some powerhouse red blends from the South Okanagan. Expect to pay for them, though; land is expensive, and that drives up the prices of the wine, too.

Also check out the terrific selection of craft beers. A new brewery seems to be opening here every week or so, and you'll find everything from the lightest of lagers to the chocolatiest of porters on tap somewhere. B.C. also has a lively artisanal distilling scene—the **Okanagan Spirits Taboo absinthe, Victoria gin,** and **Pemberton Distillery Schramm potato vodka** are just a few of the spirits that must be sampled. And be sure to have a cocktail—both cities have an exceptional craft cocktail scene.

What to Eat & Drink

Before you go home, you must try these 10 dishes and drinks:

VANCOUVER COCKTAIL: A recently rediscovered classic from the 1950s that you'll find on the city's top cocktail lists, especially at the grand **hotel bars** (gin, sweet vermouth, Benedictine, orange bitters).

FRASER VALLEY DUCK POUTINE: The city has gone crazy for poutine, a Quebecois dish of French fries, melted cheese curds, and gravy that is much, much better than it sounds. **Edible** at the Market on Granville Island serves an especially luxurious version topped with duck confit and fried eggs.

THOMAS HAAS SPARKLE COOKIES: Thomas Haas has been named 1 of the top 10 pastry chefs in North America and everything at his tiny shop in North Vancouver is sweetly perfect. But it's his humble sparkle cookies—chocolate dusted with sugar—that keep people coming back.

FISH AND CHIPS: This dish is as quintessential to life in Victoria life as a ticket on the BC Ferries. There are many, many places that do it well, but **Red Fish Blue Fish, the Guild,** and **Steamship Grill** are among the best. Best bet: Crispy fried local halibut when it's in season.

SEAFOOD CHOWDER: Forage in Vancouver makes their version with cream, spot prawns, and quail eggs. The **BC Ferries'** simple tomato-based clam chowder is legendary. And **Spinnakers Gastro Brewpub** in Victoria makes a version that is decadently creamy and loaded with seafood. A West Coast must.

BONE LUGE: Take a roasted, cracked marrow bone, raise it to your lips, then shoot a tot of sherry down its length, scooping up every little bit of silky, salty marrow as it makes its way to your ecstatic taste buds. That's the bone luge, a delicious if undignified must at **Wildebeest** in Vancouver.

KFC: Not the Colonel's fried chicken, but the Korean Fried Cauliflower at **Hawksworth Restaurant** in Vancouver. It's one of the bar snacks in the swish little cocktail lounge: chunks of cauliflower tossed in spicy hot sauce then flash fried until crispy and caramelized.

XIAO LONG BAO: These tender Shanghainese pork or crab dumplings form a delicate broth inside the wrapper as they steam. Try them at **Shanghai River** in Richmond or at **Dinesty** on Robson Street in Vancouver.

SALTED CARAMEL GELATO: The creamy, frozen treats from **Bella Gelateria** near the Vancouver Convention Center were voted the best gelato in the world by the Italians, the people who invented it. You cannot go wrong with any of the flavors, but the salted caramel is especially divine.

OKANAGAN VALLEY RIESLING OR PINOT NOIR: There are many exceptional wines being produced in B.C.'s Okanagan Valley, but two varietals that seem to have consistent success are the delicate dry Rieslings and bright Pinot Noirs. Try the **Tantalus Riesling,** named by critic Jancis Robinson one of the best in the world, and the **Blue Mountain Reserve Pinot Noir** from one of the province's oldest family-owned vineyards.

SUGGESTED ITINERARIES

This chapter is a guide to planning your stay in Vancouver and Victoria. I've provided several different itineraries in each city to help you schedule your time. While you can follow these itineraries to a T, you can also mix, match, and meander off on your own adventure. Just be sure to leave plenty of time to enjoy a pint on a patio or watch the world go by from a sunny spot on a beach somewhere.

In addition to the main attractions, I've also provided itineraries for families and foodies. If you're staying in the city center, you can get around easily by foot or by transit. But if you plan to venture farther afield, you may want to rent a car, so be prepared and plan accordingly.

ICONIC VANCOUVER IN 1, 2 & 3 DAYS

Vancouver's downtown core—which includes some of its oldest, most historic neighborhoods—is clustered on a peninsula caught between the North Shore Mountains and the Salish Sea. You can explore this area on foot, and cover most of it in a day, though you may want to spend a little bit longer than that to really feel at home here. If you have more than a day, venture south to the funky hoods of Kitsilano and Main Street, or north to the mountains of the North Shore. In any case, bring your best walking shoes and be prepared to work up an appetite.

DAY 1

1 Canada Place ★★

The distinctive sails of Canada Place are one of Vancouver's most famous sights, and this is as good a place as any to start exploring the city. Canada Place is home to Vancouver's two convention centers, the cruise ship and seaplane terminals, the **FlyOver Canada** attraction, and the **Olympic Cauldron.** It also offers unbeatable views of the **North Shore Mountains, Lions Gate Bridge,** and the busy Port of Vancouver. Tourism Vancouver has a visitor center here, so you can pick up any info you need, and numerous tours depart from the area, including the **Vancouver Trolley Company** city tours (p. 101). And from here, it's just a short walk east to historic **Gastown,** and a slight longer walk west along a seaside pathway to **Stanley Park.** See p. 82.

2 Stanley Park ★★★

This 400-hectare (1,000-acre) public park is one of Vancouver's greatest attractions—a wilderness area encircled by a scenic seawall and featuring gardens, a lagoon where swans glide, beaches, concession stands, playgrounds, totem poles, statuary, a miniature railway, and much more. One of the best ways to explore it is via horse-drawn carriage ride. See p. 84.

3 Vancouver Aquarium ★★★

While you're in Stanley Park, be sure to drop by the aquarium, one of the best such facilities in North America. Visit the tuxedo-clad birds at Penguin Point, discover the critters of the Pacific Northwest in the Wild Coast Gallery, and stay for the daily beluga and dolphin shows. See p. 86.

4 English Bay Beach ★★

If the weather is nice, head over to English Bay Beach, located at the south entrance to the park. Stretch out on the sand and check out the views of Kitsilano and, off in the distance, misty Vancouver Island. This is a good place for lunch: Try **Raincity Grill** (p. 72), one of Vancouver's first places to promote a local, sustainable cuisine, or any of the fun noodle bars along Denman Street.

5 Robson Street & the West End ★

Once you've refueled, you can meander by foot across the charming residential neighborhood of the West End. As you walk along the shady, tree-lined streets of cozy old brick walkups, you'll find it hard to believe this friendly and livable community is one of the most densely populated in North America. Davie Street is still the heart of the city's vibrant gay village, while Denman is a cluster of restaurants from every corner of the world. Head over to **Robson Street** for some window-shopping, and if time allows, pop into the **Vancouver Art Gallery** to check out the paintings by local legend **Emily Carr** (p. 86). If time is short, though, you can always jump on a bus—either one of the hop-on, hop-off tours or the No. 5 city bus—or catch a cab to Chinatown.

6 Chinatown ★

Vancouver's Chinatown is one of the largest and oldest in North America. Although many of the original families that once lived here have moved on to the suburb of Richmond in recent years, it's still a vibrant spot filled with cafes, noodle houses, markets, and increasingly, hip cocktail lounges. Don't miss the **Dr. Sun Yat-Sen Classical Chinese Garden.** See p. 87.

7 Gastown & the Steam Clock ★★

Near Chinatown you'll find Vancouver's oldest neighborhood, **Gastown.** The city got its start here back in the late 1860s when a saloonkeeper named **Gassy Jack Deighton** (p. 40) first set up shop to keep the local sawmill workers lubricated. This low-rise brick neighborhood has often flirted with the disreputable—and sometimes plunged headlong into flat-out bad behavior—but these days it's best known for its funky cocktail bars, independent restaurants, First Nations galleries, and trendy boutiques featuring local designers like **John Fluevog** (p. 113). Be sure to stop and watch the famous **Gastown Steam Clock** whistle out the quarter hour. See p. 87.

8 L'Abattoir ★★

There is no shortage of great places to dine in Gastown, but one of my favorites is **L'Abattoir** (so named because it sits on the edge of Blood Alley, once home to the city's butchers). A modern restoration of a 120-year-old brick-and-beam space, with ornate French tile work and twiggy light fixtures, this is a chic little spot to enjoy chef Lee Cooper's French-influenced West Coast fare and head barman Shaun Layton's creative cocktails. Then, if you're up for a little nightlife, you can hit the neighborhood's clubs and bars afterward. See p. 69.

DAY 2

Today you'll leave the downtown peninsula, with its shimmering glass towers and cozy brick walkups, and head south to Kitsilano, False Creek, the University of British Columbia, and Main Street. You can cross either the Burrard or Granville Street Bridge, or you can take the funky little foot passenger ferry called the Aquabus. On this side of False Creek (which is actually an inlet), you'll find Craftsman-style houses, glorious gardens, beaches aplenty, and loads of delicious things to whet your appetite.

---

1 Granville Island ★★★

This sandbar under the Granville Street Bridge was once an industrial site where factories churned out barrels, paint, nails, roofing tiles, and heavy machinery. Today you'll find artisan shops, theaters, an art school, marina, several restaurants, a brewery, sake maker, and distillery, and the very popular **Granville Island Public Market.** Browse among the many food stalls to find breakfast—perhaps a rustic peach-and-rosemary tart at Terra Breads or one of the Montreal-style bagels at Siegel's—then explore the shops and galleries. See p. 88.

2 Vanier Park ★

If you're on foot, you can easily walk to Vanier Park along a scenic seaside pathway. The park itself is a wide-open space with spectacular views of downtown and the North Shore Mountains, perfect for picnicking or kite flying when it's not busy hosting a festival like the summer-long **Bard on the Beach** (p. 118). It's also home to the **Museum of Vancouver** (p. 90), where you can find the flickering vestiges of Vancouver's neon past, as well as the **H. R. MacMillan Space Centre** (p. 90) and nearby **Vancouver Maritime Museum** (p. 91).

3 Kitsilano ★★

You have two options, both of which will take you into the neighborhood of Kitsilano. Back in the 1960s and '70s, this was hippie central; today, it's a bit more yuppified, but it's still a cool area to explore. If you continue along the seaside walk, you'll come to **Kits Beach,** with its massive outdoor saltwater pool, busy concession stands, and wide, sandy stretches. Head up the hill through the shaggy old houses, though, and you'll arrive on 4th Avenue, a busy thoroughfare lined with shops and restaurants. One great lunch option is **Fable Kitchen** (p. 75), a casual downhome eatery known for exceptional farm-to-table fare. And if you need a caffeine break, head straight to 49th Parallel for the best beans around town.

4 UBC & the Museum of Anthropology ★★★

From here, you'll need wheels. Hop in your car or aboard the No. 4 bus to the University of British Columbia and the outstanding **Museum of Anthropology.** The building alone is worth the visit—designed by celebrated Vancouver architect **Arthur Erickson** (p. 19), it's a sleek vision of concrete and glass perched on a cliff above the clothing-optional Wreck Beach. Step inside and you'll discover a collection of aboriginal art that is among the biggest and best in the world, especially when it comes to the totem poles, spirit masks, and sculptures of the Pacific Northwest First Nations. See p. 90.

5 Main Street & Brassneck Brewery ★

If you have time, head back the way you came and meander on over to Main Street. This is the city's hip new-old hood, where the traditional (antiques stores and bridal shops) rubs shoulders with the oh-so-trendy. You'll find gourmet donuts, tiki drinks, upscale eateries like the exceptional Burdock & Co, and local designer boutiques here. See p. 120.

6 Vij's? Or Tojo's? ★★★

And then to dinner. You are spoiled for choice in this area, where you can find exceptional cuisine from every part of the globe, but if you are only here for 1 night, then it really comes down to one of two choices: Tojo's or Vij's. It really depends on what you're hungry for—and whether you have the patience to wait. **Tojo's** is exceptional sushi in a cool room, where you can sip on chilled sake while the master prepares his immaculate works of culinary art (p. 74). **Vij's** is South Asian food, but don't expect your typical Indian curry-in-a-hurry. Instead, think shiitake mushrooms in cream curry, wine-marinated lamb popsicles in fenugreek sauce, and an award-winning wine list. It does not, however, accept reservations, so go early and prepare to wait—it'll be worth it once you're inside this fragrant jewel box of a restaurant (p. 75).

DAY 3

If Day 2 was all about museums, shops, and restaurants, today is all about the great outdoors. You'll head north to the mountains that overlook Vancouver, where you will find ski hills and hiking trails galore as well as old-school English-style pubs and some breathtaking attractions. It helps if you have a car, but if you don't, there are plenty of other ways to get yourself up into them thar hills, including shuttles, tour buses, city buses, and the foot-passenger ferry called the SeaBus. See p. 43.

1 Lions Gate Bridge ★★

This graceful green span, officially known as the First Narrows Bridge, was built in 1938 to connect the communities of North and West Vancouver to the City of Vancouver. It has three reversible lanes, which are the bane of many commuters' existence, but the inevitable traffic jams do offer lots of opportunity to take in those magnificent views of the North Shore Mountains. If you're driving, your route will take you through **Stanley Park** and across the nearly 1,800m (6,000-ft.) bridge span; at its northern end, you can choose to take the exit left to West Vancouver and on to Whistler Mountain Resort or right to North Vancouver and **Capilano Road.** Point yourself up Capilano Road. See p. 84.

2 Capilano Suspension Bridge Park ★★★

About halfway up Capilano Road, you'll come across one of British Columbia's most famous—and famously terrifying—attractions. It's a simple wood-and-cable footbridge that stretches 140m (460 ft.) across a deep gorge, gently swaying 70m (230 ft.) above the Capilano River so very, very far below. The bridge is the main attraction, but the park also features a Treetops Adventure, cantilevered Cliffwalk, gift shop, interpretive story center, and First Nations exhibits. One of the best times to go is during the holidays, when the park is lit up with hundreds of thousands of Christmas lights. See p. 91.

3 Grouse Mountain ★★

Keep going up Capilano Road and you'll reach the parking lot for Grouse Mountain, one of three ski hills on the North Shore (the other two are Cypress Mountain and Mount Seymour). If you feel energetic, take the Grouse Grind, a tough 2.9km (1.8-mile) hike that goes straight uphill. Otherwise, hop aboard the Skyride for a leisurely journey to "The Peak of Vancouver." At the top, you can explore hiking trails, go zip lining, and visit the grizzly bears in the wildlife refuge; in winter, you can also ski, snowboard, skate, or take a sleigh ride. You can also enjoy a romantic gourmet dinner at **The Observatory** or a casual burger at the **Rusty Rail BBQ.** Above all—quite literally—you'll enjoy the spectacular views of Vancouver, the Salish Sea, and the Gulf Islands. See p. 92.

4 Lighthouse Park ★

From Grouse Mountain, you can head east to North Vancouver or west to West Vancouver. (And yes, all those "wests" are confusing for locals, too.) If you choose to explore West Vancouver, drive down to Marine Drive and turn right, but be careful not to get caught up in the bridge traffic or you'll end up back in Vancouver. West Van is a series of small seaside villages such as Ambleside and Dundarave that have combined to become one of the wealthiest addresses in Canada. Keep following Marine Drive to **Lighthouse Park,** a 75-hectare (185-acre) cliffside park of towering old-growth rainforest, easy hiking trails, and scenic picnic areas. See p. 93.

5 Lynn Headwaters Regional Park ★★

If you decide to go east to North Vancouver instead, you'll find this spectacular park gathered around the rushing waters of Lynn Creek. You'll find **another suspension bridge** here, and, while this one doesn't have a gift store or interpretive center, it is free. The park itself is riddled with terrific hiking trails that range from easy ambles to rugged backcountry treks, as well as lakes, rivers, waterfalls, majestic forests, and towering mountain peaks. And all of this is just minutes from the heart of the city. See p. 97.

6 Dinner with a View ★

While the North Shore isn't known for its gourmet dining, it does offer a handful of decent casual-upscale restaurants with spectacular views. If you're ending your day in West Vancouver, the **Beach House** at Dundarave (p. 79) is a great place to nibble on local seafood, sip a glass of wine, and enjoy the beachside view of Lions Gate Bridge and Stanley Park. Should you be in North Vancouver, **Pier 7** (p. 79) next to the Lonsdale Quay is also a good place for dinner. It, too, offers a seafood-intense menu, with classic cocktails and interesting wine selection, with a lively view of downtown Vancouver and the busy port.

VANCOUVER FOR FAMILIES

From its world-class children's festival to its children's theaters, markets, parks, and playgrounds, this city has plenty to keep the whole family busy. I've provided 2 days of action-packed fun for kids big and small.

Day 1: Stanley Park & North Shore

Before you start your adventure, visit **Mink Chocolates** (p. 78) for the sweet taste of the city's most luxurious hot chocolate. Once everyone's sugar levels are nicely topped up, head over to Canada Place to swoop across the country (virtually, at least) on the **FlyOver Canada** attraction (p. 82).

From there, board one of the hop-on, hop-off tours, and roll on over to **Stanley Park** (p. 84). You can easily find enough to keep the little ones entertained all day here. One of the most popular experiences is the **Miniature Train,** an open-air replica of the first transcontinental passenger train to arrive in Vancouver back in the 1880s, which chugs around a pretty pond in the middle of the park's lush rainforest. Nearby is the **Vancouver Aquarium,** with its penguins, dolphins, belugas, jellyfish, finny critters, and tanks full of wiggly things to touch. The aquarium not only offers plenty of stuff to see, it's also got plenty of stuff to do, so you can expect to spend a good few hours here. Just past the aquarium is **Lumberman's Arch,** where your little ones can splash in the water park and fuel up on hot dogs and fish and chips at the popular concession stand. While you're in the park, you can also visit the totem poles at **Brockton Point,** splash around in the **heated outdoor pool** at Second Beach, wander along the **forest trails** or the **paved Seawall,** and take a ride in a **horse-drawn carriage.**

If you still have time and energy in the afternoon, cross Burrard Inlet to the North Shore, where you can swing across a deep, narrow canyon on the **Capilano Suspension Bridge** (p. 91), then race through the branches of an ancient rainforest on a wooden boardwalk known as Treetops Adventure. Then visit **Maplewood Farm** (p. 100), a rural heritage farm where you can visit the 200-plus animals, ride a pony or tractor, enjoy a picnic, and play at being a farmer for a day.

If you're still on the Shore at dinnertime, hit the **Tomahawk Barbecue** (p. 80), a kitschy old-school diner, where you can enjoy a "Skookum Chief" burger, mile-high lemon meringue pie, and First Nations souvenirs. If, on the other hand, you're back in the city for dinner, check out **Cardero's Restaurant** (p. 72), a fun, kid-friendly, boisterous place perched on a wharf overlooking Coal Harbour, with a huge menu and lots of running-around space.

Day 2: False Creek

There are three main kid-friendly destinations in False Creek, and two of them are accessible by **Aquabus or False Creek Ferries,** the tiny little ferryboat service that may prove to be the funnest part of all. At the far eastern end of the inlet is **Science World at TELUS World of Science** (p. 91), where kids of all ages can create fantastic vehicles out of Lego, power drums with their heartbeat, watch IMAX movies, learn about bodily secretions, and build cool things in the science park.

Once you've exhausted your inner mad scientist, you can hop back onto the ferry and bob on over to **Granville Island** (p. 88), which is home to the **Kids**

Market, with its giant indoor Adventure Zone and dozens of kid-friendly shops. On the island, you'll also find Canada's largest free outdoor waterpark and plenty of other fun, free stuff to see and do, including watching artisans at work and wandering through the marina. You'll also find the **Carousel Theatre for Young People,** which offers great kids' programming year round. Each May, the island also hosts the annual **Vancouver International Children's Festival.** This is one of the top juvenile performing arts festivals in the world, featuring many of the greatest names in the biz, such as Fred Penner and Rick Scott. And, of course, there are loads of delicious things to nibble on at the **Granville Island Public Market** itself. Be sure to try the peanut brittle and saltwater taffy made in the big copper cauldrons at **Olde World Fudge.**

Finally, if you haven't run out of steam, you can take the 20-minute seaside stroll to Vanier Park and the **H. R. MacMillan Space Centre** (p. 90), where you can gaze at the starry, starry skies, learn how to build a Rover like the one that landed on Mars, and watch films that introduce you to the wonders of the universe. While you're there, you can also visit the **Museum of Vancouver** (p. 90) and the nearby **Maritime Museum** (p. 91), then head up the hill to 4th Avenue for an early dinner at **Sophie's Cosmic Café** (p. 77). This Kitsilano institution is stuffed with toys, memorabilia, and quirky bric-a-brac and serves up simple burgers, salads, and the like. Don't even try to resist the Cosmic apple pie and served á la mode.

VANCOUVER FOR FOODIES

This city is crazy about food, especially when it comes to anything local, seasonal, and organic. It is, after all, where Alisa Smith and J.B. MacKinnon wrote the book "The 100-Mile Diet: A Year of Local Eating," which popularized the concept of dining from one's own back yard. It's also where OceanWise, the seafood conservation program, was created, as well as Greenpeace. And with its vibrant mix of Asian and European cultures, passionate chefs, talented bartenders, and super-savvy diners, you just know there are going to be some fine eats (and drinks) to be had here. Be sure to bring your appetite—and your credit card. Here are just some of the places to check out while you're in town.

Start with a visit to the **Granville Island Public Market** (p. 115), making sure you arrive early, before the crowds do. But first, swing by **Beaucoup Bakery & Café** (p. 78) near the entrance to the island to fuel up on pastry chef Jackie Ellis's mouthwatering pain au chocolat and a perfectly frothy cappuccino. Then, at the market itself, browse through the stalls selling produce, pastries, seafood, exotic spices, and more, until you find the longest lineup, which will lead you to the exceptional charcutière **Oyama Sausage Co.** Pick up a slab of their irresistible Belgian truffle pâté and a toothsome baguette from nearby **Terra Breads,** then head out onto the wharf to enjoy it along with the marina view—just watch out for the hungry seagulls, who know a good thing when they see it.

After that, wander over to **Edible Canada** (p. 75), a bistro and boutique celebrating all things deliciously local. This is a good place to stock up on foodie gifts like bacon-flavored sea salt, West Coast smoked salmon, and Vista d'Oro craft beer jam and other preserves. If you're still peckish, you can also stop in at the bistro for the Fraser Valley duck poutine topped with duck confit and eggs. On the island, also check out **Finest at Sea** for sustainable seafood, the **Granville Island Brewing Co.** for their classic

lager, **Artisan Sake Maker** for a taste of locally made sake, the **Liberty Distillery** for a splash of gin, and, near the entrance to the island, **Fisherman's Wharf,** where you can pick up sweet, buttery spot prawns during their short spring season. Also nearby is **Barbara-Jo's Books to Cooks** (p. 110), where you can find cookbooks by local chefs such as Rob Feenie or Vikram Vij.

Speaking of Vij, this is a good opportunity to venture up South Granville Street to **Rangoli** (p. 75), the casual sister to his more famous restaurant, for a savory snack of lentil, paneer, and chickpea samosas with cilantro-jalapeño chutney. South Granville is also home to a number of kitchenware chain stores such as Cookworks and Williams-Sonoma, but at this point I suggest you hop in your car or on a bus and head down to **Gourmet Warehouse** (p. 115) on East Hastings Street. Here you will find an epic selection of everything from spices, prepared foods, artisanal potato chips, and cocktail bitters to pots, pans, baking sheets, platters, and glassware.

Next, it's over to **Chinatown** and the quirky little **Harvest Community Foods** on Union Street, where you can pick up a glass jar of **Earnest Ice Cream,** locally made small-batch ice cream that comes in flavors like salted caramel and strawberry basil. From there it's a short stroll to the **Keefer Bar** (p. 81) and cocktail hour—try an apothecary-inspired cocktail like the Opium Sour. For a quick snack before dinner, visit the hip little modern Chinese joint **Bao Bei** (p. 70) two doors up for the truffled pork dumplings or *shao bing,* a sesame flatbread with lamb sirloin.

Finally, dinner. Vancouver has many choices for all budgets and tastes, but for a truly unforgettable culinary experience, go directly to **PiDGin** (p. 69) in Gastown. Chef Makoto Ono prepares true fusion cuisine, where east meets west, vegan meets carnivorous, and the flavors are vibrant, exciting, and like nothing you've tasted before. I love the *dan dan* raw rutabaga salad, the pickling spice half squab, the grilled octopus with romesco, and the duck-fat-washed Sazerac cocktail. Just order the tasting menu, and try them all. Afterward, should you find yourself in need of a nightcap, wander down the street to **the Diamond** (p. 81) for a handcrafted whisky cocktail.

If You Have Time

GO NORTH: In North Vancouver, visit **Thomas Haas Patisserie;** he has been named 1 of the top 10 pastry chefs in America, and his croissants, pastries, and whimsical chocolates are worth the trip across the bridge. See p. 78.

GO SOUTH: The suburb of **Richmond** is home to some of the best **Chinese restaurants** in the world and is just a 20-minute ride from downtown via Canada Line. Climb aboard for gourmet dim sum at one of the Cantonese dining palaces such as Sea Harbour, Fisherman's Terrace, or Sun Sui Wah. See p. 98.

ICONIC VICTORIA IN 1 & 2 DAYS

Victoria lies at the southern tip of Vancouver Island, and the scenic trip by ferry or plane is just part of the adventure. Victoria is much smaller and more relaxed than Vancouver, and is a terrific walking city and an even better cycling one, so you don't really need a car unless you want to explore the outlying areas. Note that my Day 1 itinerary is especially action-packed and while you can cover all this ground in 1 day, you may want to spread it out over two.

DAY 1

1 Inner Harbour

The city is built around the scenic Inner Harbour, a busy working port where fishing boats, floatplanes, ferries, and whale-watching tours chug all day long. One could easily spe nd a day watching all the action from the walkway around the inlet, but it's even better to hop aboard one of the cute little **Victoria Harbour Ferries** (p. 142) and check out the view from the water. That includes the historic **Fairmont Empress Hotel** (p. 161) and the magnificent **BC Parliament Buildings** (p. 165). The ferries operate tours that travel throughout the harbor and offer a number of stops, including the one at Fisherman's Wharf.

2 Fisherman's Wharf

Hop off the ferry here and wander through the gaily painted floating homes, the funky little shops, and the ecotour operators based here. Stop for fish and chips or ice cream, and check out the fresh seafood on display at the fish markets. See p. 176.

3 Steamship Terminal Building

From Fisherman's Wharf, it's an easy stroll along the harbor back into the city. Along the way, you will pass a magnificent Beaux Arts building that old-timers will remember as once housing a spectacularly cheesy wax museum. It was originally built in 1924, designed by Victoria's famous architect, **Francis Rattenbury** (p. 20), who also designed the Parliament Buildings across the street, and it was, indeed, the city's steamship terminal back in the day. Today it is home to a restaurant and the **Robert Bateman Centre** (p. 166). Climb up to the second floor to find a gallery of the legendary wildlife painter's works. See p. 166.

4 Royal BC Museum ★★★

Keep walking past the Parliament Buildings and the buskers and souvenir stalls along the water. On your left you will see the Fairmont Hotel Empress ruling from the end of the harbor, and on your right you will see the sprawling **Royal BC Museum.** Outside it is the retro-looking Carillon Tower, where 62 bells musically announce each hour, and just past the museum, in Thunderbird Park, is the Mungo Martin carving shed where First Nations carvers work on a myriad of projects. Step into the museum, and you will discover an ever-changing array of shows and interactive presentations such as 2014's much-anticipated Vikings exhibit. The permanent collections, too, are well worth a visit, especially the First Peoples Gallery, an absorbing and thought-provoking showplace of First Nations art and culture. This is truly an impressive museum experience, and it's quite easy to spend several hours here. See p. 166.

5 Tea at the Empress

Truly, there is no more iconic experience in Victoria than taking tea at the **Fairmont Empress Hotel.** This grand old dame of Victorian architecture, with its lovely rose gardens and elegant public rooms, is a must-visit no matter what, but it's so much better to enjoy it from the plush, rose-and-cream Tea Lobby with a pot of Empress Blend tea and a tiered tray of little sandwiches and teensy baked goods. Be sure to reserve your spot well ahead of time, especially during the busy summer months. See p. 161.

6 Whale-Watching

Few experiences are as breathtaking as watching a sleek, black-and-white orca arc out of the waters right beside your boat. And that's why Victoria's whale-watching tours are among its most popular activities. They run year-round, and range from short trips in a Zodiac to full-day adventures that cross over to the Mainland. Along the way, you're sure to see porpoises, seals, eagles, herons and ospreys, whales (including the orca, humpback, and minke), and, of course, the magnificent scenery of the Gulf Islands. See p. 171.

7 Downtown

Your whale-watching tour will drop you back in the Inner Harbour, and from there, you can explore the city's pretty, historic downtown on foot as you meander over to dinner. Start by wandering up **Government Street** (p. 175), which is home to the city's biggest collection of souvenir shops as well as Victoria's own **Roger's Chocolates, Murchie's Tea & Coffee,** and the legendary **Munro's Books,** arguably Canada's best bookstore, which is housed in a gorgeous neoclassical building that was once a bank. When you reach Johnson Street, turn left into what's known as **LoJo** (for Lower Johnson; p. 177), where you will find a whole collection of funky little boutiques and restaurants clustered around Market Square.

8 Dinner at Spinnakers

Cross the Johnson Street Bridge into the community of **West Victoria.** Take the seaside path that hugs the Inner Harbour, and keep going until you reach what looks like a big, shambling old house but is actually **Spinnakers Gastro Brewpub.** Spinnakers is Canada's oldest brewpub and is renowned not just for craft beers like the Northwest Ale and Hoptoria, but for a menu that celebrates the best of what's local. The rich, creamy seafood chowder is among the best on the coast. See p. 154.

9 Don't Forget Your Nightcap!

Still going? Then head back downtown and drink in Victoria's small but mighty cocktail scene. The best cocktails are being shaken up at **Veneto Tapa Lounge** (p. 157), **Little Jumbo** (p. 156), and **Clive's Classic Lounge in the Chateau Victoria** (p. 179). You can try a classic cocktail or a modern creation, or let the talented bartenders at any of these establishments create a drink just for you.

DAY 2

After spending Day 1 exploring the city center, today you're going to venture a bit further afield. It's easy if you have a car, but there are plenty of buses and tours as well. Perhaps the best way to explore the city, though, is on two wheels—Victoria, after all, is known as the cycling capital of Canada. It's mostly flat, with scenic trails, short distances to travel, cautious drivers, and plenty of rental shops and bike tour operators.

1 Butchart Gardens ★★★

Next to taking tea at the Empress, exploring this four-season garden—considered one of the gardening wonders of the world—is the most iconic of Victoria's experiences. More than 100 years ago, Jennie Butchart started planting sweet peas and roses in an old limestone quarry on the Saanich Peninsula. Today the estate boasts 22 hectares (55 acres) of gardens and has been named a National Historic Site of Canada. Nearly a million people visit each year, strolling through the magnificently perfumed rose garden or the serene Japanese garden and searching for the elusive Himalayan blue poppy. The site also includes a restaurant and gift shop, and features fireworks on summer nights and lighted displays on winter ones. See p. 173.

2 Saanich Peninsula ★

If you are visiting Butchart Gardens by bike or by car, spend a little time exploring the Saanich Peninsula where it is located. You'll find lots of little farms, wineries, and the town of **Sidney-by-the-Sea,** famous for its many new and used bookstores as well as the **Shaw Ocean Discovery Centre** (p. 169).

3 Oak Bay Village

Meander back toward the city, but instead of going directly to the center, turn off toward **Oak Bay Village.** Spend a little time exploring the high-end **shops and boutiques** along Oak Bay Road, then venture down to the shore and the **Oak Bay Beach Hotel.** Grab a table in the cozy **Snug Pub,** a painstaking reproduction of the original hotel's pub, for a pint and bite of lunch with a beautiful ocean view. See p. 178.

4 Dallas Road & Beacon Hill Park

From Oak Bay, stay to the seaside route, which is easy to follow by foot, by bike, or by car. It will turn into **Dallas Road,** every Victorian's favorite place to take the air, preferably with a dog by their side. You can follow the path all the way around Ogden Point and the cruise ship terminal, but a much prettier option is to turn off at **Beacon Hill Park** (p. 173) and cut across this 80-hectare (200-acre) green space. It is a beautifully manicured garden filled with trees and flowers, sports pitches, a children's petting zoo, band shell, horse-drawn carriages, and a 39m (130-ft.) totem pole. Keep an eye out and you may see a roving peacock.

5 On the Trail of Emily Carr

As you emerge from Beacon Hill Park, you will have several opportunities to pay homage to one of Canada's greatest artists, the painter and writer **Emily Carr** (p. 19), who was born here in 1871. On one side of the park, you can visit her family home, **Carr House** (p. 165), and take a tour with one of the passionate caretakers of her remarkable legacy. On the other side of the park, you can find a significant number of her evocative works at the **Art Gallery of Greater Victoria** (p. 167). Be sure to stop at the corner of Government and Belleville streets, where you will find a bronze statue of the "little old woman on the edge of nowhere" with her beloved dog Willie and pet monkey, Woo.

6 Dinner at Steamship Grill

Victoria has become a city of foodies as passionate about local ingredients as the great dishes they can make with them. Many of the restaurants are small, chef-owned eateries, and it's tough to choose just one. But if you're looking for a fun, not terribly expensive place to dine, with a cheerful and casual vibe as well as an unbeatable setting, then that's the **Steamship Grill** (p. 154) in the historic

Steamship Terminal Building. You can't go wrong with a crispy, beer-battered halibut burger and a glass of Vancouver Island Viogner on tap as you watch the sun set on the harbor below.

VICTORIA FOR FAMILIES

Despite its reputation as a big retirement community, Victoria is actually filled with young families, with loads of activities to keep them busy. That's good news for your family, too. You can easily while away the hours roaming the seaside pathways on a rented bike or picnicking on one of the many beaches. Or you can take the little ones to check out these great attractions, starting right in the city center.

Day 1

Step through the doors on the north side of the Fairmont Empress Hotel and enter **Miniature World,** an alternative reality of meticulously produced dioramas representing everything from famous battles to literary scenes to outer space, all in teeny-tiny scale. Don't miss the world's largest dollhouse or the miniature train chugging across historic Canada. See p. 166.

Just a block away, you will discover the creepy-crawly critters of the **Victoria Bug Zoo,** including giant walking sticks, hairy tarantulas, and Canada's largest ant farm. Expert "bug guides" are on hand and will even let you hold a tickly millipede as long as your arm. (Don't worry, it's safe!) See p. 167.

If you prefer critters with four legs rather than hundreds of them, head over to the **Beacon Hill Park Children's Farm** just a few minutes away. This petting zoo features goats, ponies, chickens and Osmund the llama. Don't miss the twice-daily goat stampedes. Note that the farm is only open during the summer, but the nearby playground is open year-round. See p. 173.

It's time for a break, so why not pop in to the **Fairmont Hotel Empress** for a spot of tea? The hotel now offers a special "Prince and Princess Tea" in its ornate Tea Lobby, replete with tiny sandwiches, scones, and attentive service for their youngest guests. Be sure to book ahead. See p. 165.

After tea, head across the street to the **Royal BC Museum.** In addition to a spectacular array of permanent and temporary collections, the museum hosts family-friendly "Wonder Sundays," sleepovers, camps, and IMAX shows. The totem poles and natural history exhibits will fill your kids with wonder, as will traveling exhibits such as the impressive Vikings collection. See p. 166.

A little further from the city center is **Craigdarroch Castle,** a 39-room turreted mansion built in the late 1800s by the wealthy coal baron Robert Dunsmuir. It is filled with lavish furnishings and is famous for its ornate stained glass and woodwork (p. 167). On the way to the castle, stop in at **Rogers' Chocolates** for one of their decadent ice cream bars (p. 176).

If you wrap things up early enough, you have time to head back to the Inner Harbour for takeout fish and chips at **Red Fish Blue Fish** (p. 155). The *tacones* with tempura cod are especially fun to eat, and even better while watching all the bustle of the harbor around you.

Day 2

Today you'll head out to the Saanich Peninsula, which has plenty of family-friendly attractions. But first stop by one of Victoria's plethora of breakfast joints, like **Willie's Bakery** (p. 159), to make sure you're fueled up for a day of fun.

To make the most of this area, you'll likely want a car, but if your kids are old enough, you can also rent bikes and cycle out there along the **Galloping Goose Trail,** which goes all the way out to the ferry terminal in Swartz Bay. The most famous attraction out here is the glorious **Butchart Gardens,** a year-round spectacle in bloom (p. 173). However, your kids may prefer the wild adventure of **Victoria Butterfly Gardens,** just 5 minutes away (p. 175). It's an indoor tropical jungle filled with flamingoes, exotic fish, rare flowers, and, of course, butterflies.

In nearby **Sidney-by-the-Sea,** the **Shaw Ocean Discovery Centre** (p. 169) is an aquarium that offers a unique glimpse of the creatures that live in the **Salish Sea** (p. 185). Your kids will especially love tickling the starfish and sea urchins in the touch pools. And if you are here in late May, Saanich is also the site of the **Island Children's Festival,** which features star performers like Fred Penner.

If the weather is nice, you can bring a picnic lunch and venture out onto the **Sidney Spit,** part of the Gulf Islands National Park Reserve. A walk-on ferry service will take you to this sandy beach park during the summer months.

On your way back to town, swing through Oak Bay Village and stop in at **Sweet Delights,** a candy store simply bursting with old-timey sugary treats from around the world (p. 178). Or drop in to Hillside Village and the family-owned **Bolen Books,** with its huge children's books section (p. 176).

Dinner should be fun, and what's more fun than burgers? Victoria has several terrific burger joints, but one of my faves is **Bin 4 Burger Lounge** (p. 158), which offers a "small bites" menu for kids 10 and under. The yummy chocolate torte should be an excellent way to end the day.

VICTORIA FOR FOODIES

Your chef is actually cooking in the kitchen—and he probably owns the restaurant, and maybe the farm where the kale is grown, too. The bartender is growing his own micro-greens in a hydroponic unit under the counter. The guy who sold you your cheese this morning is probably sitting across the room from you at dinner tonight. Your server can tell you where the beets were grown, the lamb was raised, and the fish was caught—all of it local and sustainable, of course. There's no doubt that Victoria is all over this whole local food thing.

The easiest way to explore Victoria's dynamic food scene is to join one of the culinary tours organized by **Travel with Taste** (p. 170), such as the urban walking tour of downtown Victoria, or the all-day food-and-wine tour of nearby Cowichan Valley. But if you want to explore on your own, here are some of the can't-miss foodie destinations. Bring your appetite, and wear stretchy pants.

Start by venturing across the Johnson Street Bridge to Dockside Green and **Fol Epi** (p. 160). This little organic bakery makes some of the best artisan bread you've ever tasted, all made from heritage grains ground on site and baked in a wood-fired oven. Enjoy a pastry or baguette with coffee to start your day in the best possible way.

From there, head back across the bridge into downtown and the new **Victoria Public Market** (p. 158). This beautiful market takes up the ground floor of the century-old Georgian revival-style former Hudson Bay building, now a luxury condominium complex called The Hudson. Nibble your way around the market, sampling the gourmet Indian fare at Sutra, the handmade cheeses at Salt Spring Island Cheese, the porchetta sandwich at Roast Carvery, and the sustainable smoked salmon at Cowichan Bay Seafood. Be sure to pick up some of the local *fleur de sel* from the Vancouver Island Salt Co. for your friends back home. And, if you can, plan your visit for a Wednesday, when area farmers bring their fresh produce to the market.

Then it's just a short stroll to **Chinatown and Silk Road Tea** (p. 177), where master tea blender Daniela Cubelic creates fragrant infusions such as the dark, chocolatey Velvet Potion. If you have time, join her for a tea and chocolate tasting.

If you didn't overdo it at the market, you might be thinking of lunch right about now, and a pint or two of local craft brew. You'll find some of the city's best fish and chips and local brews at **the Guild** (p. 158), a new English-style gastro-pub in a heritage building on Wharf Street. A great place to relax a while.

After lunch, continue on to **Fort Street** (p. 176). Once known for its many antique stores, this busy street is now best known as a foodie destination. Drop into the **Dutch Bakery,** where the Schaddelee family has been making croquettes and vanilla slices since 1956. Visit **Choux Choux Charcuterie** and **the Little Cheese Shop** for some savory samples.

By now, it should be cocktail hour, which means it's time to head to **Little Jumbo** (p. 156) at the foot of Fort Street for terrific handcrafted cocktails concocted from an extravagant back bar and a savory snack to go with. As for dinner, it's a tough choice: perhaps the romantic setting of **Café Brio** (p. 155)? The fab Italian food at **Zambri's** (p. 157)? Or the farm-to-table fare at **10 Acres** (p. 157)? Whichever you choose, be sure to save room for a nightcap, perhaps the smoky "Rosemary's Baby" at **Veneto Tapa Lounge** in the Hotel Rialto (p. 157).

VANCOUVER

Vancouver is, quite simply, one of the most beautiful places on Earth. But it's more than just a pretty face. "Van-groovy," the locals call it, a cheeky little nod to its laidback lifestyle and a counterculture vibe that lingers even as real estate prices soar and yummy mummies insist on sporting the local uniform of yoga pants and designer handbags. Sure, there's still plenty of well-intentioned, granola-fed earnestness to go around—after all, Greenpeace and the 100 Mile Diet were created here. Then again, so was the cosmetic application of Botox.

The climate is mild. The attitudes are tolerant. The economy is surprisingly stable. The populace is fit, obsessed with running, cycling, and climbing those big mountains to the north. It's green here year round, even when the rest of Canada is buried in snow or withered with summer drought. These days, Vancouver's very English heritage rubs along peaceably with its vibrant multicultural present, much as the shiny glass towers of Coal Harbour complement the red-brick Victorian low-rises of Gastown and the West End. The Edwardian manors of Shaughnessy, the soaring modernist homes of West Vancouver, the slice of modern Hong Kong that is Richmond's Golden Village, the spices and saris that are Little India—they all coexist in a magnificent natural landscape of parks and gardens surrounded by ocean, mountains, and wilderness.

Vancouver is routinely named one of the world's most livable cities. Which isn't bad at all for a place that not so long ago was just a big, rough, rainy mill town on the edge of nowhere.

ESSENTIALS

Arriving

BY PLANE **Vancouver International Airport (YVR; ℰ 604/207-7077;** www.yvr.ca) is a 14km (8⅔-mile) journey south of downtown—it's actually located on Sea Island in the suburb of Richmond. YVR has won numerous awards for its design, and it's a pleasant space filled with impressive works of art, especially by First Nations artists. The most popular is Bill Reid's massive bronze sculpture, "Spirit of Haida Gwaii: The Jade Canoe," in the international terminal. If you need assistance, two **Tourist Information Centres** are located in the airport's domestic and international arrivals areas.

The easiest, fastest, and cheapest way to get into Vancouver from the airport is by the **Canada Line SkyTrain,** opened in late 2009 and operated by **Translink** (ℰ **604/953-3333;** www.translink.ca). The train zips to Waterfront Station in 26 minutes, with several stops along the way. For airport passengers, there is a C$5 surcharge on top of Translink's two-zone fare, bringing the total Canada Line ticket price to C$8.75 for adults on weekdays, C$7.50 after 6:30pm weekdays and all day on weekends. Purchase tickets at the machines clustered around the Canada Line entrance.

Several hotels (most of them in Richmond) provide courtesy shuttles; check with your accommodation to see what's on offer. Otherwise, the average **taxi** fare from the airport to a downtown Vancouver hotel is approximately C$35, plus tip, but it can run up to C$40 or higher if the cab gets stuck in traffic. **Aerocar Service** (℗ **888/821-0021** or 604/298-1000; www.aerocar.ca) provides limousine service with flat rates based on destination as well as the type of vehicle and number of passengers. Rates start at C$45 for a trip downtown and C$55 to Canada Place, plus taxes and tip. Look for Aerocars and taxis in front of the terminal.

Most major **car-rental firms** have airport counters and shuttles. Drivers heading into Vancouver from the airport should take the Arthur Laing Bridge, which leads directly to Granville Street, the most direct route to downtown.

BY TRAIN & BUS VIA Rail and Amtrak trains, as well as Greyhound buses arrive at **Pacific Central Station** (1150 Station St., at Main and Terminal), the main Vancouver railway station, located just south of Chinatown. Plenty of taxis wait at the station entrance and the fare to downtown is about C$10. For more info, contact **Amtrak** (℗ **800/872-7245;** www.amtrak.com), **VIA Rail** (℗ **888/842-7245;** www.viarail.ca), or **Greyhound** (℗ **604/661-0328;** www.greyhound.ca).

BY CAR From the U.S., Interstate 5 from Seattle becomes Hwy. 99 at Peace Arch Crossing, then heads straight into Vancouver. **(Don't forget you'll need your passport to enter Canada.)** The 210km (130-mile) drive from Seattle takes about 2½ hours, depending on lineups at the border. If you're arriving from just about anywhere else, you'll arrive on the Trans-Canada Highway (Hwy. 1). It takes about 11 hours to drive from Calgary to Vancouver, a distance of 970km (600 miles).

Visitor Information

The **Tourism Vancouver Visitor Centre** (200 Burrard St., Plaza Level; ℗ **604/683-2000;** www.tourismvancouver.com) is your single-best travel information source about Vancouver and the North Shore. A helpful and well-trained staff provides information, maps, and brochures, and can help you with all your travel needs, including hotel, cruise ship, ferry, bus, and train reservations. The center also has a **half-price ticket office** (Tickets Tonight; ℗ **604/684-2787;** www.ticketstonight.ca) for same-day shows and events. The visitor center is open daily from 8:30am to 6pm (closed Sun in winter). If you're driving, a **Touristinfo Centre** is located just north of the U.S.-Canada Peace Arch border crossing. For more information, visit the **Destination BC** website at www.hellobc.com.

City Layout

With four different bodies of water lapping at its edges and miles of shoreline, not to mention a major mountain range, numerous bridges, and a handful of islands, Vancouver's geography can seem a bit complicated. At least it's always easy to orient yourself: The North Shore Mountains (which are, indeed, to the north) are visible from just about everywhere. Most of your time will likely be spent in Vancouver city proper, which covers a peninsula that comprises **Stanley Park,** the **West End, Yaletown, Chinatown,** and **Downtown.** It's bordered to the north by Burrard Inlet, the city's main deep-water harbor and port; to the west by English Bay; and to the south by False Creek, which is actually an inlet. There are four key east-west streets on the peninsula—Robson, Georgia, Hastings, and Davie—and three major north-south streets: Denman, Burrard, and Granville.

The thing to keep in mind when figuring out what's where in Vancouver is that this is a city where property is king, and the word "west" has such positive connotations that folks have gone to great lengths to associate it with their particular patch of real estate. Thus we have the West End, the West Side, and West Vancouver, which is located immediately beside North Vancouver. It can be a bit confusing for newcomers, but fortunately, each west has its own distinct character. The West End is a high-rise residential neighborhood on the downtown peninsula. The West Side is one-half of Vancouver, from Ontario Street west to the University of British Columbia. (The more working-class East Side covers the mainland portion of the city, from Ontario St. east to Boundary Rd.) Very tony West Vancouver is a city unto itself on the far side of Burrard Inlet. Together with its more middle-class neighbor, North Vancouver, it forms the North Shore.

4

Tourist information centers and most hotels can provide you with a detailed downtown **street map.** A good all-around metropolitan area map is the Rand McNally Vancouver city map. If you're an auto club member, the Canadian Automobile Association map is free to AAA and CAA members.

The Neighborhoods in Brief

Downtown Most of Vancouver's commercial and office space is found in a square patch starting at Nelson Street and heading north to the harbor, with Homer and Burrard streets forming the east and west boundaries, respectively. Canada Place, on the waterfront facing Burrard Inlet, is part of the city's huge convention center and cruise-ship terminal. The most interesting avenues for visitors are West Georgia, Robson, and Granville streets. West Georgia Street is where you'll find the Vancouver Art Gallery, the Colosseum-inspired Vancouver Public Library, and the Pacific Centre shopping mall. Robson Street is all designer chains, restaurants, and cafes. Granville Street, also known as the Entertainment District, is where you'll find many of the city's bars, nightclubs, theaters, and pubs.

Gastown Vancouver's oldest neighborhood, Gastown, was named for a voluble saloonkeeper named "Gassy" Jack Deighton, who kept the millworkers lubricated back when this was just a rough frontier settlement named Granville. In 1886, it was incorporated as the city of Vancouver—and just a few months later, burnt to the ground, only to be rebuilt from scratch shortly thereafter. And so began the first of the city's many real estate booms. In today's Gastown, you can find brick low-rises, cobblestoned streets, a certain amount of tourist tat, and plenty of quirky, vintage charm. It's increasingly become home to many creative professionals, as well as some of the city's most exciting restaurants, craft cocktail bars, First Nations art galleries, and unique boutiques, not to mention the famous Steam Clock on Water Street. Be aware, though, that Gastown borders the notorious Downtown Eastside, a desperately poor neighborhood of homeless, drug-addicted, and mentally ill residents, so it can be a bit dodgy, especially at night.

Chinatown Located southeast of Gastown, Vancouver's Chinatown was originally settled by migrant laborers brought in to build the Canadian Pacific Railway. It quickly became one of North America's most populous Chinatowns, and even today, although most of the city's huge Asian population has moved out to Richmond, thousands of Cantonese- and Mandarin-speaking Canadians still live, shop, and eat here. And, although it retains much of its original character, Chinatown is quickly evolving into one of the city's hippest neighborhoods, with trendy restaurants, cocktail bars, and condo projects moving in.

Yaletown & False Creek North Hard to believe these days, but legend has it this is where the expression "skid row" was coined. That's because a century or so ago, Yaletown was where logs were "skidded" into the harbor. It was, at any rate, a rough, tough industrial area of sawmills, cooperages, and warehouses that likely stored illegal hooch back in the dirty days of Prohibition. Today, this is a sleek, chic, urban neighborhood of trendy condos, cool restos, chic boutiques, galleries, and well-dressed young professionals walking tiny dogs along the cobblestoned streets that are all that remain of the bad old days.

West End This was Vancouver's first upscale neighborhood, settled in the 1890s by the city's merchant princes. By the 1930s, most of the grand Edwardian homes had become rooming houses, and in the late 1950s, some of the Edwardians came down and high-rise apartments went up. Expect to find bland concrete towers sitting comfortably next to brick walkups among lush gardens, tree-lined streets, pocket parks, and the gorgeous beaches of English Bay. Davie Street is Vancouver's most prominent gay neighborhood, with rainbow-painted crosswalks and rainbow banners fluttering overhead. Denman and the northern end of Robson Street are chock-a-block with cafes, takeout joints, and restaurants dishing up a global banquet of cuisines.

Granville Island Vancouver's most successful urban renewal project, and one of its most popular destinations. This sandbar under the Granville Street Bridge was once an industrial area of sawmills and factories producing everything from paint to planks to machine parts. Then, back in the 1970s, the federal government decided to transform it into a "people-friendly place," and to everyone's surprise, succeeded. Its main attraction is the Granville Island Public Market, but you'll also find theaters, pubs, restaurants, artists' studios, bookstores, crafts shops, a marina, Fisherman's Wharf, an art school, a hotel, parks, a community center, a cement plant, lots and lots of people, and just as many seagulls.

Kitsilano In the 1960s, this West Side neighborhood had fallen on hard times. Nobody respectable wanted to live there—the 1920s homes had all been converted to cheap rooming houses—so the hippies moved in. Kits became Canada's Haight-Ashbury, with coffeehouses, head shops, and plenty of patchouli and long hair. Today the patchouli and head shops are gone, and this is one of the city's priciest, most yuppified neighborhoods. It's still a fun place to wander, though, with plenty of trendy boutiques selling furniture, housewares, fashion, and snowboards. Plus, every third storefront is a restaurant, and who can resist the heated saltwater swimming pool at Kits Beach?

Commercial Drive Known as "The Drive," Commercial Drive is the 12-block section from Venables Street to East 6th Avenue. The Drive has an unpretentious, down-to-earth, fading counterculture feel to it. It's an old immigrant neighborhood that, like everyplace else in Vancouver, has been rediscovered: First, it was the Italians, who were followed by waves of Portuguese, Hondurans, and Guatemalans. Nowadays it's all young families, artists, and eccentrics of all stripes. Think Italian cafe near a Marxist bookstore across from a vegan deli and co-op grocery store, and you've got the picture.

Shaughnessy Designed in the 1920s as an enclave for Vancouver's budding elite, this is Vancouver's Westmount or Nob Hill. With its stately mansions, lush gardens, and towering trees, this a lovely place to go for a walk, a bike ride, or an afternoon drive and gaze upon the lifestyles of the rich and famous. Look on the map for the area of curvy and convoluted streets between Cypress and Oak streets and 12th and 32nd avenues. Be sure to check out The Crescent, where the poshest of the homes are, as well as South Granville Street, the luxurious shopping district between Broadway and 16th.

Richmond Not so long ago, this flat suburb was mostly farmland; about a third of it still is. But it's also become the vibrant, exciting epicenter of Vancouver's new

The Newest Hood: Southeast False Creek

Vancouverites still can't get used to seeing this sleek, sophisticated new neighborhood instead of rundown old industrial lands. Mind you, it wasn't created without a certain amount of pain. It was developed as the Vancouver Olympic Village to house the athletes during the 2010 Winter Games and was mired in controversy—the city abandoned its promise for subsidized housing, then had to take on the bills when the developer backed out of its agreement, and for a while, no one wanted to live or buy here. Now the dust has settled, and this is rapidly becoming one of the coolest hoods in the city. Located on the waterfront overlooking downtown and BC Place Stadium, it's also considered one of the greenest neighborhoods in the world, with a fab new waterfront Seawall that makes it a good place to walk, run, or cycle.

Chinatown, where wealthy, well-educated newcomers are flocking from Hong Kong, Taiwan, and all over Asia. Head to an Asian-themed mall like Aberdeen Centre or Parker Place, and you'll feel like you've landed in Hong Kong, without the jet lag. The best reason to visit, though, is the fantastic Chinese restaurants, which are considered some of the best in the world. Then, for a very different sort of experience, visit Steveston, a charming, historic fishing village that's a great place for the whole family to spend a sunny day.

Little India Most of the businesses on this 4-block stretch of Main Street from 48th to 52nd Avenue are run by and cater to Indo-Canadians, primarily Punjabis. The area is best seen during business hours, when the fragrant scent of spices wafts from food stalls, and Hindi pop songs blare from hidden speakers, while young brides hunt through sari shops or seek out suitable material in discount textile outlets.

South Main South Main Street—awkwardly dubbed SoMa—is the city's hip, new, happening neighborhood, all artist studios in converted industrial buildings, hidden theater companies, uber-trendy eateries, craft breweries, and independent eco-fashion boutiques. It still retains its old working-class and strong community feel, but with serious hipster street cred for miles. Nearby on Cambie Street lies City Hall, an Art Deco make-work project built in 1936.

North Shore Two bridges—the graceful Lions Gate and workmanlike Ironworkers Memorial Bridge—and the SeaBus connect Vancouver to the communities of North and West Vancouver and the North Shore Mountains. West Van is one of the wealthiest neighborhoods in Canada, a series of charming seaside "villages" and luxe homes with beautiful views from their aeries on the hill. North Van traditionally was more working class, and is still home to shipbuilding and a variety of light industries. It's where you'll find major attractions like the Capilano Suspension Bridge and Grouse Mountain, just one of three ski hills on the North Shore (the other two are Cypress Mountain and Mount Seymour). The North Shore Mountains are known for their hiking and biking trails, and can make for an idyllic day spent among nature.

GETTING AROUND
By Public Transit

Vancouver's public transportation system is the most extensive in Canada and includes service to all major tourist attractions, so you really don't need a car, especially if you're staying in the downtown area.

The **Translink** (℡ 604/953-3333; www.translink.ca) system includes electric trolley and diesel buses, the SeaBus catamaran ferry, and the light-rail SkyTrain. It's a reliable, safe, eco-friendly, and inexpensive system that allows you to get everywhere you want to go, including the beaches and ski slopes. Regular service runs from about 5am to 2am, although schedules vary depending on the line, and some routes have reduced service on Sundays and holidays. Schedules and routes are available online, at tourist information centers, and at many major hotels.

At some point in 2014, all the current passes and tickets will be replaced by a reloadable electronic fare card called Compass. The rollout is being done gradually, so you can expect some confusion regarding fares and how to pay them throughout the year. Until Compass is fully in place, you will still be able to pay cash on buses, buy tickets for SkyTrain and SeaBus at machines in the stations, and purchase FareSavers and DayPasses at retailers displaying the FAREDEALER sign. Fares are based on the number of zones traveled and one ticket allows you to transfer from one mode of transport to another, in any direction, within 90 minutes. A one-way, one-zone fare (everything in central Vancouver) costs C$2.75. A two-zone fare—C$4—is required to travel to nearby suburbs such as Richmond or North Vancouver, and a three-zone fare—C$5.50—is required for travel to the far-off city of Surrey. To depart the airport costs an additional C$5 over the two-zone fare. After 6:30pm on weekdays and all day on weekends and holidays, you can travel anywhere in all three zones for C$2.75. DayPasses, good on all public transit, cost C$9.75 for adults and can be used for unlimited travel.

BY BUS   Both diesel and electric-trolley buses service the city. Regular service on the busiest routes is about every 5 to 15 minutes from 5am to 1am, although hours will vary depending on the route. Wheelchair-accessible buses and bus stops are identified by the international wheelchair symbol. Some key routes to keep in mind: **no. 5** (Robson St.), **no. 6** (Davie St.), **no. 10** (Granville St.), **no. 4** (UBC), **no. 2** (Kitsilano Beach to downtown), **no. 50** (Granville Island), **no. 19** (Stanley Park), **no. 240** (North Vancouver), and **no. 250** (West Vancouver–Horseshoe Bay). The Translink site (www.translink.ca) has a handy "Next Bus" feature that lets you plug in the number of your bus stop, and it'll let you know when the next bus is due.

BY SKYTRAIN   SkyTrain is a fast, light-rail service between downtown Vancouver and the suburbs. All stations are wheelchair accessible. The **Expo Line** trains operate along a scenic 27km (17-mile) route from downtown Vancouver east to Surrey in 39 minutes. The **Millennium Line** loops from Waterfront through Burnaby, Port Coquitlam, New Westminster, and East Vancouver. Trains on both lines run every 2 to 8 minutes. **Canada Line,** the newest SkyTrain, began operating in October 2009 and links Richmond and Vancouver International Airport to downtown. Trains run every 4 to 20 minutes, and departures from YVR cost an additional C$5.

BY SEABUS   Double-ended catamaran ferries take passengers, cyclists, and wheelchair riders on a scenic 12-minute commute across Burrard Inlet between downtown's Waterfront Station and North Vancouver's Lonsdale Quay. The SeaBus travels every 15 minutes from 6am to 7:30pm on weekdays and 10am to 6:30pm on weekends; outside of peak hours, it departs every 30 minutes. There's a countdown clock in each terminal that lets you know whether you need to run or be prepared to wait for the next crossing. The crossing is a two-zone fare on weekdays until 6:30pm.

BY TAXI   Cab fares start at C$3.20 and increase at a rate of C$1.85 per kilometer. In the downtown area, you can expect to travel for less than C$12, plus tip. Taxis are easy to find in front of major hotels, but flagging one down can be tricky, especially late at night or on rainy days. Most drivers are usually on radio calls, and thanks to built-in satellite positioning systems, if you call for a taxi, it often arrives faster than if you go out and hail one. Call for a pickup from **Black Top** (℗ **604/731-1111**), **Yellow Cab** (℗ **604/681-1111**), **Vancouver Taxi** (℗ **604/871-1111**), or **MacLure's** (℗ **604/731-9211**).

BY CAR   If you're staying in Vancouver proper, you don't really need a car. But if you must drive, keep in mind that driving in Vancouver can be quite a leisurely experience—there are no freeways through the city, plus the addition of new bike lanes has meant the loss of driving lanes, which has slowed traffic even further. Add a few major construction projects and a landscape that doesn't necessarily lend itself to a grid system, and you can see why a short trip can take such a long time. At least the view is nice while you wait. Also, remember that gas is sold by the liter, not the gallon, mileage is posted in kilometers, not miles, and that seatbelts and car insurance are compulsory in British Columbia. The typical speed limit in Vancouver is 50kmh (30 mph). It's 30kmh (20mph) around parks and schools and the highway speed limit is usually 100kmh (60 mph).

You can find rental cars at **Avis** (757 Hornby St.; ℗ **800/879-2847** or 604/606-2868; www.avis.ca), **Budget** (416 W. Georgia St.; ℗ **800/472-3325** or 604/668-7000; www.budget.ca), **Enterprise** (550 Bute St.; ℗ **800/736-8222** or 604/689-7377; www.enterpriserentacar.ca), **Hertz Canada** (1270 Granville St.; ℗ **800/263-0600** or 604/606-4711; www.hertz.com), **National** (999a Canada Place; ℗ **800/387-4747** or 604/609-7160; www.nationalcar.ca), or **Thrifty** (413 Seymour St.; ℗ **800/847-4389** or 604/606-1666; www.thrifty.com). These firms all have counters and shuttle service at the airport as well.

BY BIKE   Vancouver is a cyclist's paradise. Along Robson and Denman streets near Stanley Park you will find plenty of places to rent bikes. Paved paths crisscross through parks and along beaches, plus several major thoroughfares now have designated bike lanes. Helmets are mandatory, and riding on sidewalks is illegal except on designated bike paths. SkyTrain, SeaBus, and many buses will carry your bike at no extra charge.

BY MINI FERRY   Crossing False Creek to Granville Island or Vanier Park on one of the zippy little mini-ferries is a cheap and fun way to get around. There are two lines—**Aquabus** (℗ **604/689-5858**; www.theaquabus.com) and **False Creek Ferries** (℗ **604/684-7781**; www.granvilleislandferries.bc.ca)—which dock at the south foot of Hornby Street, Granville Island, Science World, and other locations. They operate daily from about 7am to 10:30pm (9:30pm in winter) and run every 3 to 15 minutes or so, but schedules change monthly and depend on the route. They are not part of Translink, so your public transit pass or ticket is not valid. One-way fares are C$3.25 to C$5.50 for adults and C$1.75 to C$3.75 for seniors and children. Various passes are also available.

ON FOOT   Vancouver proper is a great place to explore by foot. It'll take you about half an hour to cross the peninsula from north to south, and about twice that to wander west to east from, say, Stanley Park to Chinatown. There's plenty to see while you're walking that you'll miss from a car or bus. Just make sure you have a map, comfortable walking shoes, layers, and an umbrella, because you never know what Vancouver's unpredictable weather will throw at you.

[FastFACTS] VANCOUVER

Business Hours

Vancouver **banks** are open Monday through Thursday from 10am to 5pm and Friday from 10am to 6pm. Some banks, like TD Canada Trust and Vancity, are also open on Saturday. **Stores** are generally open daily from 10am to 6pm, with many open until 9pm Thursdays and Fridays. Last call at **restaurants, bars,** and **cocktail lounges** is usually 1 or 2am and about midnight on Sundays.

Child Care

If you need to rent cribs, car seats, playpens, or other baby accessories, **Wee Travel** (© **604/222-4722;** www.weetravel.ca) delivers them right to your hotel or the airport.

Dentists

Most major hotels have a dentist on call. **Vancouver Centre Dental Clinic** (Vancouver Centre Mall, 1B11–650 W. Georgia St.; © **604/682-1601;** www.vancouver dentalclinic.com) is another option. You must make an appointment. The clinic is open Monday to Thursday 8:30am to 5pm (Wed until 6pm) and Friday 8:30am to 2pm.

Doctors

Hotels usually have a doctor on call. **Ultima Medicentre** (Bentall Centre, 1055 Dunsmuir St.; © **604/683-8138;** www.ultimamedicentre.ca) is a drop-in clinic open Monday through Friday 8am to 5pm. **Care Point Medical Centers** have a number of clinics, including one downtown (1175 Denman St.; © **604/681-5338;** www.cbi.ca), open Monday through Wednesday 8:30am to 9pm, Thursday to Saturday 9am to 9pm, and Sunday 9am to 8pm.

Emergencies

Dial © **911** for any emergency police, fire, or ambulance service.

Hospitals

St. Paul's Hospital (1081 Burrard St.; © **604/682-2344**) is the closest facility to downtown and the West End. West Side Vancouver hospitals include **Vancouver General Hospital** (855 W. 12th Ave.; © **604/875-4111**) and **BC Children's Hospital** (4480 Oak St.; © **604/875-2345**). In North Vancouver, there's **Lions Gate Hospital** (231 E. 15th St.; © **604/988-3131**).

Hotlines

Emergency numbers include the **Crisis Centre** (© 604/872-3311), **Rape Crisis Centre** (© 604/255-6228), **Rape Relief** (© 604/872-8212), **BC Drug and Poison Information Centre** (© 604/682-5050), **Crime Stoppers** (© 800/222-8477), and **SPCA** animal emergency (© 604/879-3571).

Internet Access

Free Internet access is increasingly available at hotels, coffee shops, restaurants, and soon, in Vancouver parks. It is also available at the Vancouver **Public Library** Central Branch (350 W. Georgia St.; © **604/331-3600**).

Luggage Storage & Lockers

Lockers are available at the main Vancouver railway station (which is also the main bus depot), **Pacific Central Station,** 1150 Station St., near Main Street and Terminal Avenue (© **604/661-0328**).

Newspapers & Magazines

The two local daily papers are the broadsheet **"Vancouver Sun"** (www.vancouversun.com) and the tabloid **"Province"** (www.theprovince.com). Also check out the free weeklies, **"Georgia Straight"** (www.straight.com), and **"The West Ender"** (www.wevancouver.com).

Pharmacies

Shopper's **Drug Mart** (1125 Davie St.; © **604/669-2424**) is open 24 hours. Several Safeway supermarket pharmacies are open late; the one on Robson and Denman streets is open until midnight.

Police

For emergencies, dial © **911.** This is a free call. Otherwise, the **Vancouver City Police** can be reached at © **604/717-3321.**

Post Office

The **main post office** (349 W. Georgia St., at Homer St.; © **866/607-6301**) is open Monday through Friday from 9am to 5:30pm. You'll also find post office outlets in some Shopper's Drug Mart and 7-Eleven stores with longer open hours than the main post office.

WHERE TO STAY IN VANCOUVER

Downtown & Yaletown

VERY EXPENSIVE

Fairmont Hotel Vancouver ★   In 2014, Vancouver's grande dame is undergoing a much-needed facelift, a C$12-million renovation that will update the lobby and **900 West Restaurant,** and replace the beloved Griffins restaurant with luxury retailers. It's expected to be complete by November 2014, but it's also just the first phase of an ongoing reno that will take on the function rooms next and, finally, the guest rooms. Once one of the grand railway hotels, the Hotel Vancouver was opened in 1939, just in time for the royal visit of King George VI and Queen Elizabeth. It still retains its historic grandeur, with high ceilings, ornate moldings, and stately old elevators. The guest rooms are spacious, with luxe decor in plush gold and burgundy or blue, and dark, colonial-style furnishings. Bathrooms, admittedly, are small but well appointed. Guests have access to a spectacular indoor pool in an airy, glassed atrium. The hotel is home to several designer boutiques, including a flagship Louis Vuitton store, with more to come. And the two canine ambassadors, Mavis and Beau, will make you feel right at home.

900 W. Georgia St. ✆ **866/540-4452** or 604/684-3131. www.fairmont.com/hotelvancouver. 556 units. C$240–C$490 double, C$450–C$660 suite. Parking C$39 per day. Children 18 and under stay free in parent's room. Pets welcome (C$25 1-time fee). **Amenities:** Restaurants, bar, babysitting, concierge, executive-level rooms, health club, Jacuzzi, indoor pool, room service, sauna, spa, free Wi-Fi (with Presidents Club membership, C$15 a day without).

Fairmont Pacific Rim ★★★   Fairmont has five properties around Vancouver, including one in Whistler and another at the airport. Of them, this is the newest, the smallest, and the most coolly beautiful. It has an enviable setting right across from the convention center, with spectacular views of the harbor and North Shore Mountains from its upper floors. There is a subtle, modern, almost Asian feel to the property, from the perfumed entranceway to the Japanese serenity of the rooftop pool deck. The lobby is a bright, busy, high-ceilinged space lined with white marble, where guests can enjoy craft cocktails and exceptional sushi from the new raw bar while listening to live music most nights. Guest rooms are peaceful refuges with clean, contemporary lines, soft, earthy colors, and immaculate attention to detail: plush throws for chilly nights, comfortable leather armchairs, TVs inset into the mirrors of the granite-lined bathrooms, telescopes and free-standing Japanese-style soaker tubs in the in the luxury suites. (Be warned, though, that the many high-tech features of the rooms can be a bit confusing at times.) The hotel also features a high-end restaurant called **Oru,** which new chef Darren Brown is transitioning from Asian-themed to include fare from around the Pacific Rim, as well as the popular Italian bakery/deli/wine bar **Giovane,** and **Bella Gelateria,** which has won awards worldwide for its frozen treats. And then, for ultimate pampering, there's the signature Willow Stream Spa. Truly an exceptional place to stay.

1038 Canada Place Way. ✆ **877/900-5350** or 604/695–5300. www.fairmont.com/pacificrim. 377 units. C$450–C$650 double, C$900–C$10,000 suite. Self-parking C$43 per day, C$48 valet. Children 18 and under stay free in parent's room. Pets welcome (no charge). **Amenities:** Restaurant, cafe/deli, bar, babysitting, concierge, executive-level rooms, health club, Jacuzzi, outdoor pool, room service, sauna, spa, free Wi-Fi (with President's Club membership, C$14 a day without).

Fairmont Waterfront ★   Just down the street from the Fairmont Pacific Rim is its slightly older and somewhat overshadowed sister. It, too, has an enviable location, right across the street from the convention center and the cruise ship terminal. In 2014, it has seen some significant (and much-needed) renovations on its Gold Floor, Fairmont's luxurious "hotel within a hotel," as well as its lobby restaurant and bar, which was recently renamed ARC. It's part of an ongoing update throughout the property: Some guest rooms may still retain the old, dark, heavy traditional look, but most have transitioned to a lighter, cleaner, contemporary West Coast design, with features like pale leather headboards, rounded glass lamp bases, cheerful floral throw pillows, and shimmery wallpapered statement walls. Some of the rooms from this triangle-shaped tower have spectacular views of the big cruise ships, and others have views of the garden terrace, where chef raises bees and grows herbs for the kitchen.

900 Canada Place Way. ✆ **866/540-4509** or 604/691-1991. www.fairmont.com/waterfront. 457 units. C$379–C$560 double, C$550–C$1,150 suite. Parking C$44. Children 18 and under stay free in parent's room. Pets welcome (C$25/day). **Amenities:** Restaurant, bar, babysitting, concierge, executive-level rooms, health club, Jacuzzi, outdoor pool, room service, sauna, free Wi-Fi (with President's Club membership, C$14/day without).

Four Seasons Hotel ★★★ This 40-year-old property doesn't have the cool opulence of the newer Four Seasons hotels, but it does have a lovely, understated charm and some of the best service in the city. Plus, everyone who's anyone will eventually end up at the lively cocktail bar, so it's a great place just to hang out. Over the decades, the hotel has quietly and continuously updated its guest rooms and public spaces, with a major reno in 2007 that saw the transformation of its old Garden Terrace Restaurant to the buzzy Yew. (In 2014, it became **Yew Seafood,** where celebrity chef Ned Bell creates magic with sustainable fare from the ocean.) The lobby is a bit awkwardly designed—you have to climb an old escalator from the cramped and crowded driveway—but it comfortably mixes outdated elements, like the 1980s-era brass railings, with cool contemporary furniture, polished driftwood coffee tables, warm wooden paneling, and giant turquoise urns. Guest rooms are large, bright, and luxuriously comfortable, with pale, clean, cool, modern lines occasionally mixed with older, more traditional mahogany-finished furniture, tufted leather chairs, and floral draperies. Bathrooms are on the small side, but updated with marble counters and top-of-the-line fixtures and accessories. Lower floors don't have a view, but the upper ones offer glimpses of the mountains—here, it's more about the central location than the scenery. Plus nothing can beat the spectacular health club, with its huge, heated indoor-outdoor pool on a lovely terrace, one of the city's best-kept secrets.

791 W. Georgia St. ✆ **800/819-5053** or 604/689-9333. www.fourseasons.com/vancouver. 373 units. C$315–C$575 double, C$465–C$1,750 suite. Parking C$43. Pets welcome (no charge). **Amenities:** Restaurant, bar, babysitting, concierge, exercise room, indoor and heated outdoor pool, room service, sauna, free Wi-Fi.

Loden Vancouver ★★ The Loden is a luxurious little treasure of a boutique hotel just slightly off the beaten path. It's located on a side street near Coal Harbour and a short stroll from Robson Street, the West End, and the financial district. This place is all about chic comfort—the guest rooms have luscious bedding and a warm red, gold, and orange palette, and bathrooms feature chocolaty marble. Suites are dazzling in white-upon-white, with high ceilings, dramatic cream-leather headboards, deep soaker tubs, and pale sofas just waiting for a glass of red wine to spill. Throughout, floor-to-ceiling windows offer peeks of the water and North Shore Mountains, and the Garden Terrace rooms have peaceful private patios. **Tableau,** the excellent

Where to Stay in Vancouver

Blue Horizon **8**
Buchan Hotel **2**
The Burrard **33**
Coast Coal Harbour Hotel **11**
Coast Plaza Hotel & Suites **3**
Days Inn Downtown **15**
Delta Vancouver Suites **17**
Empire Landmark **5**
Executive Hotel Le Soleil **16**
Fairmont Hotel Vancouver **23**
Fairmont Pacific Rim **12**
Fairmont Waterfront **14**
Four Seasons Hotel **21**
Georgian Court Hotel **29**
Granville Island Hotel **36**
Hostelling International Vancouver
  Downtown Hostel **35**
Hostelling International Vancouver
  Jericho Beach Hostel **37**
The Kingston Hotel **26**
The Listel Hotel **7**
Loden Vancouver **10**
Metropolitan Hotel Vancouver **20**
Moda Hotel **31**
Opus Hotel **32**
Pan Pacific Vancouver **13**
Rosedale on Robson Suite Hotel **30**
Rosewood Hotel Georgia **22**

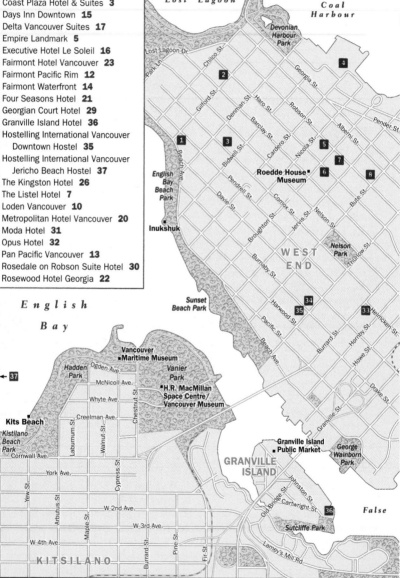

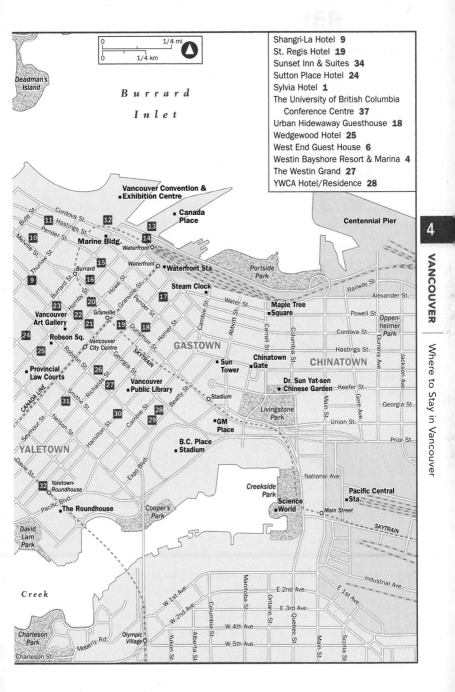

Shangri-La Hotel **9**
St. Regis Hotel **19**
Sunset Inn & Suites **34**
Sutton Place Hotel **24**
Sylvia Hotel **1**
The University of British Columbia
    Conference Centre **37**
Urban Hidewaway Guesthouse **18**
Wedgewood Hotel **25**
West End Guest House **6**
Westin Bayshore Resort & Marina **4**
The Westin Grand **27**
YWCA Hotel/Residence **28**

Deadman's
Island

B u r r a r d

I n l e t

0   1/4 mi
0   1/4 km

Centennial Pier

Vancouver Convention &
■ Exhibition Centre

■ Canada
Place

Cordova St.
Hastings St.
Pender St.
Marine Bldg.
Bute St.
Melville St.
Thurlow St.
Burrard
Hornby St.
Howe St.
Granville St.
Seymour St.
Richards St.
Homer St.
Hamilton St.
Mainland St.

11
12
13
14
15
16
10
9

Waterfront
Waterfront **■ Waterfront Sta.**

Portside
Park

Railway St.
Alexander St.
Powell St.
Cordova St.
Hastings St.

Oppen-
heimer
Park

Dunlevy Ave.
Jackson Ave.

Steam Clock

Water St.
Maple Tree
■ Square

17
20
23
22
21
19
18
24
25

Vancouver
Art Gallery
Granville
Robson Sq.
Vancouver
City Centre
Robson St.
Dunsmuir St.
Pender St.
Cambie St.
Abbott St.
Carrall St.
Columbia St.

GASTOWN

■ Sun
Tower

Chinatown
■ Gate

CHINATOWN

Gore Ave.
Main St.

Dr. Sun Yat-sen
■ Chinese Garden Keefer St.

Georgia St.

■ Provincial
Law Courts

26
27
31
30
28
29
32

Vancouver
■ Public Library

Georgia St.
Smithe St.
Nelson St.
Beatty St.
○ Stadium

Livingstone
Park

Union St.
Prior St.

■GM
Place

B.C. Place
■ Stadium

YALETOWN

CANADA LINE
SKYTRAIN
Expo Blvd.
Davie St.

National Ave.

Creekside
Park

Pacific Central
■ Sta.

Science
■ World
○ Main Street

SKYTRAIN

Yaletown-
Roundhouse
Pacific Blvd.
■ The Roundhouse

Cooper's
Park

David
Lam
Park

Creek

Industrial Ave.

E. 1st Ave.
E-2nd Ave.
E-3rd Ave.
W-1st Ave.
W-2nd Ave.
W-4th Ave.
W-5th Ave.

Manitoba St.
Columbia St.
Ontario St.
Quebec St.
Main St.
Scotia St.
Yukon St.
Alberta St.

Charleson
Park
Charleson St.
Moberly Rd.
Olympic
Village ○

West-Coast-accented French bistro downstairs, is one of the city's most underrated eateries and a real find.

1177 Melville St. (at Bute St.). ℂ **877/225-6336** or 604/669-5060. www.theloden.com. 77 units. C$230–C$350 double, C$590 suite. Parking C$35. Pets welcome (C$40 1-time fee). **Amenities:** Restaurant, bar, babysitting, concierge, exercise room, Jacuzzi, room service, sauna, free Wi-Fi.

Opus Hotel ★★★   For sheer, vibrant, grown-up fun, you cannot beat the Opus. It's the only place to stay right in Yaletown, which means it can be a bit noisy, what with all the bars, clubs, and restaurants outside. All the rooms feature spa bathrooms, in-room iPads, Frette bathrobes, Herman Miller ergonomic chairs, and a nightly amenity of retro candy, which is all pretty cool. Even cooler? Each room fits into one of five "personalities"—and the lifestyle concierge can help you decide if you're, say, "Mike," the gay New York doctor, "Pierre," the Parisian food critic, or "Susan," the Toronto fashion exec. Each has a room designed just for their personality, in vivid colors (cranberry red, foxglove blue, daring taupe, Hermes orange, Liverpool green) with glamorous decor elements like animal print armchairs, faux-fur throws, silk cushions, and funky art. The cool Opus Bar is one of Yaletown's liveliest hangouts, plus, after a few hits-and-misses (mostly misses), Opus has finally got its restaurant right: **La Pentola della Quercia** is the downtown outpost of a popular Kits eatery, with an award-winning wine list and exceptional Italian food in a bright, airy room.

322 Davie St. ℂ **866/642-6787** or 604/642-6787. www.opushotel.com. 96 units. C$250–C$550 double, from C$740 suite. Valet parking C$38. Children 17 and under stay free in parent's room. Pets welcome (no charge). **Amenities:** Restaurant, bar, bikes, concierge, small exercise room, room service, loaner iPads, free Wi-Fi.

Pan Pacific Vancouver ★★   Few locations can beat the one at the Pan: It's situated above the sails of Canada Place, right between the cruise ship terminal and the convention center. At 23 stories and 503 guest rooms, the hotel is large (for Vancouver, at least), yet somehow cozy, intimate, and comfortable at the same time. The spectacular harbor and mountain views are unsurpassed anywhere in the city. The guest rooms are spacious, serene, and modern, all blond wood and pale leather, marble bathrooms, and details like Persian carpets, potted orchids, or dramatic works of seascape art that give each room its own personality. There are numerous places to eat and drink within the hotel, and the luxurious Five Sails, with its floor-to-ceiling windows, award-winning wine list, and West Coast menu, is one of the few special-occasion restaurants left in the city. Plus there's a heated outdoor pool that overlooks the harbor and all the pampering you can stand at Spa Utopia.

300–999 Canada Place. ℂ **800/937-1515** in the U.S., 800/663-1515 in Canada, or 604/662-8111. www.panpacificvancouver.com. 503 units. C$240–C$540 double, C$450–C$7,500 suite. Self-parking C$39, valet parking C$43. Pets welcome (C$30/day). **Amenities:** 2 restaurants, bar, cafe, babysitting, concierge, health club, Jacuzzi, outdoor heated pool, room service, sauna, spa, Wi-Fi (C$5–C$15/day).

Rosewood Hotel Georgia ★★★   When it was built in 1927, the gracious Hotel Georgia quickly became Vancouver's go-to place for celebrities. Everyone stayed here, from the Queen (Elizabeth) to the King (Elvis). And then, in the late 1970s, it began its sad decline, and by the time the Rosewood group took it over, it was a shabby shadow of its former self. It took 5 years to finish the renovation, but in 2011 the Georgia reopened to retake its place among the best hotels in the city. The dark, sexy lobby retains its old glamor with high ceilings, marble floors, deep moldings, a sweeping staircase, and hints of gold detailing. The meticulously restored Spanish Ballroom, with its silvery plasterwork and minstrels' gallery, is one of the prettiest rooms you'll find anywhere. Throughout are masterworks by Canadian artists, including Douglas Coupland and Jack Shadbolt. Even the guest rooms feature original works of art—which is probably a good thing, since few have much of a view, except perhaps of the Vancouver Art Gallery. Still, the rooms are luxuriously comfortable, all decked out in hues of silver, pearl, and gold, with quilted leather bed frames, marble-topped coffee tables, velvety furnishings, and gorgeous marble bathrooms. The hotel is also home to the multiple-award-winning **Hawksworth Restaurant and Bar,** as well as the lovely 1927 Lobby Lounge, Bel Café, and, in summer, the outdoors Reflections Lounge, near the Senses spa. A jazz bar called Prohibition is expected to open in fall 2014.

801 W. Georgia St. ✆ **888/767-3966** or 604/682-5566. www.rosewoodhotelgeorgia.com. 155 units. July–Oct from $375 double, Nov–June from $295 double. Parking C$42. Small pets welcome (C$50 1-time charge). **Amenities:** Restaurant, bar, lounge, seasonal outdoor bar, babysitting, concierge, room service, fitness center, indoor pool, sauna, spa, free Wi-Fi.

Shangri-La Hotel ★★   The first North American property for Shangri-La brings with it all the style and service for which this Asian hotel chain is famous. At 62 stories, it's the tallest building in Vancouver, and has become the anchor for the city's new high-end boutique and restaurant row along Alberni Street, thanks in part to its own restaurant, **MARKET by Jean-Georges** (as in Vongerichten). The Shangri-La public spaces are all cool, airy, and serene, with floor-to-ceiling windows, blond wood, golden furnishings, and ornate Chinese screens. Guest rooms are large and furnished in contemporary style with sumptuous bathrooms and Asian accents like the bamboo-patterned gold brocade bedding or paintings of goldfish or cherry blossoms. Some rooms have interesting city views; unfortunately, though, the best views are from the top floors, which are the private residences. Still, it's a lovely place to stay. Be sure to visit Chi, the hotel's beautiful Asian-themed spa, with its menu of unique body treatments such as the martial arts-inspired Wushu.

1128 W. Georgia St. ✆ **604/689-1120.** www.shangri-la.com/vancouver. 119 units. C$355–C$405 double. Parking C$43. Pets welcome (C$50 charge every 15 days). **Amenities:** Restaurant, lounge, babysitting, concierge, health club, Jacuzzi, outdoor heated pool, room service, sauna, spa, free Wi-Fi.

Sutton Place Hotel ★★   Once the shining star among Vancouver hotels, this European-style boutique hotel has been eclipsed in recent years by some of the newer properties. Expect that to change in 2014, though, as the hotel replaces its tired Fleuri restaurant with the exciting new **Boulevard Kitchen and Oyster Bar,** which will feature some of the top culinary talent in the city. The hotel is still luxurious and comfortable, with attentive service and all the amenities. Its outside may look bland and corporate, but step inside and you'll find a bright lobby with marble floors, chandeliers, and French-style furniture. That esthetic extends to the guest rooms with their regency-stripe wallpaper, brocade wingback chairs, and botanical prints. The clubby Gerard Lounge is still one of the city's favorite hangouts, especially for lawyers from the nearby Law Courts. There's also an exceptional European-style health club and spa, with a big heated pool and sun deck, as well as a tower of apartments for long-stay guests.

845 Burrard St. ✆ **866/378-8866** or 604/682-5511. www.vancouver.suttonplace.com. 397 units. C$209–C$409 double. Parking C$40. Pets welcome (C40 1-time charge). **Amenities:** Restaurant, lounge, bakery/cafe, bikes, concierge, health club, Jacuzzi, indoor pool, room service, sauna, spa, Wi-Fi (C$15/day).

Wedgewood Hotel ★★★   This lovely little Relais & Châteaux boutique hotel is one of the city's most romantic hideaways. From the moment you step in under the navy blue awnings on busy Hornby Street, you've entered a completely different world, an elegant one that borders on the baroque, with none of that boring minimalistic restraint. Think dark, opulent wood, luxe fabrics, rich colors, and lots and lots of original art. The spacious guest rooms all have balconies, fireplaces, top-quality bedding, and limestone-and-marble bathrooms, as well as lovely details like toile dust ruffles, brocade throws, and inlaid wooden cabinetry. The spa is famous for its facial, and **Bacchus,** the plush hotel restaurant, is one of the city's fave places for ladies who lunch and lawyers who win their cases at the Law Courts across the street.

845 Hornby St. ℗ **800/663-0666** or 604/689-7777. www.wedgewoodhotel.com. 83 units. C$250–C$500 double, C$300–C$1,500 suite. Valet parking C$31. No pets. **Amenities:** Restaurant, concierge, executive-level rooms, exercise room, room service, spa, free Wi-Fi in common areas.

EXPENSIVE

Coast Coal Harbour Hotel ★
Great location, great value. This cool, comfortable, contemporary hotel opened in 2010 just in time for the Olympic Winter Games. It's steps away from Stanley Park, and not much further from most of the attractions you'll want to experience. All the guest rooms feature floor-to-ceiling windows for taking in that view—try to get a corner room to make the most if it. This is an exceptionally eco-friendly hotel, with a zero-waste policy, so you can feel good about staying here. You can also feel good while you stay here—the bright, airy lobby features white cubic stools and tables, while the guest rooms have nice, big, comfortable beds and low-slung modernist armchairs in pale leather. It looks like a much more expensive hotel than it actually is. Plus its casual eatery, **Prestons,** features a festive long table, all the better for enjoying its classics-inspired menu with friends. Note that another, older, less expensive Coast Plaza is located in the West End at 1763 Comox St. (℗ **800/716-6199** or 604/688-7711; www.coasthotels.com).

1180 W. Hastings St. ℗ **800/716-6199** or 604/697-0202. www.coasthotels.com. 220 units. C$230–C$360 double. Valet parking C$28. Pets welcome (C$25/day per pet). **Amenities:** Restaurant, concierge, fitness center, outdoor pool, room service, free Wi-Fi.

Delta Vancouver Suites ★
If you're looking for a great place to stay while you're in town for a conference or business meeting, this is exactly what you're looking for. Terrific location near Gastown, the Waterfront Centre transportation hub, and the convention center. Beautiful all-suites guest rooms with all the amenities you need, notably, an office area with desk and place to plug in all your electronics. The look throughout is luxe—beautiful wood paneling, boutique-hotel-style bathrooms, comfy linens, dramatic brick-red statement walls—without the luxe price. For a small fee, you can upgrade to the Signature Club suites, which will give you a better view and access to Signature Lounge, which serves a good continental breakfast. The hotel also has an okay casual restaurant called Manhattan, but since you're only steps from some of the best restaurants in the city you may want to dine out instead.

550 W. Hastings St. ℗ **888/890-3222** or 604/689-8188. www.deltahotels.com. 225 units. C$150–C$280 double. Children 17 and under stay free in parent's room. Valet parking C$26. Pets welcome (C$35 1-time charge). **Amenities:** Restaurant, bar, babysitting, concierge, executive-level rooms, exercise room, indoor pool, room service, free Wi-Fi.

Executive Hotel Le Soleil ★
Where most Vancouver hotels are going for the clean, contemporary look, Le Soleil is all ornate, over-the-top opulence. Think luxuriously swagged draperies, gilt-edged furniture, and plush, velvety, satiny upholstery, all in rich colors of red and gold. And patterns! You might find stripes, damask, and medallions all in the same space. This 1980s-era boutique hotel is conveniently located

midway between Robson Square and the financial district and it is a somewhat over-looked little treasure. Unfortunately, because it is surrounded by much-bigger buildings, the all-suite guest rooms don't have much of a view at all. Still, the service is exceptional, and the **Copper Chimney Restaurant & Bar** is a fine place to go for global fare—the new chef hails from India, so be sure to try the South Asian specialties, especially the naan flatbreads from the tandoor oven.

567 Hornby St.✆ **877/632-3030** or 604/632-3000. www.lesoleilhotel.com. 119 units. C$155–C$300 double. Valet parking C$29. Pets welcome (C$25/day). **Amenities:** Restaurant, concierge, access to YWCA fitness facilities next door, room service, free Wi-Fi.

Georgian Court Hotel ★   If you are in town for an event at one of the two sports stadiums, the Vancouver Public Library, or the Queen Elizabeth Theatre, then this is a great destination for you. A member of the Small Luxury Hotels of the World, the hotel was designed to evoke the grace and elegance of the 18th century, and even has a royal connection—Princess Margriet of the Netherlands was on hand for the groundbreaking ceremony back in the early 1980s. Since then, it has been updated throughout with comfortable gold-toned furniture, splashes of red accent color, great business amenities, and a pretty orchid theme. This extends to its Orchid Floor, 18 rooms especially designed for women travelers, with flat irons, curling irons, yoga mats, ladies' emergency kits, and extra skirt hangers, at no extra charge.

773 Beatty St. ✆ **800/663-1155** or 604/682-5555. www.georgiancourt.com. 180 units. C$200–C$250 double. Parking C$16. Pets welcome (no charge). **Amenities:** Restaurant, bar, exercise room, Jacuzzi, room service, sauna, downtown shuttle (drop-off only), free bike loans, free Wi-Fi.

Metropolitan Hotel Vancouver ★★   It would be worth staying here just for the complimentary downtown shuttle service in the hotel Jaguar. But the central location, great meeting facilities, and fine restaurant are also pretty swell. The hotel has been around since the early 1990s, and still retains some of the look of the era, a tad too much brass and smoky glass, but has mostly been updated throughout. That's especially true of the guest rooms, some of which can boast a sexy red velvet chaise longue, as well as marble-tiled bathrooms, Frette linens, tufted headboards, and modern art. Many have balconies, but the views aren't much; it's really all about the location here. It's also worth popping into the sleek and stylish restaurant, **Diva at the Met,** which seems to have something of a revolving door of the city's best chefs—regardless, something good is always cooking.

645 Howe St.✆ **800/667-2300** or 604/687-1122. www.metropolitan.com/vanc. 197 units. C$200–C$400 double, C$250–C$700 suite. Children 17 and under stay free in parent's room. Underground parking C$40. Pets welcome (C$30 1-time charge). **Amenities:** Restaurant, bar, concierge, exercise room, Jacuzzi, indoor pool, room service, squash court, limo service, free Wi-Fi.

Rosedale on Robson Suite Hotel ★   It's not fancy; indeed, it's perhaps a bit dated, one of those green-trimmed glassy buildings that popped up everywhere in the 1990s. But the value is great, especially if you want to stay in the area around the library, which is otherwise not terribly well served by hotels. All the rooms are either one- or two-bedroom suites, with living rooms and kitchenettes, making this a great place to stay for families or friends in town for a big concert. The First Nations and West Coast-themed art throughout adds a nice touch to what is otherwise a pretty plain and simple, but clean and comfortable, decor.

838 Hamilton St. (at Robson St.).✆ **800/661-8870** or 604/689-8033. www.rosedaleonrobson.com. 217 units. C$170–C$650 suite. Additional adult C$25. Rates include continental breakfast. Look for seasonal deals. Parking C$20. No pets. **Amenities:** Restaurant, babysitting, concierge, executive-level rooms, small exercise room, Jacuzzi, indoor lap pool, room service, sauna, kitchenette, free Wi-Fi.

St. Regis Hotel ★ The building is more than a century old, but the rooms are beautifully up to date. This lovely boutique hotel is in a great location near the financial district, SkyTrain, and shopping, and it boasts all the amenities both leisure and business travelers crave. It recently underwent a major 18-month, C$12-million renovation, reopening in December 2008 to rave reviews. Guest rooms retain historic details like the crown molding, baseboards, and windows that open, but with a contemporary coolness thanks to a soft gray palette, modern art, sleek furniture, and beautiful bathrooms with double sinks and miles of counter space. Plus this placed is truly wired, with fast, free, easy Internet access, and all the plug-ins you could possibly need for all your devices. The lobby features a curved granite counter and vibrant works of modern art, and the pub downstairs is a popular local hangout. Best of all, a stay here gets you a proper breakfast. What's not to love about that?

602 Dunsmuir St. ℂ **800/770-7929** or 604/681-1135. www.stregishotel.com. 65 units. C$170 double, C$275–C$509 suite. Rates include full breakfast. Parking C$25. No pets. **Amenities:** Restaurant, bar/pub, coffee shop, concierge, executive-level rooms, access to nearby health club, free Wi-Fi.

MODERATE

The Burrard ★★ Thousands of Vancouverites have driven by this hotel day after day, never realizing that it encloses one of the city's best-kept secrets: a lush tropical garden in its inner courtyard. Who knew? The Burrard Motor Inn first opened its doors in 1956 as the cool new kid on Vancouver's block. Now, after a major reno, it's that cool kid once again. Its location is a good one—right on busy (and noisy) Burrard Street, across the street from St. Paul's Hospital and within a short stroll of English Bay. The lobby is filled with Vancouver-centric photography and art—in fact, there are often art shows here—and the guest rooms have a cool updated retro vibe, with silver Moroccan pouffes, 1970s-style plastic molded chairs, and comfortable, contemporary beds with padded headboards. The hotel offers bikes for guests to use free of charge on the nearby bike paths and Seawall. Plus there's a casual restaurant downstairs that carries some of Vancouver's fave treats—like yummy Cadeau Bakery pastries—and since the whole place is licensed, you can take a glass of wine upstairs to enjoy in the garden.

1100 Burrard St. ℂ **800/663-0366** or 604/681-2331. www.burrardinn.com. 72 units. C$186–C$206 double. C$30 for additional adult, children under 12 stay free. Parking C$25. Pets welcome (C$25/day). **Amenities:** Restaurant, bicycles, courtyard garden, access to nearby fitness club, free Wi-Fi.

Days Inn Vancouver Downtown ★ The building is nearly a century old and has been a hotel since it opened in 1918; unfortunately, most of that historic charm has been lost amid the many updates over time. The decor is pretty much just a bland, beige, middle-of-the-road hotel style—but it's clean and functional, the price is right, and the location is fantastic. Plus every once in a while you can spot the bones of the building's history, whether it be an original fireplace or the old safe. The guest rooms have all the essential amenities (TV, Wi-Fi, comfortable beds, room for all your gear), plus there's the excellent **Butcher & Bullock** gastro pub downstairs. Note that some of rooms have showers only, and those facing east stare directly at a concrete wall.

921 W. Pender St. ℂ **877/681-4335** or 604/681-4335. www.daysinnvancouver.com. 85 units. C$105–C$219 double. Parking C$20. No pets. **Amenities:** Restaurant, bar, concierge, downtown shuttle (drop-off only), free Wi-Fi.

Moda Hotel ★★ It's hard to believe this stylish, century-old building was once the notorious Dufferin Hotel, a rough, run-down, and rowdy place famous in the 1980s

Looking for a Bed & Breakfast?

If you prefer to stay in a B&B, the **BC Bed & Breakfast Innkeepers Guild** (www.bcsbestbnbs.com) has listings of its members throughout the province. Listings include a detailed description, contact info, photos, and pricing. Since B&Bs come in all styles from sleek and urbane to frilly and flouncy, there's bound to be one that suits your needs.

for its gay bars, drag shows, and male strippers, hence the popular slogan: "Go buff at the Duff." Things have certainly changed in recent years. After a major renovation, the hotel has retained its historic charms, but enhanced them with a chic, modern, Italian-inspired new look. (The new owner's background is Italian, so it all makes sense.) You'll find marble, slate, and cornice moldings throughout, much of which was uncovered during the restoration. The lobby has a beautiful mosaic tile floor and photos of the hotel in its early days, as well as bright red contemporary chairs with swooping lines. Guest rooms are clean and elegant, with ingenious use of space, and a modern Italian design aesthetic in black, gray, and white with splashes of red in pieces like the chic rounded accent chairs. There are also a handful of upscale suites in the building across the street, ideal for entertaining large groups. The hotel has several excellent places to eat and drink, including the award-winning **Cibo Trattoria, Uva Wine & Cocktail Bar,** and **Red Card,** a sports bar that is more soccer than hockey. Moda is right across the street from the Orpheum Theatre, making this a popular spot for culture vultures.

900 Seymour St. © **877/683-5522** or 604/683-4251. www.modahotel.ca. 67 units. C$100–C$230 double, C$220–C$290 suite. Parking C$20. Pets welcome (C$15/day). **Amenities:** 2 restaurants, sports bar, free Wi-Fi.

INEXPENSIVE

Hostelling International Vancouver Downtown Hostel ★   Traveling on a budget often means staying in dodgy, dirty, unsafe places, or in locations far away from the action. Not so with this great hostel. It is, believe it or not, a converted nunnery, located just a few blocks from the beach and most of downtown's main attractions. It's not just for kids, either, so it has no curfew, but it does have a fantastic shared kitchen, all stainless steel and commercial-quality appliances, where you can whip up a snack or a gourmet meal. Most rooms are clean, whitewashed quad dorms with simple pine bunk beds; a limited number of doubles, triples, and private rooms are also available. Most require that you share a bathroom. There's also a spectacular rooftop patio, game room with pool table, and free shuttle to the bus depot and Jericho Beach. Not too surprisingly, it's extremely busy in summer, so be sure to book ahead.

1114 Burnaby St. (at Thurlow St.). © **888/203-4302** or 604/684-4565. www.hihostels.ca. 67 units (44 4-person shared dorm rooms, 23 double or private rooms). C$30–C$33 dorm (IYHA members), C$33–C$37 dorm (nonmembers); C$72–C$86 private (members); C$80–C$95 private (nonmembers). Rates include full breakfast. Annual adult membership C$35. Limited free parking (reserve ahead). No pets. **Amenities:** Bikes, free Wi-Fi.

The Kingston Hotel ★   You can find hotels like the Kingston all over Europe, but here it's a real rarity—and a real find. This is a small, budget-friendly, family-run B&B in a 1910 heritage building in a great location right in the heart of all the action on busy Richards Street. Rooms aren't fancy, most bathrooms are shared, and you rarely see those shiny, floral bedspreads these days, but the place is immaculate, the staff is friendly, and there's a cozy character to the place. There's also a great little lounge to hang out in, and a good continental breakfast.

757 Richards St. ☏ **888/713-3304** or 604/684-9024. www.kingstonhotelvancouver.com. 52 units (13 with private bathroom). C$85–C$155 double. Additional person C$20 each. Senior discount. Rates include continental breakfast. Parking C$25. No pets. **Amenities:** Restaurant, bar, sauna, free Wi-Fi.

Urban Hideaway Guesthouse ★   This is a great little find—though it may not be for everyone. Janine and Ken, a pair of world travelers, came home from their far-flung journeys to create the kind of hotel they dreamed of. They found an old Victorian built in 1896, and quite possibly the last actual house remaining in downtown Vancouver. Then they turned it into a welcoming space for fellow adventurers. It is a quiet refuge not far from the dodgy bits of the city, where you'll share your space with your hosts, fellow guests, and three kitties. Space is small, stairs are steep, and the bathrooms are shared, but there is a gorgeous rooftop garden where you can enjoy barbecues with your fellow travelers amid a riot of flowers. The guest rooms are romantically cozy, with wicker chairs, pretty bedspreads, and potted plants—the loft suite especially is huge, and drenched with light from the skylight.

581 Richards St. ☏ **604/694-0600.** www.urban-hideaway.com. 7 units. Oct–Apr C$70–C$110 double, May–Sept C$110–C$160 double. Breakfast included. Parking lots nearby. No pets. **Amenities:** Bikes, kayaks, shared kitchen, free Wi-Fi.

YWCA Hotel ★   Newly refurbished, clean, safe, comfortable, and close to many of the main attractions—there are plenty of good reasons to choose this hotel. The fact that it's such a great bargain is just one of them. Located across the street from BC Place Stadium, it's close to many of the main attractions, and is a favorite with international travelers. Guest rooms are bright and cheerful, with simple IKEA-esque pine furniture, comfortable beds, and vibrant abstract art on the walls. Most rooms have shared bathrooms, and there are a number of communal kitchens, three TV lounges, and access to the really great YWCA Fitness Centre. (And in case you were wondering, the hotel is co-ed, so everyone is welcome.) Proceeds from the hotel support YWCA projects.

733 Beatty St. ☏ **800/663-1424** or 604/895-5830. www.ywcahotel.com. 155 units (about a third with private bathroom). C$75–C$145 double. Weeklong discounts available. Parking C$13. No pets. **Amenities:** Access to YWCA facility, coffee shop, communal kitchen, TV lounge, Wi-Fi (C$3/day).

The West End
VERY EXPENSIVE
Westin Bayshore Resort & Marina ★★   When famously reclusive billionaire Howard Hughes was on the lam from U.S. tax authorities back in 1972, he holed up at the Bayshore for a year. And why not? This cool, modern hotel has an outstanding location at the entrance to Stanley Park, with stellar views of Coal Harbour and the North Shore Mountains. Plus it's the only hotel in Vancouver with its own marina, so an easy getaway was, and is, close at hand. The original, low-rise Bayshore was built in 1961, and has since been joined by a tower. The hotel features 40 meeting rooms, so it is as popular with business travelers as it is with leisure visitors. The entire property was updated in 2009, and guest rooms now feature the Westin Heavenly Beds and Bathrooms, as well as elegant, low-slung, modern modular furniture, glass sinks, and fabulous showers, all done up in cool West Coast modern decor with lots of glass and pale wood. But the real attraction is that view, captured in the floor-to-ceiling windows. The hotel has two restaurants—**Currents** and the **Seawall Bar & Grill**—but locals

still lament the loss of the old Trader Vic's, once one of the city's top dining establishments, and the source of fabulous tiki drinks to enjoy by the outdoor pool. Note that there's also another Westin, the business-friendly Westin Grand, up near Rogers Arena and BC Place (433 Robson St.; ℭ **888/680-9393** or 604/602-1999; www.westingrand vancouver.com).

1601 Bayshore Dr. ℭ **800/937-8461** or 604/682-3377. www.westinbayshore.com. 511 units. C$460 double, C$560 suite. Children 17 and under stay free in parent's room. Self-parking C$36, valet parking C$41. Pets welcome (no charge). **Amenities:** 2 restaurants, bar, coffee shop, babysitting, concierge, health club, Jacuzzi, 2 pools (1 indoor, 1 outdoor), room service, sauna, spa, free Wi-Fi in lobby (C$15/day in room).

EXPENSIVE

The Listel Hotel ★★ In 2012, the Listel Hotel closed its faded O'Doul's Restaurant, once a popular spot for live jazz and Sunday brunch, and turned one half of it into an art gallery and the other half into a lively, local-food-obsessed bistro called Forage. It's been a winning formula, and a perfect fit for this great little boutique hotel on Robson Street. The Listel is known as Vancouver's most "art-full" hotel, and there is cool art everywhere you look, from the cast-iron statues in the lobby to the First Nations art on loan from the Museum of Anthropology on the Museum Floors to the contemporary works on the Gallery Floors. Every room is a lovely little oasis of luxury and art, with the cool, clean, comfortable lines of the decor creating a perfect frame for the paintings, and special touches like vintage-style alarm clocks or lamps that could double as sculptures. Or maybe they actually are sculptures—it's hard to say. Don't forget to visit **Forage,** where talented chef Chris Whittaker captures the essence of the West Coast on a plate.

1300 Robson St. ℭ **800/663-5491** or 604/684-8461. www.thelistelhotel.com. 129 units. C$200–C$290 double, C$400–C$600 suite. Valet parking C$39. No pets. **Amenities:** Restaurant, bar, concierge, executive-level rooms, exercise room, room service, free Wi-Fi.

MODERATE

Blue Horizon ★ This 31-story high-rise built in the 1960s towers above the rest from its lofty position on a rise. It has some pretty terrific views, especially from the upper floors. It's also a pretty sweet-looking hotel on the inside, thanks to a major reno in 2011 that included new windows and a cool, new decor. The rooms look fresh and modern, with bold colors and sleek lines, jazzed up with funky details like throws printed with tree branches, multi-colored striped carpets, and paintings of seascapes that echo the view out the windows. A good location near the shopping district of Robson Street, and a terrific value for the area.

1225 Robson St. ℭ **800/663-1333** or 604/688-1411. www.bluehorizonhotel.com. 214 units. C$100–C$220 double, C$110–C$230 superior double, C$190–C$330 suite. Children 15 and under stay free in parent's room. Parking C$16. No pets. **Amenities:** Restaurant, small exercise room, Jacuzzi, indoor pool, sauna, free Wi-Fi.

Empire Landmark ★ Every city's got to have its revolving restaurant, and Vancouver's is located here at the Empire, a 42-story tower with an uninterrupted panorama of city, sea, and mountains. Predictably, the food at **Cloud 9** isn't actually all that great, but it's a good place for a drink while you take in the beautiful view. As for the hotel itself, it's the sort of place that's popular with tour groups and as a result is a bit beige and anonymous despite a recent makeover. (The executive guest rooms at least have a few funky touches, like curvy, colorful modern accent chairs.) What sells it is the location: on popular Robson Street, near busy Denman and the entrance to Stanley Park. Note that there are a handful of smoking rooms still available, making this a real rarity in a city that was among the first to adopt a no-smoking policy.

1400 Robson St. ⓒ **800/830-6144** or 604/687-0511. www.empirelandmarkhotel.com. 357 units. C$170–C$230 double. Parking C$15/day. No pets. **Amenities:** Restaurant, bar, Wi-Fi (C$9/day).

Sunset Inn & Suites ★   One of the city's true hidden gems. The rooms are large, the parking is free, and the whole place underwent a renovation just a few years ago. This family-owned hotel is located just a few blocks from English Bay and around the corner from Davie Street, in the heart of Vancouver's vibrant gay village. All the rooms are studios or one-bedroom suites, with balconies and full kitchens, some with pullout couches ideal for families traveling with children. The beds are luxuriously comfortable and allergy-friendly and desks have ergonomic chairs. Rooms have plush oversized sofas, Persian-style rugs, sponged walls, and leather chairs that all contribute to a pleasantly homey feel. Add in the friendly staff and free parking, and you'll see why this is such a great find.

1111 Burnaby St. ⓒ **800/786-1997** or 604/688-2474. www.sunsetinn.com. 50 units. Oct–May C$90–C$160 studio, C$110–C$210 1-bedroom; June–Sept C$160–C$230 studio, C$180–$475 1-bedroom. Additional adult C$10. Children 9 and under stay free in parent's room. Rates include continental breakfast. Weekly rates available. Free parking. No pets. **Amenities:** Small exercise room, free Wi-Fi.

Sylvia Hotel ★   The Sylvia was Vancouver's first high rise, constructed back in 1912 when the rest of the West End was all houses. Now most of the houses have been replaced by much higher towers, but the ivy-clad brick Sylvia quietly continues on. This hotel is beloved by locals and by many of its guests; others are less impressed by its unpretentious, even plain, decor. The big draw is, of course, the unbeatable location right on English Bay—that, and the great room rates. Each room has its own layout, which ranges from small bargain rooms to big suites with full kitchens. You'll find more character in the old wing (coffered ceilings, crown moldings), and more convenience (king size beds, bigger bathrooms) in the new low-rise one. The best feature of all is the popular restaurant and lounge. It was Vancouver's first cocktail lounge, back in 1954, and where the classic Vancouver Cocktail was invented. Enjoy one while you take in the terrific views of the beach and English Bay.

1154 Gilford St. ⓒ**604/681-9321.** www.sylviahotel.com. 120 units. May–Sept C$160–C$255 double, Oct–Apr C$120–C$175 double. Children 17 and under stay free in parent's room. Parking C$15. Pets welcome (no charge). **Amenities:** Restaurant, bar, concierge, room service, beach across street, free Wi-Fi.

West End Guest House ★★   Tucked amid lush cedars and rhododendrons, you'll find this charming, well-kept heritage home, with its comfortable rooms and welcoming hosts. The house was built in 1906 and is one of the very few to survive the building boom of the 1950s and '60s. Located as it is on the edge of the gay village, it's not surprising that it's especially popular among the LGBT set. And why not? It's beautifully maintained and filled with antiques and historic photos of Vancouver taken by the original owners. Expect old Victrolas and damask armchairs, swagged draperies and bow windows. Each of the seven guest rooms has its own character, which could mean pretty upholstered headboards, toile comforters, or lace bed curtains, as well as wingback chairs, fireplaces, claw-foot tubs, or antique wood-framed love seats. Breakfast is a feast, and there's sherry and iced tea to sip in the garden on a sunny afternoon.

1362 Haro St. ☎ **888/546-3327** or 604/681-2889. www.westendguesthouse.com. 7 units. Oct–May C$90–C$195 double, June–Sept C$200–C$275 double. Rates include full breakfast. Free off-street parking. No pets. **Amenities:** Bikes, garden, free Wi-Fi.

INEXPENSIVE

Buchan Hotel ★   It's rumored that Errol Flynn died here. Mind you, it's also been said that he died at the Sylvia, the Georgia, and aboard a boat in the harbor; also, that he died in the arms of a young girl—or, perhaps, a young boy. No matter. The point is, this place has history. It was built in 1926 and still has many of the features of the era, like the extra wide hallways and vintage photos of Vancouver. It's on a quiet, leafy street in the West End, just 2 blocks from Stanley Park, and if the location weren't enough of a draw, the price would be: This is one of the best deals in town. The draw-back is that it's not exactly fancy. Rooms still have those 1980s-style brass lamps and floral bedspreads, veneer desks, and tiny bathrooms (and half of those are shared). Still, there are vintage radiators and inlaid hardwood floors, friendly staff, and a lounge with big, plush sofas perfect for curling up with a book on rainy days. Plus the **Adesso Bistro** downstairs serves up great northern Italian food and wine, making this a lovely, affordable refuge.

1906 Haro St. ☎ **800/668-6654** or 604/685-5354. www.buchanhotel.com. 60 units (29 with private bathroom). C$70–C$170 double. Children 12 and under stay free in parent's room. Additional person C$10. Weekly rates available. Limited parking C$10. No pets. **Amenities:** Restaurant at foot of hotel, lounge, free Wi-Fi.

The West Side
EXPENSIVE

Granville Island Hotel ★★   Just in time for the 2010 Winter Olympic Games, this great little boutique hotel underwent a renovation that saw it become a sleek, chic, modern place to stay. Certainly, its location is a good one—right on Granville Island, overlooking a marina and False Creek. It's steps from shops, theaters, playgrounds, galleries, the public market, and several eateries, including the hotel's own **Dockside Restaurant.** Plus it has one of the best patios in the city, with a fire pit, low-slung sofas, and a sort of dining cabana enclosed with dramatic black-and-white stripe drap-eries. The downside? It's a bit of a distance from downtown, and will cost you C$10 to C$15 to take a taxi into the city. Still, guest rooms are spacious, and some have balconies and soaker tubs. Decor is elegantly simple, with cool white-and-black hotel bedding, cozy duvets, nautical art on the walls, and dark wood headboards. Penthouses have fireplaces and huge patios. And that view is pretty sweet.

1253 Johnston St. ☎ **800/663-1840** or 604/683-7373. www.granvilleislandhotel.com. 82 units. Oct–Apr from C$160 double, C$400 penthouse; May–Sept from C$215 double, C$500 penthouse. Parking C$12. Pets welcome (C$25/day). **Amenities:** Restaurant, brewpub, babysitting, fitness room, Jacuzzi, room service, sauna, access to nearby tennis courts, free Wi-Fi.

INEXPENSIVE

Hostelling International Vancouver Jericho Beach Hostel   Want to stay at the beach? For next to nothing? Then this is the place for you. This hostel is located in a former military barracks, and admittedly, the decor isn't much fancier than it was back in the days when soldiers bunked here. Most of the rooms are dorms, with simple pine bunk beds and shared bathrooms. But bedding is provided, and it's clean, well-maintained, and safe. There's a cafe that serves simple food prepared by students of the North Shore Culinary School, as well as a kitchen where you can cook your own meals. And the hostel's staff can set you up with tours and activities. But the real point is the setting—right in the middle of a big park just a block away from beautiful Jericho Beach.

1515 Discovery St. ☏ **888/203-4303** or 604/224-3208. www.hihostels.ca. 252 beds in 15 dorms, 9 private family units (without private bathroom). C$27–C$32 dorm (IYHA members), C$30–C$35 dorm (nonmembers); C$60–C$98 private room (members), C$63–C$108 private room (nonmembers). Parking C$10. Bus: 4. Children 4 and under must stay in a private room. No pets. **Amenities:** Cafe, bikes, bike storage, free Wi-Fi.

Staying on the North Shore

The North Shore has great hikes, biking trails, and ski hills, as well as beautiful views and thrilling attractions like the Capilano Suspension Bridge. It's got a handful of good pubs, seafood restaurants, and bakeries. Plus it has the fabulous and ever-expanding Park Royal Shopping Centre. What it doesn't have? A lot of good accommodation. That said, there are a couple of great little finds.

Lonsdale Quay, where the SeaBus docks, was intended to be another Granville Island Public Market, but somehow that never quite worked out as planned. It's mostly takeout places, a couple of inexpensive restaurants, and the great little **Lonsdale Quay Hotel** (123 Carrie Cates Ct.; ☏ **800/836-6111** or 604/986-6111; www.lonsdalequay hotel.com). Standard rooms are pretty basic, though they have fun views of the busy harbor, but the premium executive suites are fantastic, with dark wooden sleigh beds, sunken tubs, and 180-degree harbor and city views. The hotel has 70 rooms, and doubles run C$140 to C$450.

Right next door to the quay, you'll find the relatively new, 106-room **Pinnacle Hotel at the Pier** (138 Victory Ship Way; ☏ **877/986-7437** or 604/986-7437; www.pinnaclehotelatthepier.com). Opened in 2010, this is a chic, modern addition to the waterfront, which is undergoing a major transformation over the next few years, including, quite possibly, a London Eye-style wheel. The Pinnacle has great views of Vancouver

and the harbor, and you can even soak in the view while you soak in the tub. There's an indoor pool, state-of-the-art fitness center, and several good restaurants nearby, including its own. Rates for a double room begin at C$150 in low season (Oct–May), and C$199 in high season (June–Sept).

There are also a handful of great little B&Bs on the North Shore. Among them is the beautiful, Craftsman-style **Thistle-Down House Bed & Breakfast** (3910 Capilano Rd.; ☏ **604/986-7173;** www.thistle-down.com), which is nestled up against the forests of Grouse Mountain. Surrounded by gorgeous gardens and filled with art and antiques, it's well known for its sumptuous breakfasts and lovely guest rooms. There are five of them, ranging from the petite Snuggery, with its fireplace and Persian carpets, to Under the Apple Tree, a romantic hideaway with a sunken sitting room and private patio with French doors. Rates will run you C$175 to $279 in summer, C$125 to C$189 in winter. For other North Shore B&Bs, visit the **Vancouver North Shore Bed and Breakfast Association** site at www.bbvancouverbc.com.

Note that if you decide to stay on the North Shore, there are two bridges to get into Vancouver, and traffic across them can be excruciatingly slow at peak times. There is good bus service, though, and the handy SeaBus sails from Lonsdale Quay every 15 minutes during the day, 30 minutes in the evenings.

The University of British Columbia Conference Centre ★ Admittedly, most of the year these are student dorms. And, admittedly, it's a long way from downtown, which is a good half-hour drive away. But the UBC Conference Centre is in a lovely forested setting out on Point Grey, the rooms are actually pretty nice, and the price, well, that can't be beat. The West Coast Suites are a little bit nicer, with stylish feature walls, full kitchens and balconies, and they are available year round. The other rooms vary from dormitory-style accommodation (with the kind of decor that will take you back to your freshman year) to shared rooms and private apartments. These are only available in the summer months. A continental breakfast buffet at the Student Union Building cafeteria is included with all rooms.

5961 Student Union Blvd. ✆ **888/822-1030** or 604/822-1000. www.ubcconferences.com. 1,500 units. Walter Gage Residence units available approx. May 11–Aug 25; Pacific Spirit Hostel units available May 15–Aug 15; West Coast Suites and Marine Drive Residence units available year-round. Walter Gage Residences and Marine Drive Residences C$46–C$57 single with shared bathroom, C$120–C$140 studio, C$150–C$180 suite; Pacific Spirit Hostel C$33–C$35 single, C$65–C$70 double; West Coast Suites C$160–C$200 suite. Parking C$7. Bus: 4, 14, 44, 84, or 99. No pets. **Amenities** (on campus): Restaurant, cafeteria, pub, fitness center, access to campus Olympic-size swimming pool, sauna (C$5/person), tennis courts, free Wi-Fi.

WHERE TO EAT IN VANCOUVER

You'd better arrive hungry, because Vancouver has an incredible banquet waiting for you. Dining is practically a competitive sport here; certainly, food is pretty much all anyone talks about, aside from housing prices and how the Vancouver Canucks hockey team is doing (losing, usually). In the past few years, the trend in restaurants has been moving away from fancy fine dining; instead of white tablecloths and endless tasting menus, it's all about terrific little joints led by creative young chefs and housed in funky heritage spaces. But just because the room is casual, don't expect a laissez-faire attitude to what's on the plate. Vancouver chefs are passionate about local ingredients, and they've got some of the best to work with, from the fantastic Pacific seafood to all the wild mushrooms foraged in the nearby mountains. They are also, by and large, an open-minded, creative bunch, less hung up on traditions and trends, and more willing to experiment, whether it's with old-school preserving techniques or newfangled molecular ones. And, thanks to Vancouver's spot on the edge of the Pacific Rim, you can expect to savor a joyful fusion of Asian and European flavors. Best of all, compared to other cities, Vancouver's restaurant food prices are surprisingly low, considering the high quality. (The booze is another story; thanks to exorbitant taxes and import duties, wine and spirits can be shockingly expensive.) Whatever you're hungry for, you're sure to find it, and much more. So dig in, and enjoy!

Downtown & Yaletown
VERY EXPENSIVE
Black & Blue ★ STEAKHOUSE The backlit, glass-doored meat locker has pride of place in the dining room. It's the first clue that this luxe steakhouse may not be the best place for vegetarians. Sure, there's some seafood and chicken on the menu, but really, it's all about beef: prime rib, chateaubriand, 60-ounce tomahawk steak, Japanese wagyu rib-eye. Plus you'll find all the traditional steakhouse sides, including creamed corn, scalloped potatoes, and Caesar salad made tableside, as well as add-ons of king crab or tiger prawns. Although the menu sounds old school, the room is anything but. It's all dark and sultry and modern, with cool cylindrical chandeliers and a

Where to Eat in Vancouver

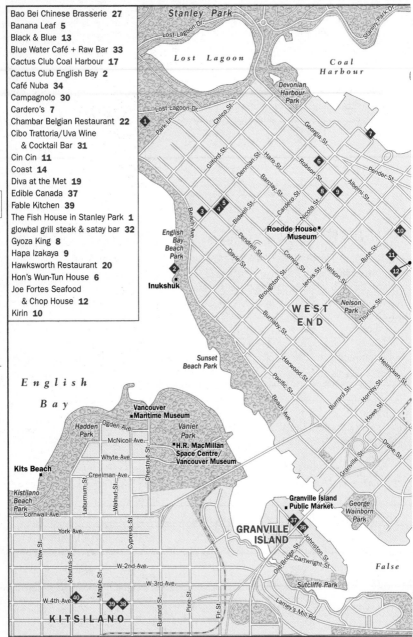

Bao Bei Chinese Brasserie **27**
Banana Leaf **5**
Black & Blue **13**
Blue Water Café + Raw Bar **33**
Cactus Club Coal Harbour **17**
Cactus Club English Bay **2**
Café Nuba **34**
Campagnolo **30**
Cardero's **7**
Chambar Belgian Restaurant **22**
Cibo Trattoria/Uva Wine
   & Cocktail Bar **31**
Cin Cin **11**
Coast **14**
Diva at the Met **19**
Edible Canada **37**
Fable Kitchen **39**
The Fish House in Stanley Park **1**
glowbal grill steak & satay bar **32**
Gyoza King **8**
Hapa Izakaya **9**
Hawksworth Restaurant **20**
Hon's Wun-Tun House **6**
Joe Fortes Seafood
   & Chop House **12**
Kirin **10**

4

VANCOUVER | Where to Eat in Vancouver

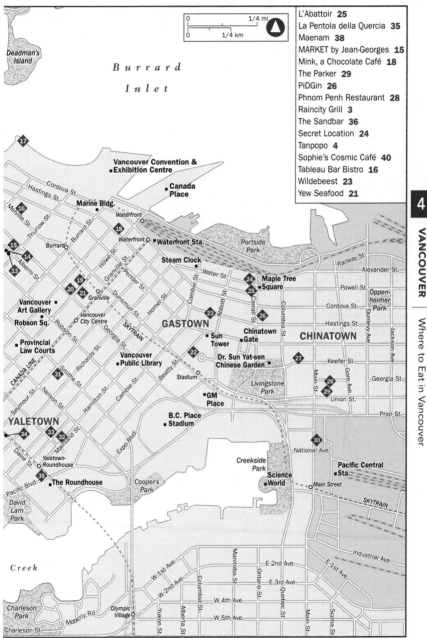

L'Abattoir **25**
La Pentola della Quercia **35**
Maenam **38**
MARKET by Jean-Georges **15**
Mink, a Chocolate Café **18**
The Parker **29**
PiDGin **26**
Phnom Penh Restaurant **28**
Raincity Grill **3**
The Sandbar **36**
Secret Location **24**
Tanpopo **4**
Sophie's Cosmic Café **40**
Tableau Bar Bistro **16**
Wildebeest **23**
Yew Seafood **21**

4

VANCOUVER | Where to Eat in Vancouver

flashy glass bar where the people who like to see and be seen hang out. Upstairs, The Roof patio is one of the best outdoor dining spots in town, a sexy space with potted plants, animal-print cushions, and social sofas gathered around fire pits.

1032 Alberni St. ☎ **604/637-0777.** www.glowbalgroup.com/blackblue. Main courses C$11–C$28 lunch, C$28–C$150 dinner. Mon–Fri 11:30am–1am, Sat–Sun 4:30pm–1am.

Blue Water Cafe + Raw Bar ★★★ SEAFOOD   In many ways, this is the quintessential Vancouver restaurant, with some of the city's greatest talents behind the bar, in the kitchen, and manning the sushi counter. Bar manager Evelyn Chick mixes up masterfully crafted cocktails behind the long bar with its excellent whiskey selection. Surrounded by ice at the end of the bar, Raw Bar chef Yoshiya Maruyama carefully crafts exquisite *nigiri* and *maki*—the Dungeness crab and avocado roll in an egg wrapper is pure heaven. And in the open kitchen way across the elegant dining room with its relaxed West Coast vibe, gleaming wood, and gorgeous, deep blue pottery plates, executive chef Frank Pabst takes a delectably creative approach to all the creatures from the sea. Try the miso-glazed sablefish, the white sturgeon in a pumpernickel crust, or, when they're in season, sweet, buttery spot prawns. One of the best times to visit is in February when Pabst serves up his "unsung heroes" menu of less popular seafood, like sardines, sea urchin, whelks, and the like. All this comes with an exceptional wine list, winner of the platinum award in 2013 and 2014 at the Vancouver International Wine Festival.

1095 Hamilton St. ☎ **604/688-8078.** www.bluewatercafe.net. Reservations recommended. Main courses C$25–C$40. Daily 5pm–midnight.

Hawksworth Restaurant ★★★ WEST COAST   Even though it's been open a few years now, Hawksworth is still the buzziest—and busiest—restaurant in Vancouver. It's a flat-out gorgeous space in a prime location on the main floor of the Rosewood Hotel Georgia, right across from the art gallery. It's worth dropping by just for a drink in the bar—it's an intimate space with rock star sofa seating, quite possibly the city's best spirits selection, and supremely talented bartenders. Try the ethereal Hotel Georgia cocktail, a long-lost recipe that was rediscovered right before the 2011 opening. The dining room is split into two spaces: The first is known as the Pearl Room and has a lovely cream-colored leather banquette and a massive, dazzling crystal light fixture; the second features a stunning custom wall art installation by BC-born artist Rodney Graham. It's a perfect setting for chef David Hawksworth's spectacular food. He mixes high and low, formal and comfort with aplomb—beef tenderloin with braised short rib, for instance, or elk strip loin with bacon and cabbage. The menu is ever changing, depending on what's in season. And his bar snacks are irresistible, especially the KFC—spicy, crispy, lightly caramelized Korean fried cauliflower. Plus, with five sommeliers on staff and an award-winning wine list, there are some spectacular choices when it comes to wine.

Rosewood Hotel Georgia, 801 W. Georgia St. ☎ **604/673-7000.** www.hawksworthrestaurant.com. Reservations essential. Main courses C$36–C$59; tasting menu C$98, C$148 with wine pairings. Mon–Fri 6:30–10:30am and 11:30am–2pm, Sat–Sun 7am–2:30pm, daily 5pm–late.

Joe Fortes Seafood & Chop House ★ SEAFOOD   This has been a favorite hangout for Vancouver's business crowd ever since it opened in 1985, and it still has a bit of an '80s feel to it—brass lamps, dark green furnishings, an ornate oak bar where guys in suits like to gather. It's always busy on the main floor, and there's excellent people-watching from the tables up on the mezzanine, but the best spots are out on the fantastic rooftop patio. Joe Fortes is named for Vancouver's first lifeguard, a big guy with an outsized personality, which is fitting for this fun, vibrant spot. (He was immortalized on a Canadian stamp in 2013.) It's considered Vancouver's best oyster bar, and the chilled seafood tower is a masterpiece of lobster, crab, oysters, clams, and more. Food is usually simply prepared and pretty traditional. The real star here, though, is the service, led by everyone's favorite maître d', the charming Frenchy, who can organize anything from calling a cab to picking up an engagement ring.

777 Thurlow St. ✆ **604/669-1940.** www.joefortes.ca. Reservations recommended. Main courses C$18–C$65, C$38 fixed-price 3-course dinner (Sun–Thurs 4–6pm). Daily 11am–11pm.

Kirin ★★ CANTONESE   Vancouver has some truly exceptional Chinese restaurants, but few of them are downtown, making this a great choice if you want a taste of what Vancouver Chinese food is all about. This is one of four in a high-end chainlet of Cantonese banquet rooms. Unlike many of the big Chinese restaurants, which are designed to serve large family groups, this one has small tables for couples and foursomes. It's a more modern, upscale Chinese eatery, with elegant screens and subtle lighting. As the style is Cantonese, you can expect mild, savory dishes, with a heavy emphasis on seafood. This location features many of the high-end ingredients beloved by well-heeled Asian gourmands, though they may be a bit exotic for some western tastes, things like sea cucumber, geoduck, birds nest, and squab roasted whole and served with the head on. Be sure to try the Peking duck, which comes in two courses, and the spicy deep-fried shrimp. Dim sum—the lunchtime meal of dumplings, noodles, and other small bites—is a great way to sample a bunch of dishes at a much more reasonable price.

1172 Alberni St. ✆ **604/82-8833.** www.kirinrestaurants.com. Main courses C$16–C$120. Daily 11am–2:30pm, 5:30–10:30pm.

Yew Seafood ★★ SEAFOOD   With chef Ned Bell in charge, the Four Seasons' always-popular restaurant has shifted its focus to seafood—and changed its name accordingly in 2014—and it couldn't be a better fit. It's been a gradual evolution after the huge changes wrought by a massive, multi-million-dollar makeover in 2008. Back then, what was a slightly fussy (yet strangely cavernous) room was transformed into a breathtaking space with high ceilings, warm wood accents, and a giant sandstone fireplace that separates the bar and restaurant. The lounge area has a huge, L-shaped bar where all sorts of interesting locals and visitors hang out. There's also a sweet little nook off to one side, with booths and high-tops for enjoying some of the city's best cocktails. As for the dining room, it's a big space, with a variety of seating options, but the best, if you're with a group, is at the big chef's table that seats 12—it's a slab cut right out of the center of a tree, with the rough bark still on. Or see if you can book the table in the glassed-in wine room that perches in the middle of the dining room. The food is gorgeous high-end seafood with a few other options—think pork belly with spot prawns, West Coast paella, lobster tacos, and the like. Wine pairings are exceptional, thanks to talented sommelier Emily Walker.

Four Seasons Hotel, 791 W. Georgia St. *Ⓒ* **604/692-4939.** www.yewrestaurant.com. Reservations recommended. Main courses C$18–C$41. Daily 6:30am–midnight.

EXPENSIVE

Chambar Belgian Restaurant ★★ BELGIAN/MOROCCAN   In 2014, one of Vancouver's favorite restaurants moved to a new location, causing both great excitement and great trepidation among local fans. Excitement because the new place is bigger and has a patio; trepidation because the old place was, quite simply, perfect. Owners Nico and Karri Schuermans have made sure the new Chambar has all the charm of the old, which wasn't too hard since they just moved next door. Besides, all the favorite dishes, like the spicy Congolese mussels and lamb tagine, are still on the menu, plus lots of new ones as well. The food is at first sight a strange combination of Belgian and Moroccan, but it's a combination that works, at least in the talented hands of Michelin-trained chef Nico Scheurmans. Chambar is also known for its exceptional wine, beer, and cocktail list, and its location close to the Queen Elizabeth Theater and the two sports arenas ensures that this is always a busy spot with a vibrantly mixed crowd.

566 Beatty St. *Ⓒ* **604/879-7119.** www.chambar.com. Reservations essential. Main courses C$26–C$45, set menu C$60–C$70. Daily 5pm–midnight.

Cibo Trattoria/Uva Wine Cocktail Bar ★★ MODERN ITALIAN   When Cibo opened in 2008, it made all the "best-of" lists. And then it sort of faded away. Meanwhile, its sister restaurant, Uva, never really caught on. Now with a talented new team behind the two restaurants, they are on fire, and are proving to be an irresistible destination for the city's foodies. (You can, for instance, expect to find chefs and bartenders from other establishments gathered around Uva's busy bar.) Chef Faizal Kassam is the talented young chef cooking for both restaurants—in Uva, it's mostly the small plates known as "cicchetti," cured meats, cheese, and nibbles such as deviled eggs and spicy chickpeas, enjoyed in a room that combines historic architectural details with modern decor. (The best seats are the white leather wingbacks by the windows.) At Cibo, where the brick walls are painted white and the modern Milanese furniture is striped green and brown, it could be ravioli with bitter greens, spaghetti with morel mushrooms, or halibut with lentils, depending on what's fresh and in season. Meanwhile, sommelier Robert Stelmachuk is curating a spectacular wine list that's heavy on terrific Italians, while at Uva, superstar bartender Lauren Mote leads a talented team shaking up some of the best—and most unusual—cocktails in the city.

Moda Hotel, 900 Seymour St. *Ⓒ* **604/602-9570** (Cibo). *Ⓒ* **604/632-9560** (Uva). www.cibo trattoria.com. www.uvavancouver.com. Main courses C$17–C$33, small bites C$4–C$17. Cibo: Mon–Fri 7–11am and 11:30am–2pm, Sat–Sun 7am–2pm, daily 5pm–late. Uva: Mon–Sat 11:30am–2am, Sun 11:30am–midnight.

Coast ★ SEAFOOD/INTERNATIONAL   Alberni Street is becoming one of the city's hot new restaurant rows, and most of the restaurants along here seem to be members of the Glowbal Group, a local chainlet of swish, sophisticated eateries with stylish decor, great food, and an action-packed social scene. (In 2013, owner Emad

Yacoub was named Canada's restaurateur of the year in the prestigious Pinnacle Awards.) Coast, the seafood-focused member of the group, is no different. The raw bar-cum-real bar sits in the middle of the lower floor, a brightly lit cylinder of shellfish and vodka bottles surrounded by happy people drinking and nibbling on sushi. Seafood ranges from casual fish and chips to sushi rolls, bowls of steamers, and fancy fare like lobster stuffed with Dungeness crab. The best bet is the chilled seafood platter or tower that lets you taste all sorts of fishies, including *nigiri,* prawns, ceviche, and more. A good wine list rounds out the experience. Note, though, that there's not much available for those who don't like seafood.

1054 Alberni St. © **604/685-5010.** www.coastrestaurant.ca. Reservations recommended. Main courses C$18–C$60. Mon–Thurs 11:30am–1am, Fri 11:30am–2am, Sat 3pm–2am, Sun 3pm–1am.

La Pentola della Quercia ★★ ITALIAN   After a couple of hits and misses, Yaletown's Opus Hotel has finally got its restaurant right with this offshoot of Kitsilano's popular La Quercia (3689 W. 4th Ave.; © **604/676-1007;** www.laquercia.ca). It's a beautiful space slightly below street level with windows that let in tons of light and offer great people-watching. The moldings, tiled floors, ornamental tin ceiling, and other features of this century-old building have remained, but they've ben brightened up with creamy paint, contemporary furnishings, and industrial-looking steel light fixtures. The food, under chef Lucais Syme's direction, is northern Italian, so you can expect excellent primi (squid ink tagliatelle, pappardelle with fennel sausage), secondi (prosciutto-wrapped rabbit loin, black cod "baccala"), and vegetable side dishes like peas with guanciale and mint. The best option, though, is to tell chef you'd like to dine family style and he'll just make a fantastic meal for you and your friends. An award-winning wine list just adds to the lovely experience.

Opus Hotel, 350 Davie St. © **604/642-0557.** www.lapentola.ca. Main courses C$12–C$48 lunch, C$26–C$65 dinner, family-style dinners C$60–C$75. Daily 7am–10pm.

MARKET by Jean-Georges ★ FUSION   In general, Vancouverites aren't big fans of celebrity chefs from elsewhere coming to town and setting up shop—Daniel Boulud's restaurant here lasted barely 2 years. But it's been a different story for the Alsatian Jean-Georges Vongerichten. For one thing, his restaurant in the Shangri-La Hotel is part of his more casual "MARKET" brand (although it's still fairly fancy for Vancouver); for another, his east-meets-west fusion fare is the way most locals like to eat anyway. Many of his most popular dishes can be found on the menu here, including the black truffle-and-fontina pizza and the rice-cracker-crusted tuna. The dining room is a serene space, with soft, gray, rounded booths and walls draped in chains of tiny gold beads, curvy glass chandeliers, and a sexy bar with funky silver seats. The glassed-in private room surrounded by urban towers is a popular place for business lunches. In summer, they open up the patio outside, and it's a great place to enjoy a cocktail or glass of wine.

Shangri-La Hotel, 1115 Alberni St. © **604/695-1115.** Reservations recommended. Main courses C$16–C$44, fixed-price lunch C$35, tasting menu C$68. Daily 6:30–11am, 11:30am–2:30pm, daily 5:30–10pm (Fri–Sat till 10:30pm).

MODERATE

Cactus Club ★★★ CASUAL/FUSION   Normally, I wouldn't bother to address chain restaurants, but Cactus Club has two unique things going for it: One of the city's most illustrious chefs, Rob Feenie, is running the show; and they've somehow managed to snag two of the most enviable view locations in the city. (No wonder founder

VANCOUVER food trucks

Before 2010, the only food trucks you'd find in Vancouver sold hot dogs (aka "tube steaks") or, in winter, roasted chestnuts. Then in 2010, the city came to its senses and allowed 17 new vendors to fire up their propane tanks. They were just the first in a whole convoy of food trucks: By the beginning of 2014, there were more than 100 food trucks cooking up everything from grilled cheese to pirogues and tacos to Thai. The best way to find a food truck is to download an app like **Streetfood Vancouver,** or visit www.streetfoodapp.com. Here are five of the best.

Japadog The original. Kurobuta, beef, or bratwurst sausage topped with "terimayo," a combination of teriyaki sauce and mayo, and sprinkled with dried seaweed. Other toppings include kimchi and meat sauce. There are four trucks as well as a restaurant location at 530 Robson St., ✆ **604/569-1158;** www.japadog.com.

TacoFino Cantina Originally from Tofino on Vancouver Island, this truck has taken the city by storm with its excellent fish, bean, or pork-jowl tacos. Look for the orange truck painted with an image of the Virgin of Guadalupe at Robson and Howe streets, or drop by the commissary at 2327 E. Hastings St., ✆ **604/253-8226;** www.tacofino.com.

Fresh Local Wild As the name suggests, this truck focuses on fresh, local ingredients. Think buttermilk-fried oyster po'boy, salmon burger, or the signature seafood chowder poutine—local shellfish and bacon in a creamy chowder poured over crisp French fries. Find the truck at the corner of Hastings and Burrard streets. www.freshlocalwild.com.

Re-Up BBQ Southern BBQ comes to the West Coast with succulent pulled pork or beef brisket sandwiches and sweet tea. Find the truck at Hornby and West Georgia streets; there's also a location inside the River Market in New Westminster. ✆ **604/553-3997;** www.reupbbq.com.

Roaming Dragon Feeding the city's hunger for pan-Asian flavors, this super-popular truck serves Chinese pork-belly sliders, Korean short rib tacos, and the ridiculously good Indonesian beef *rendang* poutine. The Roaming Dragon truck regularly shows up at charity events and farmer's markets, as well as its popular Burrard and Robson location outside the art gallery. www.roamngdragon.com.

Richard Jaffray won the Lifetime Achievement Award at the 2014 Vancouver Magazine Awards, the city's version of the Oscars.) One location is right on the beach, built atop the old 1937 English Bay Bathhouse on Beach Avenue; the other is a new, and breathtakingly beautiful building right next to the Olympic Cauldron and overlooking Coal Harbour. These two locations have a more sophisticated wine list and more extensive menu than the others. In general, the menu is a wide-ranging one, offering everything from burgers to tuna sushi cones to the very sophisticated sablefish with shiitake mushrooms. Several dishes are Feenie's signatures, including the excellent rocket salad with Parmesan-crusted chicken. Both are beautiful rooms, decorated in a cool contemporary style, and dotted with a mix of First Nations and pop art. If you visit the Coal Harbour location, try to get a seat in the atrium area that overlooks the floatplane terminal and beware that the huge lounge area turns into quite a raucous party in the evenings.

English Bay, 1790 Beach Ave. ✆ **604/681-2582.** Coal Harbour, 1085 Canada Place, ✆ **604/620-7410.** www.cactusclubcafe.com. Main courses C$14–C$31. Daily 11am–midnight.

glowbal grill steak & satay bar ★ FUSION   What are you hungry for? Satay with dipping sauce? Spaghetti and meatballs? A nice big steak? A niçoise salad? Or how about a platter that has a bit of everything on it? glowbal, is, of course, another glowbal restaurant, this one in Yaletown, where it began life in 2002 as a then-trendy satay house. In 2009 it rebranded as a steak house, and now it seems to be a little bit of everything. No matter: It's still a fun place to hang out and meet new people, especially on the lively patio on summer nights. Inside, there are luxe gold-toned leather booths, dramatic gold-colored cylindrical light fixtures, and a big glass case where the steaks are aging. glowbal also has a great weekend brunch.

1079 Mainland St. ✆ **604/602-0835.** www.glowbalgrill.com. Reservations recommended. Main courses lunch C$13–C$44, dinner C$18–C$44. Mon–Thurs 11:30am–1am, Fri 11:30am–2am, Sat 10:30am–2am, Sun 10:30am–1am.

INEXPENSIVE

Café Nuba ★ LEBANESE/VEGETARIAN   The decor isn't much, just some simple pine benches and tables in a room of cream-painted bricks. But the food is great, and the value even better. It's one of four locations (the others are in Gastown and the recently opened Kitsilano and Mount Pleasant eateries) serving up mostly vegetarian Lebanese fare. The crunchy falafel is made according to a secret recipe that involves both chickpeas and fava beans, and one of the most popular dishes is the crispy roasted cauliflower with lemon and sea salt. There are a couple of meat dishes—lamb patties and chicken skewers, mainly—and no alcohol, but the fresh-pressed juices are loaded with delicious vitamins. This is a great spot for a cheap, nutritious lunch.

1206 Seymour St. ✆ **778/371-3266.** www.nuba.ca. Main courses C$6–C$14. Mon–Fri 11:30am–9pm, Sat noon–9pm. Closed Sun.

Gastown & Chinatown

EXPENSIVE

L'Abattoir ★★ WEST COAST   The name might seem off-putting until you realize that the restaurant sits on the edge of Gastown's historic Blood Alley, named for the slaughterhouses that could once be found here. And so you might think that this is a meat-heavy sort of place, but in fact, L'Abattoir serves up some beautifully fresh, creative dishes. There's a French influence, and a slight Asian one, and maybe a dash of molecular gastronomy, but it's mostly about great West Coast ingredients. Think warm steelhead trout and crunchy potato salad, or char-grilled lamb loin with Indian spices, or a milk-braised pork shoulder with salsa verde. Oh—and the best bread basket in town, bar none. Expect a meticulously well-edited wine list and terrific creative and classic cocktails, courtesy of talented barman Shaun Layton. Expect, too, a pretty room—French tile floors, a strangely beautiful sculpture-cum-light fixture made of twigs, exposed brick walls—in one of the city's oldest buildings located right at the intersection where Vancouver got its start—Maple Tree Square.

217 Carrall St. ✆ **604/568-1701.** www.labattoir.ca. Reservations recommended. Main courses C$27–C$34. Daily 5:30–10pm. Closed statutory holidays.

PiDGin ★★ PAN-ASIAN FUSION   If it had just been a couple of doors down, or even across the street, PiDGin would have avoided all the fuss. But as luck would have it, when it opened in 2013, the restaurant attracted the attention of Vancouver's well-meaning, but at times misguided gang of anti-poverty activists. For a while, all you heard about was the protests. Then you started hearing about the food. And then the accolades started rolling in. Now the protesters are long gone, and chef Makoto Ono's food just keeps getting better and better. The cuisine is a vibrant blend of creative, Asian-inspired dishes like *dan-dan* rutabaga salad, pork-belly rice bowl, raw scallops with pomegranate curry oil, and spiced duck with carrot cake. The best way to dine is definitely to order the prix fixe, which will get you generous tastes of eight different dishes. There's also a good wine list, excellent sake selection, and creative cocktail list. It's not a fancy place—the pine furniture looks like it came from a schoolroom designed by IKEA, and the white walls and plain, black light fixtures look a bit stark— but the simplicity of the decor just emphasizes the vibrancy of the food.

350 Carrall St. © **604/620-9400.** www.pidginvancouver.com. Main courses C$15–$35, prix fixe C$55. Mon–Sat 5pm–midnight, Sun 6pm–midnight.

Secret Location ★ FUSION   It's safe to say there's nothing else like this in Vancouver. It's also safe to say Vancouverites don't know quite what to make of it, which is why it's often a bit empty, in spite of the extraordinary cuisine. The idea here was to create a concept shopping and dining experience similar to Colette in Paris. (There's a fabulously stylish shop next door.) The dining room is simply stunning. Big, bright, and opulent, with huge windows that look out onto Maple Tree Square, a backlit white onyx bar, glamorous chandeliers, and brilliant spots of color such as the fuchsia and lime-green love seats. And then there's the food. Chef Jefferson Alvarez is clearly influenced by the wild creativity of chefs like El Bulli's Ferran Adria and Noma's René Redzepi. The menu changes almost every night, depending on what's in season and what chef feels like creating. You might find maple tree blossoms in tempura batter, or a simple arrangement of asparagus with poached egg, or an elaborate concoction of shaved vegetables, fish, and various other ingredients transformed to resemble soil and leaves and flowers. Seriously beautiful. In the evening, he only offers 3-, 5-, and 10-course tasting menus, each course accompanied by wine or cocktails, although he has a more traditional lunch and brunch menu.

1 Water St. © **604/685-0090.** www.secretlocation.ca. 3-course prix fixe C$70, 5-course C$95, 10-course C$150 including wine and cocktail pairings. Mon–Fri 11am–late, Sat–Sun 10am–late.

Wildebeest ★★★ WEST COAST   Walking by, you might not even notice this dark place on a slightly sketchy street. But step inside and you'll find warm exposed brick walls, industrial-style light fixtures on pulleys, and long tables perfect for family-style dining. In 2013, Wildebeest won both Best New Restaurant and Best New Design at the Vancouver Magazine Restaurant Awards, and it's never looked back. It's all about "whole beast" eating here, which means savory off-cuts prepared in delectably interesting ways, like executive chef Wesley Young's seared rabbit loin with crispy rabbit croquettes, or chicken roasted porchetta style, or the famous "bone luge," an ounce of sherry shot down a cracked, roasted bone marrow. Fun, and delicious, with a great wine list and fantastic cocktails like the savory horseradish sour.

120 W. Hastings St. © **604/687-6880.** www.wildebeest.ca. Main courses C$16–C$45. Daily 5pm–midnight, Sat–Sun 10am–2pm.

MODERATE

Bao Bei Chinese Brasserie ★★ MODERN CHINESE   When Tannis Ling opened her little brasserie in late 2010, she wanted it to be a sentimental homage to the food she grew up eating—and at the same time she wanted to have some fun with it. And so, instead of *dan-dan* noodles, you might find "Dan-Dan Dance Revolution" noodles. The room itself is an old Chinatown storefront, with vintage floral wallpaper uncovered during the restoration, decorations found in flea markets, and black-and-white photos of Ling's own family. Food is served family style and it can be a bit random; it just arrives as it's done. You might enjoy the vegetable pot stickers or the wok-charred octopus salad, crispy pork belly with pickles, or the *shao bing,* a sesame flatbread with cumin-scented lamb. Before opening her own place, Ling was bartender at Chambar, so the cocktails are fantastic, and there's also a good selection of beer and wine. Interestingly, when Bao Bei opened, not much was happening in Chinatown; 4 years later, it's one of the city's most exciting neighborhoods, and many credit Bao Bei with leading the transformation.

163 Keefer St. ✆ **604/688-0876.** www.bao-bei.ca. No reservations accepted (except large groups). Small plates C$8–C$18. Tues–Sat 5:30pm–midnight, Sun 5:30–11pm. Closed Mon.

The Parker ★★ VEGETARIAN   The food here is so good, you will never miss the meat. Though how chef Curtis Luk manages to make such culinary magic in a kitchen so small—it's basically a single hotplate behind the bar, which itself isn't that big—is a complete mystery. Luk was a "Top Chef Canada" competitor in 2012, and later joined renowned barman Steve Da Cruz at The Parker, a tiny, minimalistic joint. While Da Cruz shakes up some impressive classic cocktails—he's a passionate cocktail historian as well as talented bartender—Luk cooks up his house-made gnudi with gremolata, or his delicate king oyster mushroom carpaccio, or risotto with asparagus and nasturtiums. All dishes are vegetarian, many are vegan, and some are gluten-free. The menu is quite small, and the best way to enjoy it is to order the chef's five-course tasting menu. There's a serious approach to sustainability here, too—furniture is made of recycled wood, and there's a zero-waste policy in place.

237 Union St. ✆ **604/779-3804.** www.theparker.com. Main courses C$11–C$17. 5-course tasting menu C$32. Daily 5:30pm–late.

INEXPENSIVE

Phnom Penh Restaurant ★ VIETNAMESE   Always busy; always good. This family-run restaurant has been serving up *pho* (beef noodle soup) and addictive chicken wings for years, and the lineups never seem to get any shorter. Year after year, Phnom Penh scoops up the Best Vietnamese title at the Van Mag Awards, and 2014 was no exception. Still, from the outside, it doesn't look like much, just a faded red-and-white awning and steamy windows. Inside, you'll find a busy room, crowded with dark chairs and tables, and not much in the way of decoration aside from the Khmer dolls in glass cases. Whatever you order will be good, but the deep-fried chicken wings are everyone's favorite, especially the ones with salt and lime. Be warned that you may need to share a table, and it's not always easy to get a server's attention.

244 E. Georgia St. ✆ **604/682-5777.** Main courses C$7–C$18. Mon–Thurs 10am–9pm, Fri–Sun 10am–10pm.

The West End
VERY EXPENSIVE

Cin Cin ★★ MODERN ITALIAN   With a new chef, Andrew Richardson, in the vast open kitchen, things are cooking once again at this Robson Street institution. Climb the stone steps and you'll find a romantic slice of Tuscany, with ceramic tile floors, white tablecloths, and beautiful Italianesque art on the sponged ochre walls. Well-dressed ladies and gents cluster around the elegant marble bar, sipping artisanal cocktails before stepping into the gracious dining room. Dinners might feature spaghetti with lobster or ravioli with truffles, followed, perhaps, by a wood-grilled bone-in rib-eye steak or roasted whole sea bass. The wine list, as one would expect, is exceptional, and heavily focused on the very best of Italy. The service is as exemplary as the food.

1154 Robson St. © **604/688-7338.** www.cincin.net. Reservations recommended. Main courses C$30–C$65. Daily 5pm–midnight.

EXPENSIVE

The Fish House in Stanley Park ★ WEST COAST   The location couldn't be better: a historic, 85-year-old old clapboard summer house near the southern entrance to Stanley Park, with lovely ocean and garden views. And it's a perennial favorite, especially with visitors. Truth is, though, the building could probably use a little work, and so could the food. Still, the afternoon tea is always lovely, with homemade scones, tea sandwiches, fragrant teas, and a selection of sweets. And the seafood platter for two is a bounteous serving of crab, scallops, prawns, tuna, and more, most of it local and Ocean Wise. Plus who can resist the drama of the popular prawns flambéed with ouzo?

8901 Stanley Park Dr. © **604/681-7275.** www.fishhousestanleypark.com. Reservations recommended. Main courses C$22–C$45, afternoon tea C$29. Mon–Fri 11:30am–late, Sat–Sun 11am–late. Closed Dec 24–26.

Raincity Grill ★★ WEST COAST   This, right here, is where the 100 Mile Diet was invented, at a dinner with the authors of the popular book and locavore manifesto. That was in 2005, but Raincity was all about local food even longer than that, dating right back to when it opened in 1992. Amazingly, it's still as popular as ever, thanks largely to a stellar location at the corner of Denman and Davie St., just a stone's throw from English Bay Beach. It's built on two levels, with a cluster of small tables on the top and curved black leather banquettes on the lower level, with a slippery tile ramp in between, and a gorgeous series of paintings that fill the back wall with an image of a sunset over rolling hills. Some of Vancouver's most illustrious chefs have been through this kitchen; these days, it's executive chef Nicholas Hipperson running the show. He celebrates local ingredients including beets from Pemberton, honey mussels from Salt Spring Island, pink salmon from Hecate Strait, and cheese from the Fraser Valley in dishes that combine simplicity with flair, and allow the natural goodness of the main ingredients to shine through. He still offers a 100 Mile tasting menu, where everything is grown, caught, or produced within 100 miles (161km) of the restaurant, and there is an impressive list of West Coast wines.

1193 Denman St. © **604/685-7337.** www.raincitygrill.com. Reservations recommended. Main courses C$13–C$17 lunch, C$25–C$34 dinner, tasting menu C$72, wine pairings C$34. Mon–Fri 11:30am–3pm, Sat–Sun 10am–3pm, daily 5pm–late.

MODERATE

Cardero's Restaurant ★ CASUAL/FUSION   Cardero's is loud and fun, with a great view, a fantastic patio, and lots of room for the kids to run around. It's located on a wharf overlooking Coal Harbour, in a building that looks like salvaged bits of wood and metal flung together to create modern art. Inside, it's all comfy caramel-colored leather sofas, exposed wood beams, floor-to-ceiling windows, curved wooden bars, and a great old cast-iron stove in one corner. The menu takes a global approach, offering Chinese stir-fries, Cajun ling cod, mussels in curry sauce, Mediterranean pastas, and North American chops and burgers. The food is not exceptional (hardly surprising with so much fusion confusion), but there is something to satisfy everyone, especially

EAST meets WEST END

The West End is riddled with inexpensive but good hole-in-the-wall ethnic eateries that cater to a diverse population. You can find ramen shops and izakayas, curry huts, Korean barbecue joints, and dumplings to go. And you can usually tell which ones are the best—or at least the cheapest—because they have the longest lines. Here are five of my favorites:

Banana Leaf If you've never tried Malaysian cuisine, you are in for a treat. It's fragrant, with a touch of heat, and satisfyingly hearty, with dishes like spicy stewed rendang beef and *mee goreng* (fried egg noodles with vegetables, beef, egg, shrimp, and tofu). Think of it as the missing link between Thai, Vietnamese, and Indian food. Banana Leaf has five locations around the city, two of them in the West End: the original one on Denman Street, and the bright, modern new one on Robson. 1096 Denman St. Ⓒ **604/683-3333.** 1779 Robson St. Ⓒ **604/569-3363.** www.bananaleaf-vancouver.com. The Robson location open daily 11:30am–10pm; Denman closes 2:45–5pm.

Gyoza King Every student on a budget loves Gyoza King—and so do the rest of us. Think of this as Japanese dim sum: Gyoza are dumplings, similar to Chinese pot stickers, filled with prawns, pork, vegetables, and other goodies. There are also Japanese noodles, soups, and other hearty but inexpensive fare. And if you find the menu confusing, the staff is happy to help you out. 1508 Robson St. Ⓒ **604/669-8278.** Fri–Sun 11:30am-2:30pm; Mon–Fri 5:30pm–1am, Sat 6:30pm–1:30am; Sun 6–11:30pm.

Hapa Izakaya This is Japanese tapas in a nightclub atmosphere. Izakaya means "eat-drink place," and that really sums it up. You'll find familiar dishes like the sushi rolls and lettuce wraps, but pretty much anything goes on the daily fresh sheets. It's all good fun, though, especially as everything is supposed to be washed down with lashings of beer or wine. 1479 Robson St. Ⓒ **604/689-4272.** www.hapaizakaya.com. Reservations recommended on weekends. Small plates C$6–C$24. Sun–Thurs 5:30pm–midnight; Fri–Sat 5:30pm–1am.

Hon's Wun-Tun House Your kids will love this big, bright, busy room with hundreds of food choices. And you'll love it, too, especially when you see the bill. The Robson location is one of four around Greater Vancouver, with a simply massive menu of pot stickers, noodles, soups stir-fries, and dumplings. You can also pick up frozen pot stickers to take home for later. 1339 Robson St. Ⓒ **604/685-0871.** www.hons.ca. Daily 11am–11pm.

Tanpopo If, like so many of us, you feel that you can never get your fill of sushi, you're going to love this place. It's Vancouver's best all-you-can eat sushi joint, where for about C$25, you can gorge yourself on California rolls, veggie tempura, tuna *nigiri*, and more. The best place to sit is at the sushi bar, so you can keep on ordering more. 1122 Denman St. Ⓒ **604/681-7777.** Daily 11:30am–11:30pm.

if you're traveling with kids, and a respectable beer and wine list to keep the grownups happy, too.

1583 Coal Harbour Quay. Ⓒ **604/669-7666.** www.vancouverdine.com/carderos. Reservations suggested. Main courses C$14–C$40 dinner. Daily 11:30am–midnight.

Tableau Bar Bistro ★★ FRENCH For some reason, this perfect little French bistro in the chic Loden Hotel has remained a bit of a hidden gem. But now, after it won a slew of awards in 2013 and 2014, the word is finally getting out, so reservations are a good idea. The room combines a dark, sleek contemporary esthetic—high ceilings, contemporary furniture, sexy Marilyn Monroe photos—with such nods to bistro tradition as the black-and-white checkered tile floor, ornately framed chalkboard menu, and blue-and-white dishtowels as napkins. It shouldn't work, but it does. What also works is the menu put together by talented executive chef Marc-Andre Choquette. It offers all the bistro favorites—steak frites, French onion soup, bouillabaisse and cassoulet—as well as some pastas, flatbreads, and creative daily specials depending on what's in season. Everything is done to perfection, even dishes that sound as simple as "mushrooms on toast," which turns out to be a rich, creamy sauté of wild mushrooms on buttery toasted brioche. Plus there are excellent cocktails and a well-executed wine list. A real find.

Loden Hotel, 1181 Melville St. ✆ **604/639-8692.** www.tableaubarbistro.com. Reservations suggested. Main courses C$16–C$22 lunch, C$18–C$25 dinner. Mon–Fri 11:30am–2:30pm, Mon–Thurs 5–11pm, Fri–Sat 5pm–midnight, Sun 10:30am–3pm.

The West Side
VERY EXPENSIVE

Tojo's Restaurant ★★★ JAPANESE   Chef-owner Hidekazu Tojo is a legend. Indeed, you can probably credit him for Vancouver's passionate love for the cool, clean flavors of sushi. He carries more than 2,000 recipes in his head, and, for good measure, invented both the crab-and-avocado-filled California roll and the B.C. roll of salmon and cucumber that you see on sushi menus everywhere. More than 25 years after it first opened, Tojo's is still as good as it ever was. The room is fantastic—in 2007, he moved from his cramped, warrenlike original space up the block to an airy, light-filled room with high ceilings, low-slung navy banquettes, decoratively gnarled branches, and a huge polished wooden sushi bar. Everything is good; nothing is cheap, though, because Tojo sources only the best. Order the *omakase,* the chef's arrangement that features his greatest hits as well as whatever chef feels like making just for you. It can be five, six, or more courses, including one designed around the exquisite (and exquisitely expensive) Japanese Wagyu beef. Be sure to try the golden roll of crab, salmon, scallops, and shrimp wrapped in a paper-thin egg crepe, as well as the unsurpassed selection of premium sakes.

1133 W. Broadway. ✆ **604/872-8050.** www.tojos.com. Reservations required. Main courses C$34–C$45, sushi/sashimi C$12–C$55, *omakase* C$80–C$225. Mon–Sat 5–10pm. Closed Christmas week.

West ★★★ WEST COAST   In the heart of tony South Granville Street near the old-moneyed Shaughnessy neighborhood—that's where you'll find this lovely little modern restaurant. It's a beautiful room, with a temperature-controlled "wall of wine," a cherry wood bar where one of the city's best bartenders, David Wolowidnyk, presides, sleek Mario Bellini-designed leather chairs, and unique works of art, including a Werner Forster installation that floats under the ceiling and a row of somewhat phallic-looking glass sculptures atop the wall that divides entrance from dining room. In the kitchen, the supremely talented Quang Dang is cooking up fresh, local fare with innovative flair: sherry-glazed chicken, herb-butter-roasted ling cod, bison short rib braised overnight. Everything is beautifully plated, and flavors perfectly balanced. West has always combined French culinary traditions with subtle Asian flavors, so you can expect that salty-sweet-sour-hot balance here. West also features one of the city's top sommeliers—Owen Knowlton, named Vancouver International Wine Festival's sommelier of the year in 2011—so there is an exceptional selection of vintages to go with your meal.

2881 Granville St. ✆ **604/738-8938.** www.westrestaurant.com. Reservations recommended. Main courses C$19–C$28 lunch, C$29–C$49 dinner, tasting menus C$68–C$95. Mon–Fri 11:30am–2:30pm, Sat–Sun 10:30am–2:30pm, daily 5:30–11pm.

EXPENSIVE

Vij's ★★★ INDIAN   In 2014, owner Vikram Vij seems to be everywhere—judging on Chopped Canada, making deals on Dragon's Den, speaking at symposia, cooking at food festivals—so, clearly, the word is out about Vancouver's best Indian restaurant. Vij's isn't your typical curry-in-a-curry place. The food is exciting and ever-changing, featuring local ingredients like the sturgeon farmed on the Sunshine Coast as well as all the exotic flavors and aromas of South Asia. That's why there's always a huge lineup to get in (Vij's doesn't take reservations); in fact, standing in line can become a party all on its own. Once you finally get inside, you'll discover a perfect little jewel box of a restaurant with soft lighting from the punched-out metal lanterns (those are actually elephants dancing on the walls) and lush patterns throughout. Must-tries include the lamb "popsicles" (rib chops) in fenugreek curry, as well as the crispy samosas, and whatever is fresh and exciting. Plus there are lots of choices for vegetarians. And, unlike most Asian restaurants, this one has an exceptional wine list—Vij himself is a sommelier, and his wine director, Mike Bernardo, was named sommelier of the year at the 2014 Vancouver International Wine Festival. This is one of Vancouver's quintessential dining experiences. In addition, in 2004 Vij opened the casual **Rangoli** next door (1488 W. 11th Ave.; ✆ **604/736-5711;** www.vijsrangoli.ca), and in 2013, launched a food truck, Vij's Railway Express (www.vijsrailwayexpress.com).

1480 W. 11th Ave. ✆ **604/736-6664.** www.vijsrestaurant.ca. Reservations not accepted. Main courses C$24–C$30. Daily 5:30–10pm.

MODERATE

Edible Canada ★★ WEST COAST   This is what Granville Island was missing—an eatery that is truly focused on local ingredients. (It's also connected to a shop selling local foodstuffs, as well as a culinary tourism operation.) The room itself is pretty simple and straightforward; in fact, it's a bit noisy and echo-y, thanks to the concrete floors, high ceilings and hard, white plastic chairs, but the long wooden tables give it warmth, and sitting under the lime green lights at the bar is always a good choice. An even better choice is to sit outside on the patio, a perfect spot for people-watching. The food itself is generally casual fare made with exceptional ingredients—a juicy burger, grilled seafood, and utterly irresistible fries cooked in duck fat. This spot is especially popular for lunch and brunch (try the poutine topped with duck confit and fried eggs), plus it has an excellent selection of beer and wine from across Canada.

Granville Island Public Market. ✆ **604/682-6681.** www.ediblecanada.com. Main courses brunch C$9–C$24, dinner C$23–C$26. Mon–Fri 11am–9pm, Sat–Sun 9am–9pm.

Fable Kitchen ★ WEST COAST   The idea for this farm-to-table eatery came to chef Trevor Bird as he was competing on "Top Chef Canada." He opened it in 2012, taking over the old Fuel/Refuel location on a busy stretch of 4th Avenue. It's got a rustic look, with chicken-wire cabinets, old kitchen tools on shelves, a wall covered with a chalkboard menu, and an open kitchen right as you walk in. The menu, as you might expect, features dishes that are simply prepared to let the flavors of the great local ingredients shine. At dinner, you might find herb-crusted halibut, roast chicken, or duck breast with creamed cabbage, and for lunch, simple salads and sandwiches, including the popular grilled cheese. It also boasts a small but good wine list and a good selection of craft beer.

1944 W. 4th Ave. ✆ **604/732-1322.** www.fablekitchen.ca. No reservations for lunch and brunch, reservations recommended for dinner. Main courses C$12–C$17 lunch, C$18–C$29 dinner. Mon–Fri 11:30am–2pm, Sat–Sun 10:30am–2pm, daily 5:30–10pm.

Farmer's Apprentice ★★★ WEST COAST   You might think from the name that this place would be as obsessed with local ingredients as every other Vancouver eatery seems to be. But no. What chef-owner David Gunawan is obsessed with is really, really good ingredients, wherever they may come from. No one else in the city is cooking like this, which is why his tiny *boîte* was named Restaurant of the Year in the 2014 Vancouver Magazine Awards. You'll find it on the bottom floor of a condo building, and it's so small it would be easy to miss if it weren't for the sweet smell of wood smoke as you walk by. Inside, the decor is pretty simple, all white walls and rustic wooden tables, with cute touches like enamel cups for water and the floral mural painted on a concrete wall. Plates are all small to medium in size and meant to be shared. The menu changes depending on what chef finds at the market—or what shows up at his back door, like the tiny Peruvian peppers that arrived one day. And everything is out of the ordinary: For instance, you might nibble on a concoction of leeks and cattails with caramelized buttermilk, or snack on smoked olives (Gunawan loves his smoker), or indulge in a tender slice of albacore tuna marinated in coconut milk and served with just a soupçon of Thai curry sauce. The wine, beer, and cocktail list is small but perfectly edited to the food. This is a great little find.

1535 W. 6th Ave. ✆ **604/620-2079.** www.farmersapprentice.ca. Reservations essential for dinner. C$10–C$45. Daily 11:30am–2pm, 5:30–10pm. Closed Mondays.

Maenam ★★ THAI   Chef-owner Angus An has worked with some of the best Thai chefs in the world, and it shows. That's why it's always so busy at this little Kitsilano eatery. The room is fairly small, without any of the kitschy beads-and-elephants decor you see in so many Southeast Asian restaurants. Instead, there are reed screens, a cool granite bar, and bright, white walls. It's all the better to showcase the gorgeous food. Expect all your favorites—pad Thai, panang curry, papaya salad—and some creative new dishes, like the duck confit salad or warm mushrooms with toasted rice powder, all prepared with exquisitely fresh ingredients and a perfect balance of flavors. There's also a respectable wine, beer, and cocktail list, and service is attentive in spite of the crush of people. The best bet is to order one of the chef's set menus—that way you don't have to make any decisions and can enjoy the best of what the kitchen produces. In 2013, An opened a second location, Longtail Kitchen, at the River Market in New Westminster (✆ **604/553-3855;** www.longtailkitchen.ca).

1938 W. 4th Ave. ✆ **604/730-5579.** www.maenam.ca. Reservations accepted. Main courses C$14–C$19. Chef's menu C$33 or C$48 per person. Tues–Sat noon–2:30pm, daily 5–10pm.

The Sandbar ★ CASUAL   This Granville Island hot spot is part of a local chainlet of restaurants with terrific view locations (the others are Cardero's on Coal Harbour, the Teahouse in Stanley Park, and Seasons in the Park in Queen Elizabeth Park). The food is casual and good, with an international menu that ranges from pizza to wok-fried squid, but aside from chef Hoshi's terrific sushi, it's not fantastic. Instead, it's all about the fun atmosphere: big, comfy leather armchairs, industrial-looking wooden beams, a patio overlooking False Creek, and nautical doodads like crab traps and even a small fishing boat. This place is busy, lively with young and middle-aged professionals drinking and chatting and enjoying the great views from under the Granville Street Bridge. There's also live music nightly in the Teredo Lounge.

1535 Johnston St., Granville Island. ℰ **604/669-9030.** www.vancouverdine.com. Reservations recommended on weekends. Main courses C$15–C$44, tapas C$8–C$17. Sun–Thurs 11:30am–midnight, Fri–Sat 11:30am–1am.

INEXPENSIVE

The Naam Restaurant ★ VEGETARIAN Step back into the 1960s and Vancouver's counterculture past. Although a number of gourmet vegetarian restaurants have opened in the last few years (see the Parker; p. 71), this is the city's original natural foods eatery. Plus it's open 24/7, so if you should have a hankering for tofu at 2am, you're good to go. Although the neighborhood has changed dramatically since it was all hippies and tie-dye, The Naam is still the same old place of funky wooden tables, slightly battered old chairs, a wood-burning fireplace, and a mish-mash of art on the walls. (There's a great garden patio out back, too.) The service is earnest, but can be a bit hit and miss. But there's live music nightly, and the food is the same hearty selection of pizzas, salads, veggie burgers, and dragon bowls. Definitely order the sesame spice fries topped with miso gravy.

2724 W. 4th Ave. ℰ **604/738-7151.** www.thenaam.com. Only group reservations accepted Mon–Thurs. Main courses C$8–C$15. Daily 24 hrs.

Sophie's Cosmic Café ★ CASUAL More than 25 years after it first started serving its famous eggs Benedict, back in 1988, this is still Vancouver's favorite breakfast spot. It's a colorful old diner, with bright ochre walls, red-and-fuchsia vinyl booths, and lime green chairs out on the patio. And the place is simply jammed with kooky toys, games, posters, and all sorts of 1950s and '60s memorabilia. Your kids will love it. It's busy, too: On weekends, get here early, or you'll be waiting an hour to get in. This is mainly a spot for breakfast and lunch, with a few casual choices (burgers, salad, pasta) for an early dinner. Breakfasts especially rule: Think fluffy pancakes, over-stuffed omelets, terrific eggs Benedict, and Sophie's classic steak and eggs.

2095 W. 4th Ave. ℰ **604/732-6810.** www.sophiescosmiccafe.com. Main courses C$8–C$16. Mon 8am–2:30pm, Tues–Sun 8am–8pm.

Main Street
EXPENSIVE

Sun Sui Wah ★★ CANTONESE Most of Vancouver's high-end Cantonese restaurants are in Richmond and this is one of the few that's in the city itself. It's always busy, so make a reservation, then expect to wait, especially if you're here for dim sum on a weekend. But it's worth the wait because this is some fine food. The space itself is bright and modern, even a little cold—stark white walls, dark chairs, white tablecloths, few decorative elements—and the curved, dark green stairs from the front door to the restaurant are always crowded with playing children. Whole families come here for the exceptionally fresh seafood. There are live tanks filled with king crabs, spot prawns, and king clams in season and, if you're up to it, you can pick the one you'd like to dine on. Or you can just go for the famous roast squab, glazed to a mahogany brown and served whole, with the head still on. Still a bit much? Then the Peking duck is a good option, any of the noodle dishes, or the steamed chicken with Chinese mushroom. Your best bet, though, is to come here for the lunchtime feast of small bites called dim sum, mostly dumplings, pork buns, noodles, and tea.

3888 Main St. ℰ **604/872-8822.** www.sunsuiwah.com. Main courses C$12–C$50. Daily 10am–3pm and 5–10:30pm.

sweet TREATS

Who doesn't like ending a meal or a journey with a sweet finish? It's easy to do at these sugary places:

Beaucoup Bakery & Café

Patissier Jackie Ellis has created a beautiful little Parisian refuge filled with croissants, brioche loaves, cookies, and seasonal treats like summer's raspberry pistachio macaron frais. **Try:** Peanut butter sandwich cookie. 2159 Fir St. ℂ **604/732-4222.** www.beaucoupbakery.com. Mon–Fri 7am–6pm, Sat–Sun 8am–6pm.

Bella Gelateria

You know that when a Canadian gelato shop takes top honors in a gelato festival in Italy, you know it's got to be some seriously good gelato. Everything here is made from scratch, from top quality natural ingredients, and it shows. Flavors are more grown up that in many gelato shops—no bubble gum or rocky road—and they change every day. **Try:** Salted caramel gelato. 100 W. Cordova St. ℂ **604/569-1010.** www.bellagelateria.com. Mon–Thu 10am–10pm, Fri 10am–11pm, Sat 11am–11pm, Sun, 11am–10pm.

Fauboug

A very French experience, from the bread and sandwiches to the viennoisserie, pastries, and cakes. But really, it's all about the macarons, those crisp little meringue sandwiches filled with buttercream. With three locations (downtown, Kerrisdale, and Park Royal).

Try: Hazelnut praline macaron. 769 Hornby St. ℂ **604/267-0769.** www.faubourg.com. Mon–Wed 7am–8pm, Thu–Fri 7am–9:30pm, Sat 8am–9:30pm, Sun 9am–8pm.

Mink Chocolates

Your kids aren't the only ones who will enjoy the luscious hot chocolate at this chocolate cafe. It arrives on a pretty silver tray, and is as dark and rich and deep as you could desire. The owner sources the world's best dark chocolate, not just for his drinking chocolate, but for the bars and tablets that come in more than 30 flavors. **Try:** Hot chocolate, with a bonbon on the side. 863 W. Hastings St. ℂ **866/283-5181** or 604/633-2451. www.minkchocolates.com. Mon–Fri 7:30am–6pm; Sat–Sun 10am–6pm.

Thomas Haas Patisserie

Thomas Haas is, quite simply, the best chocolatier and patissier in Vancouver, and one of the best in North America. He uses nothing but the highest quality ingredients, and everything is made by hand from scratch. His tiny shop in North Vancouver is always lined up with people hungry for his croissants, macarons, chocolates, and more. He recently opened a second location in Kitsilano (2539 W. Broadway; ℂ 604/738-1848). **Try:** Sparkle cookies. 998 Harbourside Dr., North Vancouver. ℂ **604/924-1847.** www.thomashaas.com. Tue–Sat 8am–5:30pm. Closed Sun–Mon.

MODERATE

Burdock & Co. ★★★ WEST COAST   Chef-owner-gardener Andrea Carlson has cooked at some of Vancouver's top kitchens. Now she's got her own place, and it's a beauty. Burdock & Co is a tiny masterpiece of rustic minimalism, with brick walls painted white, reclaimed wood tables, and industrial-looking swivel chairs. You can usually find Carlson cooking in the open kitchen at the back, where she whips up an eclectic, passionately local, vegetable-forward menu. Dishes are all small to medium in size and meant to be shared, and everything is so good, you'll end up ordering way more than you'd planned. The buttermilk fried chicken is perfectly crisp and tender, wheat berry risotto lusciously tooth-tender, and the squash gnocchi is sweetly savory.

The wine is all biodynamic and naturalist, and there are a handful of craft beers and unique cocktails on the list as well.

2702 Main St. ℂ **604/879-0077.** Burdockandco.com. Main courses C$8–C$20. Daily 5pm–late, Sat–Sun 10:30am–2pm.

Campagnolo ★ ITALIAN   The location is a bit dubious—on a dodgy bit of Main Street around the corner from the bus depot—but it's worth braving this transitional neighborhood to check out this great eatery. Step inside, and it's a cozy but minimalistic room, with pale brick walls, small tables that look like they're made of plywood, plain gray chairs, and clusters of vintage-looking light bulbs that dangle from the ceiling. Chef Robert Belcham has developed a passion for *salume,* Italian-style cured meats, and any night you can graze upon a changing selection of his house-made *crudo, mortadella,* salami, and prosciutto, as well as other antipasti nibbles. Otherwise, it's all tender-crusted pizzas like the "cardo," with artichokes and fontina, or hearty, creative pastas, such as the ricotta gnudi with stinging nettles or the tagliatelle with pork ragu. The wine list is all Italian, with some craft beers and a good selection of grappa and vermouth.

1020 Main St. ℂ **604/484-6018.** www.camoagnolorestaurant.ca. Main courses C$15–C$19. Mon–Fri 11:30am–2:30pm, daily 5pm–late.

The North Shore
EXPENSIVE

The Beach House at Dundarave Pier ★★ WEST COAST   The room is sophisticated, all dark leather chairs and rich reddish woods, a nice contemporary update for this century-old teahouse. But the decor isn't the point: The view is, and the best place to enjoy that is from the heated patio outside. The Beach House gazes out across the Burrard Inlet toward Stanley Park and the Lion's Gate Bridge; it's surrounded by gardens and is just steps from the beach. The food is good, mostly seafood, much of it Ocean Wise, with some exotic touches, like the crispy Thai prawns and pressed sushi. But mostly you'll find pretty traditional fare: fish and chips, lobster and prawn roll, lobster mac and cheese, fisherman's pie. The Beach House is also a favorite spot for Saturday and Sunday brunch (try the Dungeness crab and shrimp omelet), and has a good wine list with an exceptional selection of BC bottles.

150 25th St. ℂ **604/922-1414.** www.thebeachhouserestaurant.ca. Reservations recommended. Main courses C$18–C$32. Mon–Thurs 11:30am–10pm, Fri–Sat 11:30am–11pm, Sun 11am–10pm. Bus: 250 to Dundarave Village.

Pier 7 ★ WEST COAST   This is an exciting recent addition to the North Vancouver waterfront, right next to the Lonsdale Quay SeaBus terminal. Nowhere else do you get this amazing view of the city skyline and the busy port. Even better, the whole waterfront area is scheduled for a major makeover that will likely see a museum, shops, attractions, even a giant wheel like the London Eye. Meanwhile, there's Pier 7, a cool little contemporary space with a couple of fantastic patios—the rooftop one has sofas and fire pits, the lower one can be enclosed on rainy days. There's a kind of sleek industrial look to the building, evoking the area's shipbuilding past, with lots of exposed structural beams and sturdy metal bits. The seafood-heavy menu features mainly casual classics, such as crab cakes, poutine, seafood chowder, a reasonably priced seafood tower, bouillabaisse, and rib eye steak. This is one of the few places in North Van that you can get a properly made cocktail, and there's a good wine list to enjoy along with the sunset.

25 Wallace Mews. ℂ **604/929-7437.** www.pierseven.ca. Main course C$18–C$34. Mon–Fri 11:30am–late, Sat–Sun 10:30am–late.

The Salmon House on the Hill ★ WEST COAST   For more than 35 years, the Salmon House has been serving up its famous alder-grilled salmon from a spectacular view location high up on a hill in the middle of West Vancouver's ritzy British Properties. This restaurant has some of the best views in all of Greater Vancouver. But unlike many view restaurants, it also has excellent food. The building is designed in a classic West Coast style reminiscent of a native longhouse, with big windows and lots of cedar wood, dotted with First Nations artwork, including the etched glass windows of the bar, wall paintings of eagles and bears, totem poles, even a wooden canoe that hangs over the dining room. The menu features fairly traditional BC seafood dishes—the chefs and owners are huge supporters of all that is local and sustainable—including steamed Dungeness crab, an exceptional seafood tower for two, and, of course, the classic grilled salmon. A good BC-focused wine list rounds out the experience. The restaurant also serves a popular weekend brunch.

2229 Folkestone Way. ☎ **604/926-3212.** www.salmonhouse.com. Reservations recommended for dinner. Main courses C$27–C$40. Sat–Sun 10:30am–2:30pm, daily 5–10pm. Bus: 250 across Lions Gate Bridge to Park Royal, then transfer to 256.

INEXPENSIVE

The Tomahawk Barbecue ★ CASUAL   This place is a kick. It's a little old diner (dating back to 1926) that is jam-packed with First Nations memorabilia that ranges from ticky-tacky tourist tat to exceptional original artworks. It's all good-humored fun, and your kids will love it. You might be even more excited about the fact that they use top quality, hormone-free, mostly organic ingredients. The Tomahawk is famous for its huge breakfasts, especially the Yukon-style bacon and eggs, which comes with five hearty slices of bacon. The burgers are also excellent, and the mile-high lemon meringue pie alone is worth the trip across the bridge. Note that on weekends the breakfast lineups can be epic, and you can expect them to be even more so now that the Tomahawk has been selected to appear on Food Network TV's "Diners, Drive-ins and Dives" sometime in 2014.

1550 Philip Ave. ☎ **604/988-2612.** www.tomahawkrestaurant.com. Reservations not accepted. Main courses C$5–C$17. Sun–Thurs 8am–9pm, Fri–Sat 8am–10pm. Bus: 240 to Philip Ave.

Cocktail Culture

Some of the world's most talented bartenders are shaking things up in Vancouver, which has a craft cocktail scene to rival many much larger centers. On the one hand, you have the cocktail historians, who have a passion for classic drinks and arcane spirits; on the other, you have the wildly creative types, making their own bitters, infusions, and tinctures. And then you have some talented people who combine both skills. Many of the best bars are in the city's top hotels and high-end restaurants (Hawksworth, Uva, West, Bluewater, and Yew, for instance). And then there are these great places to try.

The Blackbird Public House & Oyster Bar   The newest addition to The Donnelly Group's many bars, pubs, and restaurants has the star power of two of the city's top bartenders behind its program: Jay Jones and Trevor Kallies. It combines several bars and restaurants in one place, including a scotch bar with 70-plus labels. Try: The Blackbird (Highland Park 12, honey, lemon, Bittered Sling Moondog Bitters).

905 Dunsmuir St. ☎ **604/899-4456.** www.donnellygroup.ca. Sun–Thurs 11am–1am, Fri–Sat 11am–2am.

The Diamond   Located on the upper floor of a historic building that was one of only three to escape the great fire of 1886, this joint has history to burn. It used to be a somewhat scandalous nightclub, and before that, a speakeasy during Prohibition, and before that, rumor has it, a brothel. Today it serves up great twists on classic cocktails and tasty snacks. Try: The Gastown (gin, grapefruit, Orancio vermouth, absinthe).

6 Powell St. ℂ **604/568-8272.** www.di6mond.com. Tues–Thurs 5:30pm–1am, Fri–Sat 5:30pm– 2am, Sun 5:30pm–midnight. Closed Mon.

The Keefer Bar   Bar manager Danielle Tatarin is inspired by the ingredients she finds in the Chinese herbalist shops around this chic little nightclub/restaurant/lounge. She makes tinctures and bitters from exotic roots, stems, and seeds to craft apothecary-style cocktails that are surely good for whatever ails you. Try: Live You Long Time, aka Kombucha Collins (gin, oolong tea syrup, lemon, sencha kombucha).

135 Keefer St. ℂ **604/688-1961.** www.thekeeferbar.com. Daily 5pm–late.

Pourhouse   It's an old building, built in 1910, with a vintage decor, and a vintage spirit to the cocktails. The bar is great—a giant slab of wood from an old barn—and the bartenders can make just about any classic you can think of, as well as some original creations Try: Touch of Evil (mezcal, reposado tequila, vermouth, maraschino, Jerry Thomas Decanter bitters)

162 Water St. ℂ **604/568-7022.** www.pourhousevancouver.com. Mon–Wed 11:30am–midnight, Thurs 11:30am–1am, Fri 11:30am–2am, Sat 5pm–2am, Sun 5pm–midnight.

Shameful Tiki Room   Open the anonymous-looking door on Main Street, and step right into a South Pacific adventure, complete with thatch roof, Fijian tapas cloth, puffer fish lamps, island music, even original artwork from the 1950s tiki room in Vancouver's historic Waldorf Hotel. Try: The Mystery Bowl (the recipe is secret, but it does involve lots of rum and fire).

4362 Main St. ℂ **604/999-5684.** www.shamefultikiroom.com. Wed–Mon 5pm–late. Closed Tues.

EXPLORING VANCOUVER

Vancouver's the sort of place where you can hike or ski in the morning, sail in the afternoon, then have a sophisticated evening out on the town at night. That seems awfully tiring, though, and besides, you'll never get to see all the city's great attractions if you're busy going up and down hill all the time. True, the magnificent natural setting is the main attraction here—those mountains to the north, the ocean to the west and all around, and the gardens, beaches, and parks throughout the city. But there are plenty of other things to see and do. Here are the best of them.

Downtown & the West End

Bill Reid Gallery of Northwest Coast Art ★★ ART GALLERY   Bill Reid was first among West Coast native artists, not just because of his immense talent, but because he managed to throw the door open for all other artists who followed. This beautiful, light-drenched exhibition space, which opened in 2008, a decade after his death, is a fitting tribute to this great man. Many of his works are on permanent display—they range from the huge bronze sculpture "Mythic Messengers," which comprises 11 intertwined figures recounting traditional Haida myths, to a tiny chalk tea set he carved as a young boy. The gallery also features ever-changing exhibitions of Northwest Coast art; for instance, the breathtaking jewelry of Morgan Green in her show "Ts'msyen Transforming." She takes images from her heritage and raw materials from nature to create works of deep beauty. There's also a great gift shop, where you can pick up First Nations art, books, jewelry, and collectibles.

639 Hornby St. ℂ **604/682-3455.** www.billreidgallery.ca. Admission C$10 adults, C$7 seniors and students, C$5 children 6–17, C$25 families. Wed–Sun 11am–5pm.

Canada Place and the Olympic Cauldron ★★ PLAZA/ATTRACTION   If you've never been to Vancouver, this is a good place to orient yourself and see some of what makes BC's largest city so special. With its five tall Teflon sails and bowsprit jutting out into Burrard Inlet, Canada Place is meant to resemble a giant sailing ship. Inside, it's a convention center on one level and a giant cruise-ship terminal below, with the Pan Pacific Hotel perched on top. Around the perimeter is a promenade, offering views across Burrard Inlet to the North Shore peaks and nearby Stanley Park, with plaques explaining the sights and providing historical tidbits. Continue around the promenade, and you'll get great city views and be able to see the older, low-rise buildings of Gastown, where Vancouver began. Bus sightseeing tours begin here, and there's a Tourism Vancouver Visitor Centre right across the street.

In 2013, Canada Place launched a spectacular new attraction, **FlyOver Canada.** Hop on board and it will whisk you across a virtual Canada, complete with wind, scents, and mist. The simulated flight inside a dome takes about 30 minutes, and is truly a remarkable experience.

Just west of Canada Place is a new addition to the Vancouver Convention Centre, **VCC West,** which opened in 2009. With its "green" roof, light-filled interior spaces, and spacious plazas and walkways, it has transformed this area. On the other side of VCC West is **Jack Poole Plaza** and the **Olympic Cauldron,** which burned brightly all during the 2010 Olympic and Paralympic Winter Games. Today it's lit only on special occasions, but the plaza itself has become a popular hangout, and a great place for taking photos of the North Shore Mountains. Note the mesmerizing trompe l'oeil sculpture at the northern end of the plaza, "Digital Orca," by Douglas Coupland. This is also the beginning of the seaside pathway that meanders along Coal Harbour and becomes the Stanley Park Seawall.

Canada Place (at the north end of Burrard and Howe sts.): Promenade daily 24 hr. Free admission. FlyOver Canada: ℂ **604/620-8455.** www.flyovercanada.com. C$20 adult, C$18 senior and student, C$15 children 12 and under. Daily 10am–9pm.

Christchurch Cathedral ★★ CHURCH   In a city that has bulldozed so many of its historic buildings, it's a delight to stumble upon one that escaped the developer's plans. It was a close call for this lovely sandstone building, though. It was built in 1895, and became the cathedral church of the Anglican Diocese of New Westminster. In 1971, its membership voted to demolish it and replace it with a high rise; the public, thankfully, objected, and the building was saved. Today it is a lively place that not only holds religious services, but also presents choral concerts throughout the year and Gregorian chant on Sunday evenings. Visitors are welcome to attend services and events.

690 Burrard St. ℂ **604/682-3848.** www.cathedral.vancouver.bc.ca. Sunday service 8am–9:30pm; Holy Communion Mon–Fri 12:10pm, Sat 9:10am. No admission.

Robson Square ★ PLAZA   The idea was to create a social space where people would congregate and hang out. That's what architect Arthur Erickson had in mind when he designed this concrete and grass modernist plaza outside his famous Law Courts building. Sadly, it's never quite worked out that way, even though there are

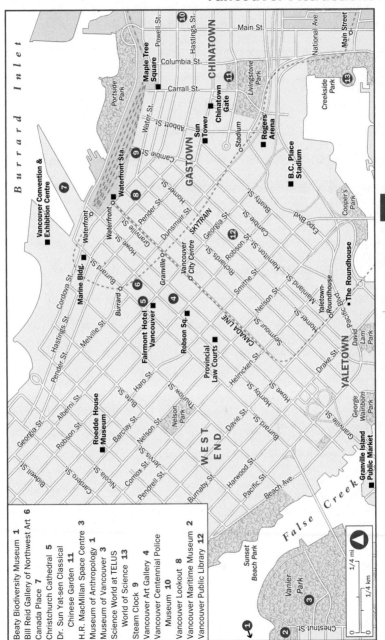

Beaty Biodiversity Museum **1**
Bill Reid Gallery of Northwest Art **6**
Canada Place **7**
Christchurch Cathedral **5**
Dr. Sun Yat-sen Classical
  Chinese Garden **11**
H.R. MacMillan Space Centre **3**
Museum of Anthropology **1**
Museum of Vancouver **3**
Science World at TELUS
  World of Science **13**
Steam Clock **9**
Vancouver Art Gallery **4**
Vancouver Centennial Police
  Museum **10**
Vancouver Lookout **8**
Vancouver Maritime Museum **2**
Vancouver Public Library **12**

often crowds of people lounging on the Vancouver Art Gallery steps across the street, as well as at the newer Library Square Plaza up the street. Still, this is where you'll find the Robson Square Ice Rink, which is a great place to lace up your skates and go for a spin, so Erickson's vision is realized at least in the chilly winter months.

800 Robson Square. ℂ **604/646-3554** (ice rink). www.robsonsquare.com. Nov–Feb daily 9am–9pm.

Stanley Park ★★★ PARK/ATTRACTION   The green jewel of Vancouver, Stanley Park is a 400-hectare (1,000-acre) rainforest jutting out into the ocean from the edge of the busy West End. Exploring the second-largest urban forest in Canada is one of Vancouver's quintessential experiences.

The park, created in 1888, is filled with towering western red cedar and Douglas fir, manicured lawns, flower gardens, placid lagoons, and countless shaded walking trails that meander through it all. The famed **Seawall** runs along the waterside edge of the park, allowing cyclists and pedestrians to experience the magical interface of forest, sea, and sky. One of the most popular free attractions in the park is the **collection of totem poles** at Brockton Point, most of them carved in the 1980s to replace the original ones that were placed in the park in the 1920s and 1930s. The area around the totem poles features open-air displays on the Coast Salish First Nations and a small gift shop/visitor information center.

The park is home to lots of wildlife, including beavers, coyotes, bald eagles, blue herons, cormorants, trumpeter swans, Brant geese, ducks, raccoons, skunks, and gray squirrels. (But no bears.) For directions and maps, brochures, and exhibits on the nature and ecology of Stanley Park, visit the **Lost Lagoon Nature House** (ℂ **604/257-8544;** www.stanleyparkecology.ca). Most Sundays at 9am or 1:30pm, rain or shine, they offer themed Discovery Walks of the park (preregistration recommended). Equally nature-focused but with way more wow is the **Vancouver Aquarium** (see below). The **Stanley Park Miniature Railway** (ℂ **604/257-8531**) is a diminutive steam locomotive that pulls passenger cars on a circuit through the woods. In December, the surrounding woods are lit up with thousands of Christmas lights, and at Halloween, it becomes the Ghost Train, haunted by vampires and ghouls.

On the cultural side, the Malkin Bowl outdoor amphitheater holds summer concerts and musical theater productions in a series called **Theatre Under the Stars** (ℂ **604/696-4295;** www.tuts.ca). Sitting on the grassy slope watching, say, "Shrek: The Musical" is a quintessential Vancouver experience for the whole family.

Swimmers head to **Third Beach** and **Second Beach** (p. 102), and for kids, there's a free **Spray Park** near Lumberman's Arch, where they can run and splash through various water-spewing fountains.

Perhaps the best way to explore the park is to rent a bike or in-line skates, and set off along the Seawall. The **horse-drawn carriage ride** operated by **AAA Horse & Carriage Ltd.** (ℂ **604/681-5115;** www.stanleypark.com) is one of the most enjoyable ways to tour the park. Carriage tours depart every 20 to 45 minutes mid-March through October from the Coal Harbour parking lot, near the Georgia Street park entrance and the park information booth. The ride lasts an hour and covers portions of the park that many locals have never seen. Also, the **Vancouver Trolley Company** (ℂ **604/801-5515;** www.vancouvertrolley.com) operates an around-the-park shuttle bus mid-June to early September.

Stanley Park. ℂ **604/257-8400.** www.vancouver.ca/parks. Free admission. Park daily 24 hr. Bus: 19. Parking Apr–Sept C$3.25/hr., C$11/day; Oct–Mar C$2.25/hr., C$6/day. Horse-drawn carriage rides C$33 adults, C$32 seniors and students, C$17 children 3–12. Vancouver Trolley shuttle C$10 adults, C$5 children 4–12, C$25 families.

Stanley Park

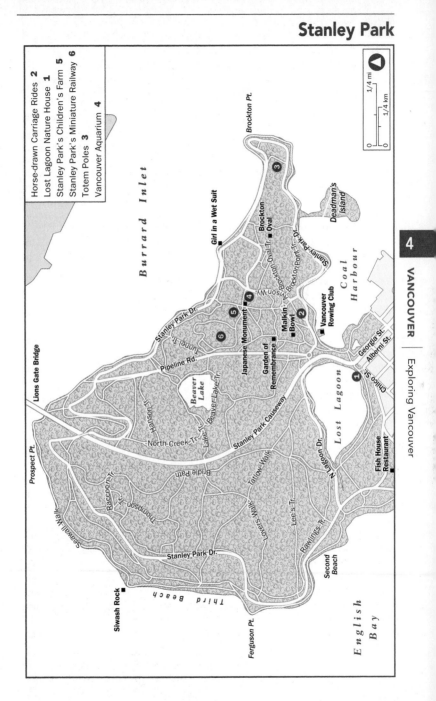

Horse-drawn Carriage Rides **2**
Lost Lagoon Nature House **1**
Stanley Park's Children's Farm **5**
Stanley Park's Miniature Railway **6**
Totem Poles **3**
Vancouver Aquarium **4**

The Park's Dark Side

Stanley Park is Vancouver's favorite place to spend a sunny afternoon. But it's still a pretty big wilderness space, and those deep, hushed forests have experienced some dark moments over the years. The plan to create the park was the first order of business for the newly formed Vancouver City Council back in 1886; only 2 years later, shortly before the park was formally dedicated, they decided to use the park's Dead-man's Island to quarantine victims of a smallpox epidemic. Their ghosts still, reportedly, haunt the island, which is now the property of the Department of National Defence. Over the years, squatters and the homeless have found refuge in the park's woods—this under-lined the plot of Timothy Taylor's novel "Stanley Park"—and in the late 1990s and early 2000s, it was the site of a num-ber of gang fights and assaults targeting gay men. But the most famous Stanley Park crime is that of the **Babes in the Woods murders.** In January 1953, the remains of two bodies were found in the Stanley Park woods, along with a hatchet and a woman's fur coat. They were found to be two boys, aged 7 and 10, who had likely been killed in 1947. Aside from that, nothing is known—not who they were, how they died, or who killed them. It's still considered one of the city's most baffling unsolved crimes. All that said, the park is a surprisingly safe and serene space. Just be careful if you venture into its shadowy places after dark.

Vancouver Aquarium ★★★ AQUARIUM   One of North America's largest and best marine facilities, the Vancouver Aquarium houses more than 70,000 critters, including white beluga whales, sea otters, Steller sea lions, and Pacific white-sided dolphins. During regularly scheduled shows, aquarium staff explain marine-mammal behavior while working with these impressive creatures. The Wild Coast area features a fascinating assortment of fish and sea creatures found in local waters, and there's always an interesting temporary exhibit or two.

For a substantial extra fee (C$160 adults, C$240 one adult and one child age 8–12), you can have a behind-the-scenes Beluga Encounter, helping to feed these giant white cetaceans, then head up to the Marine Mammal deck to take part in the belugas' regu-lar training session. Other Animal Encounter tours take visitors behind the scenes to interact with dolphins, or help feed the Steller sea lions, sea turtles, and sea otters. Call ℭ **800/931-1186** to reserve these programs ahead of time. Children must be 8 or older to participate.

There are other programs as well, including the popular sleepovers, treasure hunts, and, of course, all the various exhibits, including the new Penguin Point and the exotic Amazon Critter Corner.

845 Avison Way, Stanley Park. ℭ **604/659-3474.** www.vanaqua.org. Admission C$27 adults; C$21 seniors, students, and children 13–18; C$17 children 4–12; free children 3 and under. June–Sept daily 9am–7pm, Oct–May daily 9:30am–5pm. Bus: 19. Around-the-Park shuttle bus mid-June to early Sept. Full-day parking June–Sept C$10 or C$3 per hour, Oct–May C$5 or C$2 for 2 hr.

Vancouver Art Gallery ★★ ART GALLERY   The days, sadly, are numbered for this landmark building, at least for its role as the city's art gallery. A sleek, modern new gallery space is being designed by the architects Herzon & de Meuron, and will be unveiled in early 2015. Meanwhile, visitors can enjoy the graceful neoclassical former law court, which was designed by BC's leading early-20th-century architect, Francis

Rattenbury, and renovated by its leading late-20th-century architect Arthur Erickson. Who knows who will tackle its next incarnations? The surrounding grounds have become a popular hangout and meeting place, especially during the annual "420" marijuana smoke-in on April 20. The gallery itself is a great place to discover Canadian and West Coast art, especially the unsurpassed collection of works by Emily Carr, the great modernist painter from Victoria. It features international traveling exhibits as well, such as "The Forbidden City," an impressive display of treasures from Beijing's Palace Museum, starting October 2014. The gallery also has a friendly cafe and terrific gift shop; be sure to stop by for a stylish souvenir to take home.

750 Hornby St. © **604/662-4719.** www.vanartgallery.bc.ca. Admission C$20 adults, C$15 seniors, C$15 students, C$6 kids 5–12, C$50 families. Wed–Mon 10am–5pm, Tues 10am–9pm.

Gastown & Chinatown

Dr. Sun Yat-Sen Classical Chinese Garden ★ GARDEN/CULTURAL SITE This small reproduction of a Classical Chinese scholar's garden truly is a remarkable place, but to get the full effect, it's best to take the guided tour (included in admission). Untrained eyes will only see a pretty pond surrounded by bamboo and oddly shaped rocks. The engaging guides, however, can explain this unique urban garden's Taoist yin-yang design principle, in which harmony is achieved through dynamic opposition. To foster opposition (and thus harmony) in the garden, Chinese designers place contrasting elements in juxtaposition: Soft-moving water flows across solid stone; smooth, swaying bamboo grows around gnarled immovable rocks; dark pebbles are placed next to light pebbles in the paving. Moving with the guide, you discover the symbolism of intricate carvings and marvel at the ever-changing views from covered serpentine corridors. This is one of two Classical Chinese gardens in North America (the other is in Portland, Oregon) created by master artisans from Suzhou, the garden city of China. While you're in Chinatown, also make sure to check out the ornate China Gate on Pender Street, and the Sam Kee Building at 8 W. Pender St., at only 1.5m wide (4 ft. 11 in.), the narrowest commercial building in Canada.

578 Carrall St. © **604/662-3207.** www.vancouverchinesegarden.com. Admission C$12 adults, C$10 seniors, C$9 students, free for children 4 and under, C$25 families. Guided tour included with admission. May–June 14 and Sept daily 10am–6pm, June 15–Aug daily 9:30am–7pm, Oct–Apr Tues–Sun 10am–4:30pm. Closed Mon Nov–Apr.

Steam Clock ★ ATTRACTION The Steam Clock in Gastown is a favorite photo-op for tourists. Built by horologist Raymond Saunders in 1977 (based on an 1875 design), it was the world's first steam clock, powered by steam from an underground system of pipes that supply heat to many downtown buildings. The clock is supposed to sound its whistles (playing "The Westminster Chimes") every quarter-hour, with steam shooting out from vents at the top. Sometimes, however, it simply steams with no musical accompaniment.

Gastown, at the intersection of Water and Cambie sts. Free admission.

Vancouver Police Museum ★ MUSEUM Vancouver may seem like a pretty place, a laidback, law-abiding sort of town, but it has always had a rough, dangerous undertone to it. It's had its legendary unsolved crimes, such the Babes in the Woods murders, and scandals like the mysterious death of the actor Errol Flynn, allegedly in the arms of a 17-year-old girl (although some reports suggest it was a boy). All of that is captured here in this quaint little museum housed in the old Vancouver Coroner's Court, morgue, and crime lab. (It's where Flynn was autopsied after his untimely death

On Friday evenings at 7:30pm from mid-July through the first weekend in September, the Dr. Sun Yat-Sen Classical Chinese Garden is the scene of musical performances and dances. The eclectic repertoire includes classical, Asian, Gypsy jazz, Slavic soul, and fusion music. Shows cost about C$25 and often sell out. The website (www.vancouverchinese garden.com) provides a full listing of concerts; call *©* **604/662-3207** to reserve tickets.

in 1959.) It's not for everyone—those who aren't fascinated by crime and the people who solve it might be bored—but for the rest of us, the weapons, specimen jars, and crime-fighting memorabilia will be intriguing. Plus it offers tours, special classes for kids, and ESL programs. The museum is a proud supporter of the Vancouver Police Department Memorial.

240 E. Cordova St. *©* **604/665-3346.** www.vancouverpolicemuseum.ca. Admission C$12 adults, C$10 seniors, C$8 students and children 7–13, C$20 families. Tues–Sat 9am–5pm. Closed state holidays.

The West Side

Beaty Biodiversity Museum ★ MUSEUM   We're all thinking about biodiversity these days, even if we don't realize it, and if we're not, we probably should be. This museum explores how ecosystems work, and how they work together, whether they are in our own backyard or around the planet. Expect special speakers, tours, exhibits, and puppet shows, as well as temporary exhibits and permanent displays of fossils, skeletons, and various specimens. The most impressive of these is the massive, 26m (85-ft.) skeleton of a female blue whale—the largest creature on Earth—that floats above the displays. There are about 500 other permanent exhibits and myriad fossils and other preserved critters as well. *Note:* Unless this is an area of special interest, it may not be worth the trip out to UBC just to visit this museum.

2212 Main Mall, UBC. *©* **604/827-4955.** www.beatymuseum.ubc.ca. Admission C$12 adults, C$10 seniors and children 13–17, C$8 children 5–12. Daily 10am–5pm. Closed Mon Oct–May.

Granville Island ★★★ MARKET   Almost a city within a city, Granville Island is a good place to browse away a morning, an afternoon, or a whole day. You can wander through a busy public market jammed with food stalls, shop for crafts, pick up fresh seafood, enjoy a great dinner, watch the latest theater performance, rent a yacht, stroll along the waterfront, or simply run through the sprinkler on a hot summer day; it's all there and more. If you have only a short period of time, make sure you spend at least part of it in the **Granville Island Public Market,** one of the best in North America.

Once a declining industrial site, Granville Island started transforming in the late 1970s when the federal government encouraged new, people-friendly developments. The former warehouses and factories now house galleries, artist studios, restaurants, and theaters; the cement plant on the waterfront is the only industrial tenant left. Access to Granville Island is by harbor ferry from the West End, Yaletown, or Kitsilano or by foot, bike, or car across the bridge/causeway at Anderson Street. Avoid driving over on weekends and holidays—you'll spend more time trying to find a parking place than in the galleries.

Granville Island Attractions

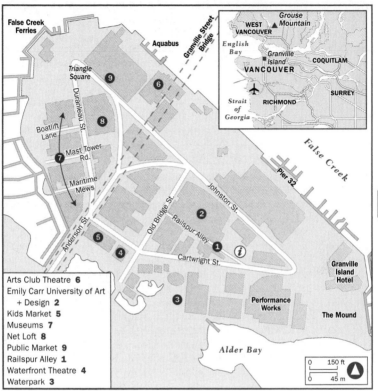

Arts Club Theatre **6**
Emily Carr University of Art
 + Design **2**
Kids Market **5**
Museums **7**
Net Loft **8**
Public Market **9**
Railspur Alley **1**
Waterfront Theatre **4**
Waterpark **3**

   While you're on the island, be sure to check out Railspur Alley, where you'll find artists' studios, cafes, fine jewelry, and the Artisan Sake Maker. You'll also find the small-batch Liberty Distillery and Granville Island Brewing on the island, as well as a terrific wine shop, Liberty Wine Merchants, and several bars and restaurants. The patios at Bridges, Edible Canada, or the Dockside Restaurant are a great place to spend a sunny afternoon.

   Also drop in on Net Loft, a sort of craftsy mall where you'll find works by local potters and other artisans at Circle Craft, as well as the great Blackberry Books, a kitchen wares shop, a fancy paper store, and First Nations fashion designs. For even more pretty, or at least interesting, things to look at, check out the Emily Carr University of Art + Design, which often has exhibits of student art.

   There are also four theaters on the island, the Kids Market, marina, kayak rentals, parks, and a farmers market on Thursdays in summer.

The south shore of False Creek (under Granville St. Bridge). ℂ **604/666-5784** (information center). www.granvilleisland.com. Public market daily 9am–7pm. Bus: 50.

H. R. MacMillan Space Centre ★ PLANETARIUM   The building is distinctive—it kind of looks like a white space ship that just happened to land in Vanier Park.
Which is only fitting, because this is the city's planetarium, which has introduced
many a budding astronomy buff to the magic of the stars. Vancouver's space center and
observatory was founded in 1968 and has since offered an exciting program of starry-
eyed displays and exhibits, as well as films that explore the universe around us. Exhibits
are hands-on and interactive, making this a great place for the kids. On Saturday
nights, visitors can scan the skies around Vancouver with the Cassegrain telescope.
The building is also home to the Museum of Vancouver (see below).

1100 Chestnut St. (in Vanier Park). ⓒ **604/738-7827.** www.spacecentre.ca. Admission C$15 adults;
C$11 seniors, students, and children 5–10; free children 4 and under; C$45 families (up to 5, max
2 adults). Evening films C$13 adults, C$10 seniors and youth 12–18, C$8 children 5–11. July–early
Sept daily 10am–5pm; early Sept–June Mon–Fri 10am–3pm, Sat–Sun 10am–5pm; evening films Sat
7:30pm and 9pm. Observatory Sat 8pm–midnight. Closed Dec 25. Bus: 22.

Museum of Anthropology ★★★ MUSEUM   If you think this is going to be
just another ho-hum museum experience, think again. It is, for starters, a purely magnificent building, a dramatic vision in concrete and glass designed by famed local
architect Arthur Erickson to soar from the cliff above Wreck Beach. Beyond that,
though, this is one of the world's truly great museums, not only capturing the past, but
celebrating the present of aboriginal peoples the world over, and especially here on the
West Coast. The Great Hall is breathtaking, with its 15m-high (50-ft.) glass walls that
surround a spectacular collection of totem poles with light. There are a number of
galleries and permanent displays, including Haida artist Bill Reid's most famous
sculpture, "The Raven and the First Men" (it's also pictured on the C$20 bill). MOA
also features special exhibits, like this summer's moving display of artworks by urban
aboriginal youth from all over the world. The grounds, too, are filled with haunting
works of First Nations craftsmanship and art, including two Haida houses, several
totem poles, and artworks by Musqueam artists in the welcome plaza. While you're on
the UBC campus, you may also want to visit the nearby UBC Botanical Garden and
Nitobe Memorial Garden (p. 96).

6393 NW Marine Dr. (at Gate 4). ⓒ **604/822-5087.** www.moa.ubc.ca. Admission C$17 adults;
C$15 seniors, students, and children 6–18; free children 5 and under; C$9 for all Tues 5–9pm. Daily
10am–5pm (Tues till 9pm). Closed Dec 25–26. Bus: 4 or 99 (10-min. walk from UBC bus loop).

Museum of Vancouver ★★ MUSEUM   Vancouver, famously, likes to forget its
past. Well, not here. All its rough, tough, neon-lit, hippy-dippy memories are captured
in this fun little museum space. In 2014, the museum celebrates 120 years of collecting
the city's artifacts, so it's a good time to come down and check out what's on display.
It starts with the early days of the city, with exhibits that include a mesmerizing movie
shot from the front of the city's first streetcar as it rolls through the streets, pedestrians
fleeing as it approaches. The 1950s Gallery is great fun, with its nod to Vancouver's
neon past—the city once had more neon lights than any other in the world, and some
of the best examples are preserved here, including the famous Smiling Buddha sign.
And, of course, there's quite the celebration of the counterculture years of the 1960s
and '70s. Note that MOV is located in the same building as the H. R. MacMillan Space
Centre (see above).

1100 Chestnut St. ⓒ **604/736-4431.** www.museumofvancouver.ca. Admission C$14 adults, C$11
seniors and students, C$8 children 5–18. Daily 10am–5pm (Thurs 10am–8pm). Bus: 2 or 22, then
walk 3 blocks south on Cornwall Ave. Boat: False Creek Ferry to Heritage Harbour.

Vancouver Maritime Museum ★ MUSEUM   You'd think it would be nothing but boats here, but the curators at this friendly space in an A-frame on the beach like to think outside the box. Recent years have seen exhibits that focused on sailors' tattoos, naughty scrimshaw carvings, and, in 2014, the evolution of the swimsuit. Yes, there are also model ships, navigational gear, maps, charts, posters, and everything to do with Vancouver's marine past, including a collection of vintage boats. But the main attraction will always be the RCMP patrol ship, *St. Roch,* especially since you actually get to climb aboard and explore the vessel. In the 1920s, it patrolled the Arctic Ocean, and was the first trip to travel both ways through the Northwest Passage. Today, it offers a glimpse of the harsh conditions in those days and in those brutal waters, something to keep in mind as you take your pleasant harbor ferry journey afterward.

1905 Ogden Ave. (in Vanier Park). ✆ **604/257-8300.** www.vancouvermaritimemuseum.com/about-us. Admission C$11 adults, C$9 seniors and children 6–18, free children 5 and under, C$30 families. Late May–Aug daily 10am–5pm; Sept–May Tues–Sat 10am–5pm, Sun noon–5pm. Bus: 2 or 22, then walk 4 blocks north on Cypress St. Boat: False Creek ferries dock at Heritage Harbour.

The East Side

Science World at TELUS World of Science ★★ MUSEUM   A must visit if
you have kids. Like so many things around Vancouver, including the SkyTrain and the China Gate in Chinatown, this big, sparkly geodesic dome at the eastern end of False Creek was initially built for Expo '86. Today, it's a popular destination for parents looking for something to entertain their kids on a rainy day. And while it certainly is educational, it's also way more fun than that. For instance, in 2014, its featured exhibit is the "Science of Sports," a hands-on exploration of what it takes to be a great athlete. In the "BodyWorks" exhibit, you can do cool things like power a drum with your heartbeat, while "Eureka!" lets you answer all those "what if" questions you've always wondered about. There are also movies presented throughout the day at the OMNIMAX Theatre, as well as outdoor activities in the Ken Spencer Science Park.

1455 Quebec St. ✆ **604/443-7443.** www.scienceworld.ca. Admission C$25 adults, C$21 seniors and students, C$18 children 4–12, free children 3 and under. OMNIMAX ticket C$5 adults. July–Aug daily 10am–6pm; Sept–June Mon–Fri 10am–5pm, Sat–Sun 10am–6pm; holidays 10am–6pm. SkyTrain: Main St.–Science World.

North Vancouver & West Vancouver

Capilano Suspension Bridge Park ★★ ATTRACTION   This heart-stopping
experience is one of Vancouver's most popular tourist attractions, and has been since it first opened back in 1889. Once just a simple suspension bridge flung 137m (450 ft.) across a 70m-deep (230 ft.) canyon, today it boasts a whole lot of extra features that keep the visitors coming back. First, there is the bridge itself, just a simple series of cedar planks held up by two cables. As you cross the Capilano Canyon, it sways alarmingly, more so if any teenage boys are crossing at the same time. The bridge is surrounded by a lovely 11-hectare (27-acre) rainforest park, with a cafe, gift shop, interpretive center, carving shed, and storytelling stations. Across the bridge is the **Treetops Adventure,** a walkway set up high in the trees. And then there's the new **Cliffwalk,** a series of cantilevered walkways, some of them glass-bottomed, that jut out from the granite cliffs, giving you a unique (and dizzying) perspective on the canyon below. Overall, this is a pretty fun way to spend a day—or it would be, if the summer crowds weren't so intense and the admission price so high. One of the best times to visit is during Canyon Lights in December, when it's all sparkly with millions

Doin' the Grouse Grind

The Grouse Grind, a popular 2.9km (1.8-mile) trail, often called "Mother Nature's Stairmaster" by locals, generally opens late spring or early summer. Over 100,000 hikers per year take on the challenge of the rugged terrain and steep climb. Indeed, some people do it every day before heading off to work. By the time you reach the plateau, your ascent will have gained 853m (2,799 ft.). Average completion time is usually 1½ hours, with the fastest official completion time sitting at just over 25 minutes (the unofficial record dips under 24 min.). Once you reach the top, you can take the tram back down for just C$5 per person. For a look at the terrain, visit www.vancouvertrails.com/trails/grouse-grind.

of fairy lights and the price is about half what it normally is. Another option is to check out the free suspension bridge in Lynn Valley (p. 97).

3735 Capilano Rd. ⓒ **604/985-7474.** www.capbridge.com. Admission C$36 adults, C$34 seniors, C$30 students, C$23 children 13–16, C$12 children 6–12, free children 5 and under. May–Sept daily 8:30am–dusk, Oct–Apr daily 9am–5pm or later. Dec daily 11am–9pm. Hours change monthly. Closed Dec 25. Take Hwy. 99 north across Lions Gate Bridge to exit 14 on Capilano Rd. Bus: 236 or 246 from Lonsdale Quay. Free shuttle from Canada Place.

Grouse Mountain ★★ VIEW/PARK/ATTRACTION   This is one of Vancouver's three ski hills (the one in the middle), but it's also so much more than that. For one thing, it's the city's most visited tourist attraction, with 1.2 million visitors a year. You can see its lights at night from downtown, and in the daytime, you can see the broad strip that is the main ski run as well as the usually stationary wind turbine. There's a zippy Skyride to the 1,250m (4,100-ft.) summit of what's been branded "The Peak of Vancouver," or, if you're feeling energetic, you can hike the brutal Grouse Grind instead (see below). Once you've reached the top, you'll have a panoramic view of the city, Fraser Valley, surrounding mountains, islands, and the Strait of Georgia. On a clear day, you can see as far as Mount Baker, a snowy volcanic peak across the border in Washington State. Near the gondola station, there is a lodge with a theater that shows wildlife movies, as well as several cafes and restaurants. Among them is the fine-dining Observatory, which is only open for dinner, but the reservation includes your Skyride ticket and access to other activities. You'll find hiking trails, lumberjack shows, and ziplines in the summer, and in the winter, there's skiing, snowboarding, a skating rink, and sleigh rides. You can climb up inside the Eye of the Wind turbine for a spectacular 360-degree view at an additional fee.

6400 Nancy Greene Way. ⓒ **604/984-0661.** www.grousemountain.com. Skyride C$42 adults, C$38 seniors, C$24 children 13–18, C$14 children 5–12, free children 4 and under. Full-day ski-lift tickets C$58 adults, C$45 seniors and children 13–18, C$25 children 5–12. Skyride free with advance Observatory Restaurant reservation. Daily 9am–10pm. Take Hwy. 99 north across Lions Gate Bridge, take North Vancouver exit to Marine Dr., then up Capilano Rd. for 5km (3 miles). Parking C$6 for 3 hr. in lots below Skyride. Bus: 236 from Lonsdale Quay or 232 from Phibbs Exchange.

Parks & Gardens

Other cities may have churches and museums; what Vancouver has is nature, both wild and tamed, and the best place to discover it is in its many beautiful parks and gardens.

The big one is, of course, **Stanley Park** (p. 84), one of the biggest urban parks in the world. In addition to its wilderness, heritage, and sports areas, it also has a lovely rose garden that blooms in June, as well as a pretty stroll around Lost Lagoon. In the downtown area, the other major garden to discover is the **Dr. Sun Yat-Sen Chinese Classical Garden** in Chinatown (p. 87). Otherwise, there are little public parks throughout the West End, as well as beaches and private gardens, all lined with shady trees and fragrant with flowers.

It's when you cross to the West Side that you start to discover some of the truly remarkable gardens.

Capilano River Regional Park ★ PARK   Cross the Lions Gate Bridge, and you will find provincial and regional parks galore, with activities to delight outdoor enthusiasts year-round. For those averse to strenuous climbing, the publicly maintained **Capilano River Regional Park** has a gentle trail that meanders by the river for about 7km (4.5 miles) down to Ambleside Park and the Lions Gate Bridge, or a mile upstream to **Cleveland Dam,** a launching point for white-water kayakers and canoeists. Just below the dam, you'll find the **Capilano Salmon Hatchery,** where approximately 2 million coho and chinook salmon are hatched annually in glass-fronted tanks connected to the river by a series of channels.

4500 Capilano Park Rd. ✆ **604/224-5739.** www.metrovancouver.org. Free admission. Hatchery daily 8am–7pm (Oct–Apr until 4pm). Drive across Lions Gate Bridge and follow signs to North Vancouver and the Capilano Suspension Bridge. Bus: 236 from Lonsdale Quay.

Cypress Provincial Park ★ PARK   Driving up-up-up will eventually get you to the top of **Cypress Provincial Park.** Stop halfway at the scenic viewpoint for a sweeping vista of the Vancouver skyline, the harbor, the Gulf Islands, and Washington State's Mount Baker, which peers above the eastern horizon. To reach the park, turn off the stretch of Hwy. 1 known as the Upper Levels Highway onto Cypress Bowl Road, then travel along 12km (7½ miles) of steep, scenic switchbacks that are popular with iron-thighed road cyclists. Cypress Provincial Park has trails for hiking during the summer and autumn, and **Cypress Mountain** grooms slopes for downhill and cross-country skiing during the winter.

Cypress Mountain, West Vancouver. ✆ **604/926-5612.** www.cypressmountain.com. Daily 24/7. Free admission. Lift tickets C$62 adult, C$40 senior, C$46 youth, C$26 child.

Lighthouse Park ★ PARK   Head to West Vancouver and keep going for about 10km (6 miles) along the twisty, narrow, and very pretty Marine Drive West, and eventually you'll reach Lighthouse Park. This 75-hectare (185-acre) rugged-terrain forest has 13km (8 miles) of groomed trails and—because it has never been clear-cut—some of the largest and oldest trees in the Vancouver area. One of the paths leads to the **Point Atkinson Lighthouse,** on a rocky bluff overlooking the Strait of Georgia and a fabulous view of Vancouver.

Dundarave, West Vancouver. ✆ **604/925-7000.** www.lighthousepark.ca. Daily 24/7. Free admission. Bus 250.

Mount Seymour Provincial Park ★ PARK   Rising 1,449m (4,754 ft.) above Indian Arm, the peaks of **Mount Seymour Provincial Park** and its ski hill **Mount Seymour** offer another view of the area's Coast Mountains range. Higher than Grouse Mountain, Mount Seymour provides a spectacular view of Washington State's Mount Baker on clear days. It has challenging hiking trails that go straight to the summit, where you can see Indian Arm, Vancouver's bustling commercial port, the city skyline,

Greater Vancouver

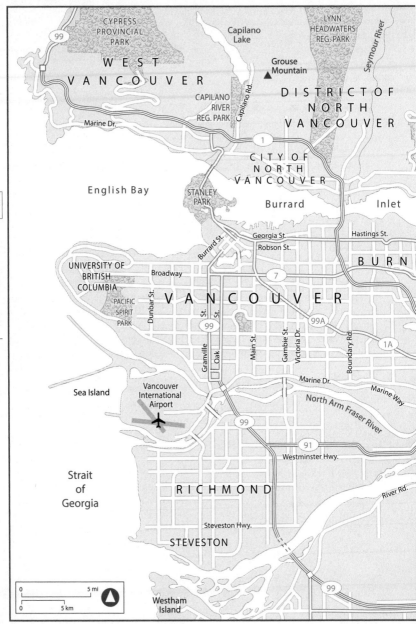

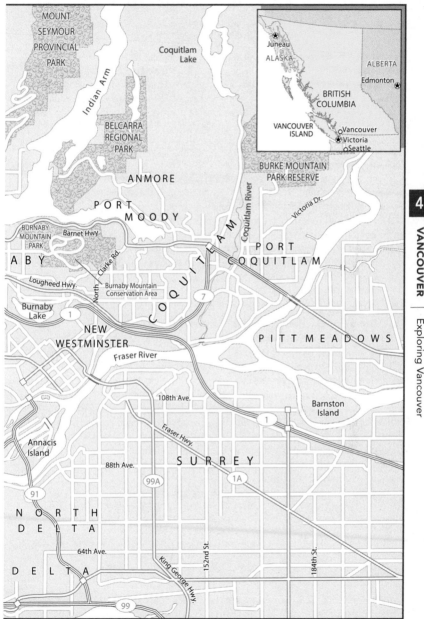

the Strait of Georgia, and Vancouver Island. The trails are open all summer for hiking; during the winter, the paths are maintained for daily skiing, snowboarding, and snowshoeing.

1700 Mt. Seymour Rd. ☏ **604/986-2261.** www.mountseymour.com. Daily 24/7. Free admission. Lift tickets C$53 adult, C$39 senior, C$45 youth, C$25 child.

Pacific Spirit Regional Park ★★ PARK   Adjoining the University of British Columbia (UBC) on the city's west side at Point Grey, **Pacific Spirit Regional Park,** usually called the **Endowment Lands** by longtime Vancouver residents, is the largest green space in Vancouver. Comprising 754 hectares (1,885 acres) of temperate rainforest, marshes, and beaches, the park includes more than 50km (30 miles) of trails ideal for hiking, riding, mountain biking, and beachcombing.

University of British Columbia. www.metrovancouver.org. Free admission. Daily 24/7.

Queen Elizabeth Park ★★★ GARDEN   Flowers run riot in this 52-hectare (130-acre) green space on a hill that is the city's highest point south of downtown (it's thought to be an extinct volcano). The big attraction is the gorgeously landscaped, flower-filled quarry garden, but the arboretum, featuring trees from all over the world, is also a big draw, as are the Henry Moore sculptures that dot the place. There are also areas for lawn bowling, tennis, disc golf, pitch-and-putt, and picnicking. The dome-shaped **Bloedel Conservatory,** which stands next to the quarry garden, houses a tropical rainforest with more than 100 free-flying tropical birds.

Cambie St. and W. 33rd Ave. ☏ **604/257-8584** (Bloedel Conservatory). www.vancouver.ca. Conservatory admission C$7 adults, C$5 seniors and youth, C$3 children 3–12. Gardens free admission. May–Sept Mon–Fri 9am–8pm, Sat–Sun 10am–8pm; Oct–Apr daily 10am–5pm. Bus no. 15.

UBC Botanical Garden & Nitobe Memorial Garden ★ GARDEN   Serious plant lovers will love the University of British Columbia. The prime attraction on campus, besides the must-see Museum of Anthropology, is the 44-hectare (110-acre) **UBC Botanical Garden,** home to more than 8,000 species of trees, shrubs, and flowers grouped into a BC native garden, a physic (or medicinal) garden, a food garden, and several others. (Spring, when the flowering trees bloom, is the best time to visit.) Energetic kids will love the **Greenheart Canopy Walkway,** a series of platforms suspended on wires at up to 18m (57 ft.) high, which move in waves as you walk along them. Nearby is the **Nitobe Memorial Garden,** a beautiful traditional Japanese garden considered among the top-five Japanese gardens in North America and one of the most authentic. Cherry blossoms peak in April and May, the irises bloom in June, and autumn brings colorful leaf displays.

Botanical Garden: 6804 SW Marine Dr., Gate 8. ☏ **604/822-4208.** www.ubcbotanicalgarden.org. Admission C$9 adults; C$7 seniors, students, and children 13–17; C$5 children 6–12; free children 5 and under. With Greenheart Canopy Walkway: C$20 adults; C$15 seniors, students, and children 13–17; C$10 children 6–12. Family rates available. Nitobe Memorial Garden: 1895 Lower Mall. ☏ **604/822-6038.** www.nitobe.org. Admission C$7 adults, C$6 seniors and children 13–17, C$4 children 6–12, free children 5 and under. Pass for all 3 attractions: C$24 adults; C$18 seniors, students, and children 13–17; C$12 children 6–12. UBC Botanical Garden open year-round; Nitobe Memorial Garden closed during winter.

VanDusen Botanical Gardens ★★ GARDEN   Just a few blocks from Queen Elizabeth Park, this lush, 22-hectare (54-acre) garden concentrates on whole ecosystems. From towering trees to little lichens on the smallest of damp stones, the gardeners at VanDusen attempt to re-create the plant life of a number of different environments. Depending on which trail you take, you may find yourself wandering

The Other Suspension Bridge

Lynn Canyon Park—between Grouse Mountain and Mount Seymour Provincial Park in North Vancouver—offers a free alternative to the Capilano Suspension Bridge. True, the **Lynn Canyon Suspension Bridge ★** is both shorter and a little lower than Capilano (p. 91), and it doesn't have all the extra features like the Cliffwalk and Treetops Adventure, but the waterfall and swirling whirlpools in the canyon below add both beauty and a certain fear-inducing fascination. Plus, did I mention it's free?

The park is located in a gorgeous 250-hectare (617-acre) rainforest of cedar and Douglas fir and is also home to an **Ecology Centre** (3663 Park Rd.; _Ⓒ_ **604/990-3755;** www.dnv.org/ecology), which presents natural-history films, tours, and displays that explain the local ecology. Staff members lead frequent walking tours. The park is open daily from 7am to 7pm in spring and fall, 7am to 9pm in summer, and 7am to dusk in winter; it's closed December 25 and 26, and January 1.

About 4km (2½ miles) up Lynn Valley Road from the highway is **Lynn Headwaters Regional Park ★★** (_Ⓒ_ **604/985-1690** for trail conditions), one of the best places close to the city where you can experience the breathtaking nature of the Northwest. Until the mid-1980s, this was inaccessible wilderness and bear habitat, but the park and the bears are now managed by the Greater Vancouver Regional Parks Department. Some of the 14 marked trails and scrambles of various levels of difficulty meander by the riverbank, while others climb steeply up to various North Shore peaks, and one trail leads to a series of cascading waterfalls.

To get to Lynn Canyon Park, take Hwy. 1 to the Lynn Valley Road exit, then follow Lynn Valley Road to Peters Road and turn right. For Lynn Headwaters Park, continue to the end of Lynn Valley Road. Or take bus no. 229 from Lonsdale Quay.

through the Southern Hemisphere section, the Sino-Himalayan garden, or the glade of Giant Redwoods. Should all this tree-gazing finally pall, head for the farthest corner of the garden to the devilishly difficult Elizabethan garden maze.

5251 Oak St., at W. 37th Ave. _Ⓒ_ **604/878-9274.** www.vandusengarden.org. Admission Apr–Sept C$11 adults, C$8 seniors and children 13–18, C$6 children 3–12, free children 2 and under, C$25 families. Reduced admission Oct–March. Daily 10am to dusk. Bus: no. 17.

Outlying Attractions

Burnaby Village Museum ★ HISTORIC SITE   Step back into the 1920s in this living history museum with costumed "townspeople" to show you the way. An entire town has been recreated here, and you may want to slip into a cloche or spats as you stroll along the boardwalk past the general store, vintage ice cream parlor, and one-room schoolhouse. One of the biggest attractions is the restored 1912 carousel—be sure to take a spin—it's only $2.50 per ride! In 2014, the park will be heading to the movies, with its special exhibit focusing on Burnaby's film and TV industry. It's always fun to visit this historic site, but one of the best times to drop by is at Christmas, when the whole village is aglow in lights and Victorian decorations. If you have time, explore the neighborhood, which is filled with big old mansions turned into art galleries.

6501 Deer Lake Ave., Burnaby. _Ⓒ_ **604/293-6501.** www.burnabyvillagemuseum.ca. Free admission. Open seasonally: May–Sept 1 Tues–Sun 11am–4:30pm; "Haunted Village" late Oct; "Holiday Village" mid-Nov to Dec Tues–Sun 1–5:30pm; mid-Dec to Jan 1 Tues–Sun 1–9pm. Closed Mon (open holidays) and Dec 24–25. Bus: 144 SFU (from Metrotown SkyTrain Station) to Deer Lake.

THE riches OF RICHMOND

If you arrive in Vancouver by plane, you'll actually be landing in the city of Richmond. It's just too bad that the airport is all that many visitors—and, indeed, locals—ever see of this fascinating community.

Richmond is by way of being **Vancouver's new Chinatown.** Some of the residents moved here from the old Chinatown in downtown Vancouver, but the population really exploded in the mid-to-late 1990s, around the time of the transfer of Hong Kong's sovereignty back to China, when thousands of wealthy, well-educated Chinese immigrated to Canada. Today, 50% of Richmond's population identifies as Chinese, although there is also a sizable population of Japanese, Filipinos, Koreans, and South Asians as well.

If you visit the heart of Richmond, the so-called **Golden Village,** you'll feel like you landed in a pocket of Hong Kong without paying for airfare. It's modern, sophisticated, and high-tech, with several malls that cater specifically to Asian customers, including Aberdeen Centre, Yaohan Centre, and Parker Place. (Even more exciting for fashionistas is the new **McArthur Glen Designer Outlet Mall,** www.mcarthurglen.com, set to open in Spring 2015 near the airport.)

The shopping is fun, but an even better reason to visit is the food: Richmond is said to have the best Chinese food in the world, a result of the felicitous combination of top-notch Chinese chefs and the exceptional local ingredients they get to work with. The Chinese call the food "clean." It's also delicious, whether you're enjoying the lunch of nibbles known as dim sum, a 10-course Cantonese banquet, the delectable Shanghai soup dumplings called *xiao long bao*, spicy Szechuan *dan-dan* noodles, a sizzling hot pot, the quirky English-Chinese fusion of the Hong Kong cafes, or simply a bowl of mild, comforting congee.

On the other hand, if you prefer traditional, English-style fare, you can head to the historic fishing village of **Steveston** and enjoy a pint and a basket of crispy halibut and chips on a sunny patio along the marina. This is still one of Canada's busiest fishing ports—at the turn of the 20th century, it was the busiest in the world—and it's great fun to watch the boats chugging in and out of the harbor, and the customers lining up for salmon, crab, halibut, or spot prawns in season. The village itself is quaint and cute and fun to explore. Be sure to check out the **Gulf of Georgia Cannery National Historic Site** (12138 4th Ave., Richmond; © **604/664-9009;** www.gulfofgeorgia cannery.com). It's the last remaining cannery of the dozens that once lined this coast, where Europeans, Chinese, Japanese, and First Nations lived and worked together preparing herring and salmon for a hungry marketplace.

Fishing has always been a big industry here, and so is farming—even today, more than a third of Richmond is farmland. A great place to explore the past and future of farming is at **Terra Nova Rural Park** (www.richmond.ca), where several community-minded farming projects are underway, as well as an ongoing restoration of a historic farm and orchard. You can reach it via the easy, flat dyke pathway that circles most of Richmond. The trail is just one of the many parks, gardens, and green spaces in what is nicknamed the "Garden City."

For more information, **Tourism Richmond** (© **604/821-5474;** www. tourismrichmond.com) has an excellent dining guide to the best restaurants, as well as a comprehensive visitor's guide to all the community's many attractions.

Fort Langley National Historic Site ★★ HISTORIC SITE In 1827, the brave adventurers of the Hudson's Bay Company established a settlement in this spot, which became the birthplace of British Columbia. Today, it's a living history museum that offers an intriguing glimpse into the past. Costumed characters demonstrate how to do old-timey things like blacksmithing and making barrels. Younger visitors can join the "Company of Adventurers," and learn those skills, too. All visitors can pan for gold, climb the fort's towers, listen to stories, enjoy a historic afternoon tea, and explore this site. Also worth exploring is nearby Fort Langley Village, where the main street, Glover Road, has great little antiques shops, a bookstore, and cafes, just a short stroll away.

23433 Mavis Ave., Fort Langley. ✆ **604/513-4777.** www.pc.gc.ca/fortlangley. C$8 adults, C$7 seniors, C$4 children 6–16, free children 5 and under; family pass C$20. Daily 10am–5pm. Closed Dec 25–26, Jan1. Take SkyTrain to Surrey Central Station and transfer to bus 501, 502, or 320 to Langley Centre, and then C62 from Walnut Grove to 6th Ave. and Glover Rd.

Especially for Kids

Vancouver is a family-friendly city (well, except for some bits of Granville Street after dark), and there's always something for the kids to do, and it's usually something that has them burning off energy.

To give kids an overview of the city, with clanging bells for special effect, take the trolley tour offered by **Vancouver Trolley Company** (✆ **888/451-5581** or 604/801-5515; www.vancouvertrolley.com). Gas-powered trolleys run through Downtown, Chinatown, the West End, and Stanley Park.

Stanley Park (p. 84) offers a number of attractions for children, including a fabulous and free **Spray Park** near Lumberman's Arch. Some of the most popular options include the **Miniature Railway,** the totem poles at **Brockton Point,** and the immense oceanside pool at **Second Beach.** Oh—and don't forget the **horsedrawn carriage rides** that begin near Lost Lagoon. Your kids will also get a kick out of what appear to be giant bronze trolls, but are actually a sculpture called **"A-maze-ing Laughter,"** by Chinese artist Yue Minjun. It comprises several giant figures making faces (laughing hysterically, according to the artist) in a ring near the south entrance to the park. People tend to love it or hate it, but your kids will probably find it as funny as the artist did.

Also in Stanley Park, the **Vancouver Aquarium** (p. 86) has sea otters, sea lions, whales, penguins, and numerous other marine creatures, as well as many exhibits and special programs geared to children. If you can, see if you can join one of the fun slumber parties.

On the East Side and easily accessible by SkyTrain, **Science World at TELUS World of Science** (p. 91) is a terrific interactive kids' museum where budding scientists can get their hands into everything. Afterwards, they'll love hopping onto one of the small foot passenger ferries that scoot around False Creek to destinations like the **Museum of Vancouver** in Vanier Park (p. 90) and **Granville Island** (p. 88).

Granville Island especially provides enough activities to keep the whole family busy for the whole day. In May, it's the site of the annual **Vancouver International Children's Festival,** which is a great time for the short set to visit. Even if you can't make it to the fest, the **Carousel Theatre for Young People** offers terrific children's programming year round. The **Kids Market** has playrooms and shops filled with toys, books, kites, clothes, and food, and the nearby **waterpark** has movable water guns and sprinklers as well as water slides and a wading pool. There are loads of yummy snacks to be had at the Granville Island Public Market (plus candy and ice cream), and seagulls to chase on the wharf outside. And there are always boats to explore in the busy marina if you get bored of everything else.

Meanwhile, over at Vanier Park, there are three great venues to explore: the **Museum of Vancouver** (p. 90), **Vancouver Maritime Museum** (p. 91), and **H. R. MacMillan Space Centre** (better known as the planetarium; p. 90).

Over on the North Shore, **Maplewood Farm** (405 Seymour River Place, North Vancouver; ✆ **604/929-5610;** www.maplewoodfarm.bc.ca) has more than 200 barnyard animals from cows to chickens living on its 2-hectare (5-acre) farm. Your kids will love playing farmer for a day. There's also the **Capilano Suspension Bridge Park** (p. 91) and the **Lynn Canyon Suspension Bridge** (p. 97), as well as the hiking trails (in summer) and ski slopes (in winter) of **Mount Seymour** (p. 93), **Cypress Mountain** (p. 93), and **Grouse Mountain Resort** (p. 106).

In **Richmond** (see above), they'll enjoy the interactive learning experience—it involves hooking and tossing fake fish, and who doesn't enjoy that?—of the **Gulf of Georgia Cannery National Historic Site,** as well as the fun of hanging out at the marina in the fishing village of Steveston. It's also a good spot to hop aboard a whale-watching excursion (p. 108). Further out in Fraser Valley, a couple of great historic sites offer lots of fun for the whole family: **Burnaby Village Museum** and the **Fort Langley National Historic Site** (see above).

And if you're in town during the summer months, head to **Playland at the Pacific National Exhibition** grounds (Hastings and Renfrew sts.; ✆ **604/253-2311;** www.pne. ca). There are rides, games, stuffed animals to be won, a special area for the littlest kids, and those little donuts everyone loves so much. What could be more fun in the summertime? One-day "Playpass" C$33. Open May through September daily 10am to 6pm.

For even more ideas, pick up Tourism Vancouver's **Kids' Guide** at Granville Island's Kids Market and the visitor center at 200 Burrard St.

Organized Tours

BY AIR   **Harbour Air** (✆ **800/665-0212** or 604/274-1277; www.harbour-air.com) offers daily floatplane flights from the downtown Vancouver terminal next to the Canada Place cruise ship terminal. The 20-minute "Vancouver Panorama" tour (C$114 per person) flies over Stanley Park, the North Shore Mountains, and all around the metro region, giving you an unparalleled bird's-eye view of the magnificent terrain. A variety of other tour options are available, as well as scheduled flights to many destinations around the province.

BY BOAT   **Harbour Cruises** (✆ **604/688-7246;** www.boatcruises.com) will take you on a sunset buffet dinner cruise with onboard entertainment (C$80) or a 4-hour luncheon cruise up the Indian Arm inlet (C$65) for a blend of the scenic and the savory. If time is tight, Harbour Cruises also conducts a 1-hour narrated harbor tour aboard the MPV *Constitution,* a 19th-century sternwheeler with a smokestack (C$30 adults, C$25 seniors and children 12–17, C$10 children 5–11, free for children 4 and under).

Accent Cruises (✆ **800/993-6257** or 604/688-6625; www.accentcruises.ca) runs a sunset cruise most nights from Granville Island, departing at 6pm depending on availability, with a chicken-and-salmon buffet (C$65 per person).

Paddlewheeler Riverboat Tours (✆ **604/525-4465;** www.vancouverpaddle wheeler.com) offers sunset dinner cruises that depart from New Westminster Quay and sail along the mighty Fraser River aboard the 19th-century vessel SS *Native* (C$65 adults, C$60 seniors, C$50 children 6–12), as well as day trips to historic Fort Langley, Steveston, and Harrison Hot Springs.

BY BUS   **Big Bus** (© **877/299-0701** or 604/299-0700; www.bigbus.ca) runs a fleet of double-decker buses on a 90-minute "hop-on, hop-off" sightseeing loop around the city. A good place to start the tour is at Canada place, and buses roll by frequently. Two-day passes C$45 adults, C$40 students and seniors, and C$25 children 6 to 12, free for children 5 and under, and C$115 family pass.

Landsea Tours (© **877/669-2277** or 604/255-7272; www.vancouvertours.com) offers a wide array of tour options, including a 4-hour city highlights tour through Vancouver in a 24-person van. Offered daily year-round at 10am, and April to early November at 2pm as well (C$75 adults, C$45 children). You can also take a tour up to Grouse Mountain and the Capilano Suspension Bridge well as tours of wineries, Victoria, Whistler, and the new Sea to Sky excursion.

Vancouver Trolley Company (© **888/451-5581** or 604/801-5515; www.vancouver trolley.com) operates gas-powered trolleys on a route through downtown, the West End, Stanley Park, Kitsilano, Yaletown, and Chinatown. Tours depart every 20 minutes from 30 stops, where passengers can get on and off, explore, and catch another scheduled trolley. Onboard, drivers provide detailed commentary. Purchase 1-day and 2-day tickets from the driver or, in summer, at the Gastown ticket booth at 157 Water St. Two-day fare C$45 adults, C$40 seniors and children 13 to 18, and C$25 children 4 to 12.

FIRST NATIONS TOURS   The Tsleil-Waututh Nation of North Vancouver leads a number of cultural and eco tours that provide an introduction to both First Nations culture and the stunning Indian Arm fjord. Their company, **Takaya Tours** (© **604/904-7410;** www.takayatours.com) operates from the Cates Park Paddling Centre in North Vancouver in summer (© **604/985-2925**), and conducts a roster of outdoor tours ranging from nature walks to cultural boat excursions. Prices run from C$35 to C$95, with dinner options available for groups.

GOURMET TOURS   Vancouver Foodie Tours (© **877/804-9220** or 604/295-8844; http://foodietours.ca) offers walking tours of some of the city's best dining options—there's a food truck tour (C$49 per person), "guilty pleasures" gourmet tour (C$69), and a Granville Island Market tour (C$49). Tours are led by well-informed and passionate local foodies, and are a great way to discover the delectable tastes of the city.

Chef and Chauffeur (© **604/267-1000;** www.chefandchauffeur.com) runs several tours of the Fraser Valley, located an hour east of the city, and the more distant Okanagan Valley, famed for its fruit, produce, meats, cheeses, and wines. Participants start the day with coffee, fresh orange juice, and cinnamon buns or berry scones while their guide maps out the day's adventures. The tours, in a luxury SUV, visit a variety of wineries, farms, bakeries, and cheese makers. Optional dinner and overnight add-ons are available. Tours range from C$200 to C$3,000 per person.

Swallow Tail Tours (© **778/855-9453;** www.swallowtail.ca) offers a variety of gourmet tours of Vancouver and the surrounding area. For instance, the Canapé Crawl visits three top restaurants where participants get to sample tasting plates paired with beer, wine, and craft cocktails (C$100 per person). Other tours might head into wine country, go foraging in the forest, or crabbing on the beach.

WALKING TOURS   **Forbidden Vancouver** (© **604/839-3126;** http://forbidden vancouver.ca) takes you on a journey into Vancouver's dangerous, disreputable past with a number of entertaining walking tours. The Lost Souls of Gastown tour, for instance, resurrects the wild frontier days of the 1800s; Prohibition City introduces you to the speakeasies, gangsters, corrupt pols, and dirty cops of the 1920s. Tours are led by expert storytellers in costume. The cost is C$22 adults, C$19 seniors and students, more for "special event" tours.

During the summer months (July–Aug), the **Architectural Institute of BC (𝒸 604/683-8588,** ext. 306; www.aibc.ca) offers a number of **architectural walking tours** of downtown Vancouver neighborhoods, including Chinatown and Granville Island, for only C$10 per person. The 2-hour tours run on a rotating basis Tuesday through Saturday, departing at 1pm sharp from the AIBC Architecture Centre at 440 Cambie St. Call or visit the website for details and to book.

If you want to organize your own walking tour—say, through the West End, Shaughnessy, or Gastown/Chinatown—**Tourism Vancouver** has lots of tips, maps, and advice for you. Drop by the visitor center at 200 Burrard St., call 𝒸 **604/682-2222,** or visit www.tourismvancouver.com.

4 | Outdoor Activities

BEACHES Vancouver is surrounded by beaches, and there has to be one that suits your style, whether it's the see-and-be-seen Kits Beach, the clothing-optional Wreck Beach, or the family-friendly Spanish Banks. And even though Vancouver has a reputation for endless rain, the summers here are actually quite dry and sunny, so there's lots of opportunity to soak in the sun. Here are some of the best.

English Bay Beach at the end of Davie Street, off Denman Street and Beach Avenue, is a busy spot, where all the residents of the West End flock on sunny weekends. Everyone, and just about everything, goes here. Its centerpiece is the historic Art Deco bathhouse, built in 1932, now the site of a Cactus Club Café, and in summer, a huge playground slide is mounted on a raft just off the beach. This is a great spot to walk the dog or watch the sunset.

On **Stanley Park**'s western rim, **Second Beach** is a short stroll north from English Bay Beach and features a playground, snack bar, and an immense heated oceanside pool that's open from Victoria Day weekend through Labour Day weekend. This is a convenient and fun spot for families. Farther along the seawall, due north of Stanley Park Drive, lies secluded **Third Beach,** a popular spot for summer barbecues. Oddly enough, there's no First Beach.

South of English Bay Beach, near the Burrard Street Bridge, is **Sunset Beach.** Running along False Creek, it's actually a picturesque strip of sandy beaches filled with enormous driftwood logs that serve as windbreaks and provide a little privacy for sunbathers and picnickers. A snack bar, basketball courts, and a long, gently sloping grassy hill are available for people who prefer lawn to sand.

On the West Side, **Kitsilano Beach,** along Cornwall Street near Arbutus Street, is affectionately called Kits Beach. It's an easy walk from the Maritime Museum and the False Creek ferry dock. If you want to do a saltwater swim but can't handle the cold, head to the huge, heated **Kitsilano Pool.**

Farther west on the other side of Hastings Mill Park is **Jericho Beach** (Alma St. off Point Grey Rd.), another local after-work and weekend social spot. **Locarno Beach,** at the north end of Trimble and Tolmie streets, and **Spanish Banks,** on Northwest Marine Drive, lead to the Point Grey Foreshore that wraps around the northern point of the UBC campus and University Hill. (Note that the beachside restrooms and concessions end abruptly at Spanish Banks East.)

Below UBC's Museum of Anthropology is **Point Grey Beach,** a restored harbor-defense site. The next beach is **Wreck Beach,** Canada's largest nude beach. You get down to Wreck Beach by taking the steep Trails 4 or 6 on the UBC campus, which lead down to the water's edge. Extremely popular with locals and maintained by its own preservation society, Wreck Beach is also the city's most pristine and least-developed sandy stretch, bordered on three sides by towering trees.

For information on any of Vancouver's many beaches, call ✆ **604/738-8535** (summer only).

On the North Shore, the coastline tends to be rocky and inhospitable, more cliff than beach, but **Ambleside Park** is one popular spot where you can shake out your towel. It's located at the northern foot of the Lions Gate Bridge, facing Burrard Inlet.

CANOEING, KAYAKING & PADDLEBOARDING Both placid, urban False Creek and the beautiful 30km (20-mile) North Vancouver fjord known as Indian Arm have launching points that can be reached by car or bus.

Ecomarine Ocean Kayak Centre (1668 Duranleau St., Granville Island; ✆ **888/425-2925** or 604/689-7575; www.ecomarine.com) has 2-hour, daily, and weekly kayak rentals, as well as courses and organized tours. The company also has an office at the **Jericho Sailing Centre** (1300 Discovery St., at Jericho Beach; ✆ **604/224-4177;** www.jsca.bc.ca). In North Vancouver, **Deep Cove Canoe and Kayak Rentals** (2156 Banbury Rd., at the foot of Gallant St.; ✆ **604/929-2268;** www.deepcovekayak.com) is an easy starting point for anyone planning an Indian Arm run. It offers hourly and daily rentals of canoes and kayaks, as well as lessons and customized tours. Prices range from about C$40 per 2-hour minimum rental to C$80 per 4 hours for single kayaks and about C$60 for canoe rentals. Customized tours range from C$75 to C$150 per person. Paddleboards generally run C$19 per hour, or C$29 for 2 hours.

Lotus Land Tours (2005–1251 Cardero St.; ✆ **800/528-3531** or 604/684-4922; www.lotuslandtours.com) runs guided kayak tours on Indian Arm that come with hotel pickup, a barbecue salmon lunch, and incredible scenery. The wide, stable kayaks are perfect for first-time paddlers. One-day tours are C$200 adults, C$190 seniors, C$130 children 5 to 12.

CYCLING & MOUNTAIN BIKING Cycling in Vancouver is fun, scenic, and very, very popular. It helps that there are so many bike paths around the city, including along many of the busiest streets. Cycling maps are available at most bicycle retailers and rental outlets. Some West End hotels offer guests bike storage and rentals, even free bikes to tootle around on. Rentals run around C$8 to C$16 an hour for a mountain or city bike, C$30 to C$60 for a day; helmets and locks are included. Popular shops that rent city and mountain bikes, child trailers, child seats, and in-line skates (protective gear included) include **Spokes Bicycle Rentals & Espresso Bar** (1798 W. Georgia St.; ✆ **604/688-5141;** www.spokesbicyclerentals.com) and **Bayshore Bicycle and Rollerblade Rentals** (745 Denman St.; ✆ **604/688-2453;** www.bayshorebikerentals. ca), both right near the entrance to Stanley Park. *Note:* Be advised that wearing a helmet is mandatory, and one will be included in your bike rental.

The most popular cycling path in the city runs along the **Seawall** around the perimeter of Stanley Park. Offering magnificent views of the city, the Burrard Inlet, the mountains, and English Bay, this flat, approximately 10km (6¼-mile) pathway attracts year-round bicyclists, in-line skaters, and pedestrians. (*Note:* Runners and cyclists have separate lanes on developed park and beach paths.) Another popular route is the

seaside bicycle route, a 15km (9-mile) ride that begins at English Bay and continues around False Creek to the University of British Columbia. Some of this route follows city streets that are well marked with cycle-path signs.

Serious mountain bikers also have a wealth of world-class options within a short drive from downtown Vancouver. The trails on **Mount Fromme** near Grouse Mountain are some of the Lower Mainland's best. Local mountain bikers love the cross-country ski trails on around **Hollyburn Lodge** in **Cypress Provincial Park,** just northeast of Vancouver on the road to Whistler on Highway 99. Closer to downtown, both **Pacific Spirit Park** and **Burnaby Mountain** offer excellent beginner and intermediate off-road trails.

ECOTOURS **Lotus Land Tours** runs guided kayak tours on Indian Arm (see "Canoeing, Kayaking & Paddleboarding," above). From late November to the end of January, this small local company also offers unique float trips on the Squamish River to see the large concentration of bald eagles up close.

Rockwood Adventures (© **888/236-6606** or 604/741-0802; www.rockwood adventures.com) has 4-hour **guided walks of the North Shore rainforest,** complete with a trained naturalist, stops in Capilano Canyon and at the Lynn Canyon Suspension Bridge, and lunch. Cost is C$95 adults, C$85 seniors and students 12 to 25, and C$60 children 4 to 11.

Sewell's Marina in Horseshoe Bay (© **604/921-3474;** www.sewellsmarina.com) offers **"sea safari"** Zodiac tours of Howe Sound, its islands, and its population of seabirds and marine mammals. Two-hour sea safari C$85 adults, C$75 seniors and students, C$55 children 5 to 12. Shuttle transfer available at C$18 per person. Daily, April to October. Reservations required.

GOLF With five public 18-hole courses, half a dozen pitch-and-putt courses in the city, and dozens more courses nearby, golfers are never far from their love. For discounts and short-notice tee times at more than 30 Vancouver-area courses, contact the **A-1 Last Minute Golf Hot Line** (© **800/684-6344** or 604/878-1833; www.lastminutegolfbc.com).

A number of excellent public golf courses, maintained by the **Vancouver Board of Parks and Recreation** (© **604/280-1818** to book tee times; www.vancouver.ca/parks), can be found throughout the city. **Langara Golf Course** (6706 Alberta St., around 49th Ave. and Cambie St.; © **604/713-1816;** www.vancouver.ca/parks/golf/langara), built in 1926 by the Canadian Pacific Railway and recently renovated and redesigned, is one of the most popular golf courses in the province.

The public **University Golf Club** (5185 University Blvd.; © **604/224-1818;** www.universitygolf.com) is a great 6,300-yard, par-72 course with a clubhouse, pro shop, locker rooms, bar and grill, and sports lounge.

Leading private clubs are situated on the North Shore and in Vancouver. Check with your club at home to see if you have reciprocal visiting memberships with one of the following: **Capilano Golf and Country Club** (420 Southborough Dr., West Vancouver; © **604/922-9331;** www.capilanogolf.com), **Marine Drive Golf Club** (7425 Yew St.; © **604/261-8111;** www.marine-drive.com), **Seymour Golf and Country Club** (3723 Mt. Seymour Pkwy., North Vancouver; © **604/929-2611;** www.seymourgolf.com), **Point Grey Golf and Country Club** (3350 SW Marine Dr.; © **604/261-3108;** www.pointgreygolf.com), and **Shaughnessy Golf and Country Club** (4300 SW Marine Dr.; © **604/266-4141;** www.shaughnessy.org). Greens fees range from C$42 to C$75.

HIKING   Great trails for hikers of all levels run through Vancouver's dramatic environs. You can pick up a local trail guide at any bookstore. Good trail maps are also available from **International Travel Maps and Books** (12300 Bridgeport Rd., Richmond; ℂ **604/273-1400;** www.itmb.com), which also stocks guidebooks and topographical maps. The retail store is open Monday to Saturday 9:30am to 5pm, or you can order maps online.

If you're looking for a challenge without a longtime commitment, hike the aptly named **Grouse Grind** from the bottom of **Grouse Mountain** (p. 92) to the top; then buy a one-way ticket (C$5) down on the Grouse Mountain Skyride gondola.

Lynn Canyon Park, Lynn Headwaters Regional Park, Capilano River Regional Park, Mount Seymour Provincial Park, Pacific Spirit Park, and **Cypress Provincial Park** (see "Parks & Gardens," p. 92) have good, easy-to-strenuous trails that wind through stands of Douglas fir and cedar, and contain a few serious switchbacks. Pay attention to the trail warnings posted at the parks (some have bear habitats) and always remember to sign in with the park service at the start of your chosen trail.

A little farther outside the city, the 9- to 12-hour hike to **Black Tusk** is one of the finest hikes in North America and is often completed over 2 days, overnighting at the primitive campground on Garibaldi Lake. Located in **Garibaldi Provincial Park** (ℂ **604/898-3678**), the trailhead is 34km (21 miles) north of Squamish, which is 65km (40 miles) north of downtown Vancouver along Highway 99 on the road to Whistler. The park has five access points; Black Tusk/Garibaldi Lake is the second marked turnoff (it takes about an hour to get there). The trail switchbacks up nearly 1,000m (3,300 ft.) in about 9km (5.5 miles), then levels onto a rolling alpine plateau with fabulous views before another 850m (2,800 ft.) climb over 7km (4 miles) to Black Tusk. The best time to make this climb is for the wildflowers in late July and August, although the trail is usually clear through October.

ICE SKATING   The highest ice-skating rink in Canada is located on **Grouse Mountain** (p. 92); it's an outdoor pond rink, and with the altitude and all, can be quite chilly in winter, so be sure to bundle up. Skating is free with your Skyride ticket, and you can rent skates on location. In the city, **Robson Square Ice Rink** (p. 82) also offers free outdoor skating in winter.

The **Richmond Olympic Oval** (6111 River Rd., Burnaby; ℂ **778/296-1400;** www. richmondoval.ca), home to the long-track speed skating events during the 2010 Winter Games, now has two Olympic-size rinks available year-round for drop-in skating. It's a gorgeous building, and a fantastic, state-of-the art facility. Another good venue is the enormous **Burnaby 8 Rinks Ice Sports Centre** (6501 Sprott St., Burnaby; ℂ **604/291-0626;** www.icesports.com/burnaby8rinks), which is also open year-round, and offers lessons and rentals. Call ahead to check hours for public skating at all these rinks.

PARAGLIDING   In Surrey, **Deimos Paragliding Flight School** (ℂ **877/359-7413** or 604/200-2029; www.deimospg.com) offers tandem flights from Burnaby Mountain and other locations starting at C$200 per person. No experience is necessary for this unforgettable adventure; the actual flights, controlled by an experienced instructor, take 10 to 30 minutes.

RUNNING   Local runners traverse the **Stanley Park Seawall** and the park paths around **Lost Lagoon** and **Beaver Lake.** If you're a dawn or dusk runner, take note that this is one of the world's safer city parks. However, if you're alone, don't tempt fate—stick to open and lighted areas. Other prime jogging areas are **Kitsilano Beach, Jericho Beach,** and **Spanish Banks** (see "Beaches," earlier in this chapter); all of them offer flat running paths along the ocean. You can also take the seawall path from English Bay Beach south along **False Creek.** If you feel like doing a little racing, competitions take place throughout the year; ask for information at any runners' outfitters such as **Forerunners** (3504 W. 4th Ave.; ✆ **604/732-4535**) or **Running Room** (679 Denman St., near the entrance to Stanley Park; ✆ **604/684-9771**). Check www.runningroom. com for information on clinics and events around Vancouver and British Columbia.

SKIING & SNOWBOARDING
World-class skiing lies outside the city at the **Whistler Blackcomb Ski Resort,** 110km (70 miles) north of Vancouver; see chapter 5. However, you don't have to leave the city to get in a few runs. It seldom snows in the city's downtown and central areas, but Vancouverites can ski before work and after dinner at the three ski resorts in the North Shore mountains. These local mountains played host to the freestyle and snowboard events in the 2010 Winter Games.

Grouse Mountain Resort (6400 Nancy Greene Way, North Vancouver; ✆ **604/984-0661,** or 604/986-6262 for a snow report; www.grousemountain.com) has four chairs, 26 alpine runs, and a Magic Carpet for beginners. The resort has night skiing, special events, instruction, and a spectacular view, as well as a terrain park for snowboarders. All skill levels are covered, with 3 beginner trails, 15 blue trails, 6 black-diamond runs, and 2 double-black-diamond runs. Rental packages and a full range of facilities are available. Lift tickets good for all-day skiing are C$58 adults, C$45 seniors and children 13 to 18, C$25 children 5 to 12, and free for children 4 and under. Lift prices do not include your gondola ride to the summit.

Mount Seymour Provincial Park (1700 Mt. Seymour Rd., North Vancouver; ✆ **604/986-2261;** www.mountseymour.com) has the area's highest base elevation; it's accessible via four chairs and a tow. In addition to 39 runs for day or night skiing, the facility offers snowboarding, cross-country, and tobogganing as well as 10km (6 miles) of snowshoeing trails. The resort specializes in teaching first-timers. Camps for children and teenagers, and adult clinics, are available throughout the winter. Mount Seymour has one of Western Canada's largest equipment rental shops, which will keep your measurements on file for return visits. All-day lift tickets are C$53 adults, C$39 seniors, C$45 children 13 to 19, and C$25 children 6 to 12. Nighttime skiing (4–10pm) costs less. Shuttle service is available during ski season from various locations on the North Shore, including the Lonsdale Quay SeaBus.

Cypress Bowl (top of Cypress Bowl Rd.; ✆ **604/926-5612,** or 604/419-7669 for a snow report; www.cypressmountain.com) was home to the 2010 Winter Games freestyle skiing (moguls and aerials), snowboarding (half-pipe and parallel giant slalom), and new ski-cross events. In the leadup to the Games, Cypress opened nine new runs for intermediate and expert skiers and snowboarders, a new quad chairlift, and a new day lodge. Cypress has the area's longest vertical drop, challenging ski and snowboard runs, and 19km (12 miles) of track-set cross-country ski trails. Lift tickets are C$62 adults, C$40 seniors, C$46 youth, and C$25 children.

TENNIS
The city maintains more than 180 outdoor hard courts that operate on a first-come, first-served basis (with a 30-min. time limit when all courts are full) from 8am until dusk. Predictably, heavy usage times are evenings and weekends. With the exception of the Beach Avenue courts, which charge a nominal fee in summer, all city courts are free.

Stanley Park has four courts near Lost Lagoon and 17 courts near the Beach Avenue entrance, next to the Fish House Restaurant on Stanley Park Drive. During the summer season (May–Sept), six courts are taken over for pay tennis and can be

OLYMPIC legacy

One of the best legacies of the 2010 Winter Olympic and Paralympic Games was the venues that remained after the athletes left. It wasn't just the Canada Line and an improved Sea to Sky Highway that were the result, but several world-class places to walk, skate, ski, or snowboard. Want to work out like an Olympian? You can, at these venues:

- **Richmond Olympic Oval** (p. 105), a venue for speed skating during the 2010 Winter Games, now offers multiple skating rinks, ball courts, and a first-class fitness center. The facility is open Monday through Friday 6am to 11pm, and weekends 8am to 9pm.

- **Cypress Mountain** (p. 93). For many winters to come, you'll be able to ski and snowboard the Olympic runs on Cypress Mountain, home of Canada's first gold medal of the 2010 Winter Games.

- **Vancouver Olympic Centre** (4575 Clancy Loranger Way; www.vancouver.ca/parks/info/2010olympics/hillcrest.htm). Home to the Olympic and Paralympic curling events, this is now an aquatic center, although eight curling ice sheets still remain.

- **BC Place Stadium** (777 Pacific Blvd.; ✆ **604/669-2300;** www.bcplacestadium.com). You may remember the stadium from the opening and closing ceremonies—if not, the Olympic memorabilia in the BC Sports Hall of Fame & Museum (✆ **604/687-5520;** www.bcsportshalloffame.com) may remind you. Find Olympic and Paralympic torches, medals, and uniforms, as well as artifacts from other sporting events. Open daily; C$15 adult; C$12 seniors, students, and children 6–17; free children 5 and under.

- **Olympic Village (Southeast False Creek).** Once where the athletes stayed, this is now Vancouver's hottest new neighborhood. Walk the False Creek seawall from Science World toward Granville Island and check out the new Creekside community center, inviting public spaces, and historical Salt Building at 85 W. 1st Ave., which has been converted into a restaurant.

- **Whistler Sliding Centre** (4910 Glacier Lane, Whistler; ✆ **604/964-0040;** www.whistlerslidingcentre.com). If you ever wanted to hurl yourself head first at insane speeds down a narrow, winding, icy chute, then this is the place for you. Site of the bobsled, skeleton, and luge events during the Games, this is now a training facility that is also open to the public. A tour with one ride down the track is about C$90 a person. For more Whistler Olympic venues, see chapter 5.

pre-booked by calling ✆ **604/605-8224. Queen Elizabeth Park**'s 17 courts service the central Vancouver area, and **Kitsilano Beach Park**'s 10 courts service the beach area between Vanier Park and the UBC campus.

The **UBC Tennis Centre** (6160 Thunderbird Blvd.; ✆ **604/822-2505;** www.tennis.ubc.ca) re-opened in 2011 with 12 indoor courts and one outdoor court. Indoor courts are C$25 to C$31 per hour, depending on the time.

WILDLIFE-WATCHING **Orcas, or killer whales,** are the largest mammals to be seen in Vancouver's waters (except for the odd gray whale, such as the one that swam into False Creek in May 2010). Three pods (families) of orcas, numbering about 80 whales, return to this area every year to feed on the salmon that spawn in the Fraser River starting in May and continuing into October. From April through October, daily excursions offered by **Vancouver Whale Watch** (12240 2nd Ave., Richmond; ✆ **604/ 274-9565;** www.vancouverwhalewatch.com) focus on the majestic whales, plus Dall's porpoises, sea lions, seals, eagles, herons, and other wildlife. The cost is C$130 adult, C$100 seniors and students, C$75 children 4 to 12. **Steveston Seabreeze Adventures** (12551 No. 1 Rd., Richmond; ✆ **604/272-7200;** www.seabreezeadventures.ca) also offers whale-watching tours for about the same price. Both companies offer a shuttle service from downtown Vancouver.

Thousands of **migratory birds** following the Pacific flyway rest and feed in the Fraser River delta south of Vancouver, especially at the 300-hectare (740-acre) **George C. Reifel Bird Sanctuary** (5191 Robertson Rd., Westham Island; ✆ **604/946-6980;** www.reifelbirdsanctuary.com), which was created by a former bootlegger and wetland-bird lover. Many other waterfowl species have made this a permanent habitat. An observation tower, 7km (4 miles) of paths, birdseed for sale, and picnic tables make this wetland reserve an ideal outing spot from October to April, when the birds are wintering in abundance. The sanctuary is wheelchair accessible and open daily from 9am to 4pm. Admission is C$5 adults, C$3 seniors and children.

The **Richmond Nature Park** (11851 Westminster Hwy.; ✆ **604/718-6188**) was established to preserve the **Lulu Island wetlands bog.** It features a Nature House with educational displays and a boardwalk-encircled duck pond. On Sunday afternoons at 2pm, knowledgeable guides give free tours. Admission is by donation.

To connect with local Vancouver birders, try the **Vancouver Natural History Society** (✆ **604/737-3074;** www.naturevancouver.ca). This all-volunteer organization runs birding field trips most weekends; many are free.

During the winter, thousands of **bald eagles**—in fact, the largest number in North America—line the banks of the Squamish, Cheakamus, and Mamquam rivers to feed on spawning salmon. To get there by car, take the **scenic Sea-to-Sky Highway** (Hwy. 99) from downtown Vancouver to Squamish and Brackendale; the trip takes about an hour. Contact the **Squamish Adventure Centre** (✆ **604/815-5084;** www.adventure centre.ca) for more information.

The annual **summer salmon runs** attract more than bald eagles. Tourists flock to coastal streams and rivers to watch the waters turn red with leaping coho and sockeye. The salmon are plentiful at the **Capilano Salmon Hatchery** (p. 93), **Goldstream Provincial Park** on Vancouver Island, and numerous other fresh waters.

Stanley Park (p. 84) is home to a **heron rookery** and you can see these large birds nesting just outside the Vancouver Aquarium. Ravens, dozens of species of waterfowl, raccoons, skunks, beavers, gray squirrels, and even coyotes are also full-time residents. For more information, drop by the **Lost Lagoon Nature House.**

WINDSURFING Windsurfing is not allowed at the mouth of False Creek near Granville Island, but you can bring a board to **Jericho** (p. 102) and **English Bay beaches** (p. 102), or rent one there. Equipment sales, rentals (including wet suits), and instruction can be found at **Windsure Windsurfing School** (1300 Discovery St., at Jericho Beach; ✆ **604/224-0615;** www.windsure.com). Rentals start at about C$20 per hour, wet suit and life jacket included. Windsure also rents skimboards, C$22 per day, which can be used on the sandy flats along the Point Grey Foreshore.

SHOPPING

Vancouver is becoming a great shopping town, in spite of all the taxes, duties, and mysteriously higher prices on this side of the U.S. border. Suddenly, high-end retailers are building flagship stores here. A luxury outlet mall is opening near the airport. The much-anticipated Nordstrom is, at long last, opening on Granville Street. Every day seems to bring a new designer boutique to Robson, Burrard, or Alberni Street. Sadly, the funky old shops selling tchotchkes, clogs, roach clips, and magazines in foreign languages, well, they're all vanishing. But I bet you'll find something great to take home with you nonetheless. Just be sure to bring your credit cards and start by exploring these main shopping areas.

Robson Street

Once known as "Robsonstrasse" for all its German and Eastern European delis, bakeries, cobblers, and bookstores, this is now designer fashion central. Indeed, it's been said that the intersection of Robson and Burrard streets gets more foot traffic than any other corner in Canada; the Tiffany store at the corner of Alberni Street reportedly has the highest sales per square foot of any of the jeweler's stores. You can expect to find well-known high-end international brand names here, and even more down Alberni Street, which runs parallel to Robson.

South Granville

The 10-block stretch of Granville Street, from 6th Avenue up to 16th Avenue, is where Vancouver's old-money enclave of Shaughnessy comes to shop. Classic and expensive clothiers, and housewares and furniture boutiques, predominate. This is also the heart of the gallery district.

Gastown

Not so long ago, pretty much all you could find here was tacky souvenir and head shops. Now Water, Cordova, and the side streets in between are filled with cute boutiques and local designer ateliers. Look for antiques, trendy decor pieces, modern furniture, First Nations art, and edgy local fashions. Be sure to visit the treasure trove (or piles of junk, depending on your perspective) that is Salmagundi West on Cordova Street, as well as the over-the-top fabulousness that is the concept store Secret Location on Water Street.

Main Street

This is still the city's antiques row, but gradually the Art Deco lamps and mid-20th-century dining sets are being edged out by local designers, trendy eateries, and contemporary decor shops. Still, you can find everything from Art Nouveau to country kitchen to fine Second Empire, and every store seems to have its own specialty.

Granville Island

The Granville Island Public Market is a fantastic place to shop for foodie souvenirs like smoked salmon, handmade chocolate art, or dried BC morel mushrooms. But the rest of the island also features tons of great shopping, include arts and crafts, maritime gear, cookbooks, hats, jewelry, fancy paper, kitchen gear, and local wine, beer, sake, and spirits. Two places to check out: Kids Market, a kind of mini-mall for children; and Edible Canada at the Market, which features foodstuffs from all over BC.

Richmond

The Golden Village—the commercial area around Richmond's No. 3 Road, between Capstan and Alderbridge roads—is a little slice of modern Hong Kong, with four malls and countless small shops that cater to Vancouver's Asian communities. **Aberdeen Centre** (4151 Hazelbridge Way; ✆ **604/270-1234**; www.aberdeencentre.com) and the adjacent **Yaohan Centre** (3700 No. 3 Rd.; ✆ **604/231-0601**; www.yaohancentre.com) are the best of the lot. Both malls have large food courts and specialty shops selling everything from cellphones to candied ginseng and the fake sushi you can often see in restaurant windows, plus Aberdeen Centre is home to **Daiso,** the crazy-awesome Japanese $2 store that's worth a trip all on its own. Note that the malls are all on the Canada Line, so they're easy to get to.

SHOPPING A to Z

ANTIQUES

Bakers Dozen Antiques   This charming shop specializes in antique toys, model ships and boats, folk art, and unusual late 19th- and early-20th-century furniture. 3520 Main St. ✆ **604/879-3348.**

DoDa Antiques   A colorful and eclectic collection of mid-20th-century pieces—costume and estate jewelry, art glass, pottery, paintings, and curios—fills this shop. 434 Richards St. ✆ **604/602-0559.** www.dodaantiques.com.

Uno Langmann Limited   Catering to upscale shoppers, Uno Langmann specializes in European and North American paintings, furniture, silver, and objets d'art from the 18th through early 20th centuries. 2117 Granville St. ✆ **604/736-8825.** www.langmann.com.

Vancouver Flea Market   OK, so it's more likely to be junk than antiques, but it's still fun to spend the day wandering through the more than 350 stalls. Go early, or the savvy shoppers will have already cleaned out the gems. Open weekends and holidays 9am to 5pm. 703 Terminal Ave. ✆ **604/685-0666.** www.vancouverfleamarket.com.

ART

Buschlen Mowatt   This is the city's leading "establishment" gallery. Look for paintings, sculptures, and prints from well-known Canadian and international artists. 111–1445 W. Georgia St. ✆ **604/682-1234.** www.buschlenmowatt.com.

Monte Clark Gallery   This cutting-edge gallery—in the otherwise slightly staid confines of South Granville's gallery row—is one of the best spots to look for that rising superstar without the rising prices. 2339 Granville St. ✆ **800/663-8071** or 604/730-5000. www.monteclarkgallery.com.

BOOKS

Barbara-Jo's Books to Cooks ★   This Kitsilano store near Granville Island has a huge selection of cookbooks and books about food and drink. It also hosts numerous events and cooking classes throughout the year—any celebrity chef who comes through town is sure to pay a visit. There's always something cooking here. 1740 W. 2nd Ave. ✆ **604/688-6755.** www.bookstocooks.com.

Blackberry Books   Although this small Granville Island store tends toward general interest and fiction, they have a healthy selection of books about art, architecture, and, above all, cuisine. They're in the Net Loft, a sort of crafty mall right across from the public market. 110–1666 Johnston St. ✆ **604/685-6188.** www.bbooks.ca.

Chapters   Chapters is Canada's big chain bookstore (along with its sister, Indigo) and you're sure to find all the current titles on the shelves here, along with all the accessories to go with. Think gourmet snacks, music, pretty throws, desk decor, coffee mugs, handbags and the like. Oh, and books, too. 788 Robson St. ℂ **604/682-4066.** 2505 Granville St. ℂ **604/731-7822.** www.chapters.indigo.ca.

International Travel Maps and Books   This store has the best selection of travel books, maps, charts, and globes in town, plus an impressive selection of special-interest British Columbia guides. This is the hiker's best source for detailed topographic charts of the entire province, making it worth the trip to Richmond. 12300 Bridgeport Rd., Richmond. ℂ **604/273-1400.** www.itmb.ca.

Kidsbooks   The largest and most interesting selection of children's literature in the city also has an amazing collection of puppets, games, and toys, and holds regular readings. 3083 W. Broadway. ℂ **604/738-5335.** 3040 Edgemont Blvd. ℂ **604/986-6190.** www.kidsbooks.ca.

Macleod's Books   The kind of dusty, old-fashioned, used bookstore true book-lovers and bibliophiles love to explore, stacked high with reasonably priced books covering every conceivable subject. 455 W. Pender St. ℂ **604/681-7654.**

Pulpfiction Books   New, used, and out-of-print books in a busy and growing independent store with three locations. 2422 Main St. ℂ **604/876-4311.** 2754 W. Broadway. ℂ **604/873-4311.** 1830 Commercial Dr. ℂ **604/251-4311.** www.pulpfictionbooksvancouver.com.

CERAMICS, CHINA, SILVER & CRYSTAL

Gallery of BC Ceramics   This Granville Island gallery is owned and operated by the Potters Guild of British Columbia and features a collection of sculptural and functional ceramic works from more than 100 BC potters. Note that they are closed Mondays in January. 1359 Cartwright St. ℂ **604/669-3606.** www.bcpotters.com.

Martha Sturdy Originals ★★   Local designer Martha Sturdy—once best known for her dramatic jewelry and collectible glassware trimmed in gold leaf—is now creating a critically acclaimed line of cast-resin housewares, as well as limited-edition couches and chairs, and stunning sculptures. Expensive, but, if you've got the dough, the furniture is well worth it. Gallery open by appointment only. 12 W. 5th Ave. ℂ **604/872-5205.** www.marthasturdy.com.

CHINESE GOODS

Cheung Sing Herbal & Birds Nest Co.   If you've never been to a Chinese herbalist, this is the one to try: jars, bins, and boxes full of such exotic things as dried sea horse, thinly sliced deer antler, and bird's nest. It's fun to explore and potentially good for what ails you. Chinese remedies can have side effects, however, so before ingesting anything unfamiliar, consult the on-site herbalist. 5838 Victoria Dr. ℂ **604/322-8063.**

Silk Road Art Trading Co.   This store, with an entrance on Columbia Street and another within Dr. Sun Yat-Sen Park in the Chinese Cultural Centre, sells reproductions of Chinese art objects, including the ancient terra-cotta warriors unearthed in a Chinese emperor's tomb. 561 Columbia St. ℂ **604/688-9305.**

T&T Supermarket   You'll discover racks and racks of goods you won't find at home (unless your home is China), especially in the seafood (live fish, frogs' legs, eels) and produce departments (fire-dragon fruit, lily root, durian). Best of all are the takeout counters where you can pick up noodles, dumplings, sushi, and sweets to go.

One of the most delicious things to do in Vancouver in the summer months is to head out to Richmond and browse your way through one—or both—of its Asian night markets. The tradition of the night market is a longstanding one in many Asian countries and now it has happily been exported to Vancouver. Vendors set up stalls that sell everything from Hello Kitty socks to diamanté iPhone cases, watches, purses, and Chinese art at vastly discounted prices. There's usually live music and games for the kids. But the real attraction is the food: dozens and dozens of stalls serving up sizzling chicken skewers or smoky turkey legs, tender dumplings, sweet fruit drinks, curly "Ro-tatoes," spicy grilled squid, fragrant noodles, crispy bubble waffles and, oh, so much more.

Sadly, the short-lived Chinatown Night Market is no more—it never did really catch on with locals—but there are two popular ones in Richmond: the **Richmond Night Market** (8351 River Rd.; ℂ **604/244-8448;** www.richmondnightmarket. com) and the **International Summer Night Market** (12631 Vulcan Way, Richmond; ℂ **877/278-8008** or 604/278-8000; www.summernightmarket.com). These busy markets are loads of fun, and have the feel of a summer festival, only with amazing food. They run mid-May through Mid-September, open Fridays through Sundays 7pm to midnight (the International Summer Night Market closes an hour earlier on Sun).

There are several locations around Vancouver, including one in Chinatown. 179 Keefer Place. ℂ **604/899-8836.** www.tnt-supermarket.com.

Ten Ren Tea & Ginseng Co.   Whether you prefer the pungent aroma of Chinese black tea or the exotic fragrance of chrysanthemum, jasmine, or ginger flower, you must try the numerous varieties of drinking and medicinal teas in this Chinatown shop. It also carries Korean and American ginseng for a lot less than you might pay elsewhere. 550 Main St. ℂ **604/684-1566.** www.tenren.com.

CIGARS & TOBACCO

City Cigar Company   Stocking extensive selection of Cubans along with brands from the Dominican Republic, Honduras, Spain, and Jamaica, City Cigar Company claims to be the largest cigar shop in the country. There's also a room purely dedicated to pipes and hookahs. Americans, remember: If they're Cuban, you can't bring them home. 888 W. 6th Ave. ℂ **604/879-0208.** www.citycigarcompany.com.

La Casa del Habano   Casa del Habano has Vancouver's largest walk-in humidor. Cigars range in price from a few dollars to more than a hundred. 402 Hornby St. ℂ **604/609-0511.** www.lacasadelhabano.ca.

DEPARTMENT STORES

Hills of Kerrisdale   This neighborhood department store in central Vancouver is a city landmark. Carrying full lines of quality men's, women's, and children's clothes, as well as furnishings and sporting goods, it's a destination for locals because the prices are often lower than those in the downtown core. 2125 W. 41st Ave. ℂ **604/266-9177.** www.hillsofkerrisdale.com.

Holt Renfrew This high-end trend-stocker can be accessed through Pacific Centre shopping mall and features all the hottest designers in a luxury department store setting. 737 Dunsmuir St. ℂ **604/681-3121.** www.holtrenfrew.com.

Hudson's Bay From the establishment of its early trading posts during the 1670s to its modern coast-to-coast department-store chain, Hudson's Bay has built its reputation on quality goods. You can still buy a Hudson's Bay woolen "point" blanket (the colorful stripes originally represented how many beaver pelts each blanket was worth in trade), but you'll also find designer fashions, costume jewelry, housewares, and more. The flagship store downtown has undergone an impressive renovation in the past couple of years, and has become an exciting new-old shopping destination, in part due to the success of its line of Olympic apparel. 674 Granville St. ℂ **604/681-6211.** www.thebay.com.

FASHION FOR CHILDREN

Isola Bella This store imports an exclusive collection of rather expensive, high-fashion newborn and children's clothing from mostly European designers like Bonpoint, Tartine et Chocolat, and Mann. 5692 Yew St. ℂ **604/266-8808.** www.isolabellakids.com.

Please Mum This Kitsilano store sells attractive Canadian-designed toddler's and children's cotton clothing. 3071 W. Broadway. ℂ **604/559-7894.** www.pleasemum.com.

FASHION FOR MEN & WOMEN

Vancouver has the Pacific Northwest's best collection of clothes from Paris, London, Milan, and Rome, in addition to a great assortment of locally made, cutting-edge fashions. It seems that almost every week a new designer or independent boutique opens in Yaletown, Kitsilano, Gastown, along Robson, or on Main Street. International designer outlets include **Chanel Boutique** (inside Holt Renfrew at 737 Dunsmuir St.; ℂ 604/682-0522), **Salvatore Ferragamo** (918 Robson St.; ℂ 604/669-4495), and **Louis Vuitton** (Fairmont Hotel Vancouver, 730 Burrard St.; ℂ 604/696-9404). Note that the **McArthurGlen Designer Outlet Mall** (www.mcarthurglen.com) is expected to open near the Vancouver International Airport in Spring 2015. It's the first North American site for the European outlet chain, and will bring with it top luxury brands like Prada, Gucci, and Valentino at affordable prices. Also opening in Fall 2015 is **Nordstrom,** in the old Eaton's location on Granville Street (www.nordstrom.com). Meanwhile, here are some other great places to shop for designer fashion:

Dream Apparel Big-name designs can be found anywhere, but this little shop is one of the few places to show early collections of clothing and jewelry by local designers. 356 Water St. ℂ **604/683-7326.** www.dreamvancouver.com.

Forge & Form Master Granville Island metal designer Jürgen Schönheit specializes in customized gold and silver jewelry. Renowned for his gold and silver bow ties, he also creates unique "tension set" rings, which hold a stone in place without a setting. The studio (open by appointment) is located just past the False Creek Community Centre. 1334 Cartwright St. ℂ **604/684-6298.**

John Fluevog Boots & Shoes Ltd. This native Vancouverite has a growing international cult following of designers and models clamoring for his funky, urban creations. You'll find outrageous platforms and clogs, Angelic Sole work boots, and a few bizarre experiments for the daring footwear fetishist. You may even meet the designer at one of his two stores. 65 Water St. ℂ **604/688-6228.** 837 Granville St. ℂ **604/688-2828.** www.fluevog.com.

Leone Shop where the stars shop. Versace, Donna Karan, Byblos, Armani, and fabulous Italian and French accessories are sold in this very elegant building; valet parking is provided, as well as private after-hours shopping by appointment for VIPs. Sinclair Centre, 757 W. Hastings St. ℂ **604/683-1133.** www.leone.ca.

Roots Canada Proudly Canadian, this chain features sturdy casual clothing, including leather jackets and bags, footwear, outerwear, and athletic wear for the whole family. 1001 Robson St. (corner of Burrard St.). ℂ **604/683-4305.** www.roots.com.

Secret Location This "concept store" based on the likes of Colette in Paris is unique in Vancouver. It mixes fashion, decor, fine dining, and everything you need to make life utterly fabulous. There is nothing ordinary here, from the David Koma frocks to the Linda Farrow sunglasses. It's a bit of a peacock in rugged Gastown, and a fun place to browse and buy. 1 Water St. ℂ **604/685-0090.** www.secretlocation.ca.

Swimco Located near Kitsilano Beach, this store sells a large variety of bikinis and other bathing suits in the latest styles for men, women, and children. There are a number of locations around Vancouver, but the best is the one in Kitsilano. 2166 W. 4th Ave. ℂ **604/732-7946.** www.swimco.com.

Zonda Nellis Design Ltd. Rich colors and intricate patterns highlight this Vancouver designer's imaginative hand-woven separates, pleated silks, sweaters, vests, and soft knits. Nellis has also introduced a line of hand-painted silks and sumptuous, sheer, hand-painted evening wear. 2203 Granville St. ℂ **604/736-5668.** www.zondanellis.com.

FIRST NATIONS ART & CRAFTS

Coastal Peoples Fine Arts Gallery There are two locations for this showcase of fine First Nations art and jewelry, one in Yaletown and one in Gastown. You can pick up a silver or gold pendant, earrings, or cuff with an image of the Bear, Salmon, Whale, or Raven, drawn from local myths and legends. You can also find Inuit sculptures and items made of glass or wood, as well as precious bentwood boxes, masks, even totem poles. Custom orders can be filled quickly and shipped worldwide. 312 Water St. ℂ **604/684-9222.** 1024 Mainland St. ℂ **604/685-9298.** www.coastalpeoples.com.

Hill's Native Art ★ In a re-creation of a trading post interior, this shop, established in 1946 and claiming to be North America's largest Northwest Coast native art gallery, sells ceremonial masks, Cowichan sweaters, moccasins, wood sculptures, totem poles, silk-screen prints, soapstone sculptures, and gold, silver, and argillite jewelry. 165 Water St. ℂ **604/685-4249.** www.hillsnativeart.com.

Shopping Especially for Kids

Probably the only mall in North America dedicated to kids, the **Kids Market** on Granville Island features a Lilliputian entryway that opens on to toy, craft, and book stores, as well as play areas and services for the younger set, including a "fun hairdresser." 1496 Cartwright St.; ℂ **604/689-8447;** www.kidsmarket.ca.

Kites on Clouds is a little Gastown shop with every type of kite. Prices range from C$10 to C$20 for nylon or Mylar dragon kites to around C$200 for more elaborate ghost clippers and nylon hang-glider kites. The Courtyard, 131 Water St.; ℂ **604/669-5677.**

Inuit Gallery of Vancouver This store is home to one of Canada's foremost collections of Inuit and First Nations art. Prices are for serious buyers, but it's worth a visit. 206 Cambie St. ✆ **604/688-7323.** www.inuit.com.

Khot-La-Cha Art Gallery & Gift Shop Hand-tanned moose-hide crafts; wood-carvings; Cowichan sweaters; porcupine-quill jewelry; and bone, silver, gold, and turquoise accessories are just a few of the selections at this Coast Salish crafts shop on the North Shore. 270 Whonoak St. ✆ **604/987-3339.** www.khot-la-cha.com.

Lattimer Gallery This beautiful gallery showcases museum-quality Pacific Northwest First Nations art, including ceremonial masks, totem poles, limited-edition silk-screen prints, argillite sculptures, and expensive gold and silver jewelry. 1590 2nd Ave. ✆ **604/732-4556.** www.lattimergallery.com.

Marion Scott Gallery/Kardosh Projects For more than 30 years, this gallery has been well regarded for its Inuit and First Nations art collections and recently shifted to showcase more contemporary works by northern artists. 2423 Granville St. ✆ **604/685-1934.** www.marionscottgallery.com.

Museum of Anthropology The recently expanded museum gift shop features excellent and elegant works by contemporary First Nations artisans, as well as books about the culture, and publications on identifying and caring for Pacific Northwest crafts. University of British Columbia, 6393 NW Marine Dr. ✆ **604/822-5087.** www.moa.ubc.ca.

FOOD & KITCHEN GEAR

Chocolate Arts The works at this chocolatier are made with exquisite craftsman-ship. Seasonal treats include pumpkin truffles around Halloween or eggnog truffles for Christmas. They've even made chocolate toolboxes filled with tiny chocolate tools. Look for the all-chocolate diorama in the window—it changes every month or so. 1620 W. 3rd Ave. ✆ **604/739-0475.** www.chocolatearts.com.

Cookworks This attractive Canadian store stocks a finely tuned selection of high-quality, well-designed kitchenware and accessories for the table. 1548 W. Broadway. ✆ **604/731-1148.** 377 Howe St. ✆ **604/662-4918.** www.cookworks.ca.

Edible Canada at the Market This cool little enterprise combines a bistro, shop, and culinary tourism company, all of it supporting locally grown and produced food. This is a great spot to pick up gifts for your foodie friends back home: flavored sea salt, Fraser Valley jam, spice blends by Vikram Vij, Thomas Haas chocolates, and the like. 1596 Johnston St. ✆ **604/682-6681.** www.ediblecanada.com.

Gourmet Warehouse Fancy food, pots, baking sheets, spices, platters, cocktail bitters, gadgets, gear, whatever gourmet thing you're craving, Caren McSherry's huge, well-stocked store will carry it. This store has everything you'd like to have (or could even imagine) in your kitchen. 1340 E. Hastings St. ✆ **604/253-3022.** www.gourmetwarehouse.ca.

Granville Island Public Market ★★★ This huge public market features pro-duce, meats, fish, wines, cheeses, arts and crafts, and lots of unique fast-food counters offering a little of everything. A great place to pick up foodie gifts, like smoked salmon in attractive wooden boxes, as well as a snack for right now. 1669 Johnston St. ✆ **604/666-6477.** www.granvilleisland.com.

The Lobsterman Live lobsters, Dungeness crabs, oysters, mussels, clams, geo-ducks, and scallops are just a few of the varieties of seafood swimming in the saltwater tanks at this Granville Island fish store. The staff steams the food fresh on the spot, free. Salmon and other seafood can also be packed for air travel. 1807 Mast Tower Rd. $\mathcal{C}$ **604/687-4531.** www.lobsterman.com.

Murchie's Tea & Coffee   This Vancouver institution has been the city's main tea and coffee purveyor for more than a century. You'll find everything from Jamaican Blue Mountain and Kona coffees to Lapsang Souchong and Kemun teas. The knowledgeable staff will help you decide which flavors and blends fit your taste. A fine selection of bone china and crystal serving ware, as well as coffeemakers and teapots, are also on sale. 110–1501 W. Broadway. $\mathcal{C}$ **604/733-2281.** 825 W. Hastings St. $\mathcal{C}$ **604/669-0783.** www.murchies.com.

River Market at Westminster Quay   A smaller version of the Granville Island Public Market, this market is located 25 minutes away by SkyTrain from downtown Vancouver. Here, you'll find a variety of gift shops, specialty stores, a food court, a delicatessen, and produce stands. Once you're finished browsing, make sure to have a gander at the neighboring Fraser River. A walkway extends along the river and allows great views of the waterfront, the busy boat traffic, and the occasional seal or sea lion. 810 Quayside Dr., New Westminster. $\mathcal{C}$ **604/520-3881.** www.rivermarket.ca.

HOME FURNISHINGS & ACCESSORIES

The Cross Decor & Design   This lovely Yaletown store is loaded with charm, not to mention irresistible finds like silver Moroccan pouffes, pretty floral teacups, chandeliers, luxury bedding, and a host of things you never needed, but once you discover, you won't be able to live without. 1198 Homer St. $\mathcal{C}$ **604/689-2900.** www.thecross design.com.

Inform Interiors   Chances are you won't be lugging a sofa back home, but this classy interior-design store in Gastown has contemporary lighting, home accessories, and design books, in addition to furniture. A second showroom is right across the street at 97 Water St. 50 Water St. $\mathcal{C}$ **604/682-3868.** www.informinteriors.com.

Parliament Interiors   The store is filled with crisp whites, glimmering metals, and punchy color accents. From bed frames to cushions to jewelry, Parliament stocks a regularly changing rotation of items for all budgets (and luggage restrictions). 115 Water St. $\mathcal{C}$ **604/689-0800.** www.parliamentinteriors.com.

SPORTING GOODS

The 2-block area around the **Mountain Equipment Co-Op** (130 W. Broadway; $\mathcal{C}$ **604/872-7858;** www.mec.ca) at Main and Columbia streets has become "outdoor central," with at least a half-dozen stores, such as **Valhalla Pure Outfitters** (222 W. Broadway; $\mathcal{C}$ **604/872-8872;** www.vpo.ca) and **AJ Brooks** (147 W. Broadway; $\mathcal{C}$ **604/874-1117;** www.ajbrooks.com). Just down the street, you'll find **Taiga** (301 W. Broadway; $\mathcal{C}$ **604/875-8388;** www.taigaworks.ca), which carries inexpensive fleece and other quality outdoor gear.

Meanwhile, the corner of 4th Avenue and Burrard Street has become the spot for high-quality snow/skate/surfboard gear, as well as the place to see top-level boarders and their groupies hanging out. Shops here include **Pacific Boarder** (1793 W. 4th Ave.; $\mathcal{C}$ **604/734-7245;** www.pacificboarder.com), **Showcase** (1766 W. 4th Ave.; $\mathcal{C}$ **604/731-6449;** www.showcasesnowboards.com), and **Westbeach** (1758 W. 4th Ave.; $\mathcal{C}$ **604/734-7252;** www.westbeach.com), as well as Comor Sports (1980 Burrard St.; $\mathcal{C}$ **604/736-7547;** www.comorsports.com).

ENTERTAINMENT & NIGHTLIFE

Vancouver's evening social calendar is filled with a variety of events. Local theater ranges from productions by cutting-edge companies to a Shakespeare festival. There's also top-notch opera, a popular symphony, and folk, film, and jazz festivals that draw people from all over the world. For a late-night crowd, there are the bars, lounges, pubs, clubs, and cafes—lots of them—for every taste, budget, and fetish.

For the best overview of Vancouver's nightlife, pick up a copy of the weekly **"Georgia Straight"** (www.straight.com). The Thursday edition of "The Vancouver Sun" contains the weekly tabloid-format entertainment section **"Westcoast Life."** The monthly **"Vancouver"** magazine (www.vanmag.com) is filled with listings and strong views about what's really hot in the city. Or get a copy of **"Xtra! West"** (www. xtra.ca), the free gay and lesbian biweekly tabloid, available throughout the West End. The **Alliance for Arts and Culture** (100–938 Howe St.; ✆ 604/681-3535; www. allianceforarts.com) is also a great information source for all performing arts, literary events, and art films.

Ticketmaster (✆ 855/985-5000; www.ticketmaster.ca) has an outlet at the **Tickets Tonight** booth in the Tourism Vancouver Visitor Centre, where you can find half-price tickets (200 Burrard St.; ✆ 604/684-2787 for recorded events info; www.tickets tonight.ca). The Touristinfo Centre is open daily from 8:30am to 6pm.

The Performing Arts

Three major theaters in Vancouver regularly host touring performances. The **Orpheum Theatre** (601 Smithe St.; ✆ 604/665-3050; www.vancouver.ca/theatres) is a 1927 theater that originally hosted the Chicago-based Orpheum vaudeville circuit. The theater, which got a much-needed interior makeover for the 2010 Winter Games, now hosts the Vancouver Symphony and pop, rock, and variety shows. The **Queen Elizabeth Theatre** (650 Hamilton St.; ✆ 604/665-3050; www.vancouver.ca/theatres) is home to the Vancouver Opera and Ballet British Columbia. Located in a converted turn-of-the-20th-century church, the **Vancouver East Cultural Centre** (the "Cultch" to locals; 1895 Venables St.; ✆ 604/251-1363; http://thecultch.com) coordinates programs of avant-garde theater productions, performances by international musical groups, and children's programs.

Meanwhile, on the UBC campus, the **Chan Centre for the Performing Arts** (6265 Crescent Rd.; ✆ 604/822-2697; www.chancentre.com) showcases the work of UBC music students and local choirs, and hosts various concert series. Designed by local architectural luminary Bing Thom, the Chan Centre's crystal-clear acoustics are the best in town.

Theater & Dance

Arts Club Theatre Company The 450-seat **Granville Island Stage** presents dramas, comedies, and musicals, with post-performance live music in the Backstage Lounge. The Arts Club **Revue Stage** is an intimate, cabaret-style showcase for small productions and musical revues. The Art Deco **Stanley Industrial Alliance Theatre** plays host to longer-running plays and musicals. Granville Island Stage: 1585 Johnston St. Stanley Industrial Alliance Stage: 2750 Granville St. ✆ **604/687-1644.** www.artsclub.com. Tickets C$29–C$74.

Ballet British Columbia ★ This established company strives to present innovative works, such as those by choreographers William Forsythe, Jean Grande-Maître, and artistic director Emily Molnar, along with more productions by visiting companies from Alberta and Winnipeg. Performances are usually at the Queen Elizabeth Theatre. 677 Davie St., 6th Fl. ℂ **604/732-5003.** www.balletbc.com. Tickets C$48–C$70.

Bard on the Beach ★★★ Every summer, from June to September, Vanier Park comes alive with men in tights crossing swords—it's the annual Shakespeare festival Bard on the Beach, and one of Vancouver's favorite events. Each year sees four shows performed—in 2014, it's "The Tempest," "A Midsummer Night's Dream," "Cymbeline," and "Equivocation," a new work featuring Bill Shakespeare trying to solve the Gunpowder Plot. Bring a picnic and enjoy the antics. Vanier Park. ℂ **604/739-0559.** www.bardonthebeach.org.

Theatre Under the Stars From mid-July to mid-August, favorite musicals like "Annie," "Singin' in the Rain," and "Bye Bye Birdie" are performed outdoors by a mixed cast of amateur and professional actors. Bring a blanket (it gets chilly once the sun sets) and a picnic for a relaxing evening. Malkin Bowl, Stanley Park. ℂ **877/840-0457** or 604/734-1917. www.tuts.ca.

Vancouver TheatreSports League ★★ Part comedy, part theater, and partly a take-no-prisoners test of an actor's ability to think extemporaneously, TheatreSports involves actors taking suggestions from the audience and spinning them into short skits or full plays, often with hilarious results. The Improv Centre, 1502 Duranleau St. ℂ **604/738-7013.** www.vtsl.com.

Cinema

Thanks to the number of resident moviemakers (both studio and independent), Vancouver is quite a film town. First-run theaters show the same Hollywood movies seen everywhere in the world, but for those with something more adventurous in mind, plenty of options can be found.

Attendance at the **Vancouver International Film Festival** (ℂ 604/685-0260; www.viff.org) reaches about 150,000, plus the celebs who drop in. This highly respected October event screens nearly 250 new feature-length films and 150 short films, representing filmmakers from 80 countries. Asian films are particularly well represented.

Since 1972, the **Pacific Cinematheque** (1131 Howe St.; ℂ 604/688-8202; www.thecinematheque.ca) has featured classic and contemporary films from around the world. Screenings are organized into themes, such as "Jean-Luc Godard's Early Efforts," film noir, or the "Hong Kong Action Flick: A Retrospective." Schedules are available in hipper cafes, record shops, and video stores around town, and on the website. Annual membership, required to purchase tickets, is C$3.

In addition, a gargantuan screen at the **OMNIMAX** Theatre at Science World (ℂ 604/443-7443; www.scienceworld.ca) features flicks about empty, wide-open spaces, outer space, and colorful coral reefs.

Classical Music & Opera

Vancouver Bach Choir ★★ Vancouver's international, award-winning amateur choir, a 150-voice ensemble, presents five major concerts a year at the Orpheum Theatre. Specializing in symphonic choral music, the choir's sing-along performance of

Handel's "Messiah" during the Christmas season is a favorite. 304–3102 Main St. *C* **604/872-8789.** www.vancouverbachchoir.com.

Vancouver Cantata Singers ★ This semiprofessional, 40-person choir special- izes in works by Bach, Brahms, Monteverdi, Stravinsky, and Handel, as well as East- ern European choral music. Seasons can include up to six programs, all at various locations, with a popular Christmas concert at the Holy Rosary Cathedral. 1254 W. 7th Ave. *C* **604/730-8856.** www.vancouvercantatasingers.com.

Vancouver Chamber Choir ★★★ Western Canada's only professional choral ensemble presents an annual concert series at the Orpheum Theatre, the Chan Centre, and Ryerson United Church. Under conductor Jon Washburn, the choir has gained an international reputation. 1254 W. 7th Ave. *C* **604/738-6822.** www.vancouverchamberchoir.com.

Vancouver Opera ★★★ The company produces both concert versions and fully staged operas, often sung by international stars, October through April, with performances in the Queen Elizabeth Theatre. 835 Cambie St. *C* **604/683-0222.** www. vancouveropera.ca.

Vancouver Symphony ★★★ At its home in the Orpheum Theatre during the fall, winter, and spring, Vancouver's excellent orchestra, under the baton of maestro Bramwell Tovey, presents a variety of year-round concerts. The box office is open from 6pm until showtime. 601 Smithe St. *C* **604/876-3434.** www.vancouversymphony.ca.

Live Music

The Commodore Ballroom ★ Every town should have one, but sadly very few do: a huge old-time dance hall, complete with a suspended hardwood dance floor. And though the room and floor date back to the Jazz Age, the lineup nowadays includes many of the best modern bands coming through town. In fact, the Commodore is one of the best places to catch a midsize band. 868 Granville St. *C* **604/739-4550.** www. commodoreballroom.ca.

Fanclub This new joint on Granville Street in the heart of the Entertainment District is part dance club, part live music venue, part restaurant, all with a decadent New Orleans-style vibe. Come out and groove to local bands like Brickhouse, or get your Rock-A-Oke on (if you ever wanted to sing with your own backup band, this is the gig for you). There's live music nightly. 1050 Granville St. *C* **604/689-7720.** www.vancouver fanclub.ca.

The Roxy Live bands play every day of the week in this no-holds-barred club, which also features bartenders with Tom Cruise "Cocktail"-style moves. Theme nights and other events add to the entertaining and sometimes raucous scene. On weekends, the lines are long, the patrons often soused. Dress code: No bags, backpacks, track suits, or ripped jeans, but everything else is OK. 932 Granville St. *C* **604/331-7999.** www. roxyvan.com.

TD Vancouver International Jazz Festival This huge festival, which features names big and small in the world of jazz, funk, and blues takes over many venues and outdoor stages around town every June. In addition to the big shows, the festival includes a number of free concerts. Various venues. *C* **604/872-5200.** www.coastaljazz.ca.

Vancouver Folk Music Festival Everyone who's anyone in the world of folk, roots, and world music comes out to this big outdoor show every July near Jericho Beach. Jericho Park. *C* **604/602-9798.** www.thefestival.bc.ca.

Bars, Pubs & Watering Holes

Not too surprisingly, given that the city originated with a saloonkeeper, Vancouver has more than a few joints where you can wet your whistle. That's in spite of some pretty restrictive liquor laws that are a nasty hangover from the days of Prohibition—for instance, until recently, in many establishments you couldn't drink standing up or without "having the intention" to eat (which explains the once-popular lunch of beer and toast). The laws have been gradually loosening up and 2014 is seeing a major overhaul of the entire provincial liquor policy, so expect lots of change that will make it easier to enjoy a drink.

Mind you, it's not that hard now, given how many bars, pubs, lounges, and "food-primary" (but booze-forward) establishments there are in the city.

In the early days, it was all about the pubs—not surprising, given Vancouver's British heritage. These days, we're seeing gastropubs like the **Irish Heather** (210 Carrall St.; ✆ **604/688-9779;** www.irishheather.com) or **Alibi Room** (157 Alexander St.; ✆ **604/623-3383;** www.alibi.ca), or brewpubs like **Steamworks** (375 Water St.; ✆ **604/689-2739;** www.steamworks.com) or **Yaletown Brewing Company** (1111 Mainland St.; ✆ **604/681-2739;** www.markjamesgroup.com). In addition, craft breweries are popping up all over the place, and some, such as **Brassneck Brewery** (2148 Main St.; no phone; www.brassneck.ca), allow patrons to hang around and enjoy a beer in the tasting room.

Those who can't imagine their pint without a big-screen TV will want to head to one of the city's sports bars, such as **Shark Club** (180 W. Georgia St.; ✆ **604/687-4275;** www.sharkclubs.com) or **Red Card** (Moda Hotel, 560 Smithe St.; ✆ **604/689-4460;** www.redcardsportsbar.ca).

Hipsters may want to check out the cool bars along Main Street, including **The Cascade Room** (2616 Main St.; ✆ 604/709-8650; www.thecascade.ca), **The Whip** (209 E. 6th Ave.; ✆ 604/874-4687; www.thewhiprestaurant.com) and the **Shameful Tiki Room** (4362 Main St., ✆ 604/999-5684; www.shamefultikiroom.com). Stylish trendsters, on the other hand, may want to head to one of Yaletown's "ultra-lounges," such as **Afterglow** (1082 Hamilton St.; ✆ 604/602-0835; www.globalgroup.com) or **George** (1137 Hamilton St.; ✆ 604/628-5555; www.georgelounge.com).

Dance Clubs

Generally, clubs are open until 2am every day but Sunday, when they close at midnight. In the summer months (mid-June through Labour Day), open hours at some clubs extend to 4am. The city's clubs and discos are concentrated around two "entertainment zones," downtown around Granville Street, and along Water and Pender streets in Gastown.

AuBAR An address is unnecessary for AuBAR; the long Seymour Street line of those not-quite-beautiful-enough for expedited entry immediately gives it away. Inside, this downtown bar is packed with beautiful people milling from bar to dance floor to the table nooks and back again. 674 Seymour St. ✆ **604/648-2227.** www.aubarnightclub.com.

Caprice Upstairs, it's the Lounge, with dark wood, a fireplace, and couches. Downstairs, it's the Nightclub, a large room with a funky semicircular glowing blue bar, big comfy wall banquettes, a secluded circular passion pit in one corner, and a medium-size dance floor. Earlier in the week, the DJ spins house, but on weekends, when the older, richer 25-and-overs come out to play, the cover goes up and the DJ retreats to the safety of Top 40. 967 Granville St. ✆ **604/685-3288.** www.capricenightclub.com.

The Cellar The Cellar inhabits that netherworld between dance club, bar, meat market, and personals ads. Dance-club characteristics include a cover charge, small dance floor, and a DJ who mostly spins Top 40. But Cellar patrons are far less interested in groovin' than they are in meeting other Cellar dwellers, a process facilitated by a wall-length message board upon which pickup lines are posted. 1006 Granville St. ✆ **604/605-4350.** www.cellarvan.com.

Empire Nightclub Located in the heart of Gastown, one of Vancouver's biggest and most legendary rooms (it was formerly Fabric, and before that, Sonar), has been revitalized after a year-long renovation. With a 500-plus capacity, it features audiovisual theatricals and big-name DJs from around the world. 66 Water St. ✆ **604/683-6695.** www.empirenightclub.ca.

The Red Room This basement warren has two bars, numerous intimate cubbyholes, and a DJ that does progressive house and hip-hop, plus a live band sometimes on the weekend. And if that weren't enough, there are also two pool tables. 398 Richards St. ✆ **604/687-5007.** www.redroomonrichards.com.

Shine This downstairs cellar in Gastown plays house and hip-hop, with occasional forays into other genres such as reggae. 364 Water St. ✆ **604/408-4321.** www.shinenightclub.com.

Gay & Lesbian Bars

BC's enlightened attitude—remember, same-sex couples can wed in Canada—has had a curious effect on Vancouver's queer dance-club scene: It's so laid-back and attitude-free that it's often hard to tell straight from gay, male go-go dancers and naked men in showers notwithstanding. Most bars and clubs are in the gay village of the West End, especially along Davie Street. Many clubs feature theme nights and dance parties, drag shows are ever popular, and every year in early August, as Gay Pride nears, the scene goes into overdrive. **QMUNITY,** BC's Queer Resource Centre (1170 Bute St.; ✆ **604/684-5307;** www.qmunity.ca) has information on the current hot spots, but it's just as easy to pick up a free copy of **"Xtra West!,"** available in most downtown cafes.

Celebrities Vancouver's largest gay and lesbian nightclub, but with a wildly mixed crowd all here for the great local and international DJs. 1022 Davie St. ✆ **604/681-6180.** www.celebritiesnightclub.com.

1181 A great little sophisticated lounge space, with terrific cocktails and a mellow crowd. Perfect for an aperitif before dinner or a night of dancing. 1081 Davie St. ✆ **604/687-3991.** www.1181.ca.

The Fountainhead Pub Reflecting the graying and mellowing of Vancouver's boomer-age gay crowd, one of the hottest hangouts these days is this relaxed pub that offers excellent microbrews on tap, decent food, and a pleasant atmosphere until the morning's wee hours. 1025 Davie St. ✆ **604/687-2222.** www.thefountainheadpub.com.

Numbers A multilevel dance club with five floors and three bars, Numbers hasn't changed much over the years. Extroverts hog the dance floor while admirers look on from the bar above. On the third floor, carpets, wood paneling, pool tables, darts, and a lower volume of music give it a neighborhood-pub feel. 1042 Davie St. ✆ **604/685-4077.** www.numbers.ca.

WHISTLER

Less than 2 hours' drive from Vancouver, up the winding, scenic Sea-to-Sky Highway, you will find the city's favorite place to play: the mountain resort of Whistler-Blackcomb. Widely considered one of the world's greatest ski resorts, Whistler-Blackcomb hosted the 2010 Olympic and Paralympic Winter Games, which brought with it a slew of new hotels, a vastly improved telecommunications system, a better highway (p. 136), and the attention of the entire world.

The resort is actually two mountains—Whistler and Blackcomb—and between them lies **Whistler Village,** which is where you can find most of the off-slope action. And, although the resort is best known for its winter sports, there's just as much to do here in summer.

In winter, the skiing is epic. The resort has more vertical runs, lifts, and varied ski terrain than any other in North America. In addition to downhill skiing and snowboarding, there's backcountry, cross-country, and heli-skiing, as well as sleigh riding, snowshoeing, and even bobsledding at the **Whistler Sliding Centre.**

In summer, Whistler is a mecca for mountain bikers, with a world-class mountain bike park to match its world-class winter skiing. There's also river rafting, hiking, golfing, wildlife-watching, and horseback riding, as well as the more leisurely pursuits of shopping and fine dining.

The Village itself is a cute, compact, colorful mountain community of hotels, restaurants, and shops. It only dates back to the 1970s, when a group of locals set about designing a resort town with a carefully planned infrastructure and aesthetic. The result is a safe, friendly, easily walkable town where everything is within easy reach. Yes, it's expensive, and it can be a bit of a party, but who doesn't like a party once in a while?

ESSENTIALS

Getting There

BY CAR   Whistler is about a 2-hour drive from Vancouver along **Hwy. 99,** also called the **Sea-to-Sky Highway.** The spectacular drive winds first along the edge of Howe Sound before climbing through the mountains. Ample pay parking is available for day skiers and visitors in the Village; most hotels charge a minimum of C$20 for underground parking.

BY BUS   **Perimeter Whistler Express** (8695 Barnard St.; ✆ **888/717-6606** or 604/717-6600; www.perimeterbus.com) operates bus service from Vancouver International Airport and downtown Vancouver hotels to Squamish and the Whistler Bus Loop, as well as drop-off service at most Whistler hotels and properties. The trip takes 2½ to 3 hours; round-trip

Whistler Valley

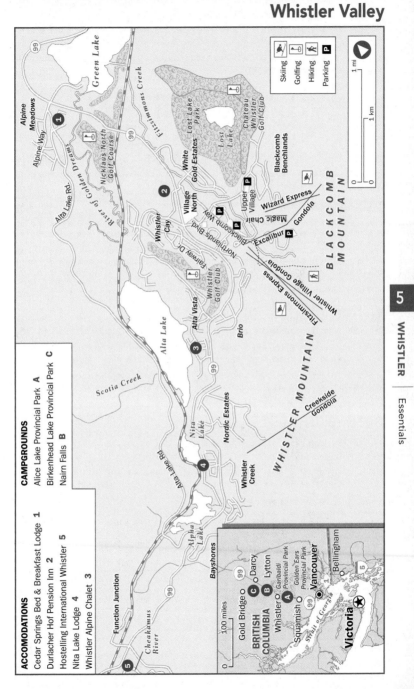

ACCOMODATIONS

Cedar Springs Bed & Breakfast Lodge **1**
Durlacher Hof Pension Inn **2**
Hostelling International Whistler **5**
Nita Lake Lodge **4**
Whistler Alpine Chalet **3**

CAMPGROUNDS

Alice Lake Provincial Park **A**
Birkenhead Lake Provincial Park **C**
Nairn Falls **B**

Skiing Golfing Hiking Parking **P**

1 mi
1 km

fares from Whistler Village are C$150 adults, C$80 children 2 to 12, and free for children 1 and under. Reservations are required year-round.

Whistler Direct Shuttle (✆ **888/405-2410;** www.whistlerdirectshuttle.com) operates year-round deluxe highway coach service between Vancouver and Whistler. The service is by reservation only and picks up from the airport and all downtown Vancouver hotels. Adult one-way fare from a Vancouver hotel is C$49; the fare from the airport is C$65.

Greyhound Bus Lines (✆ **800/661-8747** or 604/683-8133; www.greyhound.ca) operates daily bus service from the downtown Vancouver bus depot to Whistler Village and Whistler Creekside. The trip takes about 2½ hours; round-trip fares are C$56 to C$63 adults, C$42 to C$48 children 2 to 11, and free for children 1 and under.

BY PLANE   From mid-May through September, **Whistler Air** (✆ **888/806-2299;** www.whistlerair.ca) offers two daily flights from Vancouver's Coal Harbour to the Whistler area. Fares start at C$150.

BY TRAIN   From May through September, **Rocky Mountaineer** (✆ **877/460-3200** or 604/606-7245; www.rockymountaineer.com) offers Thursday to Monday service between North Vancouver and Whistler on the **Whistler Mountaineer,** a refurbished train with vintage dome observation cars. Trains depart North Vancouver early in the morning and return in the afternoon, though if you want to stay overnight of course you can do so. Breakfast is served on the way up, and a light meal on the return. Standard adult round-trip fare starts at C$270.

Visitor Information

For planning and accommodations deals, contact **Tourism Whistler** (✆ **800/944-7853** or 604/932-0606; www.whistler.com). The **Whistler Visitor Info Centre** (4230 Gateway Dr., off Village Gate Blvd. from Hwy. 99) is open daily 8am to 10pm (till 8pm during spring and fall), and can answer questions about the area, as well as help you find accommodations. Another good website for general information and mountain updates is **www.whistlerblackcomb.com**.

Getting Around

BY FOOT   Compact and pedestrian-oriented, Whistler Village has signed trails and pathways linking hotels, shops, and restaurants with the gondolas up to Whistler and Blackcomb mountains. If you're staying in the Village, you can park and leave your car for the duration of your stay. Remember that the resort is divided into **Whistler Village** (where you get gondolas for both Whistler and Blackcomb mountains) and the **Upper Village** (where you get the gondola for Blackcomb); it takes about 5 minutes to walk between the villages. At some hotels, you can ski from the front door right to the hill. There's also the **Valley Trail System,** more than 40km (25 miles) of paved pathway that connects all of Whistler's neighborhoods.

BY BUS   Whistler and Valley Express (WAVE; ✆ **604/932-4020;** www.bctransit. com), a year-round public transit service, runs from the Gondola Transit Exchange to the neighboring districts of Whistler Creekside, Alpine Meadows, and Emerald Estates. Service from the Village to Village North and Upper Village accommodations is free.

BY TAXI   Whistler Taxi (✆ **800/203-5322** or 604/932-3333; www.whistlertaxi.com) runs 24 hours.

BY CAR   Rental cars are available from **Avis** (4315 Northlands Blvd.; ✆ **800/230-4898** or 604/932-1236).

WHERE TO STAY IN WHISTLER

Very Expensive

The Fairmont Chateau Whistler ★★   Designed in a modern interpretation of the classic old railway lodges, this is Whistler's landmark hotel. It's huge, and offers every amenity from ski rentals in the basement to its own top-notch golf course, plus four restaurants and a bar. Step into the lobby, and it'll immediately evoke the A-frame ski chalets of the 1970s, only on a grand scale with lots of stone details and exposed wooden beams. The guest rooms are large, quiet, and comfortable, many with fireplaces and all with beautiful views and comfy upholstered furniture in cheerful plaids, florals, and stripes. The hotel is located in the Upper Village at the foot of Blackcomb Mountain, which means it's far from the noise of the Village—but that also means it's far from all its amenities, which is why everything you need can be found within the hotel. Eateries range from the casual **Portobello Market,** perfect for a coffee and pastry before your first run, to the posh **Grill Room. The Mallard Lounge & Terrace** is an exceptional spot for après ski.

4599 Chateau Blvd. ℭ **800/606-8244** or 604/938-8000. www.fairmont.com. 550 units. Spring–fall C\$240–C\$330 double, C\$320–C\$1,400 suite; winter C\$360–C\$800 double, C\$440–C\$3,160 suite. Valet parking C\$35, self-parking C\$30. Pets welcome, C\$50 per night. **Amenities:** 4 restaurants; bar; babysitting; children's programs; concierge; health club; Jacuzzi; 2 heated outdoor pools; room service; sauna; spa; 2 tennis courts; golf course; Wi-Fi free with President's Club membership, C\$15 without.

Four Seasons Resort Whistler ★★★   The ultimate in rustic-elegant luxury and top-notch service. The Four Seasons is located outside the bustle of the Village, in the relatively serene Upper Village near the base of Blackcomb Mountain. Its decor is a lovely mélange of modern-mountain-Craftsman style, its lobby a gracious space with a huge stone fireplace at one end and clusters of cushy leather chairs and sofas gathered under the large cast iron chandeliers. Guest rooms are spacious, among the biggest in Whistler, with elegant but comfortable furnishings—think caramel leather recliners, coffee-colored plaid throws, stone fireplaces, lots of warm wood trim, and spectacular views. Each also has a deep soaker tub for easing any post-ski aches and pains. The hotel is home to an excellent steakhouse (**Sidecut**), and casual bistro (**Fifty Two 80 Eatery + Bar**), as well as a relaxing spa. Every amenity you can think of is available, including ski concierge service and free bikes to borrow. Plus, your best friend is welcome at no extra charge.

4591 Blackcomb Way. ℭ **888/935-2460** or 604/935-3400. www.fourseasons.com. 273 units and 37 residences. Spring–fall C\$305–C\$465 double, C\$525 suite; winter C\$405–C\$650 double, from C\$720 suite. Pets welcome (no charge). Underground valet parking C\$33. **Amenities:** 2 restaurants, bar, babysitting, concierge, executive-level rooms, health club, Jacuzzi, heated outdoor pool, room service, sauna, spa, free Wi-Fi.

Nita Lake Lodge ★★   If you're arriving via Whistler Mountaineer, this is likely where you will want to stay because the train station is right next door. It's also a good place for anyone seeking a quiet refuge in the woods. The lodge is located south of Whistler Village in the community of Creekside, perched on the edge of pretty little Nita Lake. (It is the only lakefront hotel in Whistler.) The hotel has a graceful urban-contemporary-meets-rustic feel to it, with lots of exposed wood, river stone, and cast-iron fittings. Guest rooms are simply elegant, with gas fireplaces, navy or leather sofas, spa-style bathrooms, and some have balconies with views over the lake. There's an on-site spa, yoga classes, and three restaurants: the luxe and innovative **Aura,** casual

Whistler Village

ACCOMMODATIONS ■
The Fairmont Chateau Whistler 3
Four Seasons Resort Whistler 1
Pan Pacific Whistler Mountainside 4
Pan Pacific Whistler Village Centre 13
The Westin Resort & Spa Whistler 8

DINING ◆
Alta Bistro 24
Araxi 14
Bearfoot Bistro 22
Caramba! Restaurant 11
Citta Bistro 21
Dubh Linn Gate Irish Lounge/Pub 4
Il Caminetto 17
Ingrid's Village Café 15
Trattoria di Umberto 7
Whistler BrewHouse 9
Wild Wood Bistro & Bar 26

NIGHTLIFE ●
Buffalo Bills 20
Cinnamon Bear Bar 19
Dubh Linn Gate Irish Lounge/Pub 4
Garfinkel's 12
Maxx Fish 15
Moe Joe's 18
Tapley's 16
Tommy Africa's 14
Whistler BrewHouse 9

OTHER ATTRACTIONS ●
Blackcomb Gondola 5
Maurice Young Millennium Place 10
Squamish Lil'Wat Cultural Centre 2
Tourism Whistler Info Center 23
Whistler Museum & Archives Society 25
Whistler Village Gondola 6

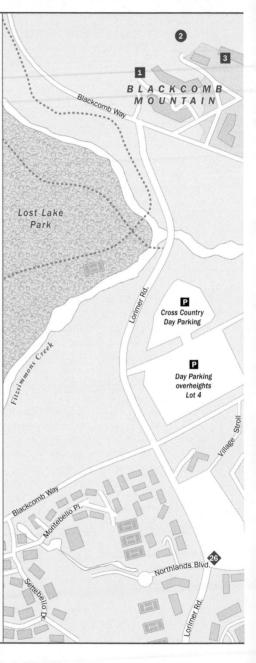

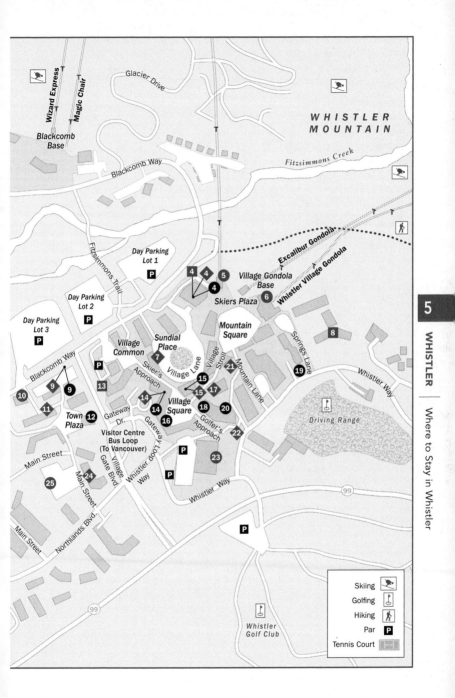

WHISTLER MOUNTAIN

Glacier Drive

Wizard Express

Magic Chair

Blackcomb Base

Blackcomb Way

Fitzsimmons Creek

Fitzsimmons Trail

Excalibur Gondola

Day Parking Lot 1

Day Parking Lot 2

Day Parking Lot 3

Village Gondola Base

Skiers Plaza

Whistler Village Gondola

4 4 5

4

6

8

Mountain Square

Sundial Place

Village Common

Village Lane

Village Stroll

Mountain Lane

Springs Lane

Whistler Way

7

21

19

Skier's Approach

Blackcomb Way

13

15

15 17

9

9

14

14

18 20

10

Village Square

Golfer's Approach

22

11

Town Plaza

12

16

Driving Range

Gateway Dr.

Gateway Loop

23

Visitor Centre Bus Loop (To Vancouver)

Whistler door Way

Village Gate Blvd.

P

P

99

Main Street

25

24

Whistler Way

Main Street

Northlands Blvd.

99

Whistler Golf Club

Skiing	
Golfing	
Hiking	
Par	P
Tennis Court	

Fix Café for all your breakfast and coffee needs, and **Cure Lounge,** which specializes in charcuterie, drinks, and après ski, and has a gorgeous patio overlooking the lake. It's worth noting that, although the hotel is outside the Village, it's just a short drive to town or a slightly longer walk along the pleasantly meandering paved Valley Trail.

2131 Lake Placid Rd. ✆ **888/755-6482** or 604/966-5700. www.nitalakelodge.com. 77 units. C$230–$600 studio, C$270–C$650 1-bedroom. Valet parking C$30, self-parking C$20. **Amenities:** Restaurants, bar, cafe, concierge, health club, room service, Jacuzzi, sauna, spa, bikes, fishing rods, free Wi-Fi.

Expensive

Pan Pacific Whistler ★★   The Pan has two excellent locations in Whistler: one right in the Village (but fortunately, slightly outside party central), and the Mountainside location just steps from the Blackcomb and Whistler gondolas. At Mountainside, you can ski right from the front door to the lift. Both feature excellent service, all-suites accommodation, ski valet and storage services, and lovely rooms with lots of warm wood, gas fireplaces, and full kitchens. Both locations have huge heated outdoor pools, with Mountainside's overlooking the slopes. Even the smallest studio suites, which feature a murphy bed, feel luxuriously comfortable, thanks to features like the leather ottomans and granite countertops. The Village location includes a free breakfast; Mountainside is home to the popular **Dubh Linn Gate Old Irish Pub,** which is one of the town's favorite après ski spots. Both properties are especially popular with families.

Mountainside: 4320 Sundial Crescent. ✆ **888/905-9995** or 604/905-2999. 121 units. **Village Centre:** 4299 Blackcomb Way. ✆ **888/966-5575** or 604/966-5500. www.panpacificwhistler.com. 83 units. Spring–fall C$140–C$230 studio, C$190–C$360 suite; winter C$200–C$770 studio, C$250–C$1,170 suite. Breakfast included at Village Centre. Pets welcome at Village Centre (C$25/day); no pets at Mountainside. Underground valet parking C$25. **Amenities:** Restaurant and pub (Mountainside), breakfast room/lounge (Village Centre), concierge, fitness center, Jacuzzi, heated outdoor pool, room service, in-room kitchen, free Wi-Fi.

The Westin Resort & Spa Whistler ★★   This lovely, big hotel was completely refurbished for the 2010 Winter Games, when it was the host hotel for the alpine, Nordic, and sliding events. It's also been twice named by Condé Nast as the **top ski resort hotel in North America,** so you know they're doing something right. It starts with a handy location near the Whistler gondola, and continues with the airy lobby, all lined with river stone and sunny pine trim, where swooping contemporary furniture clusters around the big fireplace. The same look extends to the guest rooms, which have well-appointed kitchenettes with granite countertops, as well as fireplaces; most also have balconies. What sets this place apart are all the little extras—like the ski valet, boot-warming services, an exceptional fitness center, a workout gear-lending program, and a truly great full-service spa, Avello. Then there is the cozy **FireRock Lounge** and **Grill & Vine,** a sleek update of a classic bar and grill serving wood-fired pizza and wines by the glass in a high-ceilinged room with a fabulous patio. There's also a village-level shopping plaza in case you left any of your essentials behind.

4090 Whistler Way. ✆ **888/634-5577** or 604/905-5000. www.westinwhistler.com. 419 units. C$160–C$900 junior suite, C$210–C$1,100 1-bedroom suite. Children 17 and under stay free in parent's room. Underground valet parking C$34. Pets welcome (no charge). **Amenities:** 2 restaurants, bar, babysitting, concierge, health club, indoor and outdoor Jacuzzi, indoor-outdoor pool, room service, sauna, spa, ski rentals, Wi-Fi (C$15/day).

Whistler can be a pricy place to stay, but there are options besides the big, fancy hotels, especially if you don't mind staying outside the Village. There are condos and suites to rent, a couple of small inns, B&Bs, a hostel, even a campground or two. Visit **Whistler Accommodation Reservations** (© **800/ 944-7853;** www.whistler.com) to find the best fit for you and your travel plans. They can help you book your accommodation and provide a custom- ized package with lift tickets and trans- portation from and to Vancouver. Here are some of your options:

Whistler Alpine Chalet (3012 Alpine Crescent; © **800/736-9967** or 604/935- 3003; www.whistleralpinechalet.ca) and **Durlacher Hof Pension Inn** (7055 Nesters Rd.; © **877/932-1924** or 604/932-1924; www.durlacherhof.com) are a couple of

small, European-style inns. **Cedar Springs Bed & Breakfast** (8106 Camino Dr.; © **800/727-7547** or 604/938-8007; www.whistlerinns.com) is one of the few local B&Bs to welcome children— they stay and eat free here.

Hostelling International Whistler (1035 Legacy Way; © **866/762-4122** or 604/962-0025; www.hihostels.ca) was built as part of the athletes' village for the 2010 Winter Games and is one of the few truly inexpensive places to stay in Whistler. Most rooms and bathrooms are shared, but there are a handful of private ones with ensuites.

There are a number of campgrounds in the area, including the one at the very popular **Alice Lake Provincial Park.** You can reserve spots for campgrounds through **Discover Camping** (© **800/ 689-9025;** www.discovercamping.ca).

WHERE TO EAT IN WHISTLER
Very Expensive

Araxi ★★★ WEST COAST   Executive chef James Walt has been a pioneer in the farm-to-table movement, and this sophisticated restaurant is a perfect expression of both his passion and his immense talent. The room is elegant but warm, with comfort- ably plush, curvy chairs and lots of wood details, including the long, glossy, cedar- colored bar. (If it looks familiar, that might be because it was featured on Gordon Ramsay's "Hell's Kitchen" back in 2009.) He features many local producers on his menu, and he's certainly got some excellent options, especially from the nearby Pem- berton Valley. But don't expect anything rustic here: Everything is prepared with a beautiful attention to detail, from the exquisite small plates (many of which are sushi- inspired, like the octopus and prawn *chirashi* on sushi rice) to the well-composed mains, such as the local prawn risotto or beef cheeks slow cooked in red wine. Speaking of wine: Wine director Samantha Rahn picked up the sommelier-of-the-year award at the 2013 Vancouver International Wine Festival and oversees Araxi's impressive 11,000-bottle cellar. If you can, try to join one of the al fresco long-table dinners Walt hosts in the summer.

4222 Village Sq. © **604/932-4540.** www.araxi.com. Reservations recommended. Main courses C$25–C$68, small plates C$13–C$22. Daily 11am–3pm and 5–11pm.

Bearfoot Bistro ★★★ INTERNATIONAL   It's all about excess at the Bearfoot, from the Belvedere room with its ice walls, where you can do frosty shots of vodka, to the 20,000-bottle wine cellar where you can savor a bottle of Champagne. Hard to believe this was once just a simple little bistro. It's now a sprawling space, filled with funky wrought iron and leather chairs, interesting works of art, and the sense that naughty behavior is always just one more glass of bubble away. The centerpiece of the room is the open kitchen where superstar chef Melissa Craig works her magic. Her dinners are tasting menus that take you on a journey to some wild and wonderful places, depending on what's fresh, in season, and beautiful: Think lobster bisque, steelhead trout with spring onion cream, lamb T-bone with tabbouleh-style quinoa. Plus you can always top things up with a slab of foie gras or a spoonful of local sturgeon caviar. And with that huge cellar, you know the wine selection is bound to impress.

4121 Village Green. ✆ **604/932-3433.** www.bearfootbistro.com. Reservations essential. Tasting menus C$49–C$159. Daily 5–10pm.

Expensive

Alta Bistro ★★ WEST COAST   At first glance, this little bistro doesn't look like much—it's small for Whistler (although it recently expanded) and the room is plain, with all white walls, round pine tables, and simple black and red chairs—though that cedar bar is pretty great, and the shelves filled with jars of house-made pickles and preserves give you an idea of how passionate the team here is about authentic, local food. Alta Bistro has the best cocktail program in Whistler, thanks to the talents of barman Scott Curry, who makes all his own syrups and bitters. Then there is the food. Rooted in French tradition, but dedicated to local ingredients, the ever-changing dinner menu might feature roast lamb shoulder with faro risotto, elk tartar with duck liver parfait, or clams and bacon with white beans. There is charcuterie, cheese, and a well-edited wine list. Seductive sweets round out the list at what is one of the best dining experiences in Whistler.

4319 Main St. ✆ **604/932-2582.** www.altabistro.com. Reservations recommended. Mains C$25–C$32. Daily 5:30–10pm.

Trattoria di Umberto ★ ITALIAN   Umberto Menghi once had something of an Italian restaurant empire in Vancouver. Now that he's "retired," he's got his two places in Whistler. And the cooking school in Tuscany. And there are rumors he's reopening

---

Go Casual

Whistler is well known for its high-end fare—and for the plethora of chain restaurants throughout the Village—but there are a handful of great casual places with a bit more personality. **Ingrid's Village Cafe** (✆ **604/932-7000;** www.ingridswhistler.com) on the Village Square is a local favorite for quality and price; it's been around for over 20 years, making it one of Whistler's oldest businesses. Right across from Ingrid's, **Citta Bistro** (✆ **604/932-4177;** www.citta bistro.com) is a favorite dining and night spot that serves thin-crust pizzas, gourmet burgers, and good appetizers. For excellent craft beer and casual food, try the family-friendly **Whistler BrewHouse** (✆ **604/905-2739;** www. drinkfreshbeer.com), located just over the creek in Village North. Equally fun indoor dining can be had at the **Dubh Linn Gate Old Irish Pub** (✆ **604/905-4047;** www.dubhlinngate.com) in the Pan Pacific Mountainside hotel. The Gate offers pub classics like Irish corned beef and shepherd's pie, as well as live music.

his beloved Il Giardino in downtown Vancouver. Until that happens, Trattoria and its sister restaurant, **Il Caminetto** (© 604/932-4442) on the Village Stroll, are the only places you can sample his classic dishes. Both have an exuberant Tuscan look, Trattoria being the more rustic of the two, with exposed wooden beams and ceramic pigs to keep things real. The menu features all the usual pastas and antipasti, as well as fish, steaks, and game, all prepared Italian style. The wine list features plenty of big Italian reds, and the friendly servers are happy to welcome your bambino.

4417 Sundial Place. © **604/932-5858.** www.umberto.com. Reservations recommended. Mains C$20–C$39. Daily 5:30–10pm (call ahead for seasonal lunch hours).

Moderate

Caramba! Restaurante ★ MEDITERRANEAN   Bright and cheerful, with a wood-fired pizza oven, and a big wooden rooster overlooking the tiled open kitchen, this is a great spot for a casual meal. The food is pretty straightforward—spaghetti and meatballs, fettuccine with vodka cream sauce, salad, rotisserie chicken—but the wood-fired pizzas are pretty great, and the kids will love it. The menu is Mediterranean-ish, hearty and satisfying, especially after a day on the slopes.

12–4314 Main St., Town Plaza. © **604/938-1879.** www.caramba-restaurante.com. Main courses C$13–C$39. Summer daily 11:30am–10:30pm; winter Mon–Thurs 5–10pm, Fri–Sun 11:30am–10pm.

Wild Wood Bistro & Bar ★★ WEST COAST   This is a favorite among locals, a best-kept-secret type of place. It's off the beaten track by the Whistler Tennis Club, with a recently opened second location in Function Junction, Whistler's industrial park south of town (this one is only open for breakfast and lunch). The room is warm and inviting, with tall Craftsman-style seats pulled up to a curved wooden bar and floor-to-ceiling windows for taking in the magnificent view outside. Expect hearty soups and fresh salads, burgers on brioche buns and terrific tacos, as well as more substantial mains like ribs and steak. If you're looking for good food and good value, it's worth going out of your way to this space.

4500 Northlands Blvd., Village North. © **604/935-4077.** www.wildwoodrestaurants.ca. No reservations. Main courses C$15–C$25. Daily 7am–3pm and 5–9pm.

OUTDOOR ACTIVITIES

Winter Pursuits

DOWNHILL SKIING & SNOWBOARDING   Your ski pass gives you access to both Blackcomb and Whistler mountains (© 800/766-0449; www.whistlerblackcomb.com), as well as the Peak 2 Peak Gondola—the longest in the world—that links the two mountains. Whistler is generally considered better for beginners and middle-range skiers, while steeper Blackcomb is geared to the experienced. **Whistler Mountain** has more than 1,500m (5,000 ft.) of vertical (and more than 100 marked runs) serviced by two high-speed gondolas and seven high-speed chairlifts, plus 10 other lifts and tows. Helicopter service from the top of the mountain provides access to another nearly 500 runs on nearby glaciers. The peak has cafeterias, gift shops, and a restaurant. **Blackcomb Mountain** has more than 1,600m (5,300 ft.) of vertical (and more than 100 marked runs) serviced by one high-speed gondola, nine high-speed chairlifts, plus seven other lifts and tows. The cafeteria, restaurant, and gift shop aren't far from the peak. Both mountains also have bowls and glade skiing, with Blackcomb Mountain offering glacier skiing well into July. Family-friendly Tube Park, located at Base II on

Blackcomb, offers a 300m (1,000-ft.) run with eight lanes, accessed by a carpet-style lift. Winter lift tickets are C$109 adults, C$93 seniors and children 13 to 18, C$55 children 7 to 12, and free for children 6 and under. Depending on weather and conditions, lifts operate daily noon to 6pm. *Note:* You can save about 20% on your multiday lift tickets by booking online. You can also **rent ski and snowboard gear** at the base of both Whistler and Blackcomb just prior to purchasing your lift pass.

BACKCOUNTRY SKIING   The **Spearhead Traverse,** which starts at Whistler and finishes at Blackcomb, is a well-marked backcountry route that has become a local classic. **Garibaldi Provincial Park** maintains marked backcountry trails at **Diamond Head,** with additional trails at **Singing Pass,** and **Garibaldi Lake.** These are ung-roomed and unpatrolled rugged trails, and you have to be at least an intermediate skier and bring (and know how to use) appropriate clothing and avalanche gear. Several access points to the trails are along Hwy. 99 between Squamish and Whistler. If you're not sure of yourself off-*piste,* hire a guide through **Whistler Alpine Guides Bureau** (🕿 **604/938-9242;** www.whistlerguides.com).

CROSS-COUNTRY SKIING   Well-marked, fully groomed cross-country trails run throughout the area. The 30km (20 miles) of easy-to-very-difficult marked trails at **Lost Lake** start a block away from the Blackcomb Mountain parking lot. Passes are C$20 per day. Contact **Lost Lake Cross Country Connection** (🕿 **604/905-0071;** www.crosscountryconnection.ca). **Whistler Olympic Park** (🕿 **877/764-2455** or 604/964-0060; www.whistlerolympicpark.com) in the **Callaghan Valley** hosted Nordic events during the Winter Games and has more than 90km (55 miles) of groomed cross-country trails. Day passes cost C$24 for adults. The **Valley Trail System** in the village becomes a well-marked (and free) cross-country ski trail during winter.

HELI-SKIING   For intermediate and advanced skiers who can't get enough fresh powder on the regular slopes, there's always heli-skiing. **Whistler Heli-Skiing** (🕿 **888/435-4754** or 604/905-3337; www.whistlerheliskiing.com) offers a three-run day, with 1,400–2,300m (4,600–7,500 ft.) of vertical helicopter lift, for C$930 per person. Longer trips are also available.

SLEIGH RIDES   For a horse-drawn sleigh ride, contact **Blackcomb Horsedrawn Sleigh Rides** (🕿 **604/932-7631;** www.blackcombsleighrides.com). In winter, tours go out every evening from the base of Blackcomb Mountain and cost C$65 adults, C$39 children 3 to 12, free for children 2 and under. Other options include daylight, romantic, and dinner sleigh rides.

SNOWMOBILING & ATVS   Year-round, hop on either an ATV or a snowmobile for a tour of mountain trails with **Canadian Wilderness Adventures Ltd.** (🕿 **604/938-1616;** www.canadianwilderness.com). All tours are weather- and snow-conditions permitting. **Blackcomb Snowmobile** (🕿 **604/932-8484;** www.blackcombsnowmobile.com) offers a variety of guided snowmobile tours, including family tours on Blackcomb Mountain. Either adventure starts at around C$150 for the driver, C$120 for a passenger.

SNOWSHOEING   Snowshoeing is the world's easiest and most environmentally friendly form of snow-commotion; it requires none of the training and motor skills of skiing or boarding, and it's quiet, so it truly lets you appreciate nature. You can wear your own shoes or boots, provided they're warm and waterproof, strap on your snowshoes, and off you go. One of the best rental and trail companies is **Lost Lake Cross Country Connection** (🕿 **604/905-0071;** www.crosscountryconnection.ca). **Whistler**

Truly breathtaking. A long, swooping, gondola ride links the peaks of Whistler (elevation 2,180m/7,160 ft.) and Blackcomb (elev. 2,290m/7,490 ft.) mountains. It's the longest free-span lift in the world, with a total length of 4.4km (2¾ miles). The **Peak 2 Peak Gondola** is also the highest detachable lift in the world, at 440m (1,430 ft.) above the valley floor. The gondola has 28 cars, each carrying up to 28 passengers, and leaves about once every minute. (If you're lucky, you'll get one with a glass floor so you can see the world rush by under your feet.) The lift takes 11 minutes to travel from peak to peak. The gondola offers skiers greater flexibility for skiing the highest runs of both mountains and provides summer visitors with one of the most thrilling gondola rides in the world. The price for a gondola ride is included in your winter lift ticket; if you want to skip the skiing and just ride on the gondola, the cost is around C$50 adults, C$45 seniors and children 13 to 18, and C$26 children 7 to 12.

Olympic Park (✆ **877/764-2455** or 604/964-0060; www.whistlerolympicpark.com) in the **Callaghan Valley** also maintains snowshoeing trails and rents equipment. A day pass costs C$10 to C$14 and renting a pair of snowshoes costs C$22.

Summer Pursuits

CANOEING & KAYAKING   The 3-hour River of Golden Dreams Kayak & Canoe Tour is a great way for novices, intermediates, and experts to get acquainted with the beautiful stretch of slow-moving glacial water running between Green Lake and Alta Lake behind the village of Whistler. Contact the **Whistler Visitor Information Centre** (✆ **877/991-9988**) for information. Packages begin at C$49 per person, unguided, and include all gear and return transportation to the village center. The information center can also assist with booking lessons and clinics, as well as windsurfing rentals.

GOLFING   There are four world-class golf courses in and around Whistler, making this Canada's top golf resort. All the information you need regarding greens fees and tee times, plus golf packages and a passport, can be found through **Golf Whistler** (✆ **866/723-2747;** www.golfwhistler.com).

Robert Trent Jones, Jr.'s, **Fairmont Chateau Golf Club,** at the base of Blackcomb Mountain, is an 18-hole, par-72 course that traverses mountain ledges and crosses cascading creeks. **Nicklaus North at Whistler** is a 5-minute drive north of the Village on the shores of Green Lake with spectacular mountain views. **Whistler Golf Club,** designed by Arnold Palmer, features nine lakes, two creeks, and magnificent vistas. And 20 minutes north of Whistler, **Big Sky Golf & Country Club,** designed by Robert Cupp, lies in the shadow of snow-capped Mount Currie.

A-1 Last Minute Golf Hotline (✆ **800/684-6344** or 604/878-1833) can arrange a next-day, last-minute tee time at Whistler golf courses and elsewhere in BC at more than 30 courses.

HIKING   There's every sort of hiking around Whistler, from an easy stroll along the Valley Trail to rugged, multi-day backcountry treks. You can also take a ski lift up to the alpine areas, or even hop aboard a helicopter to get into the true backcountry. Here are just a few of the best hikes:

5

WHISTLER

Outdoor Activities

Lost Lake Trail features 30km (20 miles) of marked trails that wind around creeks, beaver dams, blueberry patches, and lush cedar groves. The **Valley Trail System** is a well-marked, paved trail that connects parts of Whistler. Garibaldi Provincial Park's **Singing Pass Trail** is a 4-hour hike of moderate difficulty. The fun way is to take the Whistler Mountain gondola to the top and walk down the well-marked path that ends on an access road in the Village. **Nairn Falls Provincial Park,** about 30km (20 miles) north of Whistler on Hwy. 99, features a 1.5km-long (1 mile) trail that leads you to a stupendous view of the glacial Green River and Mount Currie.

On Hwy. 99 north of Mount Currie, **Joffre Lakes Provincial Park** has an intermediate-level hike that leads past several brilliant blue glacial lakes up to the very foot of a glacier. The **Ancient Cedars** area of Cougar Mountain, near the north end of Green Lake, is an awe-inspiring grove of towering cedars and Douglas firs, some of which are more than 1,000 years old.

Contact the **Whistler Visitor Information Centre** (✆ **877/991-9988** or 604/938-2769; www.tourismwhistler.com) for guided hikes and interpretive tours available through various Whistler operators.

MOUNTAIN BIKING Whistler Mountain Bike Park (✆ **866/218-9688;** www.whistlerblackcomb.com/bike) offers some of the best mountain-biking trails, skill centers, and jump parks in the world. When the snow melts, the slope is reconfigured for biking—with more than 200km (125 miles) of marked trails, open mid-May to early October. The variety of trails can accommodate almost all ages and experience levels. Single-day ticket prices with gondola are C$55 to C$63 adults, C$49 to C$55 seniors and children 13 to 18, and C$33 to C$37 children 7 to 12. You can rent mountain bikes and body armor at **Lost Lake Cross Country Connection** (✆ **604/905-0071;** www.crosscountryconnection.ca).

The **Crankworx Whistler Freeride Mountain Bike Festival** takes place in August, bringing hundreds of mountain bikers to town for some gnarly rides (✆ **800/944-7853;** www.whistler.com/crankworx).

RAFTING Wedge Rafting (✆ **888/932-5899** or 604/932-7171; www.wedgerafting.com) offers whitewater rafting tours that range from easy short trips to full-day adventures, and range in price from C$109 to C$169. **Sun Wolf Outdoor Centre** (✆ **877/806-8046** or 604/898-1537; www.sunwolf.net) leads family float trips as well as summer rafting trips and winter eagle-viewing trips on the Cheakamus and Squamish rivers. Full-day summer rafting trips cost C$165 per person, and the winter eagle trips cost C$100 per person.

Zipping with Ziptrek ★★

One of Whistler's most exciting year-round adventures is offered by **Ziptrek Ecotours** (✆ **866/935-0001** or 604/935-0001; www.ziptrek.com). On guided 3-hour tours, you're taken through Whistler's ancient temperate rainforest on a network of up to 10 zipline rides joined by canopy bridges, boardwalks, and trails. Along the way, you're harnessed into a safety contraption that lets you whiz out on cables suspended hundreds of feet above glacier-fed Fitzsimmons Creek. It sounds hair-raising, but it's completely safe for all ages and abilities, and you'll never forget the experience. Tours cost C$89 to C$119 adults, C$79 to C$99 for seniors 65 and older and children 14 and under.

TENNIS The **Whistler Racquet Club** (4500 Northlands Blvd.; $\textcircled{C}$ **604/932-1991;** www.whistlertennis.com) has three covered courts, seven outdoor courts, and a practice cage. The **Fairmont Chateau Whistler Resort** (Fairmont Chateau Whistler Hotel, Upper Village; $\textcircled{C}$ **604/938-8000;** www.fairmont.com/whistler) also offers courts to drop-in players. **Free public courts** ($\textcircled{C}$ **604/935-7529**) are located at Alpha Lake, Meadow, Millar's Pond, Brio, Balsam, and White Gold parks.

Indoor Pursuits

ARTS & CULTURE Admittedly, Whistler isn't exactly the place to go for high culture. Musical performances, ranging from classical and choral to folk and blues are held at the **Maurice Young Millennium Place** community center ($\textcircled{C}$ **604/935-8410**). There are also frequent outdoor concerts in summer, as well as festivals and events year round; your best bet is to check the Tourism Whistler events calendar to see what's coming up (www.whistler.com).

Believe it or not, Whistler does have a museum. The **Whistler Museum** (4333 Main St.; $\textcircled{C}$ **604/932-2019;** www.whistlermuseum.org) covers the story of the area from the First Nations to the early British settlers and right up to the Olympics. More First Nations culture is on offer at the **Squamish Lil'wat Cultural Centre** (4584 Blackcomb Way; $\textcircled{C}$ **866/441-7522;** www.slcc.ca), a beautiful new glass-and-stone building filled with haunting artifacts. There are displays, events, a cafe, a gift shop, and more.

SHOPPING The **Whistler Marketplace** (in the center of Whistler Village) and the area surrounding the **Blackcomb Mountain lift** brim with clothing, jewelry, crafts, specialty, and equipment shops that are generally open daily 10am to 6pm. One of the best things to shop for is art; for a list and map of all the galleries in town, as well as information on events, contact the **Whistler Community Arts Council** ($\textcircled{C}$ **604/935-8410;** www.whistlerartscouncil.com).

SPAS After a tough day on the slopes (or in front of the fire), nothing makes you go ahhh like a trip to the spa. And Whistler has several excellent options.

The **Taman Sari Royal Heritage Spa** ($\textcircled{C}$ **604/938-8836;** www.tamansarispa.com) at the Hilton offers an unusual array of Javanese and European spa treatments. The Westin's **Avello** ($\textcircled{C}$ **604/935-3444;** www.whistlerspa.com) has a variety of signature treatments, including hot rock, Thai, and Satago massage. The **Vida Wellness Spa** at **Fairmont Chateau Whistler Resort** ($\textcircled{C}$ **604/938-8000;** www.vidaspas.com) provides massage therapy, skin care, and body wraps. And the **Scandinave Spa** $\textcircled{C}$ **604/935-2424;** www.scandinave.com) offers Finnish-style saunas, steam room, hot pools, and cold showers, as well as massages.

If something didn't quite go right on the slopes or on the trails, **Whistler Physiotherapy** (339–4370 Lorimer Rd.; $\textcircled{C}$ **604/932-4001;** www.whistlerphysio.com) specializes in sports therapy.

Especially for Kids

Whistler Village and the Upper Village sponsor daily activities for kids of all ages near the base of the mountains. Mountain-bike races; an in-line skating park; trapeze, trampoline, and wall-climbing lessons; summer skiing; snowboarding; snowshoeing; bungee jumping; and a first-run multiplex movie theater are just a few of the options.

Based at Blackcomb Mountain, the **Dave Murray Summer Ski and Snowboard Camp** ($\textcircled{C}$ **604/902-2600;** www.skiandsnowboard.com) is North America's longest-running summer ski camp. Junior programs cost C$2,300 for 8 days or C$1,250 for a

5-day package; both are available from mid-June to mid-July. Packages include food, lodging (day-camp packages without the hotel are also available), lift passes, and tennis, trapeze, and mountain biking options. Days are spent skiing, boarding, or free-riding on the excellent terrain parks and half-pipes. Camps accommodate a range of abilities, from beginners to champion-level skiers and riders; the age group is 7 to 18 years. The comprehensive instruction and adult supervision at this activity-oriented camp are excellent.

WHISTLER AFTER DARK

For a town of just 10,000, Whistler has a pretty good nightlife scene. Of course, it *is* considered the preeminent ski resort in North America and attracts millions of year-round visitors. Bands touring through Vancouver regularly make the trip up the Sea-to-Sky Highway; some even make Whistler their Canadian debut. Concert listings can be found in the free weekly **"Pique"** (www.piquenewsmagazine.com).

Tommy Africa's (© **604/932-6090;** www.tommyafricas.com), beneath the Rexall at the entrance to the Main Village, and the dark and cavernous **Maxx Fish** (© **604/932-1904;** www.maxxfish.com), in the Village Square below the Amsterdam Cafe, cater to the 19-to-22-year-old crowd. The crowds at **Garfinkel's** (© **604/932-2323;** www.gibbonshospitality.com/garfinkels), at the entrance to Village North, and **Moe Joe's** (© **604/935-1152;** www.moejoes.com) on Golfer's Approach are similar, though perhaps appropriate for *slightly* older ages.

The **Cinnamon Bear Bar** in the Hilton (© **604/966-5060;** www.hiltonwhistler.com), **Buffalo Bills** (© **604/932-6613;** www.gibbonshospitality.com/buffalobills) across from the Whistler Gondola, and sports bar **Tapleys** (© **604/932-4011;** www.gibbonshospitality.com/tapleys), off the Village Square, cater to the 30-something set. Bills is bigger, with a pool table, video ski machine, a small dance floor, and music straight from the 1980s. Tapleys has multiple screens for airing hockey games, and the Cinnamon Bear is a slick, tranquil spot.

For a short visit, try the four- or five-bar **Whistler Club Crawl** (© **604/722-2633;** www.whistlerclubcrawl.com) to skip the lines and save on cover. Guided tours run on Thursday and Saturday nights. The C$60 cost covers dinner, five drinks, and cover for each adult.

If all you want to do is savor a beer and swap ski stories, try the **Whistler BrewHouse** (© **604/905-2739;** www.mjg.ca/brewhouse) in Village North or the fun and very Irish **Dubh Linn Gate Old Irish Pub** (© **604/905-4047;** www.dubhlinngate.com) in the Pan Pacific Whistler Mountainside hotel, which often features live musicians.

SEA-TO-SKY HIGHWAY

The Sea-to-Sky Highway is the scenic 135km (85-mile) portion of Hwy. 99 that stretches from Horseshoe Bay to Pemberton, including Whistler. The road is famously beautiful, with views of Howe Sound and towering mountains along the route. And it's famously dangerous, with narrow, winding, single-lane stretches that go through deadly avalanche country. One of the conditions of winning the bid for the 2010 Olympic and Paralympic Games was upgrading the highway, and it's a much better, safer trip now. Whistler, of course, is the most popular destination along the road, but there are some other stops worth checking out.

Britannia Beach is a tiny community where workers at the Britannia Mining and Smelting Company were housed between 1900 and 1904. Some of the old clapboard houses are still standing, but these days, they're more likely to be art galleries or ice cream shops. The big attraction in the village, and worth a stop if you have restless kids in the car, is the **Britannia Mining Museum** (✆ **800/896-4044;** www.britannia minemuseum.ca). It offers a fascinating peek at what it was like to work as a miner back in the day. The best part of the experience is the little train that runs around the old mining tracks.

For a long time, **Squamish** was little more than a bedroom community where people who worked in Whistler could actually afford to live. Now it's considered the outdoor recreation capital of Canada. There's serious biking, hiking, and killer windsurfing here, plus just about any other activity you can imagine. There are two major natural attractions: the 335m-high (1,100-ft.) **Shannon Falls,** and the continent's tallest mono-lithic rock, the 700m (2,300-ft.) **Stawamus Chief.** The Chief is a favorite destination for rock climbers who scale its face, and hikers who clamber up one of three tough trails at the back.

As of spring 2014, there's an exciting, brand-new manmade attraction in between these two natural ones: the **Sea-to-Sky Gondola** (✆ **604/892-2550;** www.seatosky gondola.com). Eight-person cars whisk you on a 10-minute journey up the mountain in between the Chief and the falls; at the top there is a lodge where you can get a bite to eat, hiking trails to explore in summer, cross-country trails to ski in winter, and, of course, an absolutely stunning view of Howe Sound and the surrounding mountains. Tickets are C$35 adult, C$33 senior, C$23 youth 13 to 18, C$14 children 6 to 12, and free for kids 5 and under.

For more information on Squamish, contact the **Squamish Adventure Centre** (✆ **604/815-5084;** www.adventurecentre.ca) or **Tourism Squamish** (✆ **866/333-2102;** www.tourismsquamish.com).

Around **Brackendale** during the winter, thousands of bald eagles—the largest num-ber in North America—line the banks of the **Squamish, Cheakamus,** and **Mamquam** rivers to feed on spawning salmon. Local outfitters, including **Sun Wolf** (✆ **877/806-8046** or 604/898-1537; www.sunwolf.net) run tours.

The mountain town of **Pemberton,** about 30km (20 miles) north of Whistler, is famous for its organic farms and passionate foodie culture. There's a popular Slow Food cycle here every August, when thousands of people hop on their bikes for a tour of local farms (www.tourismpembertonbc.com). It's also home to the **Pemberton Distillery,** which makes vodka and other spirits from local organic potatoes. Drop by for a tasting (✆ **604/894-0222;** www.pembertondistillery.com).

VICTORIA

At first glance, Victoria is a pretty, quiet, well-behaved sort of place, all quaint and charming with historic houses, lush gardens, and a definite British accent. But Victoria is also so much more than that. For one thing, its setting at the rocky southern tip of Vancouver Island makes this not just a spectacularly beautiful landscape, but also one that lends itself to sailing, kayaking, whale-watching, hiking, biking, and rugged outdoor pursuits of all sorts. For another, this city has an exciting and distinctive culinary culture that goes well beyond the traditions of high tea and pub fare. Victoria, in short, is full of delicious surprises.

Victoria is not only the provincial capital, it is also one of the oldest cities in British Columbia, older than Vancouver by more than 20 years. And, unlike Vancouver, a city always eager to embrace the new and forget the past, Victoria has hung on to its lovely old buildings and its cherished traditions.

Back in the 19th century, Victoria was primarily a merchant city, supplying the crews of seafaring vessels roaming the Pacific Ocean as well as adventurers on their way to the Fraser Canyon and Klondike gold rushes. It was a very proper place, taking its role as an outpost of Queen Victoria's empire seriously. Even so, it has always had its surprising, even scandalous side: It was, for instance, a major importer and manufacturer of opium, and back in the day had a Barbary Coast neighborhood of gambling dens and brothels that was as dangerous and decadent as any in the empire.

Victoria is still a busy port, although these days the biggest industry in the area is advanced technology, followed by government and tourism. Visitors are drawn to the spectacular Butchart Gardens, one of the world's most impressive show gardens, and the romance of horse-drawn carriage rides through the city's historic streets. Beyond the charm, though, there is a vibrant city of talented young chefs, mixologists, artists, writers, and creative professionals of all sorts. And beneath all the prettiness thrums the haunting history of the First Nations people, in evidence all around if you look closely.

Yes, Victoria is as pretty and romantic as you imagine. But it's also rugged and adventurous, lively and fun, occasionally naughty, and always delicious.

ESSENTIALS

Arriving

BY PLANE **Victoria International Airport (YYJ)** is located on the Saanich Peninsula, about 25km (15 miles) northwest of Victoria (© **250/953-7533;** www.victoriaairport.com). It's a small, single-terminal airport that is undergoing a number of improvements in 2014, including a bigger pre-security clearance area and new food and shopping opportunities post-security.

From the airport, the most economical way to get into town is by the **YYJ Airport Shuttle** (© **778/351-4995** or 855/351-4995; www.yyjairportshuttle.com). It leaves at least hourly and more frequently during peak periods, starting at 7:35am and continuing to midnight, with stops at most of the major downtown hotels. Pickup from the hotels to the airport starts at 3:30am and ends at 7:45pm. The entire trip takes about an hour and the fare is C$24 one-way (C$20 each way if you have a return ticket, C$22 per person for a party of two, and C$15 for children).

A limited number of **hotel courtesy buses** also serve the airport.

By **taxi,** expect to pay around C$50, plus tip, for the trip downtown.

In addition, several car rental firms have desks at the airport, and if you plan to explore beyond the city center, a car may be your best option. They are **Avis** (© **800/ 879-2847** or 250/656-6033; www.avis.ca), **Budget** (© **800/668-9833** or 250/953-5300; www.budgetvictoria.com), **Hertz** (© **800/263-0600** or 250/657-0380; www.hertz.ca), and **National** (© **800/227-7368** or 250/656-2541; www.nationalcar.ca). From the airport, take Hwy. 17 south for the half-hour drive to Victoria; it becomes the city's main thoroughfare, Douglas Street, as you enter downtown.

BY FERRY Most people arrive in Victoria by ferry, and there are three different options, depending on where you're coming from, and how you are traveling.

The most popular service is **BC Ferries** (© **888/223-3779**; www.bcferries.com), a fleet of vast, drive-aboard ferries that ply the waters between Tsawwassen south of Vancouver and Swartz Bay to the north of Victoria. The ferry trip itself is 1 hour and 35 minutes through the scenic Gulf Islands, then another 45 minutes' drive into the city. If you aren't driving, you can also take a **Pacific Coach Lines** bus, climbing aboard a luxury coach either in downtown Vancouver or on the ferry for a comfortable, stress-free journey with free Wi-Fi (© **800/661-1725** or 604/662-7575; www.pacificcoach.com). Note that bus service is not available on all ferries, and that reservations are required.

In addition, two U.S. ferry services offer connections: The **Victoria Clipper** is a foot-passenger-only service that travels from Seattle to Victoria's Inner Harbour daily year-round, and twice daily from May through September (© **800/888-2535**; www.clippervacations.com). **Black Ball Transport's MV Coho** carries both vehicles and foot passengers from Port Angeles to Victoria Harbour at least twice daily year round (© **800/993-3779**; www.cohoferry.com). Check the websites for the latest in scheduled sailings, reservations, and fares. And don't forget you'll need a valid passport to enter Canada.

Visitor Information

Tourism Victoria Visitor Centre (812 Wharf St.; © **800/663-3883** or 250/953-2033; www.tourismvictoria.com) is located on the Inner Harbour, across from the Fairmont Empress Hotel. The center is open daily September through April 9am to 5pm, and May through August 8:30am to 7:30pm.

For details on the **after-dark scene,** pick up a copy of **"Monday Magazine,"** available free in cafes around the city; it's an excellent guide to Victoria's nightlife and has also driven at least one mayor from office with its award-winning muckraking journalism. The online version (www.mondaymag.com) has detailed entertainment listings.

For more information on Vancouver Island travel, visit the **Tourism Vancouver Island** site www.vancouverisland.travel. **Destination BC** has loads of information, travel stories, tips and much more for Victoria and the entire province at www. HelloBC.com. Check the **Victoria Times Colonist** site (www.timescolonist.com) for the latest news. And to see what other people are saying about Victoria, visit **www. tripadvisor.ca**.

City Layout

Victoria was born at the edge of the Inner Harbour in the 1840s and spread outward from there. The areas of most interest to visitors lie along the eastern edge of the **Inner Harbour**. North of the Johnson Street Bridge is the **Upper Harbour**, which is largely industrial but taking on new life as old buildings are redeveloped. A little farther east, the **Ross Bay** and **Oak Bay** residential areas around Dallas Road and Beach Drive reach the beaches along the open waters of the Strait of Juan de Fuca.

Victoria's central landmark is the **Fairmont Empress Hotel** on Government Street, right across from the Inner Harbour. If you turn your back to the hotel, downtown is on your right, while the **BC Parliament Buildings** (also known as the **Provincial Legislature Buildings**) and the **Royal BC Museum** are on your immediate left. Next to them is the dock for the **Seattle and Port Angeles ferries,** and beyond that the residential community of **James Bay,** the first neighborhood in the city to be developed.

MAIN ARTERIES & STREETS

Three main **north-south arteries** intersect just about every destination you may want to reach in Victoria. **Government Street** goes through Victoria's main downtown shopping-and-dining district. **Douglas Street,** running parallel to Government Street, is the main business thoroughfare, as well as the road to Nanaimo and the rest of the island. It's also Trans-Canada Hwy. 1. The "Mile 0" marker sits at the corner of Douglas Street and Dallas Road. Also running parallel to Government and Douglas streets is **Blanshard Street** (Hwy. 17), the route to the Saanich Peninsula—including the Sidney-Vancouver ferry terminal—and Butchart Gardens.

Important **east-west streets** include **Johnson Street** at the northern end of downtown, **Belleville Street** at the Inner Harbour's southern edge, and **Dallas Road,** which follows the water's edge past residential areas and beaches before it winds northward up to Oak Bay.

STREET MAPS

Street maps are available free at the **Tourism Victoria Visitor Centre** (see "Visitor Information," above). The best map of the surrounding area is the **"BC Provincial Parks"** map of Vancouver Island, also available at the Info Centre.

The Neighborhoods in Brief

Victoria starts at the Inner Harbour, which is also the oldest part of the city, and radiates outward from there. Most of the city spreads north and east, although there is a growing community in West Victoria.

Inner Harbour For most visitors, this is where it's at, and it's what those glossy tourism brochures depict. Framed by the **BC Parliament Buildings** on one side and the **Fairmont Empress Hotel** on another, the Inner Harbour is where to find cabs, horse-drawn carriage rides, double-decker tour buses, ferries, floatplanes, whale-watching outfitters, kayaking tours, fish and chips, and the main Tourism Victoria Visitor Centre. The **BC Royal Museum** is among the top attractions, as is a waterside stroll around the harbor to **Fisherman's Wharf,** with is its small community of fishing boats and floating homes. In summer, the place fills up with a myriad of artist-vendors who add to the entertainment value of your meanderings.

Downtown Also called Old Town, this area has been the city's social and commercial focal point since the mid-1800s, when settlers first arrived by ship. This is also the area of the city most popular with visitors, filled with shops, museums, heritage buildings, and lots of restaurants. The area's fascinating Barbary Coast history—which includes rum smuggling, opium importing, gold prospecting, whaling, fur trading, and shipping—is reflected in the hundreds of heritage buildings, once home to chandleries, warehouses, factories, whorehouses, and gambling dens.

Chinatown Victoria's Chinatown is tiny—only 2 square blocks—but venerable. In fact, it's the second oldest Chinese community in North America (after San Francisco). At one time, legal opium manufacturing took place in the hidden courtyard buildings flanking the 1.2m-wide (4-ft.) Fan Tan Alley, Canada's narrowest commercial street.

James Bay, Ross Bay, Rockland & Oak Bay When Victoria was a busy port and trading post, the local aristocracy would retire to homes in these neighborhoods to escape the hustle and bustle in the city center. Today, they remain beautiful residential communities. Houses are perched on hills overlooking the straits or nestled amidst lushly landscaped gardens. Golf courses, marinas, and cozy inns edge the waters, where you can stroll the beaches or take a dip if you don't mind the chilly water.

Fernwood This charming residential neighborhood may not have any oceanfront to boast of, but it makes up for it with plenty of character. Home mostly to young families and creative professionals, its tree-lined streets are filled with heritage homes, popular restaurants, quirky boutiques, and the historic Belfry Theatre.

Victoria West Once the city's industrial zone, this area across the Johnson Street Bridge is now among its trendiest neighborhoods, especially for young professionals who enjoy the proximity to downtown. Several new condo developments have gone up here, and the area has plenty of bike trails, walkways, parks, and cool eateries to feed all those newcomers.

Saanich This is the part of the city you'll drive past on your way north and east to the ferry terminal. It's largely a suburban residential area of neighborhoods such as Quadra, Gordon Head, and Cordova Bay, which may be great places to live, but don't offer many attractions to the visitor. However, if you travel further out on the Saanich Peninsula, you will come across Butchart Gardens, Sea Cider, and the charming little town of Sidney-by-the-Sea, with its many bookstores.

GETTING AROUND

ON FOOT If you're planning to spend your time in the downtown area, you can easily walk just anywhere you want to go. In fact, with its safe streets, mild climate, largely flat landscape, and compact environs, Victoria is a fantastic walking city. It's the best way to see the things you want to see, and discover all sorts of myriad unexpected treasures. Wear comfy shoes, and bring a shopping bag.

BY BUS   The **Victoria Regional Transit System** (© **250/382-6161;** www.bctransit. com) operates some 40 bus routes through greater Victoria, as well as the nearby towns of Sooke and Sidney, and as far as Butchart Gardens and the ferry terminal in Swartz Bay. Regular service on the main routes runs daily from 6am to just past midnight. BC Transit also offers trip-planning help with Google Transit through Google Maps. A single fare is C$2.50, while a book of 10 tickets is C$23, and a DayPASS, which covers unlimited travel for a day, is only C$5, making it a good deal for visitors. You can purchase tickets or passes anywhere you see a "Faredealer" sign, as well as at the Tourism Victoria Visitor Centre, where you can also pick up schedules and route maps.

The Ferry Ballet

Starting at 10:45am every Sunday from May to September, the Victoria Harbour Ferries gather in front of the Fairmont Empress to perform a must-be-seen-to-be-believed **ferry "ballet"**—and they've been doing this every weekend since the ferries first arrived here 21 years ago.

BY FERRY Crossing the Inner, Upper, and Victoria harbors aboard one of the green and yellow 12-passenger **Victoria Harbour Ferries** (☏ 250/708-0201; www.victoriaharbourferry.com) is cheap, practical, and fun. There are a number of options—a water taxi service that will take you directly to your stop, the 45-minute guided harbor tours, a 60-minute guided tour of the Gorge Water Way, private charters, and the ever-popular Pickle Pub Crawls. Between May and September, the ferries transport revelers to and from Victoria's finest harbor pubs, and every group of four will receive a free appetizer at each stop. Prices vary from C$5 for a single stop in the Inner Harbour to C$15 for the pub crawl and C$44 for a combination harbor and Gorge tour.

BY CAR If you are planning to stick to downtown and the main attractions, you can get wherever you need to go by foot or by transit. But if you do plan to venture further afield, a car will make things a lot easier. You can rent a car at the airport or downtown on Douglas Street at one of the following agencies: **Avis** (☏ 800/879-2847 or 250/386-8468; www.avis.ca), **Budget** (☏ 800/268-8900 or 250/953-5300; www.budgetvictoria.com), **Hertz** (☏ 800/263-0600 or 250/952-3765; www.hertz.ca), and **National** (☏ 800/387-4747 or 250/386-1828; www.nationalcar.ca).

Metered street parking is widely available downtown, but since many meters have a centralized location, remember that you'll need to make a note of your space number before you head to the machine. Unmetered parking is very rare, but parking rates are pretty reasonable compared to other Canadian cities. Rates are C$2.50 for an hour, free on Sundays and statutory holidays. Pay 'N Go meters accept coins, credit cards, and the new city parking card. All major hotels have guest parking and parking lots can be found throughout the downtown.

Driving in Victoria can be bafflingly frustrating, especially for such a small city without much traffic volume. The locals tend to putter along well under the speed limit, while aggressive young drivers from up-Island blast through town at warp speeds and visitors blunder along in a haze of confusion, trying to figure out the system of one-way streets that seem to randomly change names once they leave the downtown core. Meanwhile, the city's pedestrians think nothing of stepping out blindly mid-block in the middle of heavy traffic, while flocks of cyclists seem to appear from nowhere. Take a deep breath and be patient.

BY BICYCLE Victoria is considered the cycling capital of Canada, and certainly it is the easiest way to get around the downtown and beach areas. The city has numerous bike lanes and paved paths in parks and along beaches. Helmets are mandatory, and riding on sidewalks is illegal, except where bike paths are indicated. You can rent bikes starting at C$7 per hour and C$28 per day (lock and helmet included) from **Cycle BC** (685 Humboldt St.; ☏ 866/380-2453 or 250/380-2453; www.cyclebc.ca).

BY TAXI Within the downtown area, you can expect to travel to most destinations for less than C$10, plus tip. It's best to call for a cab; you won't have much luck if you try to flag one down on the street since drivers don't always stop, especially when it's raining. Call for a pickup from **Yellow Cabs** (☏ 250/381-2242) or **Blue Bird Cabs** (☏ 250/382-2222).

Embassies All embassies in British Columbia are located in Vancouver; if you lose your passport or run into other difficulties, contact the numbers on p. 208.

Emergencies Call ⓒ **911** for fire, police, and ambulance services.

Internet Access Most hotels offer Internet access and it's quite often free, at least in public areas. Many downtown cafes also offer free Wi-Fi, including the ubiquitous Starbucks chain. And the Greater **Victoria Public Library** (ⓒ **250/**

382-7241; www.gvpl.ca) also offers free Wi-Fi to the public at all its locations, including the main branch at 735 Broughton St.

Pharmacies For a 24-hour pharmacy, visit the **Shoppers Drug Mart** at 3511 Blanshard St. (ⓒ **250/ 475-7572;** www1.shoppers drugmart.ca).

Post Office Canada **Post's main Victoria office** is at 709 Yates St. (ⓒ **800/ 267-1177**). There are also postal outlets in **Shoppers Drug Mart** and other stores

displaying the "Canada Post" sign.

Safety Victoria is an exceptionally safe city, with few areas that are dangerous to explore after dark. That said, pickpockets follow wherever crowds gather, so remain alert and watch your possessions. Also, a fair number of panhandlers and homeless people tend to congregate on Douglas Street. They are rarely dangerous, but they can be unpredictable, so just be aware of your surroundings at all times.

WHERE TO STAY IN VICTORIA

Whether you are looking for a palatial room with a view or just a cheap-and-cheerful place to rest your head, Victoria has the perfect accommodation for you. Most are in the downtown area, with several of the best arrayed around the Inner Harbour and within easy walking distance of the main attractions. True, there are a lot of older hotels and motels that could use a bit of an update, but there are great choices at every price point. In fact, many prices have come down in the past 5 years, thanks to the weak economy and a fluctuating tourist base, which just leaves more cash to spend on souvenirs.

Inner Harbour

This is Victoria's prime accommodation real estate, with hotels clustered around the bustling Inner Harbour, where guests can watch the fishing boats and floatplanes during the day and enjoy the soft sea breezes at night. Most of the main attractions are nearby, but the biggest attraction is that view. And that's just what you'll be paying for.

EXPENSIVE

Fairmont Empress Hotel ★★★   Not just a place to stay, but Victoria's most legendary landmark, with the best location of all, right at the heart of the Inner Harbour. The hotel was built in 1908, designed in the Chateau style by Victoria's famous (and famously scandalous) architect, Francis Rattenbury. It still retains its colonial-era ——stepping into the clubby Bengal Lounge, with its palm trees and slow-moving , is like stepping right into the last days of the Raj—but with up-to-the-minute ntive service and amenities, including the luxurious Willow Stream Spa. Decor is tional, with pastel-colored walls, swagged draperies, dark, antique-looking furni- and vintage-style botanical prints on the walls, and the rooms can be a bit on the side, especially the bathrooms, but everything is beautifully appointed. Besides, you look out onto the harbor, you'll forget the cramped quarters. The Empress lways been Victoria's favorite meeting place and hangout, and you'll find

One of the best places to view Victoria is from the top of **Observatory Hill** in the municipality of Saanich. Until 2013, it was also the best place in the city to view the stars. This is where you'll find the century-old Dominion Astrophysical Observatory, a National Historic Site of Canada that was up until the 1960s one of the most important astrophysical research centers in the world. When the Royal Astronomical Society of Canada built the observatory between 1914 and 1918, its 72-inch aperture telescope was designed to be the largest in the world. Over the following decades many crucial discoveries were made here. Even after it was eclipsed by bigger and better observatories, its public interpretive center was a popular and informative attraction, especially for school kids. Then, in 2013, the federal government closed down the public facility, apparently for economic reasons. There are petitions to reopen it, and plans to hold some public events here during the summer months. Meanwhile, you can still watch the stars from the top of the hill. They're just a little farther out of reach. Observatory Hill and the Dominion Astrophysical Observatory are at 5071 West Saanich Rd., *(C)* **250/363-0001;** www.victoria.rasc.ca/observing/observatory.

BY PEDI-CAB   Sit back and enjoy a fully guided tour of Victoria's most popular attractions from one of these two- or four-seat bicycle-powered cabs. Special packages are available for cruise ship guests or for those who want to explore Victoria's secrets, as well as those who want to customize their own experiences. Prices vary, but start at around C$15 per guest per half-hour, depending on the experience. Contact **Victoria Pedicab Tours** to see what they have scheduled or to set up your own excursion (*(C)* **250/884-0121;** www.victoriatours.net).

[Fast FACTS] VICTORIA

Banks & ATMs   You'll find 24-hour PLUS and Cirrus bank machines throughout the city, as well as branches of the major Canadian banks (BMO Bank of Montreal, CIBC, HSBC, RBC Royal Bank, Scotiabank, and Canada Trust). Remember that if you withdraw money from a bank that is not your own, it will likely charge an additional fee; still, this is often a better option than converting foreign money to Canadian dollars.

Business Hours   Most stores and other businesses are generally open Monday through Saturday 10am–6pm. Some establishments are open later, as well as on Sundays, especially in summer. Restaurants may open only for dinner (starting at 5pm). Last call at the city's **bars** and **cocktail lounges** is 2am.

Doctors & Dentists   Most major hotels have a doctor and dentist on call. Victoria does not have any 24-hour dental or medical clinics, but it does have several hospitals for emergencies, including Royal Jubilee Hospital on / Street (*(C)* **250/370** / Some medical clin/ however, have ex/ hours and accep/ patients, such a/ **Mall Medical (**/ is open daily (3170 Tillicu**/ 381-8112;** v/ medicalclin/ the Tillicu**/ Dental C**/ **7711;** w/ is open/ extend/ throu/

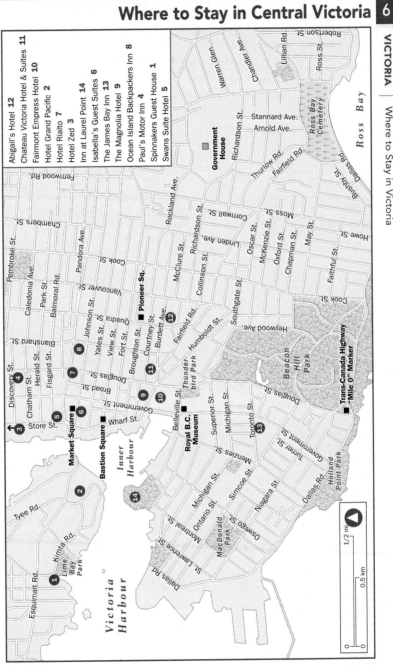

Abigail's Hotel **12**
Chateau Victoria Hotel & Suites **11**
Fairmont Empress Hotel **10**
Hotel Grand Pacific **2**
Hotel Rialto **7**
Hotel Zed **3**
Inn at Laurel Point **14**
Isabella's Guest Suites **6**
The James Bay Inn **13**
The Magnolia Hotel **9**
Ocean Island Backpackers Inn **8**
Paul's Motor Inn **4**
Spinnakers Guest House **1**
Swans Suite Hotel **5**

government staff from the legislature hobnobbing in the lounge and locals celebrating special occasions in the posh Empress Room. The decadent afternoon tea in the rosy-hued, chintz-swagged tea lobby is a must.

721 Government St. ⓒ **866/540-4429** or 250/384-8111. www.fairmont.com/empress-victoria. 477 units. C$250–C$800 standard room, C$400–C$1,200 suite, C$400–C$1,500 Gold Floor. Special rates available for seniors and AAA/CAA members, as well as seasonal offers and various getaway packages. Underground valet parking C$30/day. Up to 2 small pets accepted if not left unattended (C$25/day per pet). **Amenities:** 2 restaurants (1 open summer only), bar/lounge, tea lobby, spa, gym, indoor heated pool, babysitting, concierge, room service, executive-level rooms (Gold Floor), 24-hour business center, Wi-Fi (C$15/day; free with Fairmont President's Club membership).

Hotel Grand Pacific ★★ This is probably Victoria's best business hotel, but it's also a lot more than that. Conveniently located next to the BC Parliament Buildings and across from the ferry terminal where the Clipper and Coho dock, the Grand Pacific is a great base for any visitor to Victoria. Its guest rooms are spacious, with lovely harbor views and classically gracious decor including glossy Queen Anne-style furnishings with delicate brass fittings. Its grand public spaces include three ballrooms and several breakout meeting rooms, making this a destination for both conferences and weddings. In addition, the hotel features the popular Pacific Restaurant & Terrace, with its menu of casual fare based on local ingredients, and an exceptional tea program using Victoria's own Silk Road Tea. The hotel is also home to the Victoria Athletic Club, one of the city's best full-service fitness centers, with a pool, equipment, classes, and all the works—you might even find a local Olympian working out next to you. Swell as all this is already, note that the hotel is scheduled to get a major update in late 2014 or 2015.

463 Belleville St. ⓒ **800/663-7550** or 250/386-0450. www.hotelgrandpacific.com. 304 units. C$200–C$300 double, C$250–C$500 suite. Special bed & breakfast deal available, as well as packages for families, seniors, and others. Underground parking C$18/day self, C$24/day valet. Pets accepted (C$50 1-time fee). **Amenities:** Restaurant, bar, cafe, room service, full-service fitness center, swimming pool, spa, concierge, babysitting, squash courts, free bike loans, free Wi-Fi.

Inn at Laurel Point ★★★ With an enviable waterfront location near the entrance to the Inner Harbour, this elegant, art-filled inn is a favorite for weddings, conferences, and romantic getaways. Its sweeping, cool white lines are unusual in a city better known for the quaint and cozy—if you can, try to book a room in the Erickson Wing, designed by Vancouver's well-known modernist architect Arthur Erickson. The rooms are huge, with spacious balconies overlooking the harbor and a decor that blends the clean simplicity of contemporary furniture with rustic local materials. The bathrooms, especially in the Erickson Wing, are pure decadence, with miles of marble counter space and luxuriously deep soaker tubs. You can even enjoy a facial, massage, or pedi right in your room with the "Inn Room" spa service. Throughout, the hotel is dotted with works of First Nations, Asian, and local art, but the greatest artwork may just be outside, in the serene, seaside Japanese garden, with its waterfalls, stone paths, trees, and flowers. The inn is also home to one of the city's best restaurants, Aura, where chef Tak Ito brings Asian deftness to local ingredients.

680 Montreal St. ⓒ **800/663-7667** or 250/386-8721. www.laurelpoint.com. 200 units. C$109–C$239 standard room (Laurel Wing), C$169–C$339 suite (Erickson Wing). Bed & breakfast package available, as well as various getaway offers. Underground parking C$17/day. Pets accepted (C$30/day). **Amenities:** Restaurant, bar, room service, babysitting, concierge, fitness center and pool, in-room spa services, special treats for pets, free Wi-Fi (if you book direct with hotel).

MODERATE

Spinnakers Guesthouses ★★ You'll find this set of cozy—and affordable—guestrooms way on the other side of the harbor, in West Victoria. They're perfect for the traveler who's looking for charm and character, and doesn't mind a touch of inconvenience. Five of the rooms are tucked away in a restored 1884 heritage home; they all have private patios, fireplaces, and, thankfully, new wiring and plumbing. For couples who want to spread out a little, there is also the updated 1940s one-bedroom bungalow, with its heritage fruit trees, herb garden, and honeybees. And then there are the spacious garden suites, which were originally created as a personal residence for architectural designer Michael Cullin. They have fireplaces, living rooms, and kitchens or kitchenettes, as well as a lush garden setting, and are perfect for longer stays and families traveling together. Guests receive a complimentary beer and truffle tasting at Spinnakers Gastro Brewpub, still the city's iconic pub.

308 Catherine St. ✆ **877/838-2739** or 250/386-2739. www.spinnakers.com. 10 units. C$149–C$299. Breakfast included. Long-term stays available. Free on-site parking. Heritage House adults only; children welcome in all other rooms. **Amenities:** Restaurant/pub, fireplaces, patios, kitchen facilities in bungalow or garden suites, concierge service at the Provisions Store, free Wi-Fi.

INEXPENSIVE

James Bay Inn Hotel Suites & Cottage ★ This historic hotel isn't right on the harbor, but tucked away in the pretty residential neighborhood behind the Legislature and on the edge of Beacon Hill Park. It's not the most luxurious of accommodations, but what it lacks in luxe, it more than makes up in price and location, not to mention the friendliness of the staff. The property actually comprises three components. The four-story inn, which was built in 1911 in Victoria's signature half-timbered Tudor style, has public spaces filled with antiques and a cozy, lived-in feel. Guest rooms tend to be pretty basic, but some have fireplaces, king beds, and bay windows. The DBI Cafe and Pub are popular local hangouts, earning raves for their well-prepared casual fare, such as the exceptional creamy seafood chowder. The suites in the 1908 Heritage House are slightly more upscale (and better for families), while the crème de la crème of this property is the nearby cottage, perfect for extended stays and larger groups. Note that the inn does not have an elevator.

270 Government St. ✆ **800/836-2649** or 250/384-7151. www.jamesbayinn.com. 45 units. C$59–C$109 standard inn rooms, C$109–C$169 Heritage House suites, C$149–C$214 cottage (based on double occupancy; C$10 per extra guest). Guests receive discount at hotel restaurant; some special packages available. Free parking and secure bicycle storage. **Amenities:** Restaurant/bar, free Wi-Fi.

Downtown

The city center is where you'll likely spend most of your time, so it's a good place to stay as well. You'll find a wide array of accommodation here, from luxurious inns to backpacker hostels. Everything you want is just a short stroll away, so park the car, and start exploring.

EXPENSIVE

Abigail's Hotel ★ This may be one of the most romantic hotels in Victoria—or anywhere. Surrounded by gardens in a leafy residential neighborhood just east of downtown, it's a boutique B&B housed in a sprawling 1930s heritage Tudor-style mansion. That heritage status means there's no elevator, and if you're looking for all the mod cons, this may not be the place for you. But if you prefer antique furniture, down duvets, fireplaces, a vast library to browse, and welcoming hospitality, then you will love Abigail's. There's also a small spa if you need a little extra pampering. Plus they serve a fabulous three-course gourmet breakfast every day, and if you're lucky, it'll include the fruit-filled crêpes.

906 McClure St. ⓒ **800/561-6565** or 250/388-5363. www.abigailshotel.com. 23 units. Rates C$159–C$389 (based on double occupancy; C$30 each additional guest). 3-course breakfast included, as well as welcome cookies and nightly hors d'oeuvres. Special packages available. Free parking. Closed Jan 2–11. No pets. No children 12 and under. **Amenities:** Breakfast room, library, lounge, spa, concierge, free Wi-Fi.

Magnolia Hotel & Spa ★★★   Once you check into this discreetly gorgeous boutique hotel a block away from the harbor, you may never want to leave. A major makeover in 2013 cooled down what was a slightly fussy traditional decor, and left the rooms shimmering in elegant silver, smoke, and pearl. Tall windows let in lots of light, though it must be said, there's not much of a view, except from some of the Diamond Rooms on the 6th and 7th floors. No matter—the beds are lusciously comfortable, the marble bathrooms have deep soaker tubs and walk-in showers, some rooms have gas fireplaces, the service is warmly helpful, and it's all perfectly lovely. The hotel is also home to the beautifully appointed Magnolia Spa, which carries the Intelligent Nutrients line created by the founder of Aveda, as well as the Catalano Restaurant & Cicchetti Bar, which offers breakfast and room service for guests.

623 Courtney St. ⓒ **877/624-6654** or 250/381-0999. www.magnoliahotel.com. 64 units. C$179–C$289 double, C$229–C$389 Diamond Room, C$329–C$429 Signature Diamond Room. Continental breakfast buffet included if you book direct through hotel. Valet parking C$24/day. Pets allowed (C$60 1-time fee). **Amenities:** Restaurant, bar, room service, spa, concierge, executive-level rooms, access to fitness center, free Wi-Fi.

MODERATE

Chateau Victoria Hotel & Suites ★   Terrific location, terrific value. The Chateau Vic is an 18-story property right in the heart of all the action. It was built in 1975 as an apartment building, so many of the units are quite large and have kitchens or kitchenettes. Over the past few years, the whole property has undergone a significant makeover, and has taken on a sophisticated new look—muted colors, sleek lines, down duvets, chandeliers in the airy lobby. It's also home to the happening Clive's Classic Lounge, one of the best places in town for handcrafted cocktails, and the Vista 18 rooftop restaurant, which offers unbeatable views along with a huge "martini" list and a gourmet menu of mostly local fare.

640 Burdett Ave. ⓒ **800/663-5891** or 250/382-4221. www.chateauvictoria.com. 176 units (118 of them suites). C$129–C$185 double, C$135–C$289 suite. Parking C$15/day. Dogs allowed (C$15/day). **Amenities:** Restaurant, cocktail lounge, room service, fitness room, indoor pool, in-room spa service, concierge, some rooms feature convenience or full kitchen, free Wi-Fi.

Hotel Rialto ★★   As makeovers go, this one was a doozy. Back in the day, this was the notorious Hotel Douglas, aka the Dougie, a rough, tough, slightly scary old joint. In 2000, it was bought by new owners who have lavished it with love and oodles of money. Now it is one of Victoria's coolest boutique hotels. Located right on the edge of Chinatown—it was built in 1911 by a Chinese developer named Lim Bang—it's got a clean, airy, and spacious look, with meticulous attention to details like the Italian fresco walls in the lobby. Guest rooms are simple but chic, with a silvery color palette, dark wood furniture, subtly patterned throws on the beds, historic black-and-white photos on the walls, and bathrooms that may be small but have luxurious details like polished granite wash stands. The desks especially are well designed, with all the essentials like iPhone docking stations and free Wi-Fi. The hotel is also home to the

Veneto Tapa Lounge, one of the city's favorite hangouts and among the best places for handcrafted cocktails.

653 Pandora Ave. ✆ **800/332-9981** or 250/383-4157. www.hotelrialto.ca. 39 units. Rates C$99–C$159 double. Continental breakfast included, as well as a welcome cheese platter. Some seasonal packages available. Parking C$15/day. **Amenities:** Restaurant, bar, coffee shop, liquor store, access to gym, concierge, free Wi-Fi.

Isabella's Guest Suites ★ Beautiful and homey, this cozy downtown B&B is a rare find. It features two beautifully appointed self-contained units with full kitchens in a building that dates back to 1887. Think bold colors, French doors, bow windows, and claw-foot tubs. But what really makes this such a deal is its dream location in the heart of trendy "LoJo" (Lower Johnson Street), where it's surrounded by boutiques and restaurants. Best of all, it's right upstairs from one of the best breakfast places in town, Willie's Bakery & Café, and your room rate comes with a voucher for brekkie or lunch. Just try to resist the maple-syrup–glazed bacon.

Waddington Alley, 537 Johnson St. ✆ **250/812-9216.** www.isabellasbb.com. 2 units. C$140–C$150 double (additional rollaway bed available for 1 of the suites). Rates include C$20 credit toward breakfast or lunch; long-term rates available. Free parking. **Amenities:** Restaurant downstairs, kitchen, free Wi-Fi.

Swan's Suite Hotel ★ This funky, friendly, art-filled boutique hotel is located in a heritage building right by the Johnson Street Bridge, Market Square, and many of the city's most popular bars and pubs. In fact, one of them is right downstairs—busy Swan's Brewpub, which features live music every night. That means some of the rooms can be noisy, so be sure to ask for a quiet one if that is an issue for you. The rooms themselves are all spacious suites with full kitchens, and are graciously appointed with comfy, overstuffed furniture, bold colors, and original art on the walls. The penthouse is a truly special place, a massive suite on three levels, with wood-burning fireplace, luxurious furniture, and a rooftop terrace with spectacular harbor views.

506 Pandora Ave. ✆ **800/668-7296** or 250/361-3310. www.swanshotel.com. 29 units. C$99–C$275 double, C$895–C$1,295 penthouse suite. Romantic getaway and beer lovers' packages available. Parking C$10/day. Dogs welcome in some rooms (C$35 1-time fee). **Amenities:** Restaurant, brewpub with live music, full kitchen, original artwork, dog beds and treats, babysitting, concierge, free Wi-Fi.

INEXPENSIVE

Ocean Island Backpackers ★ If you're looking for a real bargain and don't mind sharing a room, or at least a bathroom, then this character-filled hostel is the place for you. A heritage building in the heart of downtown, it has plenty of charm to go along with its bargain price. Bright, cheerful, and clean, with simple furniture and Indonesian art throughout, this is a favorite with families, active seniors, and budget travelers, who gather in its comfy common area to swap travel tales. It offers dorm rooms and family rooms with shared bathrooms if you don't mind sharing, and private rooms, some with en-suite facilities, if you do. Plus there are three additional global-themed garden suites located in a historic house in the James Bay neighborhood if that's more your style. Be aware that there is no elevator here.

791 Pandora Ave. ✆ **888/888-4180** or 250/385-1788. www.oceanisland.com. 60 units, 6 shared bathrooms. C$20–C$29 dorm, C$30–C$100 private room (some with en-suite bathrooms), C$69–C$148 garden suite (based on double occupancy; extra charge for additional people). Special rates for extended stays. Kids 10 and under stay free. Discounts at local businesses. Parking C$10/day. Pets allowed only at Ocean Island Suites (C$11/day). **Amenities:** Lounge, shared kitchen, laundry, concierge, free Wi-Fi.

Outside the Central Area

While most of Victoria's attractions, hotels, and restaurants are downtown, some visitors prefer not to stay right in the city's urban center. For those travelers, there are basically two wildly different options. Where Hwy. 17 turns into Douglas Street, there are a number of inexpensive hotels and motels, convenient for those with early flights or whose journeys take them up island. And then there are a handful of beautiful high-end resorts in glorious natural settings dotted around the city's outskirts. Both have their charms. Here are some of the best.

EXPENSIVE

Brentwood Bay Resort & Spa ★★ This peaceful resort is tucked away on a quiet forested inlet across the bay from Butchart Gardens. It's designed in contemporary West Coast style, all clean lines, big windows, and natural materials of wood and stone, with spacious guest rooms filled with cozy furniture and decadent bathrooms with Jacuzzi tubs. This is one romantic spot, but it's also a favorite destination for eco-adventures like kayaking, scuba diving, and whale-watching. Its Seagrille Restaurant & Pub is a popular destination for seafood, especially its exceptional sushi. And for even more relaxation, there is the Essence of Life Spa. Ahh!

849 Verdier Ave. ℂ **888/544-2079** or 250/544-2079. www.brentwoodbayresort.com. 39 units. C$200–C$600 double, C$500–C$900 villa. Spa, gourmet, eco-adventure, and Butchart Gardens packages available. Free parking. From Victoria, take Hwy. 17 north to Keating Crossroads, turn left onto Saanich Road, turn right onto Verdier Ave. Not recommended for children 15 and under. **Amenities:** Restaurant, pub, spa, marina, eco-adventure center, shuttle, concierge, complimentary champagne, free Wi-Fi.

Oak Bay Beach Hotel ★★★ This luxurious seaside boutique resort property sits right at the heart of one of Canada's toniest neighborhoods. Oak Bay is known for its genteel British heritage, not to mention its many Tudor-style mansions, a charming boutique-filled village, two marinas, three golf courses, and all the accouterments of a life well lived. The hotel itself is a key part of that community. It's been owned by the same family since it first opened in 1927 and was completely rebuilt, restored, and reopened in 2012. Although the hotel is almost entirely new, many features of the original have been retained, and the feel is of a grand old manor that has been lovingly maintained. The attention to detail here is meticulous, from the luxe sheets to the perfectly soundproofed walls. All the rooms have either an ocean or residential view, fireplace, spa-inspired bathroom, kitchenette, and oversize windows. The hotel is home to The Snug Pub, a newly renovated homage to Victoria's first pub, with the original beams and customers' pint mugs, as well as the gorgeous gourmet dining room, cozy Kate's Café, and even special dinner-theater programs. Plus your stay gets you access to the mineral pools that overlook the ocean. Should you need further relaxation after a tough day on a nearby golf course, the Boathouse Spa offers nurturing treatments with a stunning view.

1175 Beach Dr. ℂ **800/668-7758** or 250/598-4556. www.oakbaybeachhotel.com. 100 units. C$179–C$429 double, C$339–C$599 suite. Special packages, including spa getaways, available year round. Free underground parking. Dogs allowed (C$30/day per dog, size and number limited). **Amenities:** Restaurant, pub, cafe, dinner theater, room service, gym, spa, outdoor mineral pools, VIP access to local golf courses, shuttle, concierge, butler and in-room chef service available for suites, fireplaces, kitchen or kitchenette, free Wi-Fi.

Sooke Harbour House ★★★ Long before barnacles and nettles and sea asparagus became a thing on every trendy menu, Sinclair and Frederique Philip had already gone full-on locavore. It was 1979 when they bought this clapboard farmhouse on a scenic spit in the village of Sooke, about a half-hour drive from Victoria, and welcomed their first guests with goodies foraged from forest, sea, and their vast, fragrant herb garden. Since then, the international accolades have showered down, and in 35 years, the quality and inventiveness have never wavered. The bright rustic-elegant guest rooms are filled with art, stone fireplaces, soaker tubs, and sumptuously comfortable furnishings. Breakfast is served in your room while you enjoy the ocean view. And then there is the incomparable local cuisine. This, right here, is exactly what life on the West Coast was meant to be.

1528 Whiffin Spit Rd. ℂ **800/899-9688** or 250/642-3421. www.sookeharbourhouse.com. 28 units. C$299–C$699 double. Breakfast included. Seasonal packages available. Free parking. About 30km (19 miles) west of Victoria along Hwy. 14. Pets allowed (C$40/day for 1, C$60/day for 2). Dining room closed Wed–Thurs. **Amenities:** Restaurant, beach, sauna, gardens, access to nearby golf course, in-room spa services, wood-burning fireplace, private balcony, art gallery, gift shop, concierge, babysitting, free Wi-Fi.

Westin Bear Mountain Victoria Golf Resort & Spa ★★ The ambience is all rustic western mountain resort, but with all the practical modern functionality you'd expect from Westin. And yes, that includes their Heavenly Beds and Baths. The hotel is part of a high-end resort-community development built around two championship golf courses designed by Jack Nicklaus and his son. It's an ideal active getaway, with hiking, cycling, swimming pool, and a fitness center if golf isn't your thing. All the rooms have kitchenettes, but there are also several good restaurants to help you refuel. And if you need a bit of pampering after all that activity, there is the luxuriously exceptional Santé Spa.

1999 Country Club Way. ℂ **888/533-2327** or 250/391-7160. www.bearmountain.ca. 165 units. C$129–C$389 double, C$209–C$699 suite. Resort fee (C$20) includes parking, fitness club access, bike rental, golf bag valet, and storage. Breakfast, golf, and family packages available. Take Hwy. 1 north to Exit 14, then follow Millstream Rd. to Bear Mountain Pkwy. **Amenities:** 2 restaurants, lounge, room service, fitness center, spa, 2 championship golf courses, outdoor pool, kitchenette, balcony, concierge, free Wi-Fi.

MODERATE

Sidney Pier Hotel & Spa ★ Sidney is a sleepy little seaside community just a few minutes from the ferry terminal, best known for its idyllic views, proximity to Butchart Gardens, the Shaw Ocean Discovery Centre, and its many, many bookstores. This cool, West Coast–style boutique hotel is a lovely and restful way to enjoy the best of the area. The first thing you'll notice is that it seems to be all windows, and why not, when the view is this beautiful? Guest rooms are bright and spacious, with muted sea-inspired colors, comfortable furnishings, and lots of glass, from the chrome-framed nightstands to the etched glass wall art to the huge windows. The hotel is also home to the upscale-casual Haro's Restaurant + Bar as well as the excellent Haven Spa.

9805 Seaport Place. ℂ **866/659-9445** or 250/655-9445. www.sidneypier.com. 55 units. C$139–C$209 double, C$189–C$344 suites. Romance and other packages available. Parking C$5/day. From Victoria, take Hwy. 17 toward ferry terminal; take Sidney exit and follow Beacon Ave. to waterfront. Dogs allowed (C$50/one-time fee). **Amenities:** Restaurant, lounge, cafe, room service, fitness center, spa, beach, shuttle, fridge or full kitchen in room, concierge, hotel dog, free Wi-Fi.

INEXPENSIVE

Hotel Zed ★ The Blue Ridge Inn was just another one of the many ubiquitous motels along Douglas Street. But in its new incarnation as the hip, happening Hotel Zed, it's something else indeed. Think the vibrant, youthful style of the mid-20th-century

Palm Springs. The whole place has been brightened up with eye-catchingly bold lines and bright colors—even the guest rooms are decked out in hues of tangerine and plum or turquoise and lime. A retro-casual restaurant and bar is scheduled to open in fall 2014, and the hotel also features a games room where guests can play Ping-Pong or Monopoly and an indoor swimming pool with a sun-drenched outdoor deck. The hotel is about a 40-minute walk from downtown, but does offer a retro VW shuttle bus for guests, and city buses stop frequently just outside. Plus the sprawling Mayfair Shopping Mall is right across the street. It's not only the coolest-looking hotel in Victoria, it's kid-friendly, bike-friendly, pet-friendly, and, best of all, budget-friendly.

3110 Douglas St. ✆ **800/997-6797** or 250/388-4345. www.hotelzed.com. 61 units. C$75–C$160 double. Free parking. Across from Mayfair Shopping Mall at Douglas St. and Finlayson Ave. 1 pet per room allowed (C$20/day). **Amenities:** Restaurant, bar, games room, pool, waterslide, shuttle, free Wi-Fi.

Paul's Motor Inn ★　This retro motel is the real deal. In fact, not a whole lot has changed since it first opened in 1958. The diner still serves home-cooked meals, the staff is as friendly as ever, and the value is just as good as always. Rooms are clean and comfortable, with in-room coffee and tea, mini-refrigerators, TV, and Wi-Fi. The decor in the guest rooms is basic motel style, but the popular diner still has all the retro cool of its 1960s heyday; be sure to pop in for a slice of lemon meringue pie and a root beer float. The motel is located within walking distance of downtown, but also with easy access to the highways.

1900 Douglas St. ✆ **866/333-7285** or 250/382-9231. www.paulsmotorinn.com. 77 units. Rates C$66–C$119 double. Children 15 and under stay for free. Free parking. On Douglas St., near Quadra, on outer edge of downtown. Pets allowed (charges may apply). **Amenities:** Restaurant, meeting rooms, concierge, free Wi-Fi.

WHERE TO EAT IN VICTORIA

Sure, we're all into local, seasonal, and organic these days, but somehow in Victoria, they just seem to do it better. Perhaps it's because the city has two great farming regions within a short drive, the Saanich Peninsula and the Cowichan Valley, as well as all the great delicacies that emerge from Pacific waters. Or maybe it's because it's still a small town, where everyone knows each other, helps each other, and inspires each other. Whatever the reason, Victoria has a uniquely delicious cuisine that is light years away from the days when the best you could hope for was a basket of fish and chips to go with your pint at the nearest pub. Though you can still enjoy that, too.

Inner Harbour
EXPENSIVE
Aura Waterfront Restaurant + Patio ★★ WEST COAST　Chef Tak Ito could just sit back and let the spectacular seaside scenery do all the heavy lifting here, but instead, he puts immaculate care and attention into every dish. His thoughtful menu mixes such local favorites as fish and chips and poutine with sophisticated, Asian-influenced dishes like the roasted duck breast served with hoisin and shiitake duck pierogi. You'll also find some real BC treasures on the wide-ranging international wine list.

Inn at Laurel Point, 680 Montreal St. ✆ **250/414-6739.** www.aurarestaurant.ca. Main courses C$13–C$19 lunch, C$16–C$35 dinner. Daily 7am–9pm.

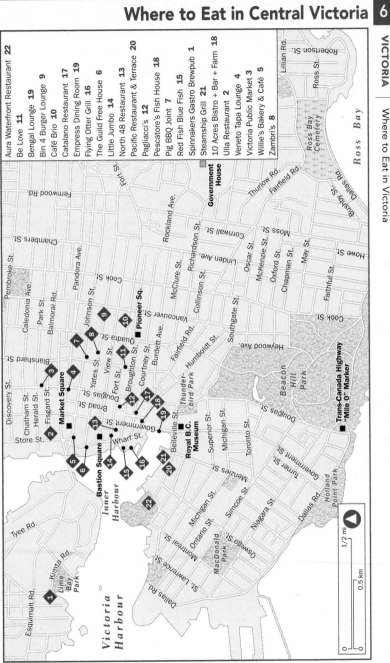

Aura Waterfront Restaurant **22**
Be Love **11**
Bengal Lounge **19**
Bin 4 Burger Lounge **9**
Café Brio **10**
Catalano Restaurant **17**
Empress Dining Room **19**
Flying Otter Grill **16**
The Guild Free House **6**
Little Jumbo **14**
North 48 Restaurant **13**
Pacific Restaurant & Terrace **20**
Pagliacci's **12**
Pescatore's Fish House **18**
Pig BBQ Joint **7**
Red Fish Blue Fish **15**
Spinnakers Gastro Brewpub **1**
Steamship Grill **21**
10 Acres Bistro + Bar + Farm **18**
Ulla Restaurant **2**
Veneto Tapa Lounge **4**
Victoria Public Market **3**
Willie's Bakery & Café **5**
Zambri's **8**

Bengal Lounge ★★ PUB FARE/INDIAN   One of Victoria's favorite meeting places. The curry buffet is a well-loved local ritual, though it isn't cheap, and it probably won't be the best curry you've had, either. Still, you do get all the butter-chicken and papadums you can eat, so there is that. Besides, this high-ceilinged colonial room is so comfortable, with its palm trees, deep leather chairs, and mementoes of the Raj, you might find it becoming your favorite hangout, too, especially once you've tried the tea-infused 1908 cocktail.

Fairmont Empress Hotel, 721 Government St. ℂ **866/540-4429** or 250/384-8111. www.fairmont. com/empress-victoria. Main courses C$19–C$28, curry buffet C$30–C$32. Daily 11:30am–11pm.

Empress Dining Room ★ CONTINENTAL   Even before the oaken drinks cart comes trundling over, you'll know that this is old-school dining at its finest. Generations of Victorians have celebrated milestone events in the hushed environs under the hand-carved wooden ceiling, so why shouldn't you? Expect classic dishes made with exceptional local ingredients, quietly attentive service, and a luxurious wine list. Note that there is a dress code of resort casual.

Fairmont Empress Hotel, 721 Government St. ℂ **866/540-4429** or 250/384-8111. www.fairmont. com/empress-victoria. Main courses C$25–C$42, 3-course prix-fixe menu C$65. Wed–Sun 6–9pm. Reservations essential.

MODERATE

Pacific Restaurant & Terrace ★ INTERNATIONAL   The location in a conference hotel right next to the Parliament Buildings makes this a busy lunch and after work spot, with one of the city's liveliest patios. The menu caters to just about every taste, with items that range from Thai soup to duck-confit pizza to classic Cobb salad, steak, and burgers. If you're looking for a satisfying entrée salad, this is the place for you.

Hotel Grand Pacific, 463 Belleville St. ℂ **800/663-7550** or 250/386-0450. www.hotelgrandpacific. com. Main courses C$15–C$21 lunch, C$15–C$38 dinner. Daily 6:30am–10pm.

Spinnakers Gastro Brewpub ★★★ WEST COAST PUB FARE   Victoria is famous for its pub culture, and if you can only visit one pub, make this the one. Spinnakers was Canada's first brewpub, and is still arguably the best. It was a leader in bringing local ingredients to casual dining, and for taking casual dining and making it extraordinary. Chef Ali Ryan has a deft hand with all the classic pub favorites—her creamy seafood chowder is among the best you'll ever taste—and the ever-changing beer selection is truly exceptional. And yes, children are welcome, too.

308 Catherine St. ℂ **877/838-2739** or 250/386-2739. www.spinnakers.com. Main courses C$13–C$25. Daily 8am–11pm, pub 11:30am–11pm.

Steamship Grill ★ WEST COAST PUB FARE   A casual eatery housed in a grand space, the glamorous Steamship Terminal Building. The Steamship Grill, which opened in late 2013, is sure to become one of Victoria's most popular restaurants—it has the location, the view, the prices, and, most importantly, the food and drink. Expect better-than-average burgers, fish and chips, chowders, and the like, as well as a good selection of local beer and wine on tap, all served in a cheerily nautical setting.

Steamship Terminal Building, 470 Belleville St. ℂ **778/433-6736.** www.steamshipgrill.com. Main courses C$14–C$34. Mon–Thurs 11am–10pm, Fri 11am–10:30pm, Sat 10am–10:30pm, Sun 10am–9:30pm.

INEXPENSIVE

Flying Otter Grill ★ PUB FARE   Victoria's only restaurant right on the water would be worthwhile visiting just for the fun of watching the floatplanes take off and land in the Inner Harbour. But it also serves up good casual-fare like burgers and poutine, as well as slightly fancier dishes like salmon Wellington. A great place to spend a sunny afternoon on the patio with an ice-cold pint.

Harbour Air Terminal, 950 Wharf St. © **250/414-4220.** www.flyingottergrill.com. Main courses C$12–C$20. Mon–Fri 11am–9pm, Sat–Sun 8am–9pm.

Red Fish Blue Fish ★★★ SEAFOOD   This is no ordinary chipper. First of all, it's a quirky joint, an outdoor eatery housed in an old cargo container on a pier. All the seating is outdoors, which means weather can be an issue. But who cares when the food is this good? Red Fish Blue Fish serves up some of the best fish you'll ever eat. It's all sustainable and mostly local, and comes in your traditional fish-and-chips format (cod, salmon, or halibut) as well as *tacones,* sandwiches, and salads. Grilled Fanny Bay oyster tacone? Yes, please!

1006 Wharf St. © **250/298-6877.** www.redfish-bluefish.com. Main courses C$10–C$20. Daily 11:30am–6:30pm, depending on weather and seasonality. No alcohol.

Downtown
EXPENSIVE

Café Brio ★★★ MEDITERRANEAN   This pretty, ivy-covered yellow house on Fort Street is one of the city's most warm, welcoming, and purely romantic restaurants. That it also serves some of the city's best food and wine just seems like a lucky bonus. Chef Laurie Munn sources the best ingredients from local farmers to create a sophisticated regional cuisine with a savory Tuscan influence. Be sure to try the house-made salumi, especially the smoky, spicy chorizo sausage. And if you come with a crowd, definitely go for the family meal of six sumptuous dishes chosen by the chef.

944 Fort St. © **866/270-5461** or 250/383-0009. www.cafe-brio.com. Main courses C$23–C$32, half orders available, family meal C$42 per person. Daily 5:30–9:30pm.

Pescatore's Fish House ★ SEAFOOD   For 20 years, this high-end seafood house has been serving up oysters, salmon, Dungeness crab, and more from an enviable location kitty-corner to the Tourism Victoria Visitors Centre. In late 2014, it will be undergoing a makeover of a dining room that was starting to look just a bit dated. But it'll be back soon, serving up chef Marcelo Najarro's local seafood with a touch of Italian panache—try the rich, creamy pasta carbonara with scallops, or the extravagant seafood dinner for two. If you're just craving a quick snack, head next door to Pescatore's sister restaurant, the Oyster Bar, for exquisite local bivalves on the half shell.

614 Humboldt St. © **250/385-4512.** www.pescatores.com. Main courses C$18–C$40, seafood dinner for 2 C$95. Mon–Fri 11:30am–11pm, Sat–Sun 11am–11pm.

Ulla Restaurant ★★ WEST COAST   The room is clean and simple, and it's all the better to show off the artistry on the plate. Ulla is tucked away on the edge of Chinatown, in an old brick building with big, arched windows; inside, it's all white walls and subtle woods, striped banquettes, moody art, and cloudlike light fixtures made of tangled strips of wood. It's restrained, but with funky touches, and makes an ideal setting for some of Victoria's most exciting food. At Ulla, chef Brad Holmes is creating beautiful compositions of local ingredients sculpted with some seriously sophisticated culinary techniques. But the food isn't just pretty, it's also lusciously flavorful. Even something that sounds as bland as "semolina cubes" proves to be a powerhouse of flavor, while the fried chicken with cheddar pierogi will make your taste buds do a happy dance. The beer, cocktail, and wine list is fairly small, but thoughtfully chosen, and offers plenty of exciting options to drink in.

509 Fisgard St. © **250/590-8795.** www.ulla.ca. Main courses C$25–C$30. Tues–Sat 5:30–10pm. Closed Sun–Mon.

MODERATE

Catalano Restaurant & Cicchetti Bar ★★ MEDITERRANEAN This friendly restaurant is a great place to experience Victoria's three main culinary passions: small plates, local ingredients, and Mediterranean flavors. It is the latest incarnation of what was a somewhat dark, gloomy steakhouse; it still has the clubby leather chairs and the multiple levels with stairs, screens, and glass dividers in between, but it's a lot brighter these days, with bright art on the walls and a terrific long, wooden bar. Try one of the excellent cocktails while you nibble on spicy chorizo puffs, polenta bites, and savory meatballs, and try to decide between the short-rib pasta or Sardinian fish stew. Catalano also serves a terrific weekend brunch, and offers a well-edited selection of interesting wines. It's owned and operated by the folks behind the popular **Ferris' Oyster Bar & Grill,** which is also well worth a visit (536 Yates St.; ℂ **250/360-1824;** www.ferrisoysterbar.com).

Magnolia Hotel & Spa, 619 Courtney St. ℂ **250/480-1824.** www.catalanorestaurant.com. Main courses C$12–C$21 lunch, C$21–C$29 dinner. Sun–Thurs 8am–11pm, Fri–Sat 8am–midnight.

Little Jumbo ★★ INTERNATIONAL When the bar grows its own herbs in a hydroponic unit under the counter, you know it's a place that takes its drinks very, very seriously. But that's no surprise when the owner is Shawn Soole, barman extraordinaire. Not only did he name his restaurant after the establishment founded by the legendary 19th-century bartender "Professor" Jerry Thomas, he's built a back bar of more than 300 bottles and offers an ever-changing list of inventive and classic hand-crafted cocktails. Still, the cocktails aren't the only reason to venture down the hall to this cozy place. The menu features hearty fare like roasted bone marrow and gnocchi in brown butter, and an ever-growing wine list.

506 Fort St. ℂ **778/433-5535.** www.littlejumbo.ca. Main courses C$12–C$15. Tues–Sat 5:30pm–midnight. Closed Sun–Mon.

North 48 Restaurant ★ MODERN DINER Dining in this sleek space near Wharf Street, with its industrial-looking exposed ducts and tables made of reclaimed wood, is sheer delicious fun. Flaming tiki drinks? You got it. House-made cheese whiz or onion soup in a jar? Sure, why not? Sister and brother owners Kelsey and Sam Chalmers (he's the chef) have taken all our childhood favorites and given them a sophisticated, grown-up twist. And despite what could seem like just a kitschy gimmick, the food is seriously well executed. Plus, in addition to a great cocktail menu, there's a dandy little wine list for even more fun.

1005 Langley St. ℂ **250/381-2428.** www.northfortyeight.com. Main courses C$15–C$26. Tues–Thurs 11:30am–2pm, 5–10pm; Fri 11:30am–2pm, 5–11pm; Sat 5–11pm; Sun 5–10pm. Closed Mon.

Pagliacci's ★ ITALIAN Pag's has been around forever, and still serves up all the homey, southern Italian dishes with punny names that made it so popular back in 1979 when it was first opened by New York ex-pat Howie Siegal. In a terracotta-colored room, cluttered with black-and-white photos and tables all jammed together, enjoy "Ravioli Paradiso" (spinach-and-ricotta ravioli with sun-dried tomatoes and gorgonzola cream sauce) or a "Salmon Enchanted Evening" dinner salad. Loud, lively, and fun, with eclectic live music, which ranges from klezmer to jazz, nightly Sundays to Wednesdays. Good value, and great for kids.

1011 Broad St. ℂ **250/386-1661.** www.pagliaccis.ca. Main courses lunch C$14–C$16, dinner C$14–C$29, half-orders available. Mon–Thurs 11:30am–10pm, Fri–Sat 11:30am–11pm, Sun 10am–10pm. Closed Christmas and Yom Kippur.

10 Acres Bistro + Bar + Farm ★★ WEST COAST   "Farm to table" takes on a whole new meaning when the restaurant actually owns the farm. And yes, at least some of the ingredients do, indeed, come from the restaurant's own farm out on the Saanich Peninsula, where they raise pigs and chickens, and grow fruit and vegetables. You can expect savory dishes like halibut poached in olive oil or pork tenderloin with spaetzle. Don't even try to resist the gooey roasted cauliflower and gruyere dip, or the many wines on a wide-ranging international list. The bright, cheerful dining room has a homey rustic vibe, with its long shared table of reclaimed wood surrounded by metal swivel stools and its chalkboard menu, but you'll probably want to head straight to the garden patio, which is among the best in the city.

611 Courtney St. ✆ **250/220-8008.** www.10acres.ca. Main courses C$13–C$15 lunch, C$17–C$28 dinner. Daily 11am–10pm, late-night menu 10pm–midnight.

Veneto Tapa Lounge ★★ TAPAS/FUSION   Let's start with the handcrafted cocktails, which are among the best in a city that is passionate about its cocktails. Choose either a classic or a new creation—you can't go wrong. Can't decide what you want? Then spin the wheel and the friendly staff will help you decide. There might even be one that involves fire. And then there's the food, an international fusion of popular tastes, mostly sharable plates of, say, Korean barbecue chicken wings, Indian butter prawns, or pulled-pork croquettes. This is a fun, lively spot with a mostly young crowd, in a beautifully renovated heritage building. Amazing to think it was once a notorious dive known as the Dougie—now the cool young people perch on chic low-backed stools around a long marble-topped bar in a room with rich wooden paneling and soft, subtle lighting.

Hotel Rialto, 1450 Douglas St. ✆ **250/383-7310.** www.venetodining.com. Tapas C$12–C$18, main courses C$12–C$24. Daily 4pm–midnight.

Zambri's ★★★ ITALIAN   After years in a tiny, cramped room in a strip mall, Peter Zambri is living it up large in this gorgeous, airy location in Victoria's Atrium Building, with its gleaming gold walls, floor-to-ceiling windows, and those round light fixtures that hang like bubbles above the bar. Zambri's is so popular, though, that no matter how much he expands, it's always crowded. And no wonder—this is some terrifically creative yet authentic Italian food. Lunch may mean an "Alpina" pizza with goat cheese, pecorino, and puréed greens. Dinner is a feast of primi like the tagliatelle with gorgonzola cream and candied walnuts followed by savory secondi such as crispy roast pork shoulder or local albacore tuna with caponata sauce. Be sure to order whatever seasonal vegetable Zambri is cooking. Don't ask—just eat! And dive right into a spectacular wine list curated from the best Italy has to offer.

820 Yates St. ✆ **250/360-1171.** www.zambris.ca. Main courses C$10–C$15 lunch, C$15–C$29 dinner. Mon–Thurs 11am–3pm, 5–9pm; Fri–Sat 11am–3pm, 5–10pm; Sun 10:30am–2:30pm, 5–9pm.

INEXPENSIVE

Be Love ★★ VEGETARIAN   "Pure nourishment," reads the tagline for this wheat-, meat-, additive-, processed-sugar- and dairy-free almost-vegan restaurant. You could add to that "pure taste," because despite all the things chef Heather Cunliffe's food does not have, what it does have is loads of vibrant, Asian-influenced flavor. She and her brother Joe also run one of Victoria's other favorite vegetarian restos, **Café Bliss** on Pandora Street. But Be Love takes vegetarian dining up a big notch with exceptional cocktails, a respectable wine list, and savory dishes like the Carmanah bowl with wild nettles, shiitake, kale, quinoa, seaweed, sauerkraut, and miso-ginger-sauce. All served in a gorgeous space filled with light, rustic furniture, and original art.

1019 Blanshard St. ℂ **778/433-7181.** www.beloverestaurant.ca. Main courses C$14–C$15 lunch, C$15–C$20 dinner. Daily 8am–9:30pm.

Bin 4 Burger Lounge ★★ BURGERS If you love burgers—and really, who doesn't?—skip the ubiquitous chain restaurants and head to this sleek, modern, and friendly place instead. There's a slight 1970s vibe to the decor, with its charcoal-and-yellow-striped banquettes, big black-and-white photos of wine glasses or butcher signs, and oval light fixtures that hover overhead like space ships. Bin 4 specializes in high-quality local ingredients, and everything is handmade with care and creativity. The house-made spiced potato chips arrive at the table when you do, and it just gets better from there. Try a wild-mushroom Angus beef burger with truffle aioli, or the minted lamb burger, or the decadent "Breakfast Club" with pork, chorizo, bacon, and a fried egg. Salads, snacks, vegetarian dishes, and a special menu for the little ones are available, along with a respectable list of affordable wine and beer.

180–911 Yates St. ℂ **250/590-4154.** www.bin4burgerlounge.com. Main courses C$11–C$15. Special kids menu. Mon–Thurs 11:30am–11pm, Fri–Sat 11:30am–midnight, Sun 11:30am–10pm.

The Guild Free House ★★ BRITISH PUB FARE Victoria has plenty of pubs, but The Guild is aiming to kick things up a notch. Chef-owner Sam Benedetto, formerly of Zambri's, spent a couple of years in England, studying the best modern gastro-pubs, and that's what he's aimed to create here. And it works. For starters, The Guild is located in a 140-year-old former warehouse with the original oak wainscoting, moldings, and ceiling, as well as a big antique bar and framed blackboard menus. A dozen ever-changing taps pour some of the West Coast's best craft ales, while beers from around the world are available by the bottle. (There's wine and cocktails, too, but this place is really all about the beer.) The menu features classic English pub fare done exceptionally well by chef-owner Sam Benedetto, formerly of Zambri's: Welsh rarebit, black pudding, fish pie, and some of the best fish and chips in the city.

1250 Wharf St. ℂ **250/385-3474.** www.theguildfreehouse.com. Main courses C$10–C$16 lunch, C$15–C$28 dinner. Wed–Thurs 11am–11pm, Fri–Sat 11am–midnight, Sun 10:30am–11pm. Closed Mon–Tues.

Pig BBQ Joint ★ BBQ This is a slow, smoky, Southern-style BBQ, just like it was meant to be. The pulled-pork sandwich is legendary—and messy, so be prepared—but you can't go wrong with the ribs, brisket, or pulled-pork poutine, either. Seating may be limited as this is more of a takeout joint than anything, but for soul-satisfying food on a budget, you cannot go wrong.

1325 Blanshard St. ℂ **250/590-5193.** Westshore Village Shopping Centre, 129–2955 Phipps Rd. ℂ **250/590-7627.** www.pigbbqjoint.com. Main courses C$7.50–C$16. Daily 11am–10pm.

Victoria Public Market ★★★ INTERNATIONAL I can't imagine a better use for the beautiful old Belle Epoque–style Hudson's Bay department store building. Upstairs, where once you could buy shoes or ladies wear, it's all condos. Meanwhile, the main floor has been transformed into Victoria's new public market, which is not only a great place to shop for foodie souvenirs, but also a great place to enjoy a grazing lunch. Try one of the succulent porchetta sandwiches at **Roast Carvery,** or the authentically Mexican cactus salad at **La Cocina de Mama Oli,** or the tangy herbed chevre at **Salt Spring Island Cheese,** or the fragrant Indian fare at **Sutra.** Cake at **Damn Fine**

Cake or pie at the **Victoria Pie Co?** Why not both? And don't forget a fine cuppa at **Silk Road Tea.** Bring your appetite.

Hudson Building, 1701 Douglas St. ⓒ **778/433-2787.** www.victoriapublicmarket.com. Main courses under C$10. Tues–Sat 9:30am–6:30pm, Sun 9:30am–5pm. Closed Mon.

Willie's Bakery & Café ★ BREAKFAST/LUNCH Victoria loves breakfast, and this is one of the best of the city's many, many places serving up toast and a cup of Joe. Located in one of Lower Johnson's heritage buildings, it has cozy vintage charm to spare, with exposed brick walls, antique counters, and a funky sort of portico detail that forms a frame for the menu boards. It can get a bit crowded, though, so if you can, sit out on the pretty garden patio. Breakfast and lunch are served all day, so if you prefer a burger for brekkie, you're good to go. But why would you when the breakfasts are this good? Try the banana-pecan French toast with a side of Willie's famous maple-syrup-glazed bacon.

537 Johnson St. ⓒ **250/381-8414.** www.williesbakery.com. Main courses C$11–C$14. Daily 9am–5pm.

Beyond the Central Area
EXPENSIVE

Seagrille Seafood & Sushi ★★ SEAFOOD/JAPANESE For a city that serves up so much seafood, it's surprising that Victoria has so few decent sushi restaurants. Seagrille is the exception. Located in the Brentwood Bay Resort in a small town on the back side of Butchart Gardens, it's an airy space of natural wood and big windows that open on to sea and forest views. Seafood is definitely the focus here, and you can order western-style dishes like the seared scallops or cioppino (a fish stew). But it's the sushi that's the star: Watch the highly trained Japanese sushi chefs prepare platters of sweet sashimi or perfectly sculpted *nigiri,* as well as a selection of plump *maki* rolls filled with tuna, spicy prawns, or candied smoked salmon.

Brentwood Bay Resort & Spa, 849 Verdier Ave., Brentwood. ⓒ **250/544-5100.** www.brentwood bayresort.com. Main courses C$24–C$30. Daily 5:30–10pm.

Sooke Harbour House ★★★ WEST COAST As Berkeley's Chez Panisse was to California cuisine, so is Sooke Harbour House to the cuisine of Canada's West Coast. Sinclair and Frederique Philip's cozy, art-filled clapboard restaurant is one of the places that first tried to define what local and regional really is—and 35 years after it first opened, is still doing it better than everyone else. Chef Olivier Kienast has recently returned from a sabbatical spent farming and foraging, and is back in the kitchen cooking with renewed energy. Expect creative and complex dishes of locally farmed, fished, and foraged food flavored with exotic combinations of herbs from the vast gardens: eucalyptus-scented crab consommé, house-made sausage, local seaweed, tender little gnocchi with fennel fronds, all paired with an exceptional list of largely BC wines. Note that Sooke Harbour House is located in the small town of Sooke, about a half-hour drive from Victoria, so you may want to book one of its guestrooms for an overnight stay.

1528 Whiffin Spit Rd., Sooke. ⓒ **250/642-3421.** www.sookeharbourhouse.com. Main courses C$14–C$34. Thurs–Mon 5:30–9pm, Sun 11:30am–3pm. Closed Tues–Wed. Hours change seasonally.

MODERATE
Pizzeria Prima Strada ★★ ITALIAN Authentic, wood-fired-baked pizza, with soft wheat crusts and savory toppings including locally made fresh buffalo mozzarella. The mosaic-tiled pizza oven takes pride of place in the Cook Street location; the

Diane Bernard is known the world over as **"The Seaweed Lady."** Since the late 1990s, she's been harvesting the succulent wild marine plants that grow in the waters off her hometown of Sooke, about a 30-minute drive west of Victoria. She eats them, cooks them, sells them to fancy restaurants, and teaches others about their culinary and health benefits. In 2001, she launched **Seaflora**, a high-end line of spa products based on the healing power of seaweed, which you can try at some of the best spas on the Island. It's organic, sustainable, anti-aging, and perfectly beautiful. For info, visit www.sea-flora.com.

Meanwhile, **Andrew Shepherd** had been working as a chef for a decade when he became intrigued by the idea of sea salt. As in, why were people harvesting it in France and England, and not from the pristine waters of the Salish Sea? And so he set about gathering buckets of water off the coast from the Cowichan Valley, where he lives, boiling it down, and harvesting the briny essence of the ocean itself. In 2010, he created the **Vancouver Island Salt Co.,** which sells a variety of flavor-infused sea salts (blue cheese, smoked paprika, balsamic vinegar) as well as a delicate fleur de sel. His products are available at a variety of retailers, including the Victoria Public Market. For more info, visit www.visaltco.com.

Bridge Street eatery is located in an old garage with cool industrial details. Go for the classics such as the Margherita with tomato and basil or the salty Napoletana with anchovies and oregano, or try your own special creation. Snacks, salads, and sweets also available, as well as a small but select wine and beer list.

2960 Bridge St. © **250/590-4380.** 230 Cook St. © **250/590-8595.** www.pizzeriaprimastrada.com. Main courses C$12–C$17. Bridge St.: Tues–Sat 11am–9pm; closed Sun–Mon. Cook St.: Sun–Thurs 11:30am–9pm, Fri–Sat 11:30am–10pm.

The Snug Pub ★ PUB FARE   The Snug in Oak Bay was the first of Victoria's many traditional neighborhood pubs, and has been given a new lease on life—not to mention a major makeover—in the recently rebuilt Oak Bay Beach Hotel. The owners have preserved the feel of the original pub, although the new version is bigger, brighter, and much less shabby. It still has the Tudor-esque plaster-and-lathe walls, though, and the old stained-glass windows at the entrance. You can expect all the classic pub favorites, like burgers, nachos and fish and chips, as well as an all-day traditional English breakfast, and, of course a decent selection of beer and wine. Although it's located in a resort hotel, it's still very much a locals' hangout, so you'll be mingling with Victorians who'll be happy to tell you about their favorite things to see and do.

Oak Bay Beach Hotel, 1175 Beach Dr. © **800/668-7758** or 250/596-4556. www.oakbaybeachhotel. com. Main courses C$12–C$21. Sun–Wed 11am–midnight, Thurs–Sat 11am–1am.

INEXPENSIVE

Fol Epi ★★★ BAKERY   You will find this gem over in the booming neighborhood of West Victoria. It shares its brick-and-pine, rustic-meets-industrial space with a great little coffee shop, so you can easily pull up a table, order a latte, then dive into the bakery's many baked delights. Fol Epi grinds its own organic flour (from rye and heritage Red Fife wheat) and bakes its bread in a wood-fired oven for some of the most flavorful artisan loaves you've ever tasted. At the same time, the bakers have a delicate hand with French-style pastries, including cookies, cannelles, tarts, and macarons. And, at lunch, they prepare individual pizzas and baguette sandwiches, perfect for tucking into your backpack as you head out on a bike ride along the nearby Galloping Goose Trail.

101–398 Harbour Rd. *℃***250/477-8882.** www.folepi.ca. Main courses under C$10. Daily 7:30am–5pm.

Tea Time

If there is one quintessential Victoria experience, it's taking afternoon tea. This was, after all, one of the most English of all cities in the vast British Empire, and many of the colonial traditions linger to this day. These days tea might mean a tea-flavored cocktail like the 1908 at the **Bengal Lounge,** or it might mean the tea-infused spa treatments at **Silk Road Tea,** where you can also pick up loose-leaf blends created by tea master Daniela Cubelic. But for a proper afternoon tea, with all the scones and finger sandwiches you can stand, try one of the following places.

Butchart Gardens ★★   What could be better after a morning of meandering through the rose gardens than sitting down to a refreshing afternoon tea? Tea is served in the serene heritage space of The Dining Room Restaurant, once part of the original Butchart family residence. (Think original Craftsman leaded glass windows, rose-pattered wallpaper in pale green lattice framework, and vases filled with flowers from the gardens.) The tea includes berry trifle, candied ginger scones, warm sausage rolls, baked delicacies, and a wide array of tea sandwiches, as well as the gardens' own signature loose-leaf teas.

800 Benvenuto Ave., Brentwood Bay. *℃* **250/652-4422.** www.butchartgardens.com. Afternoon tea C$33. Apr–Sept daily noon–3pm; tea not offered Oct–March. Admission to gardens required in addition to cost of tea. Reservations strongly recommended.

Fairmont Empress Hotel ★★★   The classic, served as it has been since 1908 in the impressive tea lobby. In a room lush with hues of green, cream, and rose, pillars topped with curvy Ionic capitals reach up to a high coffered ceiling; Persian carpets lie underfoot; potted palms, discreet screens, heavy drapes, and glossy antique furniture add to the grand Victorian look. Expect several tiers of decadent goodies that can include strawberries and cream, smoked salmon pinwheel sandwiches, fresh scones, and lemon tartlets. Bubbles and champagne cocktails are available as well as several different types of tea. You can upgrade to the Royal Tea for an additional C$30—it includes a local cheese platter and tawny Port. And there's also a Prince & Princess tea, with jam sandwiches and mini-chocolate cupcakes, for the little ones.

721 Government St. *℃* **866/540-4429.** www.fairmont.com/empress. Afternoon tea C$60 adults, C$30 children 12 and under. Daily; first seating noon, last seating 3:45pm. Reservations strongly recommended.

Murchie's Tea and Coffee ★   Murchie's is, as they say, "steeped in tradition." Since 1894, this wee West Coast company has been blending and selling exceptional teas and today, it ships all over the world, mostly online. Its Victoria store, located in a large heritage building on Government Street, is loud, busy, and one of the city's longest standing traditions. In the front section, customers order from a long counter that sits in front of a bank of antique oak drawers filled with fragrant blends under Tiffany-style stained glass. In the back is the big, bright, light-filled shop with windows facing the harbor. Murchie's doesn't have a full-on afternoon tea, but it does offer a huge tea selection and some fantastic baked goods, including light-as-air scones, hearty sandwiches, and classic sweets like opera cake and marzipan-wrapped Marie Antoinette cake.

1110 Government St. ℰ **250/383-3112.** www.murchies.com. Under C$10. Mon–Sat 7:30am–6pm, Sun 8am–6pm.

Pacific Restaurant & Terrace ★   The room has a warm, inviting traditional appeal, with a big brass-and-oak bar, gold-colored striped wallpaper, and comfortable wood-framed or wingback chairs. The tea served here features mini crab cakes, tuna *tataki,* and truffles by award-winning Vancouver pastry chef Thomas Haas, in addition to the usual scones and cucumber sandwiches.

Hotel Grand Pacific, 463 Belleville St. ℰ **800/663-7550** or 250/386-0450. www.hotelgrandpacific. com. West Coast afternoon tea C$42. Daily 2–4pm. Reservations required.

White Heather Tea Room ★★   A seriously cozy Scottish-style tea in a warm, inviting room in Oak Bay Village. It's a bit like visiting your granny's house—not terribly fancy, but with white tablecloths, simple oak furniture, and cheerfully mismatched teacups and teapots. There are lots of teas to choose from, and everyone gets their own special cup and saucer, just like you used to back in the day. "The Big Muckle" tea is huge: loads of lovely tea sandwiches, freshly baked scones and homemade preserves, a savory of the day, mini-quiches, delicious fresh baking, and lots more.

1885 Oak Bay Ave. ℰ **250/595-8020.** www.whiteheather-tearoom.com. Big Muckle tea for 2 C$54 (C$27 for each additional person). Tues–Sat 11:15am–5pm; last seating 3:45pm. Closed Sun–Mon and holidays.

EXPLORING VICTORIA

For a city that has so tenaciously hung on to its historic charms, Victoria is a surprisingly young and funky place. Yes, it has its sedate British traditions and plenty of heritage buildings to anchor it to the past, but it also has a bright, youthful, hippie-ish culture and a cheerful DIY sensibility. At the same time, Victoria is the seat of provincial government and an important business center, so it's not all silk-screened hemp frocks and organic homemade bitters. It's the mix of those ingredients that makes this city utterly unique.

For a visitor, the city's great appeal has to be its beautiful waterfront setting. The historic city center, which dates back to the 1840s, embraces the Inner Harbour, a picturesque, rocky-shored inlet that's busy with floatplanes, fishing boats, pleasure craft, whale-watching cruisers, and bustling water taxis. It's where you will find the most iconic of the city sights—including the provincial Parliament Buildings and the Fairmont Empress Hotel—and it's where any visitor should start their exploration of the city.

The harbor itself is a busy commercial port, lively with fishing boats, ferries, floatplanes, and pleasure craft. This is where most of the whale-watching adventures board and where the ferries from Washington State dock. The 12-passenger Victoria Harbour Ferries (p. 142) offer great tours of the harbor, including one to some of the area's best pubs. On land, walking around the harbor is a favorite activity for both locals and visitors. It's where you'll find the city's most famous landmarks, the B.C. Parliament Buildings and the Fairmont Hotel Empress, as well as historic warehouses, fish-and-chips stands, and, in summer, buskers, artists, souvenir sellers, and plenty of action.

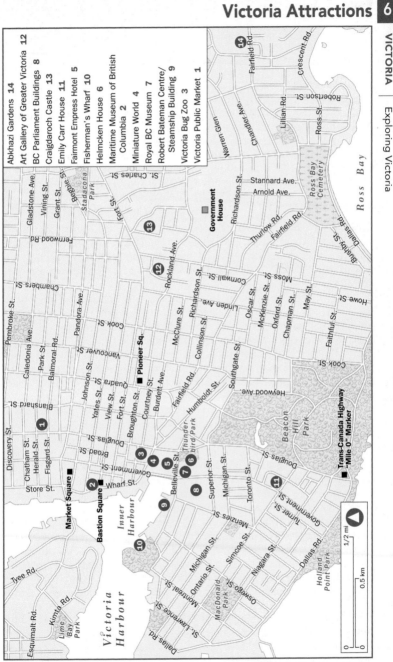

Abkhazi Gardens **14**
Art Gallery of Greater Victoria **12**
BC Parliament Buildings **8**
Craigdarroch Castle **13**
Emily Carr House **11**
Fairmont Empress Hotel **5**
Fisherman's Wharf **10**
Helmcken House **6**
Maritime Museum of British
   Columbia **2**
Miniature World **4**
Royal BC Museum **7**
Robert Bateman Centre/
   Steamship Building **9**
Victoria Bug Zoo **3**
Victoria Public Market **1**

Victoria's Chinatown may be small—only 2 blocks—but it is historically huge. A National Historic Site of Canada since 1995, it is the oldest Chinatown in Canada, and second oldest in North America, after San Francisco, dating back to the Fraser Canyon gold rush of 1858. Thousands of Chinese, most from Guangdong province, fled famine and drought back home in the hopes of finding fortune in the New World. Originally just a cluster of wooden shacks, the neighborhood quickly developed into a densely populated area of businesses, schools, temples, and a hospital—as well as opium factories, gambling dens, and brothels. Things are a bit more sedate these days, but visitors can still see the famously narrow **Fantan Alley,** the gloriously ornate **Gate of Harmonious Interest,** the old **Chinese School,** and the many shops and restaurants, including the exceptional **Silk Road Tea** on Government Street.

Although Victoria is an important city, it's a small one, which means that most of the sights you'll want to see are in a pretty compact area. You can cover the main attractions easily by foot, with just a couple of forays further afield. Most of the museums, galleries, and historic sites are in the Inner Harbour or the downtown area just a few steps away.

Downtown is the business center of the city. Here you will discover boutiques and restaurants, many of them in brightly painted century-old buildings, especially in the trendy new-old neighborhood called "Lo-Jo," for Lower Johnson Street.

Wharf Street, which runs along the waterfront, is lined with old warehouses that date back to the 19th century, when wealthy Victoria supplied prospectors heading off to the gold rushes in the Fraser Canyon or the Klondike. Government Street is where you'll find the biggest concentrations of souvenir shops and a few can't-miss boutiques. A bit further out, you'll come across the city's small but venerable Chinatown.

Cross the Johnson Street Bridge and you'll find yourself in West Victoria, once an industrial part of the city, now home to several condo developments attracting young professionals. You'll also find a huge concentration of walking and biking trails here.

Keep going east and south instead, though, and you'll find yourself in the city's older residential neighborhoods, such as pretty James Bay behind the Parliament Buildings, or wealthy Oak Bay with its manicured gardens, Tudor-style mansions, and a charming village filled with tony boutiques and eateries.

On the outskirts of Victoria lie several important attractions. The most famous of them is the legendary Butchart Gardens. It's located up north, out on the Saanich Peninsula, toward the ferry terminal and near the town of Sidney-by-the-Sea and the Shaw Ocean Discovery Centre. Then there is the bucolic Cowichan Valley, with its wineries and organic farms, just off the Island Highway to the northwest. And to the southwest, the village of Sooke, with its world-famous inn and epic hiking trails.

Victoria and its surroundings offer many attractions. Here are just a few.

Inner Harbour & James Bay

Any tour of Victoria has to begin with the Inner Harbour, its most iconic, most historic area. Here I'll include the quiet residential neighborhood of James Bay, which has a couple of attractions you won't want to miss.

British Columbia Parliament Buildings ★★ LANDMARK That's their official name; everyone else just calls them "The Leg," short for BC Legislative Assembly. The seat of provincial government is a striking neo-baroque building designed by a 25-year-old Francis Rattenbury (p. 20), the dashing young architect who created so many of the city's most distinctive structures. It was built between 1893 and 1898 and came in well over budget at a then-shocking cost of nearly C$1 million. Grand as it is on the outside—especially when it is all lit up at night—inside it is equally impressive, with fine mosaics, marble, woodwork, and stained glass, not to mention all those arguing politicians.

501 Belleville St. ✆ **800/663-7867** or 250/387-3046. www.leg.bc.ca. Free admission. Daily 9am–5pm (Oct–Apr closed Sat–Sun). Guided tour takes about 40 minutes, but the schedule changes frequently, so call ahead or plan to take a self-guided tour.

Emily Carr House ★ HISTORIC SITE On a quiet street in the leafy neighborhood of James Bay, you will find the childhood home of the great artist and writer Emily Carr. After decades of neglect, this pretty Victorian house has been restored almost to its original condition. It's surrounded by gardens and filled with antiques, books, and Carr mementoes. Best of all, it's staffed by knowledgeable people who are absolutely passionate about this most intriguing of characters, all of whom can bring her to life with just a few choice words. Stop by for tea and a chat, and say hello to the friendly house cats.

207 Government St. ✆ **250/383-5843.** www.emilycarr.com. Admission C$6.75 adults, C$5.75 seniors and students, C$4.50 children 6–18, C$17 families. May–Sept Tues–Sat 11am–4pm.

Fairmont Hotel Empress ★★★ LANDMARK Even if you aren't planning to book a room at this luxurious property, it's worthwhile taking a gander at it, starting with the pleasant rose gardens outside. (And don't forget to check out the bronze statue of artist Emily Carr with her dog Willie and monkey Woo at the corner of Government and Belleville streets.) The Empress was built from 1904–1908, designed by the architect Francis Rattenbury, who envisioned so many of Victoria's most famous buildings. It is designed in the chateau style of the great railway hotels, and is a particularly graceful example of Edwardian architecture. If you can, try to peek into the Palm Court with its ornate Tiffany-style glass ceiling. If you have time, afternoon tea at the Empress is one of Victoria's most revered traditions, and the curry buffet at the Raj-inspired Bengal Lounge is also a popular local treat (p. 154).

721 Government St. ✆ **866/540-4429** or 250/384-8111. www.fairmont.com/empress-victoria. Free admission to look around. Daily 24 hours.

Helmcken House ★ HISTORIC SITE Located in Thunderbird Park beside the Royal BC Museum, this historic home offers an intriguing glimpse back into a long-gone past. It started out as a one-story log house built in 1852 by Dr. John Sebastian Helmcken, a surgeon with the Hudson's Bay Company, when he married the daughter of Governor Sir James Douglas. Helmcken later became the first speaker of BC's elected assembly and was one of the negotiators who ushered the province into Confederation. As the family's fortunes grew, so did their house. It's not only one of the oldest houses in the province, but one of the best examples of piece-sur-piece wooden construction.

Royal BC Museum, 675 Belleville St. ✆ **250/356-7226.** www.royalbcmuseum.bc.ca. June–Sept 1 daily noon–4pm. Admission included with Royal BC Museum tickets, but C$5 donation suggested.

Robert Bateman Centre/Steamship Terminal Building ★★ ART GALLERY/ HISTORIC SITE   Yet another of architect Francis Rattenbury's iconic buildings, and perhaps the most beautiful of them all. This was, indeed, the old steamship terminal, built in 1924 in a graceful Beaux Arts style. Today, after a major renovation, the building houses an upstairs gallery with more than 100 works by the esteemed wildlife artist Robert Bateman, who lives on nearby Salt Spring Island. (It's a vastly different vibe from its previous tenant, the fabulously cheesy Royal London Wax Museum.) This is the largest collection of Bateman's works, a thought-provoking display that encourages us to explore our relationship with nature. Meanwhile, the main floor is home to a restaurant, the casual Steamship Grill (p. 154), and a gift shop selling fine Canadian crafts.

Steamship Terminal Bldg., 470 Belleville St. ⓒ **250/940-3630.** www.batemancentre.org. Tues–Sun 10am–5pm (extended hours June–Sept). Admission C$13 adults, C$8.50 seniors and students, C$6 ages 6–18. Family and group discounts available.

Royal BC Museum ★★★ MUSEUM   This is, hands down, one of the world's best regional museums, and a terrific way to learn about the peoples of coastal British Columbia. Although the museum has a serious research-and-education mandate, it's designed to be fun for the whole family. Kids will love the interactive features and super-cool dioramas, especially the one of the massive woolly mammoth in the second-floor Natural History Gallery. Don't miss the First Peoples Gallery, a remarkable display of First Nations rare artifacts including totem poles, masks, sculptures, and a full-size re-creation of a longhouse. The museum also welcomes a number of traveling shows: In 2014, for instance, it became the first North American stop for the fascinating Vikings exhibition comprising hundreds of rare artifacts that are traveling outside Scandinavia for the first time ever. The museum also has an IMAX theater, a First Nations carving shed in Thunderbird Park outside, a carillon bell tower, a cafe for a quick bite, and a fantastic gift shop. Plan to spend at least 2 hours.

675 Belleville St. ⓒ **888/447-7977** or 250/356-7226. www.royalbcmuseum.bc.ca. Daily 10am–5pm. Closed Dec 25 and Jan 1. Admission C$16 adults; C$10 seniors, students, and children 6–18; free for children 5 and under; C$40 families. Additional charge for IMAX theater.

Downtown

Stretching north and east is the downtown area, filled with great little shops, restaurants, pubs, and attractions. It's easy to explore this area by foot, but expect to find yourself carrying a few treasures home with you.

Maritime Museum of British Columbia ★ MUSEUM   Housed in a former law courts building that dates back to 1889, this museum is rich in historic tales of BC's seafaring past. It has three floors of exhibits including dozens of ship models and three full-sized vessels, among them, the Tilikum, a modified cedar log canoe that, astonishingly, was paddled from Vancouver Island across the Pacific Ocean and made it all the way to London in 1904. The museum has some 36,000 photos, plans for more than 900 vessels, as well as paraphernalia including uniforms, weapons, and gear. If you love boats and boating history, this is a must for you.

28 Bastion Sq. ⓒ **250/385-4222.** www.mmbc.bc.ca. Daily 10am–5pm. Admission C$12 adults, C$10 seniors and students, free for children 12 and under.

Miniature World ★★ ATTRACTION   Sure, it sounds cheesy, but it's actually kinda cool. The kids will love it—and it's a guilty pleasure for many grown-ups, too. Miniature World is a collection of dozens of dioramas featuring teeny-tiny figures enacting scenes from famous battles, novels, fairy tales, outer space, and more. There are incredibly detailed Victorian dollhouses, including two of the world's biggest, a vast three-ring circus, and, best of all, a miniature Canadian Pacific Railway running all the way across a miniature historic Canada. Plus, at the push of a button, you can make lights flash, bells ring, and the trains run. How much fun is that?

649 Humboldt St. ✆ **250/385-9731.** www.miniatureworld.com. Daily summer 9am–9pm, fall and winter 9am–5pm, spring 9am–7pm. Admission C$15 adults, C$11 seniors, C$10 youths, C$8 children.

Victoria Bug Zoo ★ ATTRACTION   You just haven't lived until you've held a tickly, 400-legged millipede as long as your forearm. Let the knowledgeable bug guides introduce you to more than 40 fascinatingly squiggly species of insects and spiders, including Canada's largest ant farm, glow-in-the-dark scorpions, and hairy tarantulas as big as your head. This experience is educational, but it's also creepy-crawly hands-on fun. And don't skip the gift ship, where you can pick up a "Cricket-Lick-It" bug-infused lollipop. Yum!

631 Courtney St. ✆ **250/384-2847.** www.victoriabugzoo.ca. Mon–Fri 10am–4:30pm, Sat–Sun 11am–5pm. Admission C$10 adults, C$9 seniors, C$8 youth 11–18, C$7 children 3–10. Children under 13 must be accompanied by adult.

Oak Bay, Fernwood & Fairfield

If you head east of downtown, you'll leave the city's commercial area and enter its residential neighborhoods, including posh Oak Bay and artsy Fernwood. The neighborhoods are filled with historic homes and lush gardens, and are a pleasant place to while away some time. They are also home to some of the city's important sights.

Art Gallery of Greater Victoria ★★ GALLERY   One of the best places to discover the work of Victoria's legendary artist Emily Carr, this cool little gallery combines a contemporary exhibition space with a historic 19th-century mansion. The gallery has an impressive permanent collection of more than 18,000 works from Asia, Europe, and North America, but the most popular display is the one featuring Carr and her contemporaries, which covers everything from her early watercolors to her dramatic later images of BC's wild west coast, as well as influences such as members of the Group of Seven artists and First Nations artists.

1040 Moss St. ✆ **250/384-4101.** www.aggv.ca. Mon–Sat 10am–5pm (Thurs till 9pm), Sun and most holidays noon–5pm. Sept–May closed Mon. Closed Family Day, Thanksgiving, and Christmas Day. Admission C$13 adults, C$11 seniors and students, C$2.50 children 6–17, free children 5 and under. Group rates available. See events calendar for scheduled tours. Located in Fairfield; follow Fort Street from downtown and turn right on Moss Street.

Craigdarroch Castle ★★ HISTORIC SITE   An opulent, extravagant, must-be-seen-to-be-believed "bonanza" castle built in the 1880s and '90s by the coal-mining baron Robert Dunsmuir. It was his way of showing the world that he'd made it all the way from indentured servant to richest man in British Columbia—and while he was at it, to impress his social-climbing wife, Joan. Too bad he died before it was finished; he left everything to Joan, and caused no end of family strife. The castle is located in the highlands above Oak Bay: a four-story, 39-room, multi-turreted fairy-tale house designed in the Richardsonian Romanesque style so popular in the late 19th century. Inside, it is filled with detailed woodwork, Persian carpets, loads of artworks, and 33 original stained-glass windows. Tours are self-guided and take 45 minutes to an hour.

1050 Joan Crescent. ✆ **250/592-5323.** www.thecastle.ca. Daily June 15–Labor Day 9am–7pm, Labor Day–June 14 10am–4:30pm. Closed Dec 25–26, and Jan 1. Admission C$14 adults, C$13 seniors, C$9 students, C$5 children 6–12, free for children 5 and under. Located in Rockland; follow Fort Street from downtown and turn onto Joan Crescent.

On the City Outskirts

Some of the most important aspects of Victoria aren't actually in the city, but on its outskirts—the airport, for instance, and the main ferry terminal. And so it should be no surprise that some of its biggest attractions are out there, too. From Victoria, two highways lead north: Hwy. 1, or the Island Highway, which heads up Vancouver Island to Cowichan Bay, Nanaimo, and Parksville, with arteries leading west to Sooke and Tofino; and Hwy. 17, the Patricia Bay Highway, which travels up the Saanich Peninsula to the Swartz Bay Ferry Terminal. Both roads lead to some impressive sights.

British Columbia Aviation Museum ★ MUSEUM   Out by the Victoria International Airport, you'll find a small hangar filled with a quirky collection of aircraft, engines, and historical artifacts. Among them are historic aircraft, including the strange-looking Gibson Twin Plane, the first airplane designed, built, and flown in Canada, as well as biplanes, helicopters, water bombers, and more. Most are grounded, but some occasionally go for a spin; in any case, this is a great little place to explore if you're intrigued by the magic of flight.

1910 Norseman Rd., Sidney. ☎ 250/655-3300. www.bcam.net. Daily May–Sept 10am–4pm, Oct–Apr 11am–3pm. Closed Dec 25 and Jan 1. C$10 adults, C$8 seniors and youth, C$4 children 7–12, free for children 6 and under. Follow Hwy 17 to the airport.

Fort Rodd Hill & Fisgard Lighthouse ★★ HISTORIC SITE   This fascinating National Historic Site is worth the trip just for the spectacular view. The fully restored Fisgard Lighthouse sits on a rocky outcrop from which its powerful beam (now automated) has guided ships into Victoria's safe harbor since it was built in 1873. Check out the exhibits in the lighthouse keeper's house to learn why this coastline was known as "the graveyard of the Pacific." Next to the lighthouse, Fort Rodd Hill is a well-preserved artillery fort that dates back to the 1890s. It's fun to explore, plus it has haunting audiovisual exhibits and artifact displays.

603 Fort Rodd Hill Rd. ☎ 250/478-5849. www.fortroddhill.com. Daily mid-Feb to Oct 10am–5:30pm, Nov to mid-Feb 9am–4:30pm. Admission C$4 adults, C$3.50 seniors, C$2 children 6–16, free for children 5 and under, C$10 families. Head north on Douglas St. until it turns into Hwy. 1, then take the Colwood exit (exit 10) onto Hwy. 1A toward Sooke; follow it to Ocean Blvd., then follow the signs to the site.

Hatley Park National Historic Site ★★ HISTORIC SITE   Like father, like son. In the 1880s, coal-mining magnate Robert Dunsmuir built Craigdarroch Castle (see above); 20 years later, his son James built his own wee shack, Hatley Castle, on a vast waterfront estate about 25 minutes from Victoria. His instruction to architect Samuel Maclure was, "Money doesn't matter, just build what I want." The bill came to more than C$1 million—about what the government was paying for the new Parliament Buildings. The design is a gorgeous hybrid Norman-Tudor fantasy built of local stone, with beautiful wooden interiors. (No furniture, though—it's mostly at Craigdarroch Castle.) The castle entry fee is a bit high for the experience, even with the guided tour; you might prefer to explore the castle and its beautiful heritage gardens from the outside.

Royal Roads University, 2005 Sooke Rd., Colwood. ☎ 866/241-0674 or 250/391-2666. www.hatleygardens.com. Gardens daily 10am–5pm; castle tours Mon–Fri 10am–4:30pm (last tour 4pm), Sat–Sun 10am–3:45pm (last tour 3:15pm). Gardens admission May–Sept C$9 adults, C$8 seniors, C$6 youth 13–17, free for children 12 and under, C$27 family; Oct–Apr C$4.50 adults, C$4 seniors, C$3 youth 13–17, free for children 12 and under, C$14 family. Castle admission May–Sept C$15 adults, C$14 seniors, C$9 youth 13–17, C$7 children 6–12, free for children 5 and under,

C$42 family; Oct–Apr C$17 adults, C$16 seniors, C$11 youth 13–17, C$9 children 6–12, free for children 5 and under, C$48 family. From Victoria, take Government St. north, turn left onto Gorge Rd. (Hwy. 1A) and follow about 20km (12 miles); turn left onto Sooke Rd. (Hwy. 14A) and look for signs to Royal Roads University or Hatley Park National Historic Site.

Shaw Ocean Discovery Centre ★★ AQUARIUM   Learn all about what's going on under the waters off Vancouver Island's shores at this remarkable, if small, aquarium and marine education center. It features 17 giant tanks filled with hundreds of fish, invertebrates, and plant life—including giant Pacific octopus, wolf eels, rock fish, and colorful anemones. You can take a free guided tour, join a fun class, tickle a starfish in the touch tank, or just gaze in awe at the magical creatures that fill our waters.

Sidney Pier Building, 9811 Seaport Place, Sidney. ℰ **250/665-7511**. www.oceandiscovery.ca. Daily July–Sept 10am–5pm, Oct–June 10am–4pm. Adults C$15, C$8 children 7–17, C$5 children 3–6, free for children 2 and under. From downtown, take Hwy 17 to the Sidney exit, then follow Beacon Avenue to waterfront.

Organized Tours

With its compact size, Victoria is a good place to explore all on your own. But if your time is limited, or you just want to see the city from an expert's perspective, then these tours are a great way to go.

BUS TOURS   Probably the easiest way to get an overview of the city and its main attractions is to take one of the city's bus tours. **CVS Sightseeing** (ℰ **877/578-5552** or 250/386-8652; www.cvstours.com) and **Gray Line Sightseeing Victoria** (ℰ **800/663-8390** or 250/388-6539; www.sightseeingvictoria.com) both offer regularly scheduled, fully narrated tours of Victoria and Butchart Gardens, including a Hop-On Hop-Off option in an open-air double-decker bus. Expect to pay around C$30 for an adult 1-day pass, C$40 for a 2-day pass, and about half that for kids.

   Island Time Tours (ℰ **866/477-3322** or 250/477-3322; www.islandtimetours.com) offers a variety of small, guided tours of Victoria, as well as tours that run all over Vancouver Island. Want to check out the West Coast Trail? Cowichan wine country? Saltspring Island? They've got a tour for you. In Victoria itself, they offer a private city tour (from C$75/hr. for group of 4; reservations essential), as well as regularly scheduled tours of the Villages of Victoria (C$39 all ages) and Butchart Gardens (C$69 adults, C$50 youth 13–17, C$25 children 5–12).

   How much fun is this? **Victoria Hippo Tours** (ℰ **855/884-4776** or 250/590-5290; www.victoriahippotours.com) lets you see the city from both land and sea. These amphibious vehicles travel around the city before splashing into the ocean for the grand finale. Their 90-minute tours run daily May through September, departing every hour 11am–5pm (C$43 adults, C$28 children 3–12).

WALKING TOURS   One of the best ways to discover Victoria is by foot, and there are several companies that will help you do it.

   At **Discover the Past** (ℰ **250/384-6698**; www.discoverthepast.com), local historian and raconteur John Adams leads groups on tours through Victoria's history, including its most haunted locales and special Chinatown tours. Several different tours are available, and most of the time you don't need to book ahead—just show up at the Tourism Victoria Visitor Centre in the Inner Harbour. Tours are about C$15 for adults, C$8 for children ages 6 to 11. Check the website for the latest schedule.

   At **Come See Victoria** (ℰ **778/676-0142**; www.comeseevictoria.com), amateur historian and professional architecture expert Dave Mason leads tours of Victoria's historical landmarks—including its best pubs. Tours leave from and return to the

Visitor Centre, with several tours scheduled weekly. The history tour lasts 2 hours and costs C$15 for adults, C$12 seniors and students; the historic pub tour is 3 hours, costing C$25 (adults only of course), and includes beer samples.

The **Old Cemetery Society of Victoria** (✆ 250/598-8870; www.oldcem.bc.ca) runs regular cemetery tours throughout the year. Particularly popular are the historically focused tours of Ross Bay Cemetery every Sunday at 2pm and costing C$5. See the website for scheduled tours.

The name says it all for **Walkabouts Historical Tours** (✆ 250/592-9255; www. walkabouts.ca). Charming costumed guides lead tours of the Fairmont Empress, Victoria's Chinatown, Antique Row, and Old Town Victoria, or will help you with your own itinerary. The Empress Tour costs C$12 and begins at 10am daily in the Empress Tea Lobby (11am in winter season). Other tours have different prices and starting points.

The **Victoria Heritage Foundation** (✆ 250/383-4546; www.victoriaheritage foundation.ca) offers several excellent free pamphlets for self-guided walking tours of the city's neighborhoods. They are available at the Visitor Centre.

Hosted by foodie expert Kathy McAree, **Travel with Taste** (✆ 250/385-1527; www.travelwithtaste.com) is an urban grazing experience—sample a Dutch pastry here or a truffle there, meet some of Victoria's foodiest locals, and even take a sip or two of local wine. Four-hour excursions (June–Sept) are C$89 per person; call for reservations.

Off the Eaten Track (✆ 250/380-8121; www.offtheeatentracktours.ca) also offers foodie tours including a 2-hour brunch-tour of Oak Bay Village or a flavorful excursion along Fort Street. Oak Bay Brunch Tour C$55; Knife and Fort Culinary Tour C$45.

SPECIALTY TOURS Explore Victoria the way the locals do—on two wheels. **The Pedaler Cycling Tours** (✆ 778/265-7433; www.thepedaler.ca) offers a variety of guided bicycle tours of the city, some focusing on food-and-drink cultures, others exploring its trails, and still others meandering through the scenic spots and historic neighborhoods. The Pedaler also offers bike rentals if you'd rather explore on your own. There are several tours each day, including the "Beans & Bites" coffee culture tour, and the "Hoppy Hour" tour of craft brews. Tours vary in length and cost, ranging from C$42 to C$139 per person; check the schedule online for more details.

Victoria Harbour Ferries (✆ 250/708-0201; www.victoriaharbourferry.com) offers a terrific 45-minute **harbor tour** aboard the adorable, fully enclosed 12-passenger ferries—and yes, every seat is a window seat. Harbor tours depart from seven

A Scenic Walk: Dallas Road & Ogden Point Breakwater

On any day, you can discover half the city of Victoria—and their dogs—strolling along this scenic 4km (2.5-mile) oceanfront walkway. If you start at Ross Bay, you'll pass several parks, including Beacon Hill Park, as well as the famous "Mile 0" marker of the Trans-Canada Highway and the tallest totem in the world, and end at the stunning Ogden Point Breakwater next to the cruise ship terminal. Back when it was created in 1916, the breakwater was a remarkable engineering achievement that took more than a million tons of rock and 10,000 granite blocks. Even now, it's an exhilarating experience to walk out on its 850m (½-mile) expanse as waves crash madly along its sides. For more info visit **www.ogdenpoint.org**.

stops around the Inner Harbour every 15 or 20 minutes daily 10am to 4pm (longer hours May–Sept). You can also take a 60-minute tour to the Gorge opposite the Johnson Street Bridge, where tidal falls reverse with each change of the tide, or do both tours in one trip. Harbor tours C$22 for adults, C$20 children 12 and under; Gorge tours C$26 adults, C$14 children; combination tours C$44 adults, C$21 children. Private charters available.

Seaquest Explorations (© **250/370-7500;** www.seaquestexplorations.ca) offers catamaran tours of the Inner Harbour with a special glimpse of what's under water. The Seaquest Explorer features a huge touch tank teeming with sea life, including anemones, tube worms, and Dungeness crab. Little kids will love playing with the critters; big kids will be delighted to know that beer and wine are available to sip while drinking in the scenery. Tours depart every afternoon, C$65 per adult, C$50 children 2 to 12.

Sidecar Victoria (© **250/891-3646;** www.sidecarvictoria.com) lets you take in the city's most scenic locales from the seat of a vintage Ural motorbike and sidecar. Professional drivers are behind the wheel of these sturdy Russian bikes—all you have to do is watch the view. Seriously fun! Several regular tours are available, or you can customize your own tour. The City Loop will take you to Victoria's most iconic locations for C$65 per passenger, or you can take the longer Butchart Gardens Tour for C$119 per passenger.

No doubt one of the most romantic ways to see Victoria is from the seat of a horse-drawn carriage. You'll find these dainty vehicles and their friendly steeds gathered near the Parliament Buildings in the Inner Harbour, and though you can often simply climb aboard, it's always best to reserve your spot, especially in the busy summer months. There are two main companies: **Tally-Ho Carriage Tours** (© **866/383-5067** or 250/383-5067; www.tallyhotours.com) and **Victoria Carriage Tours** (© **877/663-2207** or 250/383-2207; www.victoriacarriage.com). They offer a variety of different carriage rides and tours, so check the websites for details. But you can expect to pay about C$100 for a 30-minute waterfront tour (that's for the whole carriage, maximum six passengers).

To get a bird's-eye view of Victoria, take wing with **Harbour Air Seaplanes** (© **800/665-0212** or 250/384-2215; www.harbourair.com) and soar over the city's main attractions. The 20-minute Panorama flight is C$104 for adults, C$52 for children; or you can take the "Fly 'n Dine" excursion to the Butchart Gardens' private dock, with admission, dinner, and limousine ride back to Victoria included in the C$272 price (for adults; C$136 for children). **Hyack Air** (© **250/384-2411;** www.hyackair. ca) offer similar excursions, as well as an hour-long Gulf Islands tour, C$299 per person, C$100 extra if you stop for a wine tasting at Saturna Island Vineyards.

ECOTOURS   Just off Victoria's shores, the ocean waters are filled with marine life—sea lions, seals, porpoises, and, of course, whales, including gray, humpback, minke, and the most striking local resident, the black-and-white orca or killer whale. Getting up close and personal with these magnificent creatures is an unforgettable experience, so it's little wonder that whale-watching excursions have become such a popular activity around Victoria.

Several highly qualified tour operators offer daily trips from spring through fall in everything from open-air Zodiacs to covered expedition cruisers.

The longest-running of them is **Prince of Whales Whale Watching** (© **888/383-4884** or 250/383-4884; www.princeofwhales.com), which runs both wild-and-wet Zodiac excursions and slightly more sedate trips in its distinctive cruiser, the bright yellow Ocean Magic II. A 3-hour whale-watching journey will cost C$80 to C$110; if you take the longer trip that includes a visit to Butchart Gardens, it's C$100 to C$145.

Other companies that offer similar excursions include **Eagle Wing Whale Watching Tours** (℡ **800/708-9488** or 250/384-8008; www.eaglewingtours.com), which has a myriad of options available, including romantic sunset tours and wildlife tours in the winter months, as well as **Orca Spirit Adventures** (℡ **888/672-6722** or 250/383-8411; www.orcaspirit.com) and **Surfside Adventure Tours** (℡ **250/891-7792**; www.surfside tours.com).

Yet another option is the 2-hour wilderness cruise that departs from the marina and eco-adventure center at **Brentwood Bay Resort & Spa** (℡ **888/544-2079** or 250/544-2079; www.brentwoodbayresort.com; p. 150). It provides an enjoyably informative exploration of Finlayson Inlet, a deep fjord with a fascinating history and plentiful wildlife, including eagles, seals, and sometimes whales. June to September; C$69 per person. Reservations highly recommended.

Outdoor Activities

Victoria is, quite simply, an outdoor-lover's paradise. Its climate is mild and dry. It's riddled with parks and trails, dotted with golf courses, and surrounded by waters perfect for paddling. It's relatively flat, too, which means it's easy to run, walk, or cycle just about anywhere. Plus there are even more parks, beaches, and trails outside the city, so you can keep going as long as your energy lasts.

BEACHES   Although this coastline tends to be rocky and rugged, it also has many secluded coves and sandy beaches. Beachcombing, sunbathing, and investigating the tidal pools is a great way to spend a day, whether it's out at the **Sidney Spit, Mount Douglas Park,** or **Cordova Bay.** For those who want to venture further afield, there's also the spectacular **Botanical Beach Provincial Park,** 2 hours' drive west of the city in Port Renfrew; it's famous for its tidal pools, and for providing habitat for hundreds of species of plants and animals.

GOLF   With its Scottish heritage, lush lawns, and mild climate, it's no surprise that Victorians are crazy for golf. The season runs April to October, though many courses stay open year round. There are several public and private courses within the city, including the **Cordova Bay Golf Course** (5333 Cordova Bay Rd.; ℡ **250/658-4444;** www.cordovabaygolf.com), the 36-hole **Bear Mountain Golf and Country Club** (1999 Country Club Way; ℡ **888/533-2327** or 250/744-2327; www.bearmountain.ca), and the scenic **Cedar Hill Golf Course** (1400 Derby Rd.; ℡ **250/475-7150;** www. saanich.ca). Victoria is also the gateway to the **Vancouver Island Golf Trail,** which boasts 11 exceptional courses as far north as Campbell River. For information and golf packages, call ℡ **888/465-3239** or visit **www.golfvancouverisland.ca.**

HIKING   Botanical Beach marks the beginning of the 47km (29-mile) **Juan de Fuca Marine Trail,** just one of many great wilderness and urban trails around Victoria (www.juandefucamarinetrail.com). It is a rugged, multi-day hike along the rocky coastline, with some camping along the way, and several trailheads for those who want to hike it in smaller portions. Hiking is free, but camping is C$5 per person per night.

A somewhat more accessible—and, at 10km (6 miles), much shorter—trail with equally spectacular views is the **East Sooke Coast Trail,** located in East Sooke Regional Park, about a 40-minute drive west of Victoria (www.eastsookepark.com). Then there is the **Galloping Goose Trail** (www.gallopinggoosetrail.com), a mostly paved pathway that travels 60km (37 miles) from Sooke to Saanich and right through

Victoria. It's a rails-to-trails conversion that goes through urban, rural, and wilderness areas, ideal for hiking, running, cycling, inline skating, and even **horseback riding.** If you're looking for a more strenuous sort of hike, there are the trails in **Goldstream Park,** especially the trek up to the top of Mount Finlayson (p. 174).

KAYAKING & CANOEING   Surrounded as it is by water, Victoria is a popular place to paddle. You can rent a kayak or canoe from an outfitter like **Ocean River Adventures** (② **250/381-4233;** www.oceanriver.com) and explore the nearby lakes, rivers, coves, and even the Inner Harbour—just watch out for those floatplanes and ferries. Or set out for the serene, protected waters of the **Gulf Islands National Park Reserve** (② **866/944-1744** or 250/654-4000; www.pc.gc.ca), which comprises land and marine area on 15 islands as well as numerous islets and reefs that are home to seals and shorebirds.

Information for all of these activities and much more is available through **Tourism Victoria** (② **800/663-3883** or 250/953-2033; www.tourismvictoria.com).

Parks & Gardens

Abkhazi Gardens ★★ GARDEN   A romantic garden with an even more romantic story. It's small—less than ½ hectare (1 acre)—but exquisitely beautiful, with a modernist house set amid quiet woodlands, rocky slopes, and lovely vistas. The way the story goes is that Marjorie (Peggy) Pemberton-Carter met Russian Prince Nicholas Abkhazi in Paris in the 1920s, but they went their separate ways and didn't meet again until 1946, after they'd both been through difficult times, including spending time in prisoner-of-war camps. They married, moved to Victoria, and set about creating this lush refuge. Tea is served in their former home, which has been lovingly restored.

1964 Fairfield Rd., Oak Bay. ② **250/598-8096.** www.abkhazi.com. Daily 11am–5pm (Nov–Mar closed Mon–Tues, Dec 25, Jan 1). Admission C$10 (suggested donation).

Beacon Hill Park ★★★ PARK   The biggest, most treasured green space in the city is a lovely place for the whole family to spend a day. The park dates back to the 1880s and covers 75 hectares (190 acres) of manicured lawn, Garry oak trees, and flower gardens that stretch from Southgate Street to Dallas Road, and Douglas Street to Cook Street. It features a **children's farm** with petting zoo and daily goat stampede, as well as an aviary, tennis courts, lawn-bowling green, putting green, cricket pitch, wading pool, playground, and the world's tallest totem pole. The summit of Beacon Hill offers great views of the Strait of Georgia, Haro Strait, and Washington's Olympic Mountains. The **Trans-Canada Highway's "Mile 0" marker** stands at the edge of the park on Dallas Road.

100 Cook St. ② **250/361-0600.** www.beaconhillpark.com. Park daily 24 hours; children's farm daily 10am–5pm (closed Jan–Feb). Free admission to park; children's farm by donation.

Butchart Gardens ★★★ GARDEN   For more than a century, this former quarry has bloomed as one of the world's greatest show gardens. If there is one attraction to visit above all others in Victoria, this is it. Nearly a million people visit the gardens each year, which means it can be a bit of a stampede in the summer months (it's best to come early or late to miss the worst of the crowds). The Butchart family—which still owns it—created the gardens after they exhausted a limestone quarry near their Tod Inlet home. Jenny Butchart first created the famous Sunken Garden, which was opened to the public in 1904. To that were added a Rose Garden, Italian Garden, and Japanese Garden, and now more than a million plants fill the grounds. Among them is the rare blue Himalayan poppy, which you might spot if you visit in June and are very lucky. On summer nights, the gardens are illuminated with colored lights and fireworks; in winter, it becomes a twinkling wonderland. The Dining Room Restaurant in the historic family home serves a fine high tea (p. 161), plus there are musical events, a carousel, a terrific gift shop and much more.

800 Benvenuto Ave., Brentwood Bay. ℭ **866/652-4422** or 250/652-4422; dining reservations 250/652-8222. www.butchartgardens.com. Daily 9am–sundown (check the website for seasonal closing times). Admission C$17–C$30 adults, C$10–C$15 youth 13–17, C$2–C$3 children 5–12, free for children 4 and under; group rates available. From downtown Victoria, take Blanshard St. (Hwy. 17) north toward the ferry terminal in Saanich, then turn left on Keating Crossroads. About 20 minutes.

East Sooke Regional Park ★★ PARK About a 40-minute drive east of Victoria, you'll come to this rugged wilderness area that at 1,422 hectares (3,512 acres) is the largest in the Capital Regional District. More than 50km (31 miles) of trails let you explore the rocky coastline, windswept hills, sheltered beaches, and dark, silent rainforest. The 10km (6 miles) East Sooke Coast Trail is considered one of the best dayhikes in Canada. Along the way you'll spot fascinating marine life in the tidal pools as well as a wide range of plants and wildlife. This is also prime bird-watching territory, home to hawks, eagles, cormorants and other feathered friends who pass by on the Pacific Flyway. The park also has picnic areas and a small heritage farm.

Located in East Sook. www.eastsookepark.com. Daily sunrise to sunset. No admission. From downtown, take Hwy. 1 north to exit 14 (Langford/Sooke), then follow Hwy. 14 to Sooke; to reach the Ayland Farm entrance to the park, take Gillespie Road to East Sooke Rd., then take the first right onto Becher Bay Rd. About 37km (23 miles) from Victoria.

Goldstream Provincial Park ★★ PARK During the gold rush of the 19th century, this quiet valley was flooded with optimistic prospectors. Sadly, you're not likely to find any gold nuggets these days, but you will find a treasure of a whole different sort: a terrific little wilderness area with majestic old-growth trees, shy wildflowers, and rushing streams simply bursting with salmon. Thousands of salmon make their annual run each winter up Goldstream River, and the end of the run signals the arrival of hundreds of bald eagles. The park also features several exceptional hikes, including the trek up Mt. Finlayson and another to Niagara Falls, which is actually higher than its eastern namesake. There is limited camping in the park.

2930 Trans Canada Hwy. visitor center. ℭ **250/478-9414.** www.goldstreampark.com. Visitor Center daily 9am–4:30pm. C$3 day-use parking fee. Drive north on Hwy. 1 and you'll see the park signs on the right shortly after you leave the city limits.

Mount Douglas Park ★★ PARK This magnificent urban forest in the Municipality of Saanich offers one of the most spectacular panoramas of the Victoria area. Several trails and a paved road lead to the 213m (700-ft.) summit of Mount Douglas, with its 360-degree views of Saanich, Victoria, the Haro Strait, and Washington State's Olympic and Cascade mountains. Churchill Drive, the paved road to the top, is closed to vehicular traffic every morning, making it a safe and accessible, if steep, multi-use trail and an ideal morning workout. There are also 21km (13 miles) of trails through field and forest, as well as a sandy beach, playground, picnic areas, and plenty of plants and wildlife to check out in this 188-hectare (465-acre) suburban park.

Cedar Hill Road, Gordon Head, Saanich. ℭ **250/475-1775.** www.saanich.ca. Daily 24 hours. Free admission. From downtown, go north on Blanshard St., turn right on Hillside Ave., then left onto Cook St., and on to Cedar Hill Road. It's about 9km (5½ miles) to the parking lot.

Victoria Butterfly Gardens ★★ GARDEN   A tropical paradise filled with but-terflies—your kids will love it, sure, but so will you. It's not just butterflies you'll find here amid the orchids, palm trees, and papaya plants—you'll also spot flamingoes, parrots, turtles, frogs, and tropical fish. But it's the hundreds of colorful, fluttering butterflies that will draw you in, some 75 species from around the world. Naturalists are on hand to explain butterfly biology, and a display allows you to see how the but-terflies emerge from their cocoons.

1461 Benvenuto Ave., Brentwood Bay. ℭ **877/722-0272** or 250/652-3822. www.butterflygardens. com. Admission C$16 adults, C$10 seniors and students 13–17, C$5 children 5–12, free for children 4 and under. Family and group rates available. Daily 10am–5pm (Jun–Aug till 7pm). Closed Dec 25 and Jan 1. From downtown Victoria, follow Hwy. 17 to Keating Cross Road, then follow the signs.

Especially for Kids

Victoria offers plenty of fun stuff for kids to see and do. For one thing, the city is filled with young families who need to keep their own offspring entertained. For another, it has all sorts of parks, beaches, hills, and trails to get them moving outdoors, as well as great, kid-friendly attractions, many of them involving actual living creatures. Your kids can watch orcas and porpoises frolic on a **whale-watching** adventure (p. 171), pet the happy goats at the **Beacon Hill Children's Farm** (p. 173), play with many-legged insects at the **Victoria Bug Zoo** (p. 167) or the pretty winged ones at the **Victoria Butterfly Gardens** (see above), or check out all the squiggly critters in the touch tanks at the **Shaw Ocean Discovery Centre** (p. 169).

Of course, there are real live tide pools to investigate as well. You can find them along rocky beaches like the one in **Mount Douglas Park** (p. 174). There are also several other parks to explore, including **Goldstream Provincial Park** (p. 174) just north of the city, which has a fascinating gold rush past, easy hiking trails through old-growth forest, and a visitor center with activities geared especially for children.

If you'd rather stay in the city center, you can find plenty to keep the little ones busy there, too. The **Royal BC Museum** (p. 166) has special programming and activities just for kids—and they'll get a kick out of cool displays like the vast hall of totem poles and the life-size reconstruction of a woolly mastodon. Kids of all ages love **Miniature World** (p. 166), with its huge collection of dollhouses, model trains, and teensy circus displays. The **Prince or Princess tea** at the Fairmont Hotel Empress (p. 165) will make your kids feel like royalty. And a trip around the harbor on a **Victoria Harbour Ferry** (p. 142) is fun for the whole family—be sure to stop at **Red Fish Blue Fish** for the best ever fish and chips (p. 155).

SHOPPING

For what is such a small city, Victoria offers some pretty great shopping experiences, especially for art, antiques, homewares, food, drink, and books. Part of the fun of shop-ping here is simply meandering along the streets and peeking into one boutique after another—many of them are located in historic old buildings, which makes browsing even more fun.

Most visitors will start on **Government Street,** the main shopping strip through downtown. It's a mix of ticky-tacky souvenir shops and some great, can't-miss bou-tiques. Among them is the magnificent **Munro's Books** (ℭ **888/243-2464** or 250/382-2464; www.munrobooks.com), one of the world's truly great bookstores. Expect to spend some serious time browsing through the new releases and extensive sale tables

Back in the day, **Upper Fort Street** between Blanchard and Cook streets was known as **Antique Row** and was chock-a-block with more than a dozen antique stores selling everything from priceless Chinese artworks to well, junk. Today, the number of shops—and the selection—has been sadly diminished, but you can still find some treasures here, sometimes at astonishingly good prices. Old silverware and tea sets are particularly good buys, but you can also find glassware, jewelry, military memorabilia, furniture, and the like. There are also a handful of **galleries and auction houses** that hold regularly scheduled sales of art, antiques, and collectibles. Increasingly, the neighborhood—which has been rebranded "Mosaic Village"—is becoming a foodie destination, so while you're here, be sure to check out the bakeries and delis. Most of the shops are open Monday to Friday 10am to 6pm, Saturday 10am to 5pm, and Sunday noon to 4pm.

Bastion Square (View St., btwn. Wharf and Government sts.) is a pleasant little space with shops and restaurants, despite its somewhat grim historic past—it was once the site of Victoria's Court House, where several hangings took place. These days, you're likely to find artists displaying their works, especially during the summer months when the **Bastion Public Market** (May–Sept Thurs–Sat 11am–5:30pm, Sun 11am–4pm) features vendors and local artisans selling handmade arts and crafts, as well as live entertainment. Don't forget to check out the **boutiques of Trounce Alley** across Government Street, as well as the ceremonial arch at View Street that marks the entry to the original site of Fort Victoria.

Visiting **Fisherman's Wharf,** a cluster of floating shops, eateries, and homes on the south side of the Inner Harbour, is a great way for the whole family to spend a couple of hours, especially if you're hungry. It's even more fun if you take one of the Victoria Harbour Ferries over, though you can walk in from either Dallas Road or St. Lawrence Street. A handful of eco-adventure outfitters are located here, as well as shops selling ice cream, fish and chips, and fresh seafood, including live crab. Be sure to wander over to the colorful float homes and enjoy the views of the busy harbor while you enjoy your crispy fried halibut and a lemonade. Most shops are open daily 11am to 7pm (or until dark).

under the ornate ceiling of this neoclassical former bank building. In fact, Victoria is something of a mecca for bibliophiles: It's also home to Canada's biggest used and new bookstore, **Russell Books** on Fort Street (© 250/361-4447 or 250/360-2965; www.russellbooks.com), as well as the beloved independent **Bolen Books** in Hillside Mall (© **250/595-4232;** www.bolen.bc.ca), and the half-dozen or so specialty bookstores in nearby Sidney-by-the-Sea (p. 141), also known as "Booktown."

Aside from books, Government Street has boutiques selling **First Nations arts and crafts,** including the famous hand-knit Cowichan sweaters, at **Hill's Native Art** (© 866/685-5422 or 250/385-3911; www.hillsnativeart.com) and **Cowichan Trading Company** (© 250/383-0321; www.cowichantrading.com). You can also find fragrant loose-leaf tea at **Murchie's Tea & Coffee** (© 250/383-3112; www.murchies.com), decadent chocolate creams at **Rogers' Chocolates,** a perfect little candy box of a sweet shop (© 250/881-8771; www.rogerschocolates.com), and one-of-a-kind gifts at **Bastion Square,** which holds an artisan market in the summer months (see above).

Government Street intersects with **Fort Street,** and if you wander up a couple of blocks, you'll find the handful of stores that remain of the once-booming **Antique Row** (see box, above). It's still worth a visit, though you may find yourself spending more time in the bakeries and delis, especially **the Dutch Bakery** (© 250/385-1012; www.thedutchbakery.com) and **Choux Choux Charcuterie** (© 250/382-7572; www. chouxchouxcharc.com). Still, you can find some real treasures at shops like **Pacific Antiques** (© 250/388-5311; www.pacificantiques.com).

A bit further north, Government also intersects with **Johnson Street.** Turn left here and you'll find yourself in the funky Lower Johnson or **"LoJo"** neighborhood (see box, below). This area is crammed full of boutiques housed in brightly painted Victorian shop fronts, with the historic Market Square at the bottom by Wharf Street. Shop for edgy fashions at **Smoking Lily** (© 250/382-5459; www.smokinglily.com), eco-friendly toys at **Hip Baby** (© 250/385-8020; www.hipbaby.com), and organic, hand-made body-care products at **Salt Spring Soapworks** (© 250/386-7627; www. saltspringsoapworks.com). Explore **Market Square** (see below), then wander up Pandora Street to **Chinatown** (p. 164); be sure to peek down **Fantan Alley,** Canada's narrowest commercial street, then pop into **Silk Road Tea** (© 250/704-2688; www. silkroadteastore.com) for hand-blended teas and tea-based spa products.

Nearby you will also find the **Victoria Public Market** (© 778/433-2787; www. victoriapublicmarket.com). It only makes sense that a city so obsessed with local food would house its public market in one of its most beautiful landmark buildings. The Hudson was built in the 1920s, designed in the Beaux Arts style as one of the Hudson's Bay's grandest department stores. Now it houses condos on the upper floors, where once you could buy lingerie and housewares, and Victoria's brand, spanking new market on the main floor. This is a stunning space, all exposed beams, high ceilings, and industrial lights, and many of Victoria's most popular artisans have stalls here. Graze your way through the samples at **Salt Spring Island Cheese,** the savory porchetta sandwich at **Roast Carvery,** and the sweet treats at **Damn Fine Cake Company,** just for starters. This is also an excellent place to pick up a foodie souvenir for your friends back home, such as the gourmet blended teas at **Silk Road Tea** or the locally harvested sea salts at **Island Spice Trade.** The Public Market is open Tuesday through Saturday 9:30am to 6:30pm, Sunday 9:30am to 5pm (closed Mon). Note that the best day to visit is Wednesday, when the market holds a farmers market.

Lower Johnson Street & Market Square

"LoJo," as the locals call it, is an uber-trendy hood of designer boutiques housed in brightly painted heritage buildings. Even if you're not shopping for a pair of cool new shoes or over-priced yoga pants, it's fun to wander around, do some window shopping, and perhaps stop for a coffee or smoothie. Hours vary, but most shops are open Monday to Saturday 10am to 6pm.

You'll definitely want to check out Market Square, one of Victoria's oldest landmarks, an old brick town square built back in the 19th century to serve all the crowds coming through on their way to the Klondike gold rush. Today this two-story brick marketplace features a number of boutiques and restaurants, and is just a fun place to explore. Market Square is open Monday to Saturday 10am to 5pm, Sunday 11am to 4pm (www.marketsquare.ca).

Oak Bay is one of Canada's wealthiest neighborhoods, home to countless mansions, bounteous gardens, a marina, three golf courses, and this charming village stroll. It's one of Victoria's two "village" neighborhoods (the other is the slightly smaller Cook Street Village; www.cookstreetvillage.ca). Expect pedestrian-friendly streetscapes lined with trees, boutiques, cafes, and pubs. Oak Bay Village is a lovely place to amble and browse through the galleries and garden shops, and you'll want to stop in at the popular **Ottavio Italian Bakery & Delicatessen,** the cheery **Penny Farthing pub,** or the **White Heather Tea Room** (p. 162). And just try to resist the sweets at **Roger's Chocolates** or **Sweet Delights.** Opening hours vary from shop to shop, but you can expect most to be open Mon–Sat 10am–5:30pm, Sun 11am–4pm. For more information visit www.oakbayvillage.ca.

Outside of downtown, **Oak Bay Village** and **Cook Street Village** offer more great little boutique shopping (see above). Gardeners will dig **Dig This** (② **250/598-0802;** www.digthis.com) and anyone with a sweet tooth will adore the international and retro candies at **Sweet Delights** (② **778/430-4906;** www.sweetdelightsvictoria.com).

And don't underestimate the cool stuff you can find at the museum, gallery, and attraction gift shops. **Butchart Gardens** (p. 173) especially has a vast selection that ranges from cutesy floral doodads to stunning original works of art, while the **Royal BC Museum** (p. 166) is a treasure trove of beautiful things.

ENTERTAINMENT & NIGHTLIFE

Victoria is not exactly known for its wild and crazy nightlife. Indeed, it was once described as "God's waiting room" and "the only cemetery in the entire world with street lighting." Perhaps that's not so surprising, given its large population of young families, retirees, and government employees. It's also not as true as it once was, given that it's also home to several colleges and universities and has a booming cocktail culture that has young people partying into the wee hours, even on school nights. Besides, if there's one thing to be said about Victoria, it's that when something is going on, whether it is a festival, a concert, or a theater production, everyone really shows up.

When it comes to the performing arts, Victoria has several theaters offering a wide range of shows. The **Royal Theatre,** which was built in in the early 1900s, is the place for symphony, opera, dance, and some theater productions; the slightly smaller, century-old **McPherson Playhouse** features stage plays and performances by the Victoria Operatic Society. Both share a common box office (② **888/717-6121** or 250/386-6121; www.rmts.bc.ca).

The **Belfry Theatre** company (② **250/385-6815;** www.belfry.bc.ca) is located in a former Baptist church on Gladstone Avenue; it's a registered heritage building that dates back to 1892. It's the major landmark in the artsy neighborhood of Fernwood, where even the telephone poles and garbage cans are works of art, decorated by talented local residents. The Belfry began producing plays in 1976, and since then has performed 230 plays, nearly half of them by Canadian playwrights, and the company frequently tours across Canada, the U.S., London, and Australia. The neighborhood also features a number of cafes and restaurants for a bite before or after the show. Check the online schedule for performances. Tickets range from C$25 to C$40.

If you're visiting in late summer, you won't want to miss the **Victoria Fringe Festival,** organized by The Intrepid Theatre Company (© **250/383-2691;** www.victoria fringe.com), when more than 50 performers or small companies from around the world put on wildly inventive plays.

One of the most exciting events of the year is **Victoria Symphony Splash,** held on the first Sunday in August, when the whole harbor is turned into an outdoor concert hall. The concert always ends with Tchaikovsky's 1812 Overture, complete with bells, cannons, and fireworks. Truly a sight to be seen—and heard.

Before or after any of these performances, or, indeed, just about any evening, you'll likely want to hit one of Victoria's many excellent cocktail-centric bars and restaurants. For creative, handcrafted cocktails, the best include **Little Jumbo** (p. 156), **Veneto Tapa Lounge** (p. 157), **Clive's Classic Lounge** (Chateau Victoria; © **250/382-4221;** www.chateauvictoria.com), and the **Bengal Lounge** in the Fairmont Hotel Empress (p. 154).

If you prefer a pint to, say, a Manhattan or flaming tiki drink, you're in luck because Victoria is well known for its lively pub scene, which is where most of the city's night-life happens. You'll find a great pub in just about every neighborhood. Some of the best include **Spinnakers Gastro Brewpub** (p. 154), the **Penny Farthing Public House** in Oak Bay (© **250/370-9008;** www.pennyfarthingpub.com), **the Guild** on Wharf Street (p. 158), and **Swan's Brewpub** (p. 149), a funky joint filled with First Nations art and live music.

And then there is the boisterous **Sticky Wicket Pub at the Strathcona Hotel** (© **250/383-7137;** www.strathconahotel.com). It's part of a vast nightlife complex that includes several other bars and nightclubs: the high-tech, DJ-driven **Club 9one9,** summer-only **Rooftop Surfclub** with its "beach" volleyball and fruity drinks, the self-proclaimed "authentic hillbilly bar" **Big Bad John's,** the sporty **Games Room** with its big-screen TVs and billiard tables, and **the Clubhouse,** an upscale dance club. The city has a handful of other dance clubs as well, including **Sugar** (© **250/920-9950;** www.sugarnightclub.ca), and **Touch Lounge** (© **250/384-2582;** www.touchlounge.ca).

Unfortunately, although Victoria is generally a gay-friendly city, it doesn't offer a lot of nightlife options for the gay and lesbian community. The crowd at **Hush** (© **250/383-0566;** www.hushnightclub.ca) is 50-50 gay and straight, all there for the wicked electronic music. **Paparazzi Nightclub** (© **250/388-0505;** www.paparazzi nightclub.com) is probably the only true gay and lesbian nightclub, offering everything from top-40 nights to drag shows to karaoke and techno.

For up-to-the-minute information about clubs, concerts, and current shows, check the listings in Victoria's weekly **Monday Magazine** (www.mondaymag.com) or at the **Tourism Victoria Visitors' Centre** in the Inner Harbour (© **800/663-3883** or 250/953-2033; www.tourismvictoria.com).

SIDE TRIPS FROM VICTORIA

Once you've explored Victoria, if you have time, you'll want to discover the rest of the beautiful island where it is situated. British Columbia's capital city sits at the southwestern tip of Vancouver Island, which is a fairly big place—460km (290 miles) in length and 80km (50 miles) wide—with a huge range of landscapes and experiences to tempt the traveler. On the east coast are serene waters, misty islands, and most of the major communities. On the west, you'll find rocky fjords, wild seas, and rugged wilderness. Down the middle snakes a towering, snow-capped mountain range with vast parks and old-growth forests ideal for biking, hiking, and skiing. And here and there you will find warm, fertile valleys with vineyards, farms, fig trees, even a citrus orchard.

Here I discuss three of the Island's most unforgettable destinations: the **Cowichan Valley** just north of Victoria; the idyllic **Gulf Islands** just off the southeast coast; and the spectacular wilderness area of **Pacific Rim National Park Reserve** on the west coast.

COWICHAN VALLEY

In the Coast Salish language, *cowichan* means "the warm land," and this valley just north of Victoria has some of the mildest climate in Canada. Surrounding mountains protect it from ocean storms and northern winds, and it is warm and (relatively) sunny most of the year. It is a place of hushed forests, trickling streams, small communities, fertile organic farms, and quality vineyards. The Cowichan has become a refuge for a surprising number of talented chefs, vintners, foragers, and foodies-turned-farmers who are as passionate about sustainability as they are about flavor; that's why Slow Food International named this the first "Cittaslow" or "slow" community in North America. Indeed, the pace of life in general is pretty relaxed and easy-going, and no one is exactly in a rush to get anywhere. Still, there is plenty for the visitor to do, from browsing through the many galleries to hiking, biking, kayaking, fishing, and, of course, eating and drinking. This would be an ideal day trip from Victoria.

Essentials
GETTING THERE
The Cowichan Valley is about a 45-minute drive north of Victoria along the Island Highway (Hwy. 1), which includes the notorious Malahat Drive. The Malahat is a narrow, winding, steep stretch of mountain road that runs along the edge of a plunging cliff; it is as deadly a drive as it is beautiful,

so stay alert. Bus tours run from Victoria to the Cowichan (p. 169), and there is Greyhound bus service as well (✆ 800/661-8747; www.greyhound.ca); however, to really make the most of this area, you will want a car. See p. 142 for rental locations in Victoria.

VISITOR INFORMATION

The Tourism Victoria Information Centre (✆ **800/663-3883** or 250/953-2033; www.tourismvictoria.com) has loads of info on the Cowichan, but you can get still more details directly from Tourism Cowichan (✆ **888/303-3337** or 250/746-4636; www.cvrd.bc.ca).

Where to Stay

Fairburn Farm ★★   If you are looking for the ultimate escape from city life, then this family-owned heritage farm is the place for you. Built 130 years ago in a sunny valley protected by the Vancouver Island Ranges, it's a gabled clapboard house with a long, gracious verandah that calls you to curl up with a book and pot of tea. Guests can also meander among the endless trails that cross the property's 53 tranquil hectares (130 acres) of forest and farmland. Though the house is old and the decor traditional and slightly rustic, the rooms, thankfully, have been updated with comfy sleigh beds, fluffy duvets, and private en-suite bathrooms. In addition to five guestrooms in the house, there is also a two-bedroom farm-stay cottage, ideal for families. Best of all, you'll want to wake up to the fresh farm breakfast made from local ingredients, always including buffalo mozzarella from the owners' own herd of friendly water buffalo.

3310 Jackson Rd., Duncan. ✆ **250/746-4637.** www.fairburnfarm.bc.ca. 6 units. C$105–C$165; farm-stay cottage C$150/night or C$850 for 6 nights. Country breakfast included. Free parking. Closed mid-Oct to Easter. From Victoria, drive north on Hwy. 1 and turn left at Koksilah Road; Jackson Road is the third road after the railway bridge. No pets. Not suitable for guests with disabilities. **Amenities:** Dining room, kitchenette, walking trails, library, free Wi-Fi, no cable or satellite TV.

Oceanfront Suites at Cowichan Bay ★   Cowichan Bay is a pretty little village of gaily painted clapboard buildings all lined up along a harbor where sailboats float in serene waters. Not a bad setting for this modern, well-appointed, all-suites hotel. At first glace, it looks like any anonymous chain hotel built back in the 1970s or '80s, but it is much, much better than that. For one thing, it takes its place in a

---

Making the Best of the B&Bs

In the Cowichan Valley, there are generally two types of accommodation: chain motels (especially in Duncan, the biggest town in the area), and bed and breakfasts. If you'd rather stay in a place with personality, where you can mingle with locals and nosh on farm-fresh home-cooked meals, the B&Bs are likely what you're looking for. There are dozens in the area, offering rooms in everything from farmhouses to heritage homes to brand-new villas. Many have ocean-, garden-, or vineyard-views. One of the best places to start your search for the B&B that's best for you is through the **Cowichan Bed & Breakfast Association,** which lists some 17 properties on its website at www.southvanislebnb.com. You can find even more B&Bs (as well as those anonymous motels) through **Tourism Cowichan** (✆ **888/303-3337** or 250/746-4636; www.cvrd.bc.ca).

"Cittaslow" community seriously, offering locally grown fare in its Terrain Restaurant and kayak lessons from the dock below. For another, service is unusually attentive, especially at this moderate price range. All rooms have ocean views, some with patios perfect for enjoying a glass of wine while the sun sets, as well as kitchenettes, living areas, and a sunny, traditional-style decor with comfy leather armchairs, and glossy, maple-colored headboards.

1681 Cowichan Bay Rd., Cowichan Bay. ℂ **800/663-7898** or 250/715-1000. www.oceanfront cowichanbay.com. 56 suites. C$105–C$215 suite. Free parking. From Victoria, drive north on Hwy. 1; shortly after Mill Bay, turn right on Cowichan Bay Road, which will take you into the village of Cowichan Bay. Pet-friendly rooms available (charges apply). **Amenities:** Restaurant (closed Mon), indoor pool, fitness center, business center, private dock, reading and game room, concierge, free Wi-Fi.

Where to Eat

Amusé on the Vineyard ★★ WEST COAST   Chef Bradford Boisvert must be hoping that the third time really is the charm for his popular bistro. From the original location in Shawnigan Lake where he opened in 2005, he moved to an 1895 farmhouse in 2012, and now to Cherry Point Vineyards. The winery should prove an ideal location for this locavore chef: Long before it was producing its award-winning Gewürztraminer and blackberry dessert wine, it was a farm, and now Boisvert has a huge culinary garden where he can grow his own heirloom herbs and vegetables. He also has a bigger kitchen and bigger dining room, designed to evoke a First Nations longhouse, with lots of windows and dark support beams, which will welcome large groups and weddings. Still, most guests will likely find themselves on the sunny patio, enjoying a "Vintner's Lunch" of charcuterie, cheese, and vino, or one of his seasonal tasting menu dinners based on the freshest locally farmed and foraged fare he can find.

Cherry Point Vineyards, 840 Cherry Point Rd., Cobble Hill. ℂ **250/743-3667.** www.amuseon thevineyard.com. Main courses C$15–C$32; dinner tasting menus C$49–C$65; wine pairings extra. Wed–Sun 11:30am–5pm, Fri–Sat 5–10pm. Closed Mon–Tues.

Bistro at Merridale Cidery ★★ NORTH AMERICAN   As you meander along the country roads that crisscross the valley, be sure to visit this artisan cidery and its friendly little bistro. The dining room is a rambling, rustic space filled with cheerful local art and surrounded by windows that open out over the apple orchards. Owner Rick Pipes makes his ciders from proper heritage cider apples, and you will be surprised by the variety of flavors they can produce, from the light, dry Traditional to the strong, sharp Scrumpy, and sweet, rich, honeyed Cyser. All this gives the chefs plenty of flavors to play with as they create their menus. Expect casual but hearty fare such as sandwiches and salads, cider baby-back pork ribs, and buttermilk chicken strips. Sundays are pizza nights, when they feature live music (everything from beach rock to Irish/East Coast to indie roots) and artisan pizzas baked in a wood-fired oven—the same oven that produces all the breads, pastries, and apple pies.

Merridale Cidery, 1230 Merridale Rd., Cobble Hill. ℂ**800/998-9908** or 250/743-4293. www.merridale cider.com. Main courses C$9–C$20. Mon–Thurs noon–3pm, Fri–Sat 11am–5pm, Sun 10:30am–3pm.

Hudson's on First ★★★ WEST COAST/ENGLISH   From the highway, the city of Duncan seems like nothing but a sprawl of big box stores. But venture down its side streets and you'll find charming heritage houses like this rambling old Victorian. An even better surprise is that you'll find a Top Chef Canada alum in the kitchen cooking up some of the best food on the Island. Dan Hudson is a young, British-born chef with a passion for classic flavors and fresh, local ingredients. Think slow-cooked pork belly, mushroom-and-stilton risotto, or his popular fish and chips with apple-fennel slaw. Brunch is especially popular thanks to dishes like the house-made brioche French toast. And even if the food weren't so good, it would be worth a visit just to enjoy the beautiful dining room and lounge area, with their original fireplaces, ornate tin ceiling, tongue-and-groove paneling, and dark wooden trim, paired with comfy contemporary leather chairs and elegant white linens. Like Hudson's cooking, it's a perfect blend of old, new, and immaculate attention to detail.

163 1st St., Duncan. © **250/597-0066.** www.hudsonsonfirst.ca. Main courses C$15–C$30. Tues–Fri 11am–2pm, Sat–Sun 10am–2pm, Wed–Sat 5pm–close. Closed Mon; no dinner service Tues or Sun.

Stone Soup Inn ★ WEST COAST Over a 20-year career, chef-owner Brock Windsor has cooked at some of Canada's top restaurants. Now that he's got his own place, he's doing things his way. He's only open 3 nights a week. He only serves a five-course tasting menu. He changes the menu all the time. You get what you get. That's likely to be something farmed or foraged from nearby forests, fields, or waters. And it's likely to be something truly delicious, even if you've never heard of it before. Idiotfish? Nodding onion? Cauliflower fungus? Just trust him and enjoy a meal that is truly, and uniquely, of this one place. Enjoy, too, the elegant simplicity of this wooden structure surrounded by forest—the exposed beams, the tall stone chimney, the First Nations art on the pale walls, the supremely serene setting.

755 Cowichan Lake Rd., Lake Cowichan. © **250/749-3848.** www.stonesoupinn.ca. 5-course tasting menu C$65; additional C$35 for wine pairing. Thurs–Sat 5–9:30pm. Closed Sun–Wed. Reservations highly recommended.

True Grain Bread ★ BAKERY Truly, some of the best rustic artisan bread you'll ever try. True Grain mills its own grains, most of them organic heritage varieties like spelt, rye, and Red Fife wheat, and a small selection of wheat grown on Vancouver Island. All these go into their loaves, which are divinely dense and chewy with satisfyingly crisp crusts. There are classic loaves, like the French, ciabatta, sourdough, or German-style rye, and specialty breads, like the blue cheese and pecan baton. And don't forget the thick, chewy ginger cookies and other sweet treats. Pick up a loaf, then stop next door at Hilary's Cheese for some local goat or cow's milk fromage, and you've got yourself a perfect little picnic. (Hilary's also serves wine and a small selection of soups and sandwiches, if you prefer to eat in.) You can find both shops among the quirky little clapboard buildings on the main drag of Cowichan Bay; just look for all the blue bike planters with flowers spilling from their baskets.

1737 Cowichan Bay Rd., Cowichan Bay. © **250/746-7664.** www.truegrain.ca. C$5–C$10. Mon–Sat 8am–6pm, Sun 8am–5pm.

Exploring the Cowichan Valley

The Cowichan Valley is a bucolic region of farms, villages, forests, and many little country roads. Accept it now: You will get lost. Just go with the flow, though, and you will eventually end up where you want to go—or perhaps somewhere even better.

The biggest community in the area is the city of **Duncan,** which appears as little more than a sprawl of big box stores along the highway. Get off the main road, though, and you'll discover pretty neighborhoods filled with heritage homes and lush gardens. It's considered "The City of Totems," and you can discover some three dozen of the First Nations artworks throughout the historic downtown. For maps and other information, contact the **Cowichan Regional Visitor Centre** (© **888/303-3337** or

250/746-4636; www.tourismcowichan.com). And, for a totem of a completely different sort, Duncan is also home to The World's Largest Hockey Stick, a relic from Expo '86.

The village of **Cowichan Bay** is considered the heart of the "Cittaslow" community of foodies, famers, chefs, and winemakers; it's a quaint little cluster of shops, restaurants, and homes along a serene ocean harbor, and surrounded by organic farms. There are also the rustic villages of **Cobble Hill, Shawnigan Lake,** and **Chemainus,** with its famous murals. At the far northern end is **Ladysmith.**

Historically, this was logging country, but now it's more about tourism, agriculture, manufacturing, and marine businesses. But for millennia before the first Europeans arrived, this was home to the Coast Salish people, and there is still a thriving First Nations community here—you'll see their artworks and other legacies throughout the area. In fact, this is a popular area for artists in general, and one of the best ways to while away an afternoon is just to drive around and check out the many small studios and galleries.

This is also a great region for outdoor activities, from hiking to biking to kayaking and sailing. It's easy to spend a day or two getting a good workout as you explore the region. Or, even better, just sitting on a sunny patio, enjoying a glass of local wine and taking in the view. Ahhh.

BC Forest Discovery Centre ★ INTERPRETIVE CENTER

Sure, you'll learn about the history of forestry in British Columba, but really, it's all about hopping aboard one of the cool historic trains and chugging around the 40-hectare (100-acre) wooded site. There are a number of displays, including a blacksmith shop, sawmill, and logging trucks, plus trails to explore, a gift shop, and concessions serving up hot dogs and burgers in the summer months.

2892 Drinkwater Rd., Duncan. *C* **250/715-1113.** www.enertelligence.com/bcforestdiscovery centre/wordpress. Admission C$16 adults, C$14 seniors and students, C$11 children 3–12. Family passes and group rates available. Thurs–Sun 10am–4pm. Closed Tues–Wed, closed Nov–Mar. Located just off Hwy. 1 in Duncan, 1 hr. north of Victoria.

Chemainus Murals ★★★ OUTDOOR ART GALLERY

Downtown Chemainus has been transformed into a stunning art gallery with more than 40 larger-than-life murals painted on the sides of buildings. Highly detailed and grand in both size and scope, most of these depict historic scenes of the region's logging, mining, farming, and First Nations past. There is also a trompe l'oeil gallery inspired by the works of the great artist Emily Carr, as well as a number of sculptures along the route. Download the map at the Mural Town website, and take yourself on an unforgettable self-guided tour.

Throughout downtown Chemainus. *C* **250/246-4422** or 250/246-3944. www.muraltown.com. Free admission. Open 24/7. 20km (12 miles) northeast of Duncan, just off Hwy. 1.

Cowichan Estuary Nature Centre ★ INTERPRETIVE CENTER

Learn all about the natural and human history of the Cowichan Watershed via the center's interactive displays, activities, and programs. Check out the birds and other wildlife from the viewing towers, get a feel for the critters in the touch tanks, and use the microscopes to get really up close and personal with the smallest of living things. Mostly, this is a great way to discover the abundant marine life of this estuary.

Hecate Park, 1845 Cowichan Bay Rd., Cowichan Bay. *C* **250/597-2288.** www.cowichanestuary.ca. Free admission free but donation suggested. Thurs–Sun noon–4pm.

Wine Trail ★★

The Cowichan is home to more than a dozen wineries, cideries, distilleries, and brew pubs, and taking a self-guided tasting tour is a delicious way to spend a day. (If you plan to drink, though, do get someone else to drive.) Some of the best include **Venturi-Schulze,** known for its sparkling and dessert wines, as well as its balsamic vinegar made in the traditional Modena style; **Averill Creek,** which makes award-winning Pinot Blanc and Pinot Noir; and **Merridale Cidery,** which produces traditional English-style apple ciders. In general, wines tend to be cool-climate varietals, so don't expect any bold Cab Sauvs here. Visit **www. wines.cowichan.net** for a touring map and contact information for individual wineries. Follow the wine route signs off Hwy. 1. Most wineries will charge a small fee for tasting.

Kinsol Trestle ★★ HISTORIC SITE   The spectacular Kinsol Trestle is one of the tallest free-standing wooden rail trestles in the world, and one of the last remaining legacies of Vancouver Island's early mining and logging industries. It was built in 1920, and the last train trundled across it in 1979; since 2011, it has been the final link in the Cowichan Valley portion of the Trans Canada Trail, the world's largest network of trails, which will eventually stretch 22,000km (nearly 14,000 miles) from the Atlantic to Pacific to Arctic oceans. It offers spectacular views of the Koksilah River and trails for hiking, running, cycling, and riding.

Trans-Canada Trail, near Shawnigan Lake Village. © **250/746-2620.** www.kinsol.ca. Free admission. Open 24/7. From Hwy. 1, take exit to Shawnigan Lake Village, then continue on Renfrew Road 10km (6 miles), then turn right onto Glen Eagles Road, then right onto Shelby Road where you will find a parking lot. On foot, follow the rail bed (part of the Trans Canada Trail) to the trestle.

Whippletree Junction ★ SHOPPING   As you speed along Hwy. 1, you'll catch a glimpse of a cluster of brightly painted historic buildings of the frontier-era false-front variety. This is Whippletree Junction, and one of the most entertaining shopping experiences around. It's a collection of old buildings that were rescued from demolition some 30 years ago, restored, painted, and given new life as shops that attract both tourists and locals. Diversity is the name of the game here, and you'll find everything from old-time candies to handcrafted furniture. Even if you don't plan to shop, it's just fun to look around.

4705 Trans Canada Hwy, Duncan. © **250/746-5250.** Free admission. Daily 10am–5pm. Just south of Duncan.

GULF ISLANDS

The **Strait of Georgia,** also known as the **Salish Sea,** is scattered with hundreds of rocks, islets, and idyllic islands that have been grouped together under the name the Gulf Islands. (That's on the Canadian side of the border; on the U.S. side, they're the San Juans.) Historically, the Gulf Islands only included those up to Gabriola, halfway up Vancouver Island just off the coast of Nanaimo, but today, all the islands as far north as Quadra are included in the group, but split into the Northern and Southern Gulf Islands. They are peopled with artists, writers, artisans, farmers, winemakers, and cheese makers. The Gulf Islands are also a paradise for sailors and anyone who enjoys

The Gulf Islands

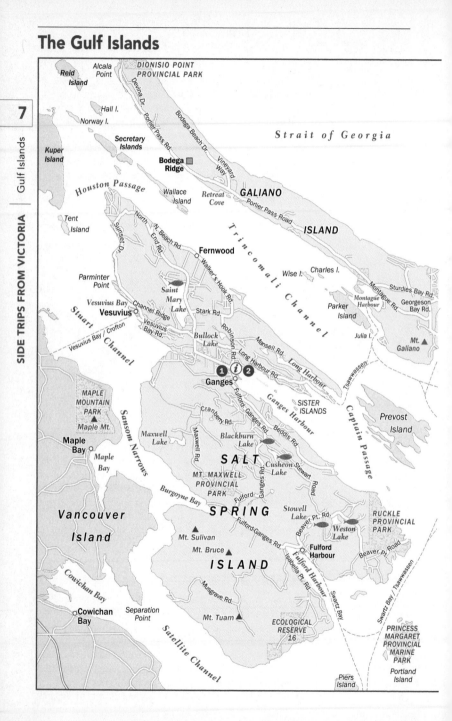

Reid Island

Alcala Point

DIONISIO POINT PROVINCIAL PARK

Hall I.

Norway I.

Devina Dr.

Porlier Pass Rd.

Bodega Beach Dr.

Vineyard Way

Strait of Georgia

Secretary Islands

Bodega Ridge

GALIANO

Kuper Island

Houston Passage

Wallace Island

Retreat Cove

Porlier Pass Road

ISLAND

Tent Island

Sunset Dr.

North End Rd.

N. Beach Rd.

Fernwood

Walker's Hook Rd.

Trincomali Channel

Wise I.

Charles I.

Sturdies Bay Rd.

Montague Rd.

Georgeson Bay Rd.

Parminter Point

Saint Mary Lake

Channel Ridge

Stark Rd.

Parker Island

Montague Harbour

Vesuvius Bay

Vesuvius

Vesuvius Bay Rd.

Robinson Rd.

Mansell Rd.

Julia I.

Mt. Galiano

Stuart Channel

Vesuvius Bay / Crofton

Bullock Lake

Long Harbour Rd.

Long Harbour

Tsawwassen

Ganges

Ganges Harbour

SISTER ISLANDS

Prevost Island

MAPLE MOUNTAIN PARK

Maple Mt.

Sansom Narrows

Cranberry Rd.

Fulford-Ganges Rd.

Beddis Rd.

Captain Passage

Maple Bay

Maple Bay

Maxwell Lake

Maxwell Rd.

Blackburn Lake

SALT

Cusheon Lake

Stewart Road

Vancouver Island

Burgoyne Bay

MT. MAXWELL PROVINCIAL PARK

Ganges Rd.

Fulford

SPRING

Stowell Lake

Beaver Pt. Rd.

Weston Lake

RUCKLE PROVINCIAL PARK

Fulford-Ganges Rd.

Mt. Sulivan

Mt. Bruce

ISLAND

Isabella Pt. Rd.

Fulford Harbour

Fulford Harbour

Beaver Pt. Road

Cowichan Bay

Separation Point

Musgrave Rd.

Mt. Tuam

ECOLOGICAL RESERVE 16

Swartz Bay

Swartz Bay / Tsawwassen

Cowichan Bay

Satellite Channel

Piers Island

PRINCESS MARGARET PROVINCIAL MARINE PARK

Portland Island

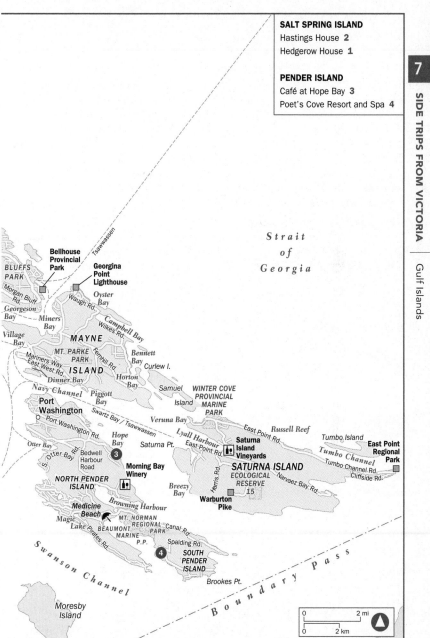

SALT SPRING ISLAND
Hastings House **2**
Hedgerow House **1**

PENDER ISLAND
Café at Hope Bay **3**
Poet's Cove Resort and Spa **4**

*Strait
of
Georgia*

Tsawwassen

Bellhouse
Provincial
Park

**BLUFFS
PARK**

Morgan Bluff
Rd.

*Georgeson
Bay*

Georgina
Point
Lighthouse

*Oyster
Bay*

Waugh Rd.

*Miners
Bay*

Campbell Bay

Wilkes Rd.

Village
Bay

MAYNE

**MT. PARKE
PARK**

Fernhill Rd.

*Bennett
Bay*

Curlew I.

Mariners Way
East West Rd.

ISLAND

Dinner Bay

*Horton
Bay*

*Samuel
Island*

**WINTER COVE
PROVINCIAL
MARINE
PARK**

Navy Channel

Piggott
Bay

Veruna Bay

**Port
Washington**

Swartz Bay / Tsawwassen

Lyall Harbour

East Point Rd.

Russell Reef

Tumbo Island

**East Point
Regional
Park**

Port Washington Rd.

Hope
Bay

Saturna Pt.

East Point Rd.

**Saturna
Island
Vineyards**

Tumbo Channel

Tumbo Channel Rd.

Otter Bay

Otter Bay Rd.

Bedwell
Harbour
Road

3

SATURNA ISLAND

Cliffside Rd.

Harris Rd.

**NORTH PENDER
ISLAND**

**Morning Bay
Winery**

*Breezy
Bay*

**SATURNA ISLAND
ECOLOGICAL
RESERVE
15**

Navaez Bay Rd.

**Medicine
Beach**

*Magic
Lake*

Browning Harbour

**MT. NORMAN
REGIONAL
PARK**

**Warburton
Pike**

Pirates Rd.

**BEAUMONT
MARINE
P.P.**

Canal Rd.

Spalding Rd.

4

**SOUTH
PENDER
ISLAND**

Swanson Channel

Brookes Pt.

Boundary Pass

*Moresby
Island*

0		2 mi
0		2 km

boating, kayaking, and generally communing with nature, or, indeed, anyone who just wants to get away from it all. If you're visiting Victoria and have an extra day or two, it's well worth hopping over to one or more of the Southern Gulf Islands.

Essentials

GETTING THERE

There are basically two ways to get to the Gulf Islands—by plane or by boat.

BY PLANE   **SaltSpring Air** (✆ 877/537-9880 or 250/537-9880; www.saltspringair.com) has a fleet of floatplanes that fly from Coal Harbour in Vancouver, near the airport in Victoria, and throughout most of the Gulf Islands. **Harbour Air** (✆ 800/665-0212; www.harbourair.com) has regularly scheduled flights from Vancouver to the Gulf Islands.

BY FERRY   Unless you have a private boat, you'll need to take a ferry, which is how most people get to the Gulf Islands. BC Ferries (✆ 888/223-3779; www.bcferries.com) has a fleet of drive-aboard ships that run regularly scheduled trips from Swartz Bay outside Victoria to Pender, Mayne, and Galiano, as well as Salt Spring Island.

VISITOR INFORMATION

You can pick up information on the Gulf Islands at the Tourism Victoria Visitors Centre (✆ 800/663-3883 or 250/953-2033; www.tourismvictoria.com) or through **Gulf Islands Tourism** (✆ 250/537-9933; www.gulfislandstourism.com). Each of the islands will also have their own info center; for instance, **Salt Spring,** the biggest of the islands (✆ 866/216-2936 or 250/537-5252; www.saltspringtourism.com). These are also your best resource for finding the area's best B&Bs.

Where to Stay

Hastings House Country House Hotel ★★★   Such a beautiful refuge. Located right on the waterfront in lovely Ganges, this small luxury property, a member of Relais & Châteaux, is definitely a getaway from the every day. The manor house is a pleasantly rambling old place loaded with charm and character, surrounded by 9 hectares (22 acres) of lush woods and pretty gardens. There are only 18 units, including a handful of cottages, as well as the highly respected Wellspring Spa, where every treatment is a customized one. Even so, the best reason to visit is the excellent cuisine—not only do guests wake up to a breakfast hamper, they then partake in a full country breakfast, plus there's afternoon tea to keep energies from flagging. Plus the dining room is legendary (p. 189). A truly unforgettable destination.

160 Upper Ganges Rd., Salt Spring Island. ✆ **800/661-9255** or 250/537-2362. www.hastings house.com. 18 units. C$285–C$495 double, C$345–C$545 suite, C$495–C$595 deluxe suites and cottage, C$595–C$745 premier suites and cottage. Breakfast, wakeup hamper, and afternoon tea included. Package and group rates available. Free parking. Dining room closed Oct 26–Feb 28. Pets allowed in select rooms only (C$50/day). **Amenities:** Restaurant, bar/lounge, room service, beach, spa, shuttles, free Wi-Fi.

Hedgerow House ★★   One of Salt Spring Island's most popular B&Bs is under new ownership, recently bought by a couple with a long history in the tourism and hospitality business. They know what they're doing, and what they're doing is offering a luxe little sanctuary on the edge of Ganges, the island's main town. The decor is a comfortable, sun-drenched mix of traditional and modern: on the one hand, sloping ceilings, hardwood floors, Persian rugs, and French doors; on the other, graphic floral print cushions, boldly colored testament walls, and round-based night table lamps.

Expect comfortable beds, fluffy towels, walks that meander through gardens and woods, a wholesome breakfast, and the sort of peace and serenity that will make you want to curl up with a good book.

238 Park Dr., Ganges, Salt Spring Island. ☏ **250/538-1716.** www.hedgerowhouse.ca. 3 units. C$130–C$190. Breakfast included. Free parking. **Amenities:** Guest lounge, walking trails, snack bar, free Wi-Fi.

Poet's Cove Resort & Spa ★ Stumbling across Poet's Cove is always something of a happy surprise. Unlike the quaint little B&Bs that pepper the islands, this is a big, beautiful, new-build luxury resort in a scenic cove on peaceful South Pender Island. It's designed in classic West Coast Craftsman style, with a lovely, high-ceilinged great room that features a massive stone fireplace and gorgeous views of the marina below. (The marina makes this a favorite destination of boaters.) There are a variety of room styles, ranging from basic lodge rooms to cottages with living rooms and kitchens and the luxe villas. All have fireplaces, overstuffed chairs and sofas where you'll want to curl up with a good book, and balconies with views. There is also a gorgeous restaurant that unfortunately seems to garner mixed reviews despite its high-end ambitions, and the excellent, award-winning Susurrus spa. Note that in early 2014, the resort was bought by new owners; look for improvements to come.

9801 Spalding Rd., South Pender Island. ☏ **888/512-7638** or 250/629-2100. www.poetscove.com. 46 units. C$139–C$319 lodge rooms, C$289–C$469 villas, C$479–C$699 executive cottage. The resort may close for part of the winter season. Free parking. Pets welcome (C$50 1-time fee for 1 pet, C$75 for 2). **Amenities:** Restaurant, lounge, fitness center, pool, business center, kitchenette, marina, spa, free Wi-Fi.

Where to Eat

Café at Hope Bay ★ WEST COAST   This casual little spot in a clapboard building overlooking the ocean is consistently the best eatery on Pender Island. It is unpretentious and friendly, with lots of options for vegetarians and those with dietary restrictions. The chef-owners work with local farmers, and make their own cheese and smoke their own meat. They serve a terrific chowder, excellent burgers, a luxurious smoked sablefish salad, and, of course, a very respectable fish and chips. Great view, great food; this is a must when you visit Pender.

Bedwell Harbour Rd., Pender Island. ☏ **250/629-2090.** www.thecafeathopebay.com. C$12–C$22. Wed–Sun 11am–3pm, Thurs–Sun 5–8pm. Closed Mon–Tues. Limited hours in winter.

Dining Room at Hastings House ★★★ CONTINENTAL   The only five-star dining experience in the Gulf Islands. Chef Marcel Kauer relies on the exceptional local bounty—including his own kitchen garden—for his fresher-than-fresh cuisine. Dinner is three courses, which could include an appetizer of seared sablefish or a green salad from the garden, entrée of grilled Salt Spring Island lamb or Pacific steelhead trout, and luscious desserts like hazelnut-apple kuchen. The wine list is exceptional, and cocktails are served on the patio on summer afternoons.

Hastings House Country House Hotel, 160 Upper Ganges Rd., Salt Spring Island. ☏ **800/661-9255** or 250/537-2362. www.hastingshouse.com. 3-course menus C$70–C$90; wine additional. Jun–Oct daily 5:30–7:30pm, Mar–Apr Wed–Sun 5:30–7:30pm. Closed Nov–Feb.

Exploring the Gulf Islands

The best part of a getaway to the Gulf Islands is simply getting away from it all. The islands are an idyllic place for wandering about and connecting with nature, so don't arrive with a big itinerary. The main islands, nearest Victoria, are Salt Spring, Pender,

Mayne, and Saturna. These are not big islands, but a car is still helpful for exploring—although they are perfect for **cycling,** so that may be an even better way to get around, and you'll find bike rental shops throughout the islands. The Gulf Islands are also hugely popular destinations for **boaters,** and on a sunny day you'll find the peaceful green waters that surround them littered with sailboats. There are numerous private marinas and kayak rentals, so you can get out on the water, too.

Salt Spring is the biggest and most populated of the islands. Its main community, **Ganges,** holds a famous farmer's market on Saturday mornings (www.saltspring market.com), where you can meet the locals and pick up fresh veggies, mouthwatering baked goods, and crafts by island artisans, of whom there are many. Historically, the island was a farming community, and it has thoroughly embraced the eat-local movement, with 23 restaurants, local cheese makers including the celebrated **Salt Spring Island Cheese** (www.saltspringcheese.com), the **Gulf Island Brewery** (www. gulfislandsbrewery.com), a **winery** (www.saltspringvineyards.com), and many small farms. The **Apple Festival** (www.appleluscious.com) each September is a sweet way to celebrate the harvest.

If time is short and you want a handy guide to the island, the **Western Splendour Tour Company** (© 778/354-1058; www.toursaltspring.com) offers several tours, including a history and culture walking tour (C$15 adults, C$10 children 12 and under), a bus tour to the best of the island (C$75 adults, C$12 children), and an artisan tour that visits farms, cheese makers, brewers, and craftspeople (C$75 adults, C$50 children 12 and under).

Saturna (www.saturnatourism.com) is a mountainous island known for its excellent wildlife-watching opportunities. More than half of it is in the **Gulf Islands National Park Reserve** (www.parkscanada.gc.ca/gulfislands), and you'll often catch glimpses of orcas and porpoises frolicking off its rocky shores. **Discovery Seatours** (© 250/539-3211; www.discoveryseatours.ca) is just one outfitter that offers whale-watching and other opportunities. The island is home to a number of popular pubs and casual eateries, as well as the **Saturna Island Family Estate Winery** (© 250/539-3521; www.saturnavineyards.com), which is known for its light, crisp white and sparkling wines.

Pender Island (www.penderislandchamber.com) is actually two islands separated by a narrow canal. It's covered in forest and farmland, with a couple of small communities. Life is slow and relaxed here, with plenty of parks, beaches, and trails to explore, as well as canoeing, kayaking, and sailing around its coves and beaches. This is where you'll find the Poet's Cove luxury resort, as well as a number of pubs and restaurants.

Mayne Island (www.mayneislandchamber.ca) is a rustic retreat, home to numerous artists and artisans, with a handful of pubs and restaurants and a number of small farms. Mayne Island is a perfect little bucolic getaway.

TOFINO, UCLUELET & PACIFIC RIM NATIONAL PARK PRESERVE

There's something magical about the stretch of Vancouver Island's west coast between **Tofino** and **Ucluelet.** For one thing, it's startlingly beautiful, with majestic old-growth forests, dramatic fjords, crashing waves, and long, silky, sandy beaches. More than that, though, there is a serenity here that attracts people searching for inspiration,

Pacific Rim National Park Reserve

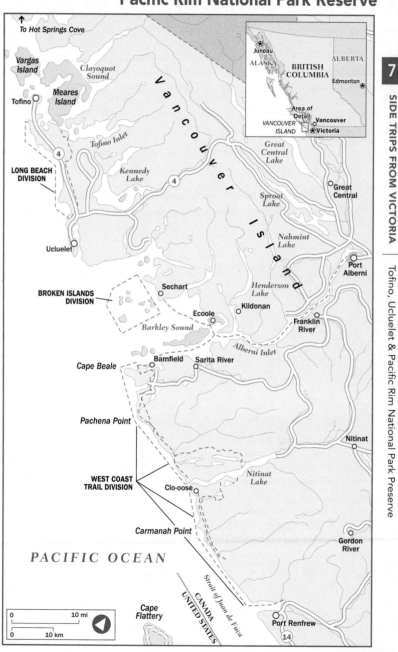

enlightenment, or inner peace. That, or just a good wave—this is, after all, prime surfing country.

This remote, rugged rainforest is home to some spectacular natural sites, including the **Clayoquot Sound UNESCO Marine Biosphere Reserve** and the pristine **Pacific Rim National Park Reserve,** Canada's first marine park, established back in 1971. That's where you will find **Long Beach,** which is actually four consecutive beaches (Radar, Long, Combers, and Wickaninnish) that total some 30km (19 miles) of surf and sand broken by rocky outcrops. About a million people visit the park each year, and from June through August the single-lane highway between Ucluelet and Tofino is a constant traffic jam. Pack your patience along with your sunscreen if you plan to drive. The crowds are just one of the reasons storm-watching season (Feb–Mar) has become so popular.

The two towns on either end of the park have distinctly different personalities. In the south, **Ucluelet** was the primary industry town, when industry meant fishing and logging instead of tourism, and it still has a way to go when it comes to amenities for visitors, despite all the new holiday homes. About a half-hour drive to the north, **Tofino** is prettier, mellower, foodier, and has more amenities for visitors, including most of the area's top restaurants, accommodations, surfer beaches, and eco-outfitters. The setting is simply stunning, with jagged mountain peaks towering above island-studded Clayoquot Sound.

Visitors come here for the hiking, the boating, the surfing, and the food. They come here to watch the sun set over the Pacific Ocean, to watch an orca leap from the waters, to listen to the soothing sound of the waves and the haunting cry of a bald eagle soaring over the mist-shrouded cedars. They come here to find a place of unsurpassed natural beauty, and might even leave having found themselves.

Essentials

GETTING THERE

The west coast of the Island is still wild and remote, and just getting there can be a serious and, at times, terrifying adventure. Back in the day, the only way in was by boat and then by floatplane. Nowadays there's a highway, but it's a narrow, winding, mostly single-lane road subject to frequent landslides, washouts, and terrible accidents. But it is a spectacularly beautiful drive, considered one of the most scenic in Canada.

BY CAR Take Hwy. 1 north from Victoria or Nanaimo to the turnoff near Parksville. From there you will follow Hwy. 4 through Port Alberni, past the towering old-growth cedars of Cathedral Grove, along a breathtakingly narrow mountain pass, and on to a T-junction. There the road splits, going south to Ucluelet or north to Pacific Rim and Tofino. The trip from Nanaimo takes about 4 hours; from Victoria, close to 6.

BY BUS There is regularly scheduled Greyhound Lines bus service year-round from Victoria and Nanaimo (© **800/661-8747;** www.greyhound.ca) as well as a service run by **Tofino Bus** (© **866/986-3466** or 250/725-2871; www.tofinobus.com) in the summer months.

BY PLANE The good news is that there's actually an airport here now, located halfway between Tofino and Ucluelet. The bad news is that it's tiny and subject to bad weather, especially fog, so flights are often diverted to Port Alberni or Qualicum and passengers bused in. **Orca Airways** (© **888/359-6722;** www.flyorcaair.com) provides daily service year-round from Vancouver, and daily service May to October from Victoria. The flight takes about an hour from either city.

VISITOR INORMATION

The **Pacific Rim Visitor Centre** (℡ 250/726-4600; www.pacificrimvisitor.ca), at the junction of Hwy. 4 and Ucluelet, serves as a general information gateway for Ucluelet, Tofino, Port Alberni, and Bamfield. It's also a good place to pick up your **day-use park pass** (C$8 adults, C$7 seniors, C$4 children 6–16, C$20 families), although you can also purchase a pass at machines in the park's parking lots.

More information is available from the **Ucluelet Visitor Info Centre** (℡ 250/726-4641; www.ucclueletinfo.com), or the **Tofino Visitor Info Centre** (℡ 250/725-3414; www.tofino-bc.com), both open June through September. For more details on the park itself, stop in at the **Kwisitis Visitor Centre** (formerly the Wickaninnish Interpretive Centre) and the **Long Beach Unit of Pacific Rim National Park Reserve of Canada** (℡ 250/726-3500; www.pc.gc.ca), which is open mid-March through mid-October.

Where to Stay

Black Rock Oceanfront Resort ★★ Finally, Ucluelet has luxe accommodation to rival almost anything Tofino has to offer. The setting of this 5-year-old property is simply spectacular—perched on a rocky cliff with waves crashing right below and the recently completed Wild Pacific Trail nearby—and its contemporary design is almost as dramatic—all rock, steel, water, wood, and the gleam of glass from floor-to-ceiling windows. The all-suite guest rooms are luxuriously comfortable, with lots of natural light, wood, and stone to provide a sense of melding with nature. The resort is a 15-minute walk from downtown Ucluelet, but is designed to provide just about anything you need on site, including the artisanal-inspired dishes of its fine-dining restaurant, Fetch, and the sense of well-being bestowed by the Drift Spa. The resort is well equipped to host weddings, elopements, and meetings, though one imagines that it would be difficult to concentrate on spreadsheets with all that natural beauty nearby.

596 Marine Dr., Ucluelet. ℡ **877/762-5011** or 250/726-4800. www.blackrockresort.com. 133 units. C$265–C$415 double, C$360–C$700 suite. Free parking. Pets allowed (C$25/day). **Amenities:** Restaurant, bar, beach, free airport transfers, fitness center, movie library, seasonal outdoor plunge pool, room service, spa, business center, free Wi-Fi.

The Inn at Tough City ★ Most of Tofino's accommodations are outside of the town itself, and what there is in town tends to be of the motel or B&B variety. The exception is this quirky little inn. "Tough" or "Tuff" City is, of course, Tofino's nickname (and the name of the excellent craft brewery, too), and this inn is quintessential Tofino. It's located right downtown with a stunning view overlooking Clayoquot Sound. Although it looks like it could date back to the 1960s, it was actually built in 1996, out of recycled and salvaged material, and filled with seafaring bric-a-brac. Don't expect a ton of luxurious amenities, but the eight cozy guest rooms are perfect romantic hideaways, some with soaker tubs and fireplaces. Plus the sushi restaurant downstairs is both excellent and affordable—try the Tofino roll made with local Dungeness crab when it's in season.

350 Main St., Tofino. ℡ **877/725-2021** or 250/725-2021. www.toughcity.com. 8 units. C$110–C$230 double. Free parking. Pets not allowed. **Amenities:** Restaurant (dinner only), free Wi-Fi.

Long Beach Lodge Resort ★★ Step through the sliding glass doors of the beachside suites and you'll find yourself on Tofino's most popular surfing beach, Cox Bay. There is something shiveringly magical about watching the black-clad surfers emerge from the early morning mist—luckily, unlike them, you can sneak back inside where it's warm and there is coffee. Long Beach Lodge is homey yet grand, with a distinctly West Coast Craftsman look to it. Its most popular feature is the great room, which truly is one of the greatest rooms on the coast, with its high ceilings, comfy armchairs, big stone fireplace, unbeatable ocean views, and award-winning martinis. The Great Room is also the resort's restaurant, and a spectacular place to enjoy local Dungeness crab or seafood chowder, though the new SandBar Bistro, opening on the beach in June 2014, is sure to be just as popular. The guest rooms are pretty great, too: They're painted the color of forest light, with rosy cedar millwork and luxurious soaker tubs, some with stone fireplaces and balconies. A handful of rainforest cottages are tucked into the woods, perfect for families.

1441 Pacific Rim Hwy., Tofino. © **877/844-7873** or 250/725-2442. www.longbeachlodgeresort. com. 61 units. C$190–C$390 double, C$320–C$630 cabin. Rates include continental breakfast. Free parking. Pets welcome (C$50). **Amenities:** Restaurant, lounge, oceanfront health club, surf center, business center, concierge, free Wi-Fi.

Middle Beach Lodge ★★ Like a middle child, Middle Beach Lodge is sometimes slightly overlooked, but that is a mistake—it is one of the most appealing resorts along the coast, and one of the best bargains to boot. It's all about unpretentious comfort here. The resort combines rustic, shabby chic with luxurious comfort in a spectacular wooded setting on a rocky headland with stunning views. There is a huge variety of guest rooms, ranging from small, simple spaces with no phone or TV to bigger, better appointed suites in the newer part of the lodge, as well as 19 family-friendly cabins tucked away in the rainforest. The centerpiece of the resort is the cozy common room (although there is nothing at all commonplace about the views from here), which is where a simple but satisfying continental breakfast is served each morning, and a seafood dinner served Wednesdays through Saturdays.

400 Mackenzie Beach Rd., Tofino. © **866/725-2900** or 250/725-2900. www.middlebeach.com. 64 units, 19 cabins. C$165–C$360 double, C$255–C$450 cabins. Rates include continental breakfast. Seafood dinner available Wed–Sat for C$30, extra for wine or beer. Surf, kayak, and other getaway packages available. Free parking. Pets welcome in some cabins (C$40 cleaning fee). **Amenities:** Dining room, exercise room, beach, kitchenette (in some), free Wi-Fi.

Pacific Sands Beach Resort ★★ Few resorts along this coast are more family friendly—or better loved. Pacific Sands is located beachfront on beautiful Cox Bay, the most popular of Tofino's surfing beaches. It is all suites with full kitchens, including a number of three-story beach houses that can sleep up to eight. The guestrooms are decked out in soft, sandy hues and comfortable furniture, with gas fireplaces, balconies for watching the waves crash on the beach, and cute nautical details like the lighthouse-shaped lamps. But the point of coming here is just how peaceful and relaxing it is. It's surrounded by forest and sea, and all you hear at night is the wash of waves on the beach. There is no restaurant or bar (although the hosts may throw an occasional beach barbecue), so it's just you and nature. Which is, after all, the point.

1421 Pacific Rim Hwy., Tofino. © **800/565-2322** or 250/725-3322. www.pacificsands.com. 77 units. C$200–C$425 suite, C$310–C$790 beach house. Free parking. Pets welcome (C$40 cleaning fee). **Amenities:** Beach, kitchen, DVD library, fireplace, business center, shuttle service, babysitting, free kids' camps July–Aug, bike rentals, free Wi-Fi.

Ucluelet Oceanfront Hostel ★ If you're looking for a steal of a deal in budget accommodation, the **Ucluelet Oceanfront Hostel** might be just the ticket. It's part of the C&N Backpackers Hotels group (they also have properties in Vancouver, Tofino, and Port Hardy), and while the accommodation is pretty minimalistic, it is clean, and above all, dry, which is not something to sneeze at if you land here during a rainstorm.

Those looking for a real bargain can book a dorm bed; there are also a handful of private rooms available. Plus the hostel has its own private beach and offers recommendations for local pubs, so you know it's going to be a fun hangout.

2081 Peninsula Rd., Ucluelet. ⓒ **888/434-6060** or 250/726-7416. www.cnnbackpackers.com/ucluelet. 3 private guest rooms plus dormitory. C$65 private room, C$25 dorm bed. Free parking. No pets. **Amenities:** Private beach, kitchen, lounge area, laundry, linens, bike and kayak rental, free Wi-Fi.

Wickaninnish Inn ★★★ For the ultimate in West Coast luxury, "the Wick" has it all. This Relais & Châteaux property was the first true luxury inn along this coast, and since the day owner Charles McDiarmid opened it in 1996, he has not stopped improving the decor, the service, or the amenities. Most recently, he's added a bike shed with free bikes for guests to use, and hired a whole new culinary team that's shaking things up in the multiple-award-winning Pointe Restaurant. The Wick's form of luxury is a subtle one—its decor is a simple, rustic-elegant West Coast style, with lots of stone, cedar, fluffy linens, and soft, misty colors. But look closer and you'll see that the wood is hand carved, the stone perfectly buffed, the sheets silky soft, and the fittings designed to slide smoothly and soundlessly. Most of all, you'll be awed by the setting, perhaps the most beautiful on a shoreline with no shortage of stunning scenery. It sits on a rocky promontory overlooking Chesterman Beach and surrounded by old-growth forests. Every view is an ocean view, even the ones from the exceptional Ancient Cedars Spa, where you can indulge in a locally harvested seaweed treatment. The inn is filled with art by local artists, and there's a First Nations carving shed on the property, where you can watch the masters at work. A stay here is an unforgettable experience that would be a once-in-a-lifetime thrill if so many guests didn't keep coming back again and again.

500 Osprey Lane (at Chesterman Beach), Tofino. ⓒ **800/333-4604** or 250/725-3100. www.wickinn.com. 75 units. C$420–C$580 double, C$540–C$620 suite, C$1,500 penthouse. Free parking. Closed Jan. Pets welcome (C$40/day for first pet, C$20/day for second; pet-sitting available). **Amenities:** 2 restaurants, bar, babysitting, concierge, fitness center, library, room service, spa, bicycles, rain gear, free Wi-Fi.

CAMPING

The whole point of the Pacific Rim area is getting back to nature, and there's no better way to do that than by setting up camp somewhere scenic. Just beware that this is a rainforest, so chances are you'll get drenched at some point during your stay.

You can even camp in the park itself. Back in the day, the flower children would camp right on the beach at Florencia Bay or Schooner Cove. Today, sadly, there is no more beach camping. But the 94 campsites at **Green Point** offer something even better: toilets, pumped well water, and fire pits. There are still no showers or hookups, but the magnificent ocean view from the bluff makes up for it. Reservations are essential in high season, and the campground will be full every day in July and August. To make a reservation, call ⓒ **877/737-3783** or visit www.pccamping.ca. The cost is C$24 per night, with an additional charge of C$7 for firewood. The campground is closed mid-October to May 1.

More camping is available at **Bella Pacifica Campground** (ⓒ **250/725-3400;** www.bellapacifica.com) near Tofino, but in this case with washrooms, showers, and laundry facilities. A beachfront site will run you C$52 in peak season, while a non-view site is C$42. Reservations are highly recommended. Closed November through February.

There is also **Surf Junction Campground** just outside Ucluelet (ⓒ **877/922-6722** or 250/726-7214; www.surfjunction.com). The campground has space for RVs and tents, and has hot showers, flush toilets, a sauna, hot tub, and covered cooking and eating area. It's popular with the surf set, and offers surf lessons and rentals, as well as a place to wash out your wet suit. Rates range from C$25 to C$55. Reservations recommended. Closed October through March.

Where to Eat

Chocolate Tofino ★★ CANDY   After a tough day of surfing, hiking, or just gazing at the scenery, nothing hits the spot quite like a sweet little treat. Chocolate Tofino has you covered, with handmade chocolates based on local ingredients—try the wild blackberry buttercream or wildflower honey ganache—as well as luscious gelatos. This is also a good place to pick up gifts for those back home, such as the chocolate bears filled with tiny chocolate salmon. Sweet.

1180 Pacific Rim Hwy., Tofino. © **250/725-2526.** www.chocolatetofino.com. Prices vary; gift boxes start at C$17. Mon–Sat 10am–6pm. Closed Sun.

Common Loaf Bakeshop ★ BAKERY/CAFE   Everyone goes to the Loaf, so if you're looking to hang out with the locals, this downtown Tofino cafe is as good a place as any. It's a great spot to grab a coffee, check your e-mail courtesy of the free Wi-Fi, and nibble on home-baked goodies. Service can be hit and miss, but the hippy vibe is cool and laid back in this cheerfully eclectic room with its randomly shaped stained-glass windows, local art on the walls, and wooden cases filled with baked goods.

180 1st St., Tofino. © **250/725-3915.** C$7–C$12. Daily 8am–9pm.

Fetch ★ INTERNATIONAL   Ucluelet has always had a tough time competing with Tofino when it comes to dining, but Fetch comes close. Sleek, modern, and cool, with swooping wooden room dividers in the dining room and low sofas in the lounge, it looks like it should be in a big city somewhere, not perched on the rugged coast. But you still get that great ocean view to remind you where you are. Expect lots of local seafood, with a wide-ranging global approach to flavor and preparation—everything from jambalaya to spaghetti *alle vongole* to mackerel grilled with *harissa* and salmon grilled with miso. There is definitely something for every taste. Perhaps the highlight of the menu, though, is the sushi in Float Lounge prepared on weekends by talented local chef Kevin Kimoto. Also expect a good wine list, perfect for enjoying on the sunny patio.

Black Rock Oceanfront Resort, 596 Marine Dr., Ucluelet. © **877/762-5011** or 250/726-4811. www.blackrockresort.com. Lunch C$12–C$15, dinner main courses C$26–C$38. Dining room daily 8am–10pm (last seating 8pm), lounge daily 3–10pm. Reservations highly recommended for dinner.

Great Room at Long Beach Lodge Resort ★★ WEST COAST   Great? This room is fantastic! High ceilings, West Coast Craftsman decor, huge stone fireplace, floor-to-ceiling windows overlooking the ocean—it's worthwhile just dropping by for a glass of wine and a snack. It's even better if you stay for dinner. The menu isn't particularly adventurous, but everything is deftly prepared and deliciously soul satisfying, such as the crisp Dungeness crab cakes or tender halibut with spot prawn croquette. Or try one of the excellent burgers or pizza with a beer or glass of wine. Also, opening in summer 2014 is the SandBar Bistro, a beachside patio that will offer casual fare like pulled-pork sandwiches and fish and chips. Perfect for après surf.

1441 Pacific Rim Hwy., Tofino. © **877/844-7873** or 250/725-2442. www.longbeachlodgeresort.com. Lunch C$15–C$20, main courses dinner C$28–C$45. Daily 7:30am–9pm. Reservations recommended for dinner.

Norwoods ★ FUSION   After working at hotels, private clubs, and high-end restaurant chains all across Canada, Asia, and Europe, chef Richard Norwood found himself at the end of the world in Ucluelet, where he opened this little gem of a bistro. It is tiny, cozy, and very friendly, with an open kitchen where guests can watch chef create his magic. He sources as much as possible locally, and changes up his menus at a whim, depending on what he can find. That could mean mussels in Thai curry, pasta with braised lamb, steamed buns filled with pulled pork, or local halibut wrapped in prosciutto. The wine list features local and international wines carefully chosen to pair with his bold flavors, and the spiced-pear cocktail is a must. A terrific find.

1714 Peninsula Rd., Ucluelet. ✆ **250/726-7001.** www.norwoods.ca. Main courses C$33–C$47. Daily 6–11pm. Reservations recommended.

The Pointe Restaurant ★★★ WEST COAST   Since the Wickaninnish Inn opened in 1996, its restaurant, The Pointe, has set the bar high for dining on this coast. And things just get better and better at this Relais & Châteaux property, even when you think that couldn't be possible. The carefully handcrafted dining room decor is deceptively simple, all the better to frame the spectacular 280-degree panorama of beach, islands, and ocean. Just as beautiful is the food on the plate, each dish a meticulous work of art, like the pretty chilled shellfish platter adorned with elderflowers and nasturtiums. Since opening, The Pointe has led the way in choosing local, seasonal, and sustainable ingredients, and that hasn't changed with the dynamic new team in the kitchen led by Executive Chef Warren Barr. You might find yourself nibbling on local ling cod, octopus, abalone mushrooms, sea lettuce, wild onions, or tip-to-tail ingredients like pig's tail or lamb tongue. Whatever it is, it will be prepared with finesse and flair, and paired with wines from one of the best cellars on the West Coast. An unforgettable dining experience. Note that The Pointe also serves a terrific value three-course set-price lunch menu, and an exceptional breakfast as well. Also well worth checking out is what might be the best-kept secret in Tofino: the inn's casual Driftwood Café, an inviting little spot where you can enjoy light meals right by the beach.

Wickaninnish Inn, 500 Osprey Lane (at Chesterman Beach), Tofino. ✆ **250/725-3100.** www.wickinn.com. Brunch C$17–C$25, 2-course lunch feature C$35, dinner main courses C$28–C$45. Daily 8am–9:30pm. Reservations essential.

The Schooner ★★ SEAFOOD   Yes, The Schooner serves other food—steaks, pasta, sandwiches, and the like—but it's mostly about the seafood here, and has been since it opened in downtown Tofino back in 1949. The room is cozy and lively, all decked out with seafaring memorabilia and jam-packed with visitors in summer months. The best dishes are the simplest ones, like the freshly shucked oysters or the grilled salmon. The classic choice is the Admiral's Plate (formerly known as the Mates Plate; clearly, it has recently received a well-deserved promotion), an extravaganza of fresh, local seafood for two to four people: Dungeness crab, snapper, salmon, prawns, scallops, mussels, clams, and oysters, all prepared simply and well. There's a decent wine list, good cocktails, and great desserts to round out the experience.

331 Campbell St., Tofino. ✆ **250/725-3444.** www.schoonerrestaurant.ca. Lunch C$11–C$29, dinner main courses C$20–C$50, Admiral's Plate C$99–C$189. Mon–Fri 11am–9pm, Sat–Sun 10am–9pm. Reservations recommended for dinner.

Shelter ★★ WEST COAST   When Shelter opened a decade ago, it was meant to offer the basics—food, wine, shelter—along with a few big-screen TVs and a lively, upscale casual feel. Since then, it has become so much more than that. Owner Jay

Gildenhuys is so serious about his food and drink, he started the Feast food fest here in 2010, and he welcomes guest chefs. (In early 2014, he welcomed Vancouver's Wildebeest restaurant and their famous "bone luge" of marrow bones and sherry shots.) You can expect the usual casual dishes, such as burgers, pizza, and Asian-inspired bowls enhanced with lots of local seafood and a good selection of libations. You can also expect everything to be exceptionally well made, and the service to be friendly and attentive. A great spot for lunch, dinner, or cocktails.

601 Campbell St., Tofino. ⓒ **250/726-3353.** www.shelterrestaurant.com. Lounge meals C$11–C$18, restaurant main courses C$13–C$32. Daily noon–midnight. Reservations recommended in summer.

SOBO ★★ FUSION   The big excitement these days at SOBO—the name is a contraction of "sophisticated bohemian"—is their new cookbook, which means you can now make their Killer Fish Tacos at home. But it's so much better to let chef Lisa Ahier make them in her shiny new restaurant in downtown Tofino. She's come a long way since she started dishing up polenta fries in a purple food truck in the Tofino Botanical Gardens back in 2003. Even then, her food made headlines—"Saveur" magazine called it "perhaps the most exciting lunch stand in North America." Now things are a lot more "SO" than "BO." For one thing, she can serve alcohol with her food, and SOBO does make a fabulous margarita. And she can serve it in a room that is sleek, modern, and airy, with big windows letting in the view of Clayoquot Sound. But the food is still terrific and just bohemian enough: Left Coast seafood stew, for instance, braised duck ramen, or the terrific wood-fired pizzas. A must on any visit to Tofino.

311 Neill St., Tofino. ⓒ **250/725-2341.** www.sobo.ca. Lunch and snacks C$5–C$21, main courses C$17–C$35. Daily 11am–9:30pm. Closed Jan and last 2 weeks of Dec. Reservations suggested.

Tacofino Cantina ★★ MEXICAN   Another little food truck that could. Tacofino now has trucks in Vancouver and Victoria, and a bricks-and-mortar commissary in Vancouver. And no wonder it's expanding: This is some ridiculously good food. Try a tempura-battered ling cod taco, or a burrito stuffed with slow-cooked pork, washed down with an icy lime-mint slush, and your taste buds will have died and gone to heaven. Look for the bright orange truck painted with an image of the Virgin de Guadalupe holding a taco at the back of the Live to Surf parking lot. You can't miss it, and you won't want to.

1184 Pacific Rim Hwy., Tofino. ⓒ **250/726-8288.** www.tacofino.com. C$4.50–C$12. Mid-May to Aug daily 11am–8pm, reduced hours Sept to mid-May.

Wildside Grill ★★ CASUAL   It's just a little wooden takeout shack with a few outdoor tables in the same mall as Chocolate Tofino and Live to Surf. But oh, this is some fine food. The owners source their ingredients from the best local providers, and the seafood couldn't be fresher if it tried. The salmon burger, pork carnitas, and gooey poutine are all great, but this place is most famous for its fish and chips, dusted with panko crumbs and served with tangy house made tartar sauce. The crispy-fried oysters, which come with chili mayo, are epic, and are even better served on a bun.

1180 Pacific Hwy. ⓒ **250/725-9453.** www.wildsidegrill.com. C$10–C$16. Daily 10am–9pm. Reduced hours in off season.

Exploring the Pacific Rim Area

The rationale for coming to the west coast of Vancouver Island is to experience the beauty of nature at its wildest and most pristine. That could mean watching a storm blow in over the Pacific Ocean while you enjoy a glass of wine in the warmth of your hotel room. Or it could mean strolling through the mist along an endless sandy beach. Or it could mean kayaking, hiking, whale-watching, or surfing. That said, there is also a cultural component to this area where so many artists live, especially First Nations carvers and painters, as well as a creative and passionate culinary community.

There are some 20 small art galleries or artists' studios in the area, and if you stop in at the Tourist Info Centre, you can pick up a pamphlet with a map and contact info, then spend a day visiting as many as possible. You can, for instance, find Sol Maya's dramatically colorful hand-blown glass sculptures at **Solart Glass Studio** (1180 Pacific Rim Hwy., Tofino; ℰ **250/725-3122;** www.solmaya.com). Or, if you drop by **Reflecting Spirit Gallery** (441 Campbell St., Tofino; ℰ **250/725-2472;** www. reflectingspirit.ca), you can discover the fiber art of Kathryn Cunningham or surf paintings by Rika. Definitely don't miss the haunting works by legendary First Nations artist Roy Henry Vickers at his longhouselike **Eagle Aerie Gallery** (350 Campbell St.; ℰ **250/725-3235;** www.royhenryvickers.com). And be sure to visit the **Himwitsa Gallery** (300 Main St., Tofino; ℰ **800/899-1947** or 250/725-2017; www.himwitsa.com) down by the waterfront—yes, there's plenty of tourist tat in here, but you can also find beautiful silver jewelry by local First Nations artists, as well as etched glass sculptures, bentwood boxes, and totem poles.

Hot Springs Cove ★ HOT SPRINGS   One of the most memorable experiences around these parts is a trip out to Hot Springs Cove. The spring is a natural thermal one that flows through five small, steamy pools. There's also a sizzling waterfall where you can wash your cares away. This can be a delightfully relaxing experience, but take note, it is clothing optional, so there can be the occasional awkward moment. It can also get incredibly crowded in summer, more of a Roman orgy than a serene bonding-with-nature experience. The springs are 67km (42 miles) north of Tofino, and getting there requires either a fairly long boat ride (90 min. each way), some of it in rocky open ocean, or a float-plane trip. Several outfitters offer trips to the springs, including **Jamie's Whaling Station** (ℰ **800/667-9913** or 250/725-3919; www.jamies.com).

Maquinna Provincial Park. Boat tour C$119 adults, C$109 seniors and students, C$89 children 4–12. Floatplane tour C$179 adults, seniors, and students; C$169 children 2–12.

Kwisitis Visitor Centre ★ MUSEUM   This center in the heart of Pacific Rim National Park focuses primarily on the First Nations culture of the area. In the Nuu-chah-nulth language, *kwisitis* means "the other end of the beach, and this center is set in the middle of apparently endless beaches. It features a nice little restaurant, the Kwisitis Feast House, which serves a good, casual lunch, as well as a small but impressive museum that covers the history of the region. It's also a good place to pick up brochures and information about the area. The center is surrounded by hiking trails, including a wheelchair-accessible boardwalk through a bog. Guided tours are available seasonally.

Pacific Rim National Park, 2040 Pacific Rim Hwy., Wickaninnish Beach exit. ℰ **250/726-3500.** www. pc.gc.ca/eng/pn-np/bc/pacificrim/activ/activkwisitis.aspx. Daily 10am–4:30pm. No admission, but if you plan to park in the park, you will need a day-use pass, C$8 adults, C$7 seniors, C$4 children 6–16, C$20 families.

Tofino Botanical Garden ★ GARDEN   This quirky 5-hectare (12-acre) garden is a good introduction to the unique ecology of this area. The garden is laid out with paths and boardwalks that wind through the forest, past sculptures by local artists, and

Tofino, Ucluelet & Pacific Rim National Park Preserve

along the shoreline. Guided walks, special workshops, and naturalist programs are offered seasonally. Also in the gardens is the **Raincoast Education Society,** which exhibits on local flora, fauna, and history, and often has guest speakers and nature walks. Off-season hours vary, so call ahead.

1084 Pacific Rim Hwy., Tofino. ℂ **250/725-1220.** www.tbgf.org. Admission C$10 adults, C$6 students, free children 12 and under. Daily 9am–dusk.

Outdoor Activities

BIRDING   The Tofino/Ucluelet area is directly in the path of the Pacific Flyway and attracts tens of thousands of birds and wildfowl; it's also home to bald eagles. The area celebrates its rich birdlife with the annual **Flying Geese & Shorebird Festival** every April and May. During those months, large flocks of migrating birds fill the skies and estuaries along Barkley Sound and Clayoquot Sound. Avid bird-lovers should contact **Just Birding** (ℂ **250/725-2520;** www.justbirding.com), which offers a variety of birding tours starting at C$99 per person.

FISHING   Fishing remains the big outdoor activity in Ucluelet, and salmon is still the most sought-after catch. Charter companies that can take you out include **Island West Resort** (ℂ **250/726-7515;** www.islandwestresort.com), **Castaway Charters** (ℂ **250/720-7970;** www.castawaycharters.ca), and **Long Beach Charters** (ℂ **877/726-2878** or 250/726-3474; www.longbeachcharters.com).

HIKING   A hike among the hushed stands of old-growth timber or along rocky, wave-dashed coastline is an unforgettable experience, and there are several great hikes along this coast for hikers of all abilities, even gentle strollers.

In Ucluelet, the **Wild Pacific Trail** (www.wildpacifictrail.com) skirts the rugged coastline with fabulous views of the Pacific Ocean and the Broken Islands; bald eagles nest along parts of the trail. For an easy and **scenic walk,** take the 2.7km (1.7-mile) gravel-paved stretch from Peninsula Road in Ucluelet to the lighthouse. This 30- to 45-minute amble passes surge channels and huge rock formations.

The 11km (6.8-mile) stretch of rocky headlands, sand, and surf along the **Long Beach Headlands Trail** is the most accessible section of the Pacific Rim National Park system, which incorporates Long Beach, the West Coast Trail, and the Broken Islands Group. To access it, take the road to the Kwisitis Visitor Centre (formerly the Wickaninnish Interpretive Centre exit) on Hwy. 4, and follow the signs. In and around **Long Beach,** there are numerous other short hikes, including the 3.3km (2-mile) **Gold Mine Trail** near Florencia Bay, where you can still see a few artifacts from an old gold mine.

If you'd prefer to have an expert guide lead you into the wilderness, you can't go wrong with **Long Beach Nature Tours** (ℂ **250/725-8305** or 250/726-7099; www.longbeachnaturetours.com). Naturalist Bill McIntyre, a retired Pacific Rim Park chief, leads **guided beach, rainforest,** and **storm walks** that explain the ecology and wildlife of the area. Half-day hikes for 1 to 5 people cost C$225; full-day hikes C$450.

For a truly memorable walk, take the 3.3km (2.1-mile) **Big Trees Trail** through the dense rainforest on Meares Island in Clayoquot Sound, just off Tofino's shores. Built in 1993 to protect the old-growth temperate rainforest, the boardwalked trail, maintained by the Tla-o-qui-aht First Nations band, has a long staircase leading up to the Hanging Garden Tree, the **province's fourth-largest western red cedar.** You can access the island by canoe or take **Tofino Water Taxi** (ℂ **866/794-2537** or 250/725-8844; www.tofinowatertaxi.com; C$30 adults, C$25 students, C$20 youth round-trip).

KAYAKING   One of the quintessential experiences of this region is paddling through the Broken Islands or Clayoquot Sound. For a region famous for its stormy weather, these waters are surprisingly calm, and as you paddle, you can see bald eagles, porpoises, even a friendly orca or two.

Several local companies offer kayak rentals, tours, lessons, and tours. Among them are **Majestic Ocean Kayaking** (✆ 800/889-7644; www.oceankayaking.com) and **Tofino Sea Kayaking Company** (✆ 800/863-4664 or 250/725-4222; www.tofinosea kayaking.com). They offer half-day harbor trips (C$67), full-day paddles to Barkley Sound (C$170) or the Broken Islands (C$260), and weeklong adventures in Clayoquot Sound (C$1,450). Single kayak rental will run you about C$58 per day.

SURFING   The wild Pacific coast is known as one of the best surfing destinations in Canada, and most surfers work in the tourism industry around Tofino, spending all their free time in the water. There are several surf schools that offer lessons, rentals, and gear. Lessons generally start at C$55 (not including gear), board rentals at C$25, and wetsuit rentals at C$20. Contact **Live to Surf** (✆ 250/725-4464; www.livetosurf. com), **Pacific Surf School** (✆ 888/777-9961; www.pacificsurfschool.com), or **Surf Sister** (✆ 877/724-7873; www.surfsister.com).

WILDLIFE-WATCHING   One of the most unforgettable experiences along this coast is a close encounter with the local wildlife. Gray whales, bald eagles, black bears, porpoises, orcas, seals, and sea lions all call this area home, and there are several outfitters that help you get up close and personal.

One of the oldest outfitters is **Jamie's Whaling Station** (✆ 800/667-9913 or 250/725-3919 in Tofino; ✆ 877/726-7444 or 250/726-7444 in Ucluelet; www.jamies. com), which departs from both Tofino and Ucluelet. It uses a glass-bottomed power cruiser, as well as a fleet of Zodiacs for tours to watch the gray whales March through October. A combined Hot Springs Cove and whale-watching trip is offered year-round. Three-hour bear-watching trips are normally scheduled around low tides, when the bruins forage for seafood on the mudflats. Fares (for this and other companies) generally start at around C$90 per person in a Zodiac and C$100 per person in a covered craft; customized trips can run as high as C$200 per person for a full day.

The best time to see the whales is in March, when about 20,000 gray whales migrate past this section of Vancouver Island as they head north to their feeding grounds. That's when the **Pacific Rim Whale Festival** (✆ 250/726-7798; www.pacificrim whalefestival.com) is held in Tofino and Ucluelet. If you want to learn more about these magnificent creatures, it's well worth checking out.

Tofino, Ucluelet & Pacific Rim National Park Preserve

PLANNING YOUR TRIP TO BRITISH COLUMBIA

Getting to the southwestern corner of British Columbia is fairly easy, but it can take time—this part of the world is a long way away from just about anywhere. But with scenery this beautiful along the way, the journey is half the fun.

GETTING TO VANCOUVER

By Plane

FROM THE U.S.

All the major American airlines serve Vancouver, though you may need to route your trip through a hub such as Denver or Seattle. Among them are **Alaska Airlines** (© 800/252-7522; www.alaskaair.com), **American Airlines** (© 800/433-7300; www.aa.com), **Continental** (© 800/231-0856; www.continental.com), **Delta Airlines** (© 800/221-1212; www.delta.com), and **United Airlines** (© 800/241-6522; www.united.com). In addition, both of Canada's major airlines, **Air Canada** (© 888/247-2262; www.aircanada.com) and **WestJet** (© 888/937-8538; www.westjet.com) fly between Vancouver and many U.S. cities.

FROM CANADA

Air Canada (© 888/247-2262; www.aircanada.com) and **WestJet** (© 888/937-8538; www.westjet.com) offer numerous daily flights from most major Canadian cities as well as many smaller communities.

FROM THE U.K.

Air Canada (© 888/247-2262; www.aircanada.com) and **British Airways** (© 800/247-9297; www.britishairways.com) offer direct daily flights from London Heathrow Airport.

FROM AUSTRALIA & NEW ZEALAND

Air Canada (© 888/247-2262; www.aircanada.com) flies direct from Sydney daily. **Qantas** (© 13-13-13; www.qantas.com.au) also flies from Sydney to Vancouver, with a stopover in Los Angeles. **Air New Zealand** (© 0800/737-000; www.airnewzealand.co.nz) flies direct from Auckland to Vancouver 3 days a week.

SAVING money ON AIRFARES

Sad but true, airfares are going up and up and up, thanks to the merger of the airlines. But there are still some savvy trips you can use to save—a hair—on airfares.

1. **Search smartly:** By which we mean don't just rely on the "name-brand" sites when you're looking for good fares. A relatively new type of airfare site called "consolidators" now search itineraries without selling them (they get a commission if a fare is bought) which means by looking at them you get a much broader search. They not only scan such online travel agencies as Orbitz and Expedia, they also search the airline sites directly as well as some of the lesser-known discount sites. The ones we would recommend are **Momondo.com** (you'll find them on the Frommers.com website), **Kayak.com,** and **DoHop.com.**

2. **Go when no one else is:** And that doesn't just mean flying in the off-season (although that can be a big money saver). Recent studies of airline booking data have shown that passengers who depart on a Wednesday (the cheapest day of the week to fly to most destinations) pay on average $40 less than those who fly on Sundays (the priciest day of the week).

3. **Book at the right time:** Perhaps it's because consumers have more time to search for airfares on the weekends, but those who book then end up paying significantly more than those who book during the week. As well, according to a study from the Airline Reporting Corporation (the company that acts as the middleman btwn. airlines and travel agents) those who book 6 weeks in advance for a domestic ticket statistically spend the least amount of money.

GETTING INTO TOWN FROM THE AIRPORT

Vancouver International Airport (YVR) is located on an island in the suburb of Richmond, about a 30-minute drive from downtown Vancouver. From there, you have a number of options for getting into the city: buses, shuttles, limos, rental cars, and taxis. Unless you have a lot of luggage, though, your best option is to take the **Canada Line rapid transit train.** It's a 25-minute trip that connects with all the major transit routes and stops near most downtown Vancouver hotels.

By Car

If you're coming from the U.S., you'll probably arrive via U.S Interstate 5 from Seattle, which becomes Highway 99 when you cross the border at Peace Arch Crossing and heads straight into Vancouver. **Please don't forget that you'll need your passport to enter Canada!** The 210km (130-mile) drive from Seattle takes about 2½ hours, depending on the lineups at the border crossing. If you're arriving from just about anywhere else, you'll be driving along the Trans-Canada Highway (Hwy. 1). It takes about 11 hours to drive from Calgary to Vancouver, a distance of 970km (600 miles).

By Boat

Vancouver is the major embarkation point for cruises going up British Columbia's Inland Passage to Alaska. The ships carry more than a million passengers annually on nearly 350 Vancouver-Alaska cruises. In summer, up to four cruise ships a day berth at Canada Place cruise-ship terminal, which is located within walking distance of many of the city's major hotels.

If you're arriving from Vancouver Island, **BC Ferries** (📞 **888/223-3779;** www.bcferries.com) offers three routes and numerous daily sailings.

By Train

The **Amtrak Cascades** service connects Seattle and Vancouver daily (📞 **800/872-7245;** www.amtrakcascades.com). **VIA Rail Canada** offers passenger rail service from Toronto to Vancouver, with numerous stops along the way (📞 **888/842-7245;** www.viarail.ca). And for the ultimate luxury train trip, there's the **Rocky Mountaineer,** which takes you on a spectacular once-in-a-lifetime journey through the Rocky Mountains (📞 **877/460-3200;** www.rockymountaineer.com).

By Bus

Greyhound Bus Lines (📞 **800/231-2222;** www.greyhound.ca) offers daily service between Vancouver and major Canadian cities as well as Seattle. **Pacific Coach Lines** (📞 **800/661-1725** or 604/662-7575; www.pacificcoach.com) provides service between Vancouver and Victoria.

GETTING TO VICTORIA

Victoria is located on the southern tip of Vancouver Island, about 100km (60 miles) west of Vancouver. Getting there usually means traveling through Vancouver. Here are the best ways to extend your trip.

By Plane

You can catch a direct flight to Victoria from Vancouver, Calgary, Portland, or Seattle via commercial airlines such as **Air Canada** (📞 **888/247-2262** or 800/661-3936; www.aircanada.com) and **WestJet** (📞 **888/937-8538;** www.westjet.com).

One of the most thrilling ways to arrive is by floatplane—**Harbour Air Seaplanes** (📞 **800/665-0212;** www.harbour-air.com) will whisk you right from downtown Vancouver to Victoria's Inner Harbour in just 30 minutes. **Kenmore Air** (📞 **800/543-9595;** www.kenmoreair.com) flies in from Seattle, and **Pacific Coastal Airlines** (📞 **800/663-2872;** www.pacific-coastal.com) wings it from YVR's South terminal in Richmond.

There's also the convenience of the **Helijet,** a helicopter service that whirrs into Victoria daily from Vancouver (📞 **800/665-4354;** www.helijet.com).

GETTING INTO TOWN FROM THE AIRPORT

Victoria International Airport is located about a half hour's drive north of Victoria, just off the Patricia Bay Highway. You can get downtown by car rental, taxi, or the AKAL airport bus service that departs every 30 minutes.

By Car & Boat

The most popular way to get to Victoria is via **BC Ferries** (📞 **888/223-3779;** www.bcferries.com). These vast drive-aboard ferries sail several times a day from the terminal in Tsawwassen, about an hour south of Vancouver, to Swartz Bay, about 45 minutes from downtown Victoria. The ferry ride itself is about 90 minutes. In busy summer months, it's best to reserve space for your vehicle ahead of time.

In addition, two **U.S. ferry** services offer connections from Port Angeles and Seattle: **Black Ball Transport** (*℃* **800/993-3779;** www.cohoferry.com) and the **Victoria Clipper** (*℃* **800/888-2535;** www.clippervacations.com).

Note: Don't forget that you'll need a passport to enter Canada from the U.S.

By Bus

Pacific Coach Lines (*℃* **604/662-7575;** www.pacificcoach.com) provides service between Vancouver and Victoria, with frequent daily departures.

GETTING AROUND
By Car

Unless you're planning to venture beyond the city center in either Vancouver or Victoria, it's best to ditch the car and travel by foot, bike, or public transit. Parking can be a hassle in both cities and is quite expensive in downtown Vancouver. But if you must get behind the wheel, here's what you need to know.

RENTALS

All the major car rental companies have offices downtown and at the airport in both cities.

DRIVING RULES

Canadians drive on the right-hand side of the road and pass on the left. Distance is measured in kilometers, which everyone calls "clicks," and speed is counted in kilometers per hour, or kmph. In the city, the average speed is usually 50kmph (30 mph) and on the highway 100kmph (60 mph).

BREAKDOWNS

Contact the **British Columbia Automobile Association** (**BCAA;** *℃* **800/222-4357;** www.bcaa.com) for emergency roadside assistance.

GASOLINE

Most service stations are self-service and open 24 hours a day. Remember that gas is measured in liters, not gallons, and is more expensive than it is in the U.S., though not as pricy as it is in Europe.

By Public Transit

Vancouver has an award-winning transit system, **TransLink,** which comprises buses, light rapid transit (Skytrain and Canada Line), and the Seabus foot-passenger ferry to North Vancouver. TransLink is in the process of switching over to Compass, a reloadable electronic fare card system, but until the transition is complete, a variety of passes, single-fare tickets, and transfers can be used. For information, call *℃* **604/953-3333** or visit www.translink.ca.

The **Victoria Regional Transit System** comprises a fleet of buses that operate frequently and cover the entire city. Call *℃* **250/382-6161** or visit www.bctransit.com to find out more about passes, fares, and schedules.

By Ferry

Both cities have charming little foot-passenger ferries that ply the waters between attractions in their watery centers. Vancouver's **Aquabus** (*℃* **604/689-5858;**

www.theaquabus.com) travels between Granville Island and other sites in False Creek, while **Victoria Harbour Ferry** (© 250/708-0201; www.victoriaharbourferry. com) operates as a water taxi around the Inner Harbour.

By Bicycle

If you want to get a Vancouverite upset, bring up the subject of bike lanes. Over the past few years, the city has gradually been replacing car lanes, parking spaces, and right-hand turns with dedicated bike lanes to make it easier for cyclists get around. While the drivers fuming in the resulting traffic jams may not appreciate it, the move certainly has made it a lot safer and more convenient to explore the city on two wheels. Several operators rent bikes, especially near Stanley Park.

Victoria is also a good cycling city, with plenty of easy routes to explore and bike rental shops to supply the gear.

Remember that **bike helmets are mandatory** for both children and adults in British Columbia, and not wearing one can cost you a hefty fine. And always be sure to lock up your bike because thefts are a problem in both cities.

For more information on cycling in B.C., visit **www.th.gov.bc.ca/BikeBC**.

By Foot

Both cities are terrific walking towns—the main downtown areas in both Victoria and Vancouver won't take more than half an hour to cross. See the city sections for more information and suggested places to explore on foot.

LODGINGS

Throughout this guide, I've tried to steer you to the types of hotels that will really offer you a great experience of the destination. But I won't sugarcoat the ugly truth about hotel pricing—rooms are not cheap, especially in downtown Vancouver and Whistler. If you'd like to save money on lodgings, consider the following strategies:

BUY A MONEY-SAVING PACKAGE DEAL. A travel package that combines your airfare and your hotel stay for one price may just be the best bargain of all. In some cases, you'll get airfare, accommodations, transportation to and from the airport, plus extras—maybe an afternoon sightseeing tour or restaurant and shopping discount coupons—for less than the hotel alone would have cost had you booked it yourself. Most airlines and many travel agents, as well as the usual booking websites (Priceline, Travelocity, Expedia) offer good packages.

CHOOSE A CHAIN. With some exceptions, I have not listed mass-volume chain hotels in this book, as they tend to lack the character and local feel that most independently run hotels have. And it's that feel, I believe, that is so much a part of the travel experience. Still, when you're looking for a deal, they can be a good option. That's because you can also pull out all the stops for discounts at a budget chain, from reward points to senior status to corporate rates. Most chain hotels let the kids stay with parents for free.

AVOID EXCESS CHARGES & HIDDEN COSTS. Use your own cellphone instead of dialing direct from hotel phones, which usually incur exorbitant rates. (But beware of roaming charges; check your service provider's plan before you leave home.) And don't be tempted by minibar offerings: Most hotels charge through the nose for water, soda, and snacks. Finally, ask about local taxes and service charges, which can increase the cost of a room by 15% or more. If a hotel insists upon tacking on an "energy surcharge" that wasn't mentioned at check-in, you can often make a case for getting it removed.

MAKE MULTIPLE RESERVATIONS. This strategy is only necessary in high season. But often then, as the date of the stay approaches, hotels start to play "chicken" with one another, dropping the price a bit one day to try and lure customers away from a nearby competitor. Making this strategy work takes vigilance and persistence, but since your credit card won't be charged until 24-hours before check-in, little risk is involved.

USE THE RIGHT ONLINE SITES. Such websites as Booking.com, HotelsCombined.com, and Trivago.ca often beat the rest because they cast a broader net when quoting prices. In the case of the latter two, that means that you'll see choices from a number of discounters, some less well-known but all reliable. Booking.com works a bit differently, but it has become known for making side deals with the small mom-and-pop hotels that many of the bigger travel agency sites skip.

BOOK BLIND. If you just want a place to sleep, consider paying before you know the name of the hotel for big savings. You can do so on either **Priceline.com** or **Hotwire.com,** and there is a way to "scoop" the system. A site called BetterBidding. com allows travelers to post how much they bid on a hotel room and which hotel they got. You'll be amazed both at how often the same hotels come up; and by the quality of these hotels (both sites only deal with major chains, so you're pretty much assured that you won't be lodged in a dump).

BOOK LAST MINUTE. An unused bed is inventory lost for a hotelier, so many are willing to play "let's make a deal" in the few days prior to a stay. And many play that game with the app **HotelTonight,** which can only be used on the day of travel. If you have the courage to wait that long, you can often get discounts of up to 70% on hotel rooms.

TRY ALTERNATIVE ACCOMMODATIONS. Strange but true, it's sometimes cheaper to rent an entire apartment, complete with a kitchen and living room, than it is to stay in a hotel room. On AirBnB, for example, you can rent a complete apartment in Vancouver's West End for just C$90 a night. If you're willing to just rent a room in an apartment (an informal B&B arrangement), you can pay as little as C$60/night in that city. Other sources that rent either full apartments and homes or rooms in private homes include **Wimdu.com, HomeAway.com, Rentalo.com, VRBO.com** and **Flip-Key.com.**

[FastFACTS] VANCOUVER & VICTORIA

ATMs & Banks   You'll find 24-hour PLUS and Cirrus bank machines just about anywhere you need to be—shopping areas, bars, nightclubs, sports arenas, and, of course, banks. The major Canadian banks include **BMO Bank of Montreal, CIBC, HSBC, RBC Royal Bank, Scotiabank,** and **TD Canada Trust.** Remember that if you withdraw money from a bank that is not your own, it will likely charge you an additional fee.

Business Hours   Business hours vary greatly, especially in Vancouver, so it's best to check ahead with the establishment you want to visit. Most shops are open 10am to 6pm, with late openings on Thursdays and Fridays. Some, however, are open 24 hours; others only open certain days. Restaurants are open for lunch between 11:30am and 2pm, then close until 5pm when they open to serve dinner until midnight; however, chains and hotel restaurant will stay open most of the day, while smaller places will not open for lunch on Saturdays and may not open at all on Sundays and Mondays, unless they offer brunch.

Customs You'll pass through **Canadian Customs** upon arrival and **U.S. Customs** if you are traveling through the U.S. on your departure. Remember that you will need a passport to enter Canada. Also, there are restrictions on alcohol, plant materials, cash, gifts, cigarettes, certain foodstuffs, and pets coming into Canada, so if you have any concerns or questions, check with **Canada Border Services** (✆ **800/461-9999;** www.cbsa-asfc.gc.ca).

Disabled Travelers Both Vancouver and Victoria have made it a priority to be as accessible as possible for people with disabilities. Indeed, the publication "We're Accessible," a newsletter for travelers with disabilities, called Vancouver **"the most accessible city in the world."** Except perhaps in some of the oldest neighborhoods, you can find

wheelchair-accessible entrances, ramps, and walkways throughout both cities, as well as beeping signals for the visually impaired. Buses and transit stations almost always have lifts for wheelchairs. All public spaces, including restaurants, must offer wheelchair-accessible restrooms, and most hotels also have specially equipped rooms for those in wheelchairs, as well as visual smoke alarms for the hearing impaired. For more information, visit the Government of Canada site **www.accesstotravel.gc.ca** (see "Tips for Travellers with Disabilities"). In addition, both Tourism Vancouver (www.tourismvancouver. com/vancouver/accessible-vancouver) and Tourism Victoria (www.tourism victoria.com/plan/travel-tips/special-needs) have resources for travelers with disabilities.

Drinking Laws British Columbia's antiquated liquor laws are undergoing a massive and keenly anticipated overhaul, so much could change in the future. Currently beer, wine, and spirits are sold in government liquor stores and a handful of private liquor or artisan-producer stores. However, in summer 2014, some farmers' markets began sampling and selling alcohol; within a year or two, alcohol will also likely be available in grocery stores. What will not change is the legal drinking age—19—and the blood-alcohol

limit for driving—0.05 mg per 100 mL, or about one drink.

Drug Stores The two main drug store chains in Western Canada are Shoppers Drug Mart and BC's own London Drugs, although some supermarkets and mass retailers also have pharmacies, and there are smaller, independent drug stores as well. For a 24-hour pharmacy in downtown Vancouver, try the Shoppers Drug Mart at 1125 Davie St., ✆ **604/669-2424;** in Victoria, go to the Shoppers at 3511 Blanshard St., ✆ **250/475-7572.**

Electricity As in the U.S., electric current is 110 to 120 volts AC (60 cycles), compared to 220 to 240 volts AC (50 cycles) in most of Europe, Australia, and New Zealand. Downward converters that change 220 to 240 volts to 110 to 120 volts are difficult to find in North America, so bring one with you. Plugs have two flat prongs, so you may need an adapter as well. Many electronics such as laptops and tablets are fine with the voltage change, but check with the manufacturer beforehand just to be sure.

Embassies & Consulates If you lose your passport or run into any other difficulties, contact your embassy or consulate for help. Here are some of the main Vancouver addresses; check the Yellow Pages for other countries. **Australia:** 2050-1075 W. Georgia St.; ✆ 604/684-1177; www.canada.embassy.gov.au

Ireland: 210–837 Beatty St.; ☎ 604/683-9233; www.embassyofireland.ca
New Zealand: 2250-1050 Pender St.; ☎ 604/684-7388; www.nzembassy.com
United Kingdom: 800–1111 Melville St.; ☎ 604/683-4421; ww2.britainincanada.org
United States: 1075 W. Pender St.; ☎ 604/685-4311; www.vancouver.usconsulate.gov

Emergencies Dial ☎ 911 for fire, police, ambulance, and poison control. This is a free call.

Family Travel Vancouver and Victoria are two of the most child-friendly cosmopolitan cities in the world. In addition to the standard attractions and sights, you'll find a lot of free, adventurous, outdoor activities that both you and your kids will enjoy. (See "Especially for Kids" on p. 99 and 175.)

Health Medical standards in Canada are very high, so should you fall ill during your visit, you will be in good hands. If you need a doctor, your hotel can help you find a reliable one. You will not have to undergo a credit check before being treated, unless you visit a private clinic rather than a public hospital, although some procedures—such as MRIs—may not be covered by your insurance. In all cases, make sure your travel insurance is up to date and that you are aware of what, exactly, it covers. Also, keep in mind that prescription drugs can be significantly less expensive in Canada.

In addition, those with food allergies and aversions will be pleased to know that both Vancouver and Victoria are world leaders in accommodating dietary restrictions. And the tap water is perfectly safe to drink in B.C.; in fact, it's some of the cleanest, tastiest drinking water around.

For a list of doctors and hospitals, see the "Fast Facts" sections for Vancouver (p. 45) and Victoria (p. 143).

Insurance For information on traveler's insurance, trip cancelation insurance, and medical insurance while traveling, please visit www.frommers.com/planning.

Internet Access Increasingly, free Wi-Fi is becoming available almost everywhere from coffee shops to hotels to public parks to the airport. The exception is some of the higher-end hotels, which still charge a substantial daily Internet fee or provide basic access for free, but charge for faster speeds and bigger bandwidths. In addition, some hotels will loan out tablets during your visit, and almost all of them will have a business center with Internet access.

Legal Aid In case of trouble with the authorities, international visitors should call their embassy or consulate. If you are accused of a serious offense, say and do nothing before consulting a lawyer.

LGBT Travelers Since 2003, when British Columbia legalized same-sex marriage,

Vancouver and Victoria have become favored sites for **gay and lesbian weddings and elopements.** Even before that, though, these hip, friendly, and open-minded cities were popular destinations for LGBT visitors—Vancouver especially has a thriving gay community and hosts one of the world's biggest and most exuberant Pride weeks, which includes a parade that attracts more than 650,000 spectators (www.vancouverpride.ca).

Mail & Postage The **Vancouver Main Post Office** is located at 349 W. Georgia St.; in **Victoria,** it's at 706 Yates St. For other locations, many of which are within other retail locations, look for a "Postal Services" sign. At press time, letters and postcards up to 30 grams cost C65¢ to mail within Canada, C$1.10 to mail to the U.S., and C$1.85 for overseas airmail service. For more information, call ☎ **866/606-6301** or visit www.canadapost.ca.

Mobile Phones Canada is part of the **GSM** (Global System for Mobile Communications), a big, seamless network that makes for easy cross-border cellphone use. GSM phones function with a removable plastic SIM card, encoded with your phone number and account information. If your cellphone is on a GSM system, and you have a world-capable multiband phone, you can make and receive calls across Canada. Just call your wireless operator and ask for "international roaming" to be activated on your account. (Many U.S. cellphones are already equipped with this capability and need no further modification to operate in Canada.) To save money on roaming charges, you can also unlock your phone and buy a prepaid Canadian SIM card.

Money & Costs Until recently, the Canadian dollar was enjoying an extended period of economic strength. In recent months, though, its value has fallen against other currencies, driving up prices for many goods and services. Vancouver especially is an expensive city, with some of the highest living costs in the world. Still, you can often find special **discounts for children and seniors,** as well as plenty of **free things to do.**

It's worth noting that the C$1 and C$2 bills have been replaced by coins known, respectively, as the "loonie" (because it has the bird known as a loon on one side) and the "toonie," because it's worth two loonies. It's wise to carry a few—you'll need them for parking meters, tips, and incidentals. Aside from that, **credit and debit cards** are widely accepted, though additional charges are often added when you use them. Most establishments will also accept American currency, but stores and restaurants typically offer poor exchange rates. Withdrawing cash from an ATM usually gives

you the best exchange rate. For the most up-to-the-minute rates, consult **www.xe.com**.

Newspapers & Magazines See "Fast Facts" in Vancouver (p. 45) and Victoria (p. 143).

Packing Tips No matter what time of year you travel to Vancouver and Victoria, you will want to pack layers, comfortable walking shoes, and rain gear, including a waterproof jacket and umbrella. For more helpful information on packing, go to **www.frommers.com** and follow the links to the **"Packing Tips"** section of the website.

Passports All international travelers entering Canada are required to carry a valid passport. U.S. citizens who are members of NEXUS or FAST programs and are entering Canada by land or sea may use their membership cards as proof of identity instead.

Police Dial ✆ **911** for fire, police, ambulance, and poison control. This is a free call. For non-emergencies, see "Fast Facts: Vancouver," p. 45; and "Fast Facts: Victoria," p. 143.

Safety Overall, Vancouver is a safe city, and Victoria is even safer. But it is worth noting that in recent years Vancouver has seen a spate of targeted, gang-related shootings, some of which have hit high-end downtown restaurants. A bigger problem for most visitors is property crime and theft. Never leave valuable items

on view in your parked car, and take care with handbags, cameras, wallets, and the like, especially in crowded areas.

It's also worth noting that, because of the mild climate and various social issues, both cities have large populations of homeless, so you can expect plenty of panhandlers in touristy areas. **Vancouver's Downtown Eastside** especially is a troubled, drug-riddled neighborhood that borders two of the city's trendiest areas, Gastown and Chinatown. Avoid the DTES if you can, especially at night, and if you somehow find yourself at the **corner of Hastings and Main,** exercise all possible caution.

Senior Travel Thanks to their mild weather, Vancouver and Victoria have become havens for older Canadians, as well as senior travelers. Senior travelers often qualify for discounts at hotels, restaurants, and attractions. Discount transit passes are also available.

Smoking Smoking is prohibited in all public areas, including restaurants, bars, and clubs, as well as public transportation. Many hotels are now entirely smoke-free. In September 2010, a ban was also instituted on smoking in public parks, including Stanley Park, and beaches.

Student Travel Obtain an **International Student Identity Card (ISIC)** and you will be eligible for a variety of discounts on accommodation, transportation, goods, and services. Visit isiccanada.ca for details.

Students will also find inexpensive accommodation at youth hostels run by Hostelling International in Vancouver, Victoria, Whistler, and Tofino. For membership information, visit the **Hostelling International** websites at **www.hiusa.org** and **www.hihostels.ca**.

Travel CUTS (© **800/ 667-2887;** www.travelcuts. com) is a great source for inexpensive accommodation, transportation, advice, and more for students and young travellers in general.

Taxes　After a brief and controversial period under a harmonized sales tax (HST), B.C. has returned to its old system of a 5% Goods and Services Tax (GST) plus a 7% Provincial Sales Tax (PST). Most goods and many services carry both taxes, but some only carry the GST and sometimes the PST is higher than 7%, so don't be surprised if you encounter confusion at the till.

Most accommodations charge an 8% PST on top of the GST, as well as a Municipal and Regional District Tax (MRDT) of up to 2%. Food at restaurants carries only the 5% GST, but alcoholic beverages come with a hefty 10% PST on top of the GST. And no, **there is no tax rebate program for visitors.**

Tipping　Service is rarely included in your bill, so expect to tip in restaurants and hotels just as you would in the U.S. In general, follow these guidelines:

In hotels, tip bellhops at least C$1 per bag, more if you have a lot of luggage or are staying in a high-end property. Leave the chamber staff at least C$2 a day, more if you are staying in a posh hotel or you have left behind a big mess. Tip the doorman or concierge only if he or she has provided you with some specific service, and tip the valet-parking attendant C$2 every time you get your car.

In restaurants, bars, and nightclubs, tip service staff and bartenders 15% to 20% of the check, tip

coatroom attendants C$2 per garment, and tip valet-parking attendants C$2 per vehicle.

As for other service personnel, tip cab drivers 15% of the fare; tip skycaps at airports at least C$1 per bag (C$2–C$3 if you have a lot of luggage); and tip hairdressers and barbers 15% to 20%.

Toilets　You won't find public toilets on the streets in either Vancouver or Victoria, or at least not any you would want to use, but they can be found in hotel lobbies, bars, restaurants, department stores, railway and bus stations, and service stations. Note that Canadians typically call these facilities "washrooms" rather than "restrooms."

Visitor Information
For tourist office locations in Vancouver, see "Visitor Information" on p. 39; for Victoria, see p. 139.

For information about travel and accommodations elsewhere in the province, contact **Destination British Columbia (© 800/435-5622;** www.hellobc.com).

General Index

A

AAA Horse & Carriage Ltd.
(Vancouver), 84
Abbottsford International Air
Show (near Vancouver), 18
Aberdeen Centre (Richmond), 110
Abkhazi Gardens (Victoria), 173
Accent Cruises (Vancouver), 100
Accommodations, 206–207.
See also Accommodations
Index; Camping
Cowichan Valley, 181–182
Gulf Islands, 188–189
Tofino and Ucluelet, 193–195
Vancouver, 4–5, 46–61
Victoria, 8–9, 144–152
Whistler-Blackcomb, 125–129
Afterglow (Vancouver), 120
Afternoon tea, Victoria, 7,
161–162
Air tours, Victoria, 171
Air travel, 202–203
Gulf Islands, 188
Tofino and Ucluelet, 192
Vancouver, 38–39
Victoria, 138–139, 204
Whistler-Blackcomb, 124
AJ Brooks (Vancouver), 116
Alibi Room (Vancouver), 120
"A-maze-ing Laughter"
(Vancouver), 99
Ambleside Park (Vancouver), 103
Ancient Cedars area, 134
Antiques
Vancouver, 110
Victoria, 176, 177
A-1 Last Minute Golf Hot Line
(Vancouver), 104
Aquabus (Vancouver), 44
Architectural Institute of BC
(Vancouver), 102
Architectural walking tours
(Vancouver), 102
Art galleries
Tofino, 199
Vancouver, 110
Victoria, 176
Art Gallery of Greater Victoria,
10, 167
Arts Club Theatre Company
(Vancouver), 117
ATMs and banks, 207
Victoria, 143
ATVs, Whistler-Blackcomb, 132
AuBAR (Vancouver), 120

B

Babes in the Woods murders
(Vancouver), 86
Backcountry skiing,
Whistler-Blackcomb, 132
Baisakhi Day Parade
(Vancouver), 17
Bakers Dozen Antiques
(Vancouver), 110

Ballet British Columbia
(Vancouver), 118
Banks and ATMs, 143, 207
Barbara-Jo's Books to Cooks
(Vancouver), 110
Bard on the Beach Shakespeare
Festival (Vancouver), 7, 18, 118
Bastion Public Market (Victoria),
176
Bastion Square (Victoria), 176
Bateman, Robert, 20–21
Bayshore Bicycle and Rollerblade
Rentals (Vancouver), 103
BC Bed & Breakfast Innkeepers
Guild, 55
BC Ferries, 139, 204
BC Forest Discovery Centre
(Duncan), 184
BC Place Stadium (Vancouver),
107
Beaches
Vancouver, 102
Victoria, 172
Beacon Hill Park (Victoria),
34, 173
Bear Mountain (Victoria), 9
Beaty Biodiversity Museum
(Vancouver), 88
Beaver Lake (Vancouver), 105
Belfry Theatre (Victoria), 178–179
Bernard, Diane, 160
Big Bus (Vancouver), 101
Big Trees Trail, 200
Biking and mountain biking, 206
Vancouver, 103–104
Victoria, 7, 9, 18, 142, 170
Whistler-Blackcomb, 134
Bill Reid Gallery of Northwest
Coast Art (Vancouver), 81–82
Bird-watching
Tofino/Ucluelet area, 200
Vancouver, 108
Bishop, John, 22
Blackberry Books (Vancouver), 110
Blackcomb Mountain, skiing,
131–132
Black Tusk (near Vancouver), 105
Bloedel Conservatory
(Vancouver), 96
Boat tours and cruises
Vancouver, 100, 203–204
Victoria, 170–171
Bone luge, 23
Bookstores, Vancouver, 110–111
Brackendale, 137
Brassneck Brewery (Vancouver),
27, 120
Britannia Beach, 137
Britannia Mining Museum, 137
British Columbia Aviation Museum
(Victoria), 168
British Columbia Parliament
Buildings (Victoria), 165
Buffalo Bills (Whistler), 136
Burnaby 8 Rinks Ice Sports Centre
(Burnaby), 105
Burnaby Mountain (Vancouver),
104

Burnaby Village Museum, 97
Buschlen Mowatt (Vancouver), 110
Business hours, 207–208
Vancouver, 45
Victoria, 143
Bus tours
Vancouver, 101
Victoria, 169
Bus travel
Tofino and Ucluelet, 192
Vancouver, 39, 43, 204
Victoria, 139, 141, 205
Whistler-Blackcomb, 122, 124
Butchart Gardens (Victoria), 7,
33–34, 173–174

C

Calendar of events, 16–19
Callaghan Valley, 132, 133
Camping
Tofino/Ucluelet area, 195–196
Whistler-Blackcomb, 129
Canada Day, 18
Canada Line SkyTrain
(Vancouver), 38
Canada Place (Vancouver), 24, 82
Canoeing and kayaking
Tofino/Ucluelet area, 201
Vancouver, 103
Victoria, 10, 173
Whistler-Blackcomb, 133
Capilano River Regional Park
(Vancouver), 93
Capilano Salmon Hatchery
(Vancouver), 93
Capilano Suspension Bridge
(Vancouver), 5
Capilano Suspension Bridge Park
(Vancouver), 28, 91
Caprice (Vancouver), 120
Carol Ship Parade of Lights
Festival (Vancouver), 19
Carousel Theatre for Young
People (Vancouver), 5, 99
Carr, Emily, 7, 19, 34, 165
Car travel and rentals, 205
Tofino and Ucluelet, 192
Vancouver, 39, 44, 203
Victoria, 139, 142
Whistler-Blackcomb, 122, 124
The Cascade Room (Vancouver),
120
Celebrities (Vancouver), 121
The Cellar (Vancouver), 121
Cellphones, 209–210
CelticFest (Vancouver), 17
Chan Centre for the Performing
Arts (Vancouver), 117
Chanel Boutique (Vancouver), 113
Chapters (Vancouver), 111
Chef and Chauffeur (Vancouver),
101
Chemainus Murals, 184
Cheung Sing Herbal & Birds
Nest Co. (Vancouver), 111

Children, families with, 209
Vancouver, 5–6, 114
attractions for, 99–100
itinerary, 29–30
Victoria, 35–36, 175
Whistler-Blackcomb, 135–136
Chinatown
Vancouver, 2, 25, 40–41
exploring, 87
restaurants, 69–71
Victoria, 141, 164
Chinese (Lunar) New Year (Vancouver), 17
Chocolate Arts (Vancouver), 115
Chocolate Tofino (Tofino), 196
Christchurch Cathedral (Vancouver), 82
Cinemas, Vancouver, 118
Cinnamon Bear Bar (Whistler), 136
City Cigar Company (Vancouver), 112
Classical music and opera, 118–119, 179
Classic Boat Festival (Victoria), 18
Clayoquot Sound UNESCO Marine Biosphere Reserve, 192
Cleveland Dam (Vancouver), 93
Cliffwalk (Vancouver), 91
Coastal Peoples Fine Arts Gallery (Vancouver), 114
Cocktail scene, Vancouver, 80–81
Commercial Drive (Vancouver), 41
The Commodore Ballroom (Vancouver), 7, 119
Consulates, 208–209
Cookworks (Vancouver), 115
Cornucopia (Whistler), 19
Coupland, Douglas, 19
Cowichan Bay, 184
Cowichan Bed & Breakfast Association, 181
Cowichan Estuary Nature Centre, 184
Cowichan Valley, 180–185
Craigdarroch Castle Historic House and Museum (Victoria), 11, 167
Crankworx Whistler Freeride Mountain Bike Festival, 134
Cross-country skiing, Whistler-Blackcomb, 132
The Cross Decor & Design (Vancouver), 116
Customs, 208
Cycling. See Biking and mountain biking
Cypress Bowl (Vancouver), 106
Cypress Mountain (Vancouver), 93, 107
Cypress Provincial Park (Vancouver), 93, 104

D

Daiso (Richmond), 110
Dallas Road (Victoria), 7, 34
Dance clubs, Vancouver, 120–121

Dave Murray Summer Ski and Snowboard Camp (Blackcomb), 135
Deep Cove Canoe and Kayak Rentals (Vancouver), 103
Deimos Paragliding Flight School (near Vancouver), 105
Dentists, Vancouver, 45
Department stores, Vancouver, 112–113
Diamond Head, 132
Dine Out
Vancouver, 17, 65
Victoria, 17
Disabled travelers, 208
Doctors and dentists
Vancouver, 45
Victoria, 143
DoDa Antiques (Vancouver), 110
Downtown
Vancouver, 40
accommodations, 46–56
exploring, 81–87
restaurants, 61–69
Victoria, 33, 141
accommodations, 147–149
exploring, 166–167
restaurants, 155–159
Dr. Sun Yat-Sen Classical Chinese Garden (Vancouver), 7, 87, 88, 93
Dream Apparel (Vancouver), 113
Drinking laws, 208
Drugstores, 208
Dubh Linn Gate Old Irish Pub (Whistler), 136
Duncan, 183–184

E

The East Side (Vancouver), 91
East Sooke Coast Trail, 172
East Sooke Regional Park, 174
Eating and drinking, 21–23.
See also Restaurants
food trucks, 68
shopping, 115–116
Vancouver gourmet tours, 101
Vancouver itinerary for foodies, 30
Victoria itinerary for foodies, 36–37
Ecology Centre (Vancouver), 97
Ecomarine Ocean Kayak Centre (Vancouver), 103
Ecotours
Vancouver, 104
Victoria, 171–172
Edible Canada at the Market (Vancouver), 115
Electricity, 208
Embassies, 208–209
Emergencies
Vancouver, 45
Victoria, 144
Emily Carr House (Victoria), 10, 165

Empire Nightclub (Vancouver), 121
Endowment Lands (Vancouver), 96
English Bay Beach (Vancouver), 2, 25, 102
Entertainment and nightlife
Vancouver, 117–121
Victoria, 178–179
Erickson, Arthur, 19

F

Fairfield (Victoria), 167
Fairmont Hotel Empress (Victoria), 165
False Creek (Vancouver), 29, 106
False Creek Ferries (Vancouver), 44
False Creek North (Vancouver), 41
Families with children, 209
Vancouver, 5–6, 114
attractions for, 99–100
itinerary, 29–30
Victoria, 35–36, 175
Whistler-Blackcomb, 135–136
Fanclub (Vancouver), 119
Fashion (clothing), Vancouver, 113–114
Fernwood (Victoria), 141, 167
Ferries
Gulf Islands, 188
Vancouver, 204, 205–206
Victoria, 139, 142, 204–206
First Nations
art and crafts
Vancouver, 114–115
Victoria, 176
tours, Vancouver, 101
Fisgard Lighthouse (Victoria), 168
Fish and chips, 23
Fisherman's Wharf (Victoria), 7, 32, 176
Fishing
Richmond, 98
Ucluelet, 200
Fluevog, John, 2, 20
FlyOver Canada (Vancouver), 5, 82
Food trucks, 68
Forge & Form (Vancouver), 113
Fort Langley National Historic Site, 99
Fort Rodd Hill & Fisgard Lighthouse (Victoria), 168
Fort Street (Victoria), 8, 10
The Fountainhead Pub (Vancouver), 121
Fraser Valley Duck Poutine, 23

G

Gallery of BC Ceramics (Vancouver), 111
Galloping Goose Trail (Victoria), 9, 172–173
Garfinkel's (Whistler), 136
Garibaldi Lake, 132
Garibaldi Provincial Park, 105, 132

Gastown (Vancouver), 25, 40
  exploring, 87–88
  restaurants, 69–71
  shopping, 109
Gastown Steam Clock
  (Vancouver), 25
Gays and lesbians, 209
  Vancouver, 18, 121
George (Vancouver), 120
George C. Reifel Bird Sanctuary
  (near Vancouver), 108
Golden Village (Richmond), 98
Gold Mine Trail, 200
Goldstream Provincial Park,
  173, 174
Golf
  Vancouver, 104
  Victoria, 9, 172
  Whistler-Blackcomb, 133
Gourmet Warehouse (Vancouver),
  115
Government Street (Victoria), 10
Granville Island (Vancouver), 26,
  41, 88–89
  for kids, 99–100
  shopping, 109
Granville Island Public Market
  (Vancouver), 88, 115
Granville Island Stage
  (Vancouver), 117
Granville Street (Vancouver),
  shopping, 109
The Great Canadian Beer Festival
  (Victoria), 19
Greenheart Canopy Walkway
  (Vancouver), 96
Green Point campground, 195
Greyhound Bus Lines, 124
Grouse Grind (Vancouver), 3, 92,
  105
Grouse Mountain (Vancouver),
  28, 92, 105
Grouse Mountain Resort
  (Vancouver), 106
Gulf Islands, 185–190
Gulf Islands National Park
  Reserve, 173, 190
Gulf of Georgia Cannery National
  Historic Site (Vancouver), 5, 98

H

Harbor tours. See Boat tours and
  cruises
Harbour Air (Vancouver), 100
Harbour Cruises (Vancouver), 100
Hatley Park National Historic Site
  (Colwood), 168
Health, 209
Heli-skiing, 132
Helmcken House (Victoria), 165
Heron rookery (Vancouver), 108
Herzog, Fred, 20
Hiking
  Tofino/Ucluelet area, 200
  Vancouver, 105
  Victoria area, 10, 172–173
  Whistler-Blackcomb, 133–134

Hill's Native Art (Vancouver), 114
Hills of Kerrisdale (Vancouver), 112
History of Vancouver and Victoria,
  14–16
Holidays, 16
Hollyburn Lodge (Vancouver), 104
Holt Renfrew (Vancouver), 113
Home furnishings and accessories,
  Vancouver, 116
Honda Celebration of Light
  (Vancouver), 18
Horse-drawn carriage rides
  Vancouver, 84, 99
  Victoria, 171
Hospitals, Vancouver, 45
Hotels, 206–207. See also
  Accommodations Index
    Cowichan Valley, 181–182
    Gulf Islands, 188–189
    Tofino and Ucluelet, 193–195
    Vancouver, 4–5, 46–61
    Victoria, 8–9, 144–152
    Whistler-Blackcomb, 125–129
Hotlines, Vancouver, 45
Hot Springs Cove (Maquinna
  Provincial Park), 199
H. R. MacMillan Space Centre
  (Vancouver), 90
Hudson's Bay (Vancouver), 113

I

Ice skating, Vancouver, 105
Inform Interiors (Vancouver), 116
Inner Harbour (Victoria), 32, 140
  accommodations, 144–147
  exploring, 164–166
  restaurants, 152
International Bhangra Celebration
  (Vancouver), 17
International Summer Night
  Market (Richmond), 112
International Travel Maps and
  Books (Vancouver), 111
Internet access, 209
  Vancouver, 45
  Victoria, 144
Inuit Gallery of Vancouver, 115
Irish Heather (Vancouver), 120
Isola Bella (Vancouver), 113
Itineraries, suggested, 24–37
  Vancouver for families, 29–30
  Vancouver for foodies, 30–31
  Vancouver in 1, 2 and 3 days,
    24–28
  Victoria for families, 35–36
  Victoria for foodies, 36–37
  Victoria in 1 and 2 days, 31–35

J

Jack Poole Plaza (Vancouver), 82
James Bay (Victoria), 141
  exploring, 164–166
Jericho Beach (Vancouver), 102
Jericho Sailing Centre
  (Vancouver), 103
Joffre Lakes Provincial Park, 134

John Fluevog Boots & Shoes Ltd.
  (Vancouver), 2, 20, 113
Juan de Fuca Marine Trail
  (Victoria), 10, 172

K

Kayaking and canoeing
  Tofino/Ucluelet area, 201
  Vancouver, 103
  Victoria, 10, 173
  Whistler-Blackcomb, 133
Khot-La-Cha Art Gallery & Gift
  Shop (Vancouver), 115
Kids. See Families with children
Kidsbooks (Vancouver), 111
Kids Market at Granville Island
  (Vancouver), 5, 99, 114
Kinsol Trestle (near Shawnigan
  Lake Village), 185
Kites on Clouds (Vancouver), 114
Kitsilano (Vancouver), 26, 41
Kitsilano Beach (Vancouver), 102,
  107
Kitsilano Pool (Vancouver), 102
Kwisitis Visitor Centre (Pacific Rim
  National Park), 199

L

La Casa del Habano (Vancouver),
  112
Landsea Tours (Vancouver), 101
Langara Golf Course (Vancouver),
  104
Lattimer Gallery (Vancouver), 115
Leone (Vancouver), 114
LGBT travelers, 209
  Vancouver, 18, 121
Lighthouse Park (Vancouver), 28,
  93
Lions Gate Bridge (Vancouver), 27
Little India (Vancouver), 42
Live music, Vancouver, 119
The Lobsterman (Vancouver),
  115–116
Locarno Beach (Vancouver), 102
LoJo (Victoria), 10
Long Beach, 192, 200
Long Beach Headlands Trail, 200
Lost Lagoon (Vancouver), 105
Lost Lagoon Nature House
  (Vancouver), 84
Lost Lake, 132, 134
Lotus Land Tours (Vancouver),
  103, 104
Louis Vuitton (Vancouver), 113
Lower Johnson Street (LoJo;
  Victoria), 177
Luggage storage and lockers,
  Vancouver, 45
Lulu Island wetlands bog, 108
Lunar New Year Celebrations
  (Vancouver), 7
Lynn Canyon Park (Vancouver), 97
Lynn Canyon Suspension Bridge
  (Vancouver), 97
Lynn Headwaters Regional Park
  (Vancouver), 28, 97

M

McArthur Glen Designer Outlet Mall (Vancouver), 98, 113
Macleod's Books (Vancouver), 111
McPherson Playhouse (Victoria), 178
Mail and postage, 209
Main Street (Vancouver), 27
    restaurants, 77–79
    shopping, 109
Maplewood Farm (Vancouver), 5, 100
Marion Scott Gallery/Kardosh Projects (Vancouver), 115
Maritime Museum of British Columbia (Victoria), 166
Market Square (Victoria), 177
Martha Sturdy Originals (Vancouver), 111
Maurice Young Millennium Place (Whistler), 135
Maxx Fish (Whistler), 136
Mayne Island, 190
Menghi, Umberto, 22
Miniature World (Victoria), 166–167
Mini-ferries (Vancouver), 44
Mobile phones, 209–210
Moe Joe's (Whistler), 136
Money and costs, 210
Monte Clark Gallery (Vancouver), 110
Mountain Equipment Co-Op (Vancouver), 116
Mount Douglas Park, 174
Mount Fromme (Vancouver), 104
Mount Seymour Provincial Park (Vancouver), 93, 96, 106
Munro's Books (Victoria), 8, 175–176
Murchie's Tea & Coffee (Vancouver), 116
Museum of Anthropology (Vancouver), 6, 27, 90, 115
Museum of Vancouver, 7, 90

N

Nairn Falls Provincial Park, 134
Neighborhoods
    Vancouver, 39–42
    Victoria, 140–141
Newspapers and magazines, Vancouver, 45
Night markets, Vancouver, 112
Nitobe Memorial Garden (Vancouver), 96
Nordstrom (Vancouver), 113
North Shore (Vancouver), 29, 42, 79–80, 104
    accommodations, 60
North Vancouver, 91–92
Numbers (Vancouver), 121

O

Oak Bay (Victoria), 141, 167
Oak Bay Village (Victoria), 10, 34, 178

Observatory Hill (Victoria), 143
Ogden Point Breakwater (Victoria), 170
Olympic Cauldron (Vancouver), 3, 82
Olympic Village (Vancouver), 107
OMNIMAX (Vancouver), 118
Orpheum Theatre (Vancouver), 117
Outdoor activities
    Pacific Rim area, 200–201
    Vancouver, 6, 102–108
    Victoria, 172–173
    Whistler-Blackcomb, 131–135

P

Pacific Boarder (Vancouver), 116
Pacific Cinematheque (Vancouver), 118
Pacific National Exhibition (Vancouver), 18
Pacific Rim National Park, 11, 192
Pacific Rim Whale Festival, 17
Pacific Spirit Regional Park (Vancouver), 96, 104
Packing tips, 210
Paddleboarding, Vancouver, 103
Paddlewheeler Riverboat Tours (Vancouver), 100
Paragliding, Vancouver, 105
Parks and gardens
    Tofino Botanical Garden, 199–200
    Vancouver, 92–97
    Victoria, 173–175
Parliament Interiors (Vancouver), 116
Passports, 210
Peak 2 Peak Gondola (Whistler Blackcomb), 11
Peak 2 Peak Gondola (Whistler-Blackcomb), 133
Pedi-cabs, Victoria, 143
Pemberton, 137
Pemberton Distillery, 137
Pender Island, 190
Perimeter Whistler Express, 122, 124
Pharmacies
    Vancouver, 45
    Victoria, 144
Philip, Sinclair, 22
Playland at the Pacific National Exhibition (Vancouver), 100
Playland at the PNE (Vancouver), 5
Please Mum (Vancouver), 113
Point Atkinson Lighthouse (Vancouver), 93
Point Grey Beach (Vancouver), 103
Polar Bear Swim (Vancouver), 17
Police, 210
    Vancouver, 45
Post office
    Vancouver, 45
    Victoria, 144
Pubs, Victoria, 22

Pulpfiction Books (Vancouver), 111
PuSh International Performing Arts Festival (Vancouver), 17

Q

QMUNITY (Vancouver), 121
Queen Elizabeth Park (Vancouver), 96, 107
Queen Elizabeth Theatre (Vancouver), 117

R

Rafting, Whistler-Blackcomb, 134
Rattenbury, Francis Mawson, 20
Red Card (Vancouver), 120
The Red Room (Vancouver), 121
Reid, Bill, 20
Restaurants. See also Restaurants Index
    Cowichan Valley, 182–183
    Gulf Islands, 189
    Tofino and Ucluelet, 196–198
    Vancouver, 3–4, 61–81
    Victoria, 8, 152–162
    Whistler-Blackcomb, 129–131
Revue Stage (Vancouver), 117
Richmond (Vancouver), 41–42, 98
    shopping, 110
Richmond Nature Park, 108
Richmond Night Market, 112
Richmond Olympic Oval (Burnaby), 105, 107
Rio Tinto Alcan Dragon Boat Festival (Vancouver), 17
River Market at Westminster Quay (Vancouver), 116
Robert Bateman Centre/Steamship Terminal Building (Victoria), 10, 166
Robert Bateman Foundation, 21
Robson Square (Vancouver), 82, 84
Robson Street (Vancouver), 25
    shopping, 109
Rockland (Victoria), 141
Rockwood Adventures (Vancouver), 104
Roots Canada (Vancouver), 114
Ross Bay (Victoria), 141
The Roxy (Vancouver), 119
Royal BC Museum (Victoria), 7, 10, 32, 166, 175
Royal Theatre (Victoria), 178
Running, Vancouver, 105–106

S

Saanich (Victoria), 141
Saanich Peninsula (Victoria), 34
Safety, 210
    Victoria, 144
Sailing, Victoria, 10
Salish Sea, 185
Salmon, summer salmon runs, 108
Salt Spring Island, 190

Salvatore Ferragamo (Vancouver), 113

Saturna, 190

Science World at TELUS World of Science (Vancouver), 5, 91, 99

SeaBus (Vancouver), 43

Seaflora (Victoria), 160

Seafood chowder, 23

Seaside bicycle route (Vancouver), 104

Seasons, 16

Sea-to-Sky Gondola, 137

Sea-to-Sky Highway (Hwy. 99), 136–137

Seawall (Vancouver), 2, 84, 103, 105

Second Beach (Vancouver), 84, 102

Secret Location (Vancouver), 114

Senior travel, 210

Sewell's Marina (Vancouver), 104

Shameful Tiki Room (Vancouver), 120

Shannon Falls, 137

Shark Club (Vancouver), 120

Shaughnessy (Vancouver), 41

Shaw Ocean Discovery Centre (Sidney), 169

Shepherd, Andrew, 160

Shine (Vancouver), 121

Shopping
Vancouver, 109–116
Victoria, 10, 175–178
Whistler-Blackcomb, 135

Showcase (Vancouver), 116

Silk Road Art Trading Co. (Vancouver), 111

Singing Pass, 132

Singing Pass Trail, 134

Skiing
Vancouver area, 106
Whistler-Blackcomb, 131–132

SkyTrain (Vancouver), 43

Sleigh rides, Blackcomb, 132

Smoking, 210

Snowboarding
Vancouver area, 106
Whistler-Blackcomb, 132

Snowmobiling, Whistler-Blackcomb, 132

Snowshoeing, Whistler-Blackcomb, 132–133

Southeast False Creek (Vancouver), 42

South Main (Vancouver), 42

Spanish Banks (Vancouver), 102

Spanish Banks Beach (Vancouver), 3

Spas, Whistler, 135

Spearhead Traverse (Whistler-Blackcomb), 132

Spinnakers (Victoria), 8

Spokes Bicycle Rentals & Espresso Bar (Vancouver), 103

Sporting goods, Vancouver, 116

Spray Park (Vancouver), 84, 99

Squamish, 137

Squamish Adventure Centre, 137

Squamish Lil'wat Cultural Centre, 135

Stanley Industrial Alliance Theatre (Vancouver), 117

Stanley Park (Vancouver), 6, 25, 29, 84–86, 93, 99
beaches, 102
tennis, 106–107

Stanley Park Miniature Railway (Vancouver), 5, 84

Stanley Park Seawall, 000m

Stawamus Chief, 137

Steam Clock (Vancouver), 25, 87

Steamship Terminal Building (Victoria), 32

Steamworks (Vancouver), 120

Steveston, 98

Strait of Georgia (Salish Sea), 185

Streetfood Vancouver, 68

Student travel, 210–211

Sunset Beach (Vancouver), 102

Sun Yat-Sen Classical Chinese Garden (Vancouver), 0m

Surfing, Tofino/Ucluelet area, 201

Surf Junction Campground (near Ucluelet), 195–196

Swallow Tail Tours (Vancouver), 101

Swiftsure International Yacht Race (Victoria), 17

Swimco (Vancouver), 114

T

Taiga (Vancouver), 116

Takaya Tours (Vancouver), 101

T&T Supermarket (Vancouver), 111–112

Tapleys (Whistler), 136

Taste (Victoria), 18

Taxes, 211

Taxis
Vancouver, 39, 43–44
Victoria, 142
Whistler-Blackcomb, 124

TD Vancouver International Jazz Festival, 7, 17

Temperatures, daily average high, 16

Tennis
Vancouver, 106–107
Whistler-Blackcomb, 135

Ten Ren Tea & Ginseng Co. (Vancouver), 112

Terra Nova Rural Park (Richmond), 98

Theatre Under the Stars (Vancouver), 7, 84, 118

Third Beach (Vancouver), 84, 102

Thom, Bing, 20

Thomas Haas Sparkle Cookies, 23

Ticketmaster (Vancouver), 117

Tipping, 211

Tofino, 190, 192

Tofino Botanical Garden, 199–200

Toilets, 211

Tojo, Hidekazu, 22

Tommy Africa's (Whistler), 136

Totem poles, Vancouver, 84

Tourism Richmond, 98

Tourism Vancouver, 102

Tourism Vancouver Visitor Centre, 39

Tourism Victoria Visitor Centre, 139

Tours
organized, Vancouver, 100–102
Victoria, 169–172

Train travel
Vancouver, 39, 204
Whistler-Blackcomb, 124

TransLink (Vancouver), 205

Translink (Vancouver), 43

Transportation, 205–206
Vancouver, 42–44
Victoria, 141–143, 205

Treetops Adventure (Vancouver), 91

U

UBC Botanical Garden (Vancouver), 96

UBC Tennis Centre (Vancouver), 107

Ucluelet, 190, 192

University Golf Club (Vancouver), 104

University of British Columbia (Vancouver), 27

Uno Langmann Limited (Vancouver), 110

V

Valhalla Pure Outfitters (Vancouver), 116

Valley Trail System, 124, 132, 134

Vancouver, 38–121
accommodations, 46–61
arriving in, 38–39
exploring, 81–102
getting around, 42–44
layout of, 39–40
neighborhoods in brief, 40–42
nightlife, 117–121
outdoor activities, 102–108
restaurants, 61–81
shopping, 109–116
traveling to, 202–204
visitor information, 39

Vancouver Aquarium, 2, 5, 25, 84, 86, 99

Vancouver Art Gallery, 6, 86–87

Vancouver Bach Choir, 118–119

Vancouver Cantata Singers, 119

Vancouver Chamber Choir, 119

Vancouver Cocktail, 23

Vancouver East Cultural Centre, 117

Vancouver Flea Market, 110

Vancouver Folk Music Festival, 18, 119

Vancouver Fringe Festival, 18

Vancouver International Airport, 38, 203

Vancouver International Children's Festival, 17, 99
Vancouver International Film Festival, 118
Vancouver International Jazz Festival, 119
Vancouver International Wine Festival, 7, 17
Vancouver International Writers and Readers Festival, 19
Vancouver Island Salt Co. (Victoria), 160
Vancouver Maritime Museum, 91
Vancouver North Shore Bed and Breakfast Association, 60
Vancouver Olympic Centre, 107
Vancouver Opera, 119
Vancouver Police Museum, 87–88
Vancouver Pride Parade & Festival, 18
Vancouver Sun Run, 17
Vancouver Symphony, 119
Vancouver TheatreSports League, 118
Vancouver Trolley Company, 84, 99, 101
VanDusen Botanical Gardens (Vancouver), 96–97
Vanier Park (Vancouver), 26
VCC West (Vancouver), 82
Victoria, 138–179
 accommodations, 144–152
 arriving in, 138–139
 entertainment and nightlife, 178–179
 exploring, 162–175
 getting around, 141–143
 for kids, 175
 layout of, 140
 main arteries and streets, 140
 neighborhoods in brief, 140–141
 outdoor activities, 172–173
 parks and gardens, 173–175
 restaurants, 152–162
 shopping, 175–178
 street maps, 140
 tours, 169–172
 traveling to, 204–205
 visitor information, 139–140
Victoria Bug Zoo, 167
Victoria Butterfly Gardens, 175
Victoria Fringe Festival, 179
Victoria International Chalk Festival, 18
Victoria International Cycling Festival, 18
Victoria Public Market, 10, 177
Victoria Symphony Splash, 18, 179
Victoria West, 141
Vij, Vikram, 22
Visitor information, 211
 Vancouver, 39
 Victoria, 139–140
 Whistler-Blackcomb, 124
Visitor inormation, Tofino and Ucluelet, 193

W
Walking
 Vancouver, 44
 Victoria, 141
 Whistler-Blackcomb, 124
Walking tours
 Vancouver, 101–102
 Victoria, 169–170
Wall, Jeff, 20
Westbeach (Vancouver), 116
West End (Vancouver), 25, 41
 accommodations, 56–59
 exploring, 81–87
 restaurants, 71–74
West Side (Vancouver)
 accommodations, 59–61
 exploring, 88–91
 restaurants, 74–77
West Vancouver, 91–92
Whale-watching
 off Steveston Harbour, 11
 Pacific Rim National Park, 17
 Tofino/Ucluelet area, 201
 Vancouver, 108
 Victoria, 7, 9, 33, 171–172
The Whip (Vancouver), 120
Whippletree Junction (Duncan), 185
Whistler Accommodation Reservations, 129
Whistler-Blackcomb, 122–137
 accommodations, 125–129
 getting around, 124
 nightlife, 136
 outdoor activities, 131–135
 restaurants, 129–131
 traveling to, 122, 124
 visitor information, 124
Whistler Blackcomb Ski Resort, 106
Whistler BrewHouse, 136
Whistler Club Crawl, 136
Whistler Direct Shuttle, 124
Whistler Museum, 135
Whistler Olympic Park, 132–133
Whistler Sliding Centre, 107
Whistler Village, 122
Wildlife-watching
 Tofino/Ucluelet area, 201
 Vancouver area, 108
Wild Pacific Trail, 200
Windsurfing, Vancouver, 108
Wineries and vineyards, 22, 23
 Cowichan Valley, 185
 Gulf Islands, 190
 Vancouver Island, 11
Wreck Beach (Vancouver), 103

Y
Yaletown (Vancouver), 41
 accommodations, 46–56
 restaurants, 61–69
Yaletown Brewing (Vancouver), 120
Yaohan Centre (Richmond), 110

Z
Ziplining, Whistler, 134
Zonda Nellis Design Ltd. (Vancouver), 114

Accommodations

Abigail's Hotel (Victoria), 9, 147–148
Black Rock Oceanfront Resort (Ucluelet), 193
Blue Horizon (Vancouver), 57
Brentwood Bay Resort & Spa (Victoria), 150
Buchan Hotel (Vancouver), 5, 59
The Burrard (Vancouver), 5, 54
Cedar Springs Bed & Breakfast (Whistler), 129
Chateau Victoria Hotel & Suites, 148
Coast Coal Harbour Hotel (Vancouver), 52
Days Inn Vancouver Downtown, 54
Delta Vancouver Suites, 52
Durlacher Hof Pension Inn (Whistler), 129
Empire Landmark (Vancouver), 57–58
Executive Hotel Le Soleil (Vancouver), 52–53
Fairburn Farm (Duncan), 181
The Fairmont Chateau Whistler, 125
Fairmont Hotel Empress (Victoria), 9, 144, 146
Fairmont Hotel Vancouver, 46
Fairmont Pacific Rim (Vancouver), 4, 46
Fairmont Waterfront (Vancouver), 46–47
Four Seasons Hotel Vancouver, 4, 47
Four Seasons Resort Whistler, 125
Georgian Court Hotel (Vancouver), 53
Granville Island Hotel (Vancouver), 59
Hastings House Country House Hotel (Salt Spring Island), 188
Hedgerow House (Salt Spring Island), 188–189
Hostelling International Vancouver Downtown Hostel, 55
Hostelling International Vancouver Jericho Beach Hostel, 59–60
Hostelling International Whistler, 129
Hotel Grand Pacific (Victoria), 9, 146
Hotel Rialto (Victoria), 9, 148–149
Hotel Zed (Victoria), 9, 151–152
Inn at Laurel Point (Victoria), 8, 146
The Inn at Tough City (Tofino), 193
Isabella's Guest Suites (Victoria), 149

James Bay Inn Hotel Suites & Cottage (Victoria), 147
The Kingston Hotel (Vancouver), 55–56
The Listel Hotel (Vancouver), 5, 57
Loden Vancouver (Vancouver), 4, 47, 50
Long Beach Lodge Resort (Tofino), 193–194
Lonsdale Quay Hotel (Vancouver), 60
Magnolia Hotel & Spa (Victoria), 9, 148
Metropolitan Hotel Vancouver, 53
Middle Beach Lodge (Tofino), 194
Moda Hotel (Vancouver), 54–55
Nita Lake Lodge (Whistler-Blackcomb), 125, 128
Oak Bay Beach Hotel (Victoria), 9, 150
Oceanfront Suites at Cowichan Bay, 181–182
Ocean Island Backpackers (Victoria), 149
Opus Hotel (Vancouver), 4, 50
Pacific Sands Beach Resort (Tofino), 194
Pan Pacific Vancouver, 50
Pan Pacific Whistler, 128
Paul's Motor Inn (Victoria), 152
Pinnacle Hotel at the Pier (Vancouver), 60
Poet's Cove Resort & Spa (South Pender Island), 189
Rosedale on Robson Suite Hotel (Vancouver), 53
Rosewood Hotel Georgia (Vancouver), 4, 50–51
St. Regis Hotel (Vancouver), 54
Shangri-La Hotel (Vancouver), 5, 51
Sidney Pier Hotel & Spa (Victoria), 151
Sooke Harbour House (Victoria), 9, 150–151
Spinnakers Guesthouses (Victoria), 147
Sunset Inn & Suites (Vancouver), 58
Sutton Place Hotel (Vancouver), 51
Swan's Suite Hotel (Victoria), 9, 149
Sylvia Hotel (Vancouver), 5, 58
Thistle-Down House Bed & Breakfast (Vancouver), 60
Ucluelet Oceanfront Hostel, 194–195
The University of British Columbia Conference Centre (Vancouver), 61
Urban Hideaway Guesthouse (Vancouver), 56
Wedgewood Hotel (Vancouver), 51–52
West End Guest House (Vancouver), 58–59

Westin Bayshore Resort & Marina (Vancouver), 56–57
Westin Bear Mountain Victoria Golf Resort & Spa, 151
The Westin Resort & Spa Whistler, 128
Whistler Alpine Chalet, 129
Wickaninnish Inn (Tofino), 195
YWCA Hotel (Vancouver), 56

Restaurants

Alta Bistro (Whistler-Blackcomb), 130
Amusé on the Vineyard (Cobble Hill), 182
Araxi (Whistler-Blackcomb), 129
Aura Waterfront Restaurant + Patio (Victoria), 8, 152
Banana Leaf (Vancouver), 73
Bao Bei Chinese Brasserie (Vancouver), 70–71
Beach House (Vancouver), 28
The Beach House at Dundarave Pier (Vancouver), 79
Bearfoot Bistro (Whistler-Blackcomb), 129–130
Beaucoup Bakery & Café (Vancouver), 78
Bella Gelateria (Vancouver), 78
Be Love (Victoria), 157–158
Bengal Lounge (Victoria), 8, 154
Bin 4 Burger Lounge (Victoria), 8, 158
Bistro at Merridale Cidery (Cobble Hill), 182
The Blackbird Public House & Oyster Bar (Vancouver), 80
Black & Blue (Vancouver), 61, 64
Blue Water Cafe + Raw Bar (Vancouver), 3, 64
Burdock & Co. (Vancouver), 4, 78–79
Butchart Gardens (Victoria), 161
Cactus Club (Vancouver), 4, 67–68
Café at Hope Bay (Salt Spring Island), 189
Café Brio (Victoria), 8, 155
Café Nuba (Vancouver), 69
Campagnolo (Vancouver), 79
Caramba! Restaurante (Whistler), 131
Cardero's Restaurant (Vancouver), 72–73
Catalano Restaurant & Cicchetti Bar (Victoria), 156
Chambar Belgian Restaurant (Vancouver), 4, 66
Cibo Trattoria/Uva Wine Cocktail Bar (Vancouver), 66
Cin Cin (Vancouver), 71–72
Citta Bistro (Whistler), 130
Coast (Vancouver), 66–67
Common Loaf Bakeshop (Tofino), 196
The Diamond (Vancouver), 81

Dining Room at Hastings House (Pender Island), 189
Dockside Restaurant, 3
Dubh Linn Gate Old Irish Pub (Whistler), 130
Edible Canada (Vancouver), 75
Empress Dining Room (Victoria), 154
Fable Kitchen (Vancouver), 75–76
Fairmont Empress Hotel (Victoria), 32, 161
Farmer's Apprentice (Vancouver), 76
Faubourg (Vancouver), 78
Ferris' Oyster Bar & Grill (Victoria), 156
Fetch (Ucluelet), 196
The Fish House in Stanley Park (Vancouver), 72
Flying Otter Grill (Victoria), 154–155
Fol Epi (Victoria), 160–161
Fresh Local Wild (Vancouver), 68
glowbal grill steak & satay bar (Vancouver), 69
Great Room at Long Beach Lodge Resort (Tofino), 196
The Guild Free House (Victoria), 158
Gyoza King (Vancouver), 73
Hapa Izakaya (Vancouver), 73
Hawksworth Restaurant (Vancouver), 3, 64
Hon's Wun-Tun House (Vancouver), 73
Hudson's on First (Duncan), 182–183
Il Caminetto (Whistler), 131
Ingrid's Village Cafe (Whistler), 130
Japadog (Vancouver), 68
Joe Fortes Seafood & Chop House (Vancouver), 64–65
The Keefer Bar (Vancouver), 81
Kirin (Vancouver), 65
L'Abattoir (Vancouver), 4, 26, 69
La Pentola della Quercia (Vancouver), 67
Little Jumbo (Victoria), 156
Maenam (Vancouver), 76
MARKET by Jean-Georges (Vancouver), 67
Mink Chocolates (Vancouver), 78
Murchie's Tea and Coffee (Victoria), 161–162
The Naam Restaurant (Vancouver), 77
North 48 Restaurant (Victoria), 156
Norwoods (Ucluelet), 197
Pacific Restaurant & Terrace (Victoria), 154, 162
Pagliacci's (Victoria), 156
The Parker (Vancouver), 71
Pescatore's Fish House (Victoria), 155
Phnom Penh Restaurant (Vancouver), 71

PiDGin (Vancouver), 4, 69–70
Pier 7 (Vancouver), 28, 79
Pig BBQ Joint (Victoria), 158
Pizzeria Prima Strada (Victoria), 159–160
The Pointe Restaurant (Tofino), 197
Pourhouse (Vancouver), 81
Raincity Grill (Vancouver), 72
Red Fish Blue Fish (Victoria), 155
Re-Up BBQ (Vancouver), 68
Roaming Dragon (Vancouver), 68
The Salmon House on the Hill (Vancouver), 80
The Sandbar (Vancouver), 76–77
The Schooner (Tofino), 197
Seagrille Seafood & Sushi (Victoria), 159
Secret Location (Vancouver), 70
Shameful Tiki Room (Vancouver), 81
Shelter (Tofino), 197–198
The Snug Pub (Victoria), 160

SOBO (Tofino), 198
Sooke Harbour House (Victoria), 159
Sophie's Cosmic Café (Vancouver), 77
Spinnaker's Gastro Brewpub (Victoria), 8, 33, 154
Steamship Grill (Victoria), 34–35, 154
Stone Soup Inn (Lake Cowichan), 183
Sun Sui Wah (Vancouver), 3, 77
Tableau Bar Bistro (Vancouver), 73–74
Tacofino Cantina, 198
TacoFino Cantina (Vancouver), 68
Tanpopo (Vancouver), 73
10 Acres Bistro + Bar + Farm (Victoria), 8, 157
Thomas Haas Patisserie (Vancouver), 78
Tojo's Restaurant, 2, 4, 27, 74

The Tomahawk Barbecue (Vancouver), 80
Trattoria di Umberto (Whistler-Blackcomb), 130–131
True Grain Bread (Cowichan Bay), 183
Ulla Restaurant (Victoria), 8, 155
Veneto Tapa Lounge (Victoria), 8, 157
Victoria Public Market, 158–159
Vij's (Vancouver), 3, 27, 75
West (Vancouver), 74–75
Whistler BrewHouse, 130
White Heather Tea Room (Victoria), 162
Wildebeest (Vancouver), 70
Wildside Grill (Tofino), 198
Wild Wood Bistro & Bar (Whistler), 131
Willie's Bakery & Café (Victoria), 8, 159
Yew Seafood (Vancouver), 65–66
Zambri's (Victoria), 8, 157